Technology as Freedom

Technology as Freedom

**The New Deal and
the Electrical Modernization
of the American Home**

Ronald C. Tobey

University of California Press
Berkeley / Los Angeles / London

University of California Press
Berkeley and Los Angeles, California

University of California Press
London, England

Copyright © 1996 by The Regents of the University
of California

Library of Congress Cataloging-in-Publication Data

Tobey, Ronald C.
　　Technology as freedom : the New Deal and the
electrical modernization of the American home /
Ronald C. Tobey.
　　　　p.　cm.
　　Includes bibliographical references and index.
　　ISBN 0-520-20421-2 (cloth : alk. paper)
　　1. Electrification—United States—History—20th
century. 2. Electrification—Social aspects—United
States. 3. Rural electrification—United States—
History—20th century. 4. Rural electrification—
Social aspects—United States. 5. New Deal,
1933–1939. I. Title.
HD9685.U5T63　1996
333.79'32'097309043—dc20　　　　　　96-23123
　　　　　　　　　　　　　　　　　　　　　　　CIP

Printed in the United States of America

1 2 3 4 5 6 7 8 9

The paper used in this publication meets the minimum
requirements of American National Standard for
Information Sciences—Permanence of Paper for
Printed Library Materials, ANSI Z39.48-1984 ∞

*To my family, Elisabeth, Amy, and David,
who, in bearing with me through this
project, modernized me continually*

Contents

Plates

Illustrations

Tables

Acknowledgments

For my understanding of the history of Riverside, California, on which several chapters of this work build, I am indebted to Tom Patterson—for his book, *A Colony for California,* cited throughout this work, and for his careful reading of chapters 3 and 5 in manuscript. I am indebted to Marguerite Duncan-Abrams for a similarly careful reading of chapter 3 and for her research for a master's thesis on the history of Riverside's planning commission. Other local historians to whom I am indebted personally or whose publications aided me are Marion Mitchell-Wilson, Harry Lawton, Allen Mawhinney, and William Myers.

A number of my university colleagues gave me valuable assistance. I am grateful to Eric Monkkonen for his careful reading of a longer version of this work and for his suggestions for revision. My debt to his theory of American urban history, *America Becomes Urban,* is apparent through this book. I appreciate the patient and generous readings of earlier versions of this work by anonymous readers, whose suggestions helped me to revise. John Phillips read chapters 2 and 4 and made numerous (and helpful) complaints about my quoting of politicians. I appreciate Sarah Stage's supportive reading of my treatment of the rational housekeeping movement. David Warren, as dean of the College of Humanities and Social Sciences, University of California, Riverside, provided years of support, as well as a vote of confidence in me and my students, for preservation and organization of the Riverside City utility records used in this research. Tom Thompson and Richard Turner have my gratitude for the hundreds of hours they sweated in a surplus university trailer physically organizing the utility records and drawing the record sample. My greatest intellectual debt is to my coauthor of chapter 6, Charles Wetherell. He has been my constant companion and critic for this project. He supervised and conducted nearly ten years of quantitative analysis on the Riverside utility readings and city directories—a truly formidable effort for which his coauthorship is inadequate acknowledgment. He produced brilliant analyses of data and methodological innovations that only a few historians can appreciate. I trust that he gained some satisfaction from their accomplishment, however invisible they are in the narrative of this book.

Over the years, my graduate students have contributed to my understanding of southern California's history through their theses and our many consultations over them. I am pleased to acknowledge what I have learned from Gabriele Carey, William Myers, and Barbara Milkovich about Orange County; Jay Brigham, Donn Headley, Joe Libby, Shola Lynch, Robert Phelps, and Trudy Selleck about Los Angeles; Ric Dias about Kaiser Steel in Fontana; Anthea Hartig, H. Vincent Moses, and Lee August Simpson about the history of citrus; C. Victor Herbin, Jr., about Riverside's African-American community; Joyce Carter Vickery about Riverside's Mexican and New Mexican pioneers; Elizabeth Leonard and Mark Rawitsch about Riverside's Japanese-American community; and Hongwei Hwang about Riverside's East Side.

My search for illustrative photographs accumulated a long list of debts among institutions around the country, in part because I made an e-mail request for assistance on H-Local, an internet discussion list. I thank especially H. Vincent Moses, Riverside Municipal Museum, Riverside, California; Steve Thomas and Edward Earle, UCR/California Museum of Photography, Riverside, California; Betty Cagle, Lee County Library, Tupelo, Mississippi; Mark Renovitch, Franklin Roosevelt Library, Hyde Park, New York; Carolyn Cole, Librarian, Los Angeles Central Public Library; Don Veasey, Birmingham Public Library, Birmingham, Alabama; and Greg Koos, McLean County Historical Society, Bloomington, Illinois. I happily acknowledge the H-Net assistance of Richard Jensen, Tracy Smith, and Robert Schweitzer. At the end of this long project, I was encouraged and aided by the director of the University of California Press's Los Angeles office, Stanley Holwitz, and by my editors, Elizabeth Knoll, Michelle Nordon, and Sheila Berg, in reducing the length of the book manuscript and preparing it for publication.

I am pleased to acknowledge thirteen years of support for voluminous copying, microfilming, research assistants' salaries, and miscellaneous tasks of computer analysis by the Academic Senate Research Committee of the University of California, Riverside. I am also grateful to the Academic Computing Center and the dean of the College of Humanities and Social Sciences of the University of California, Riverside, for posting funds to Wetherell and my bottomless computing account in the Laboratory for Historical Research in the Department of History. Grant no. SES-8708094, 1987–1989, from the National Science Foundation awarded to Charles Wetherell and me as co-principal investigators supported the initial, crucial organization of data and analysis of utility readings on which we built chapters 3 and 6.

Introduction

Did Electrical Modernization Cause a Social Revolution in the American Home in the 1920s?

In 1925 Samuel Dodsworth, captain of American industry, fantasized a $1,700 house trailer hitched to his car and bound for the wilderness. "He dreamed of a very masterwork of caravans: a tiny kitchen with electric stove, electric refrigerator; a tiny toilet with showerbath; a living-room which should become a bedroom by night—a living-room with a radio, a real writing desk; and on one side of the caravan, or at the back, a folding verandah. He could see his caravanners dining on the verandah in a forest fifty miles from any house." A generation later, Americans lived Dodsworth's dream. They owned conveniences that had once been the luxuries of the rich. Some families caravanned through the American space in silver streamlined trailers. Most households caravanned in place, enjoying nature within the screened protection of suburban patios. Americans side-saddled their domestic environment of electric appliances and electronic pleasures everywhere. In 1959, Richard Nixon held up the American standard of electrical living against Nikita Khrushchev in their famous "kitchen debate" over the relative merits of market and command economies. Standing in front of a Moscow exhibit of an American kitchen filled with electric appliances, the vice president drew out the meaning of the exhibition for the first secretary and premier. Nixon "decided that this was as good a place as any to answer the charges that had been made in the Soviet press, that only 'the rich' in the United States could afford such a house as this." Capitalism offered competing products at prices cheap enough for everyone. Competition created freedom. "To us, diversity, the right to choose, the fact that we have a thousand different builders, that's the spice of life." Thus Nixon fittingly concluded the decade of the 1950s. The affluent life won the cold war.[1] (See pl. 1.)

Plate 1. *Electrical Dream Kitchen.* ([Photographer unknown.] "L.A. Residences—Interiors—Dodge House. Student decorating cake/household training/Dodge House." Security Pacific National Bank Photograph Collection. Los Angeles Public Library.)

Scholars agree on the timing, scope, and thoroughness of electricity's transformation of the American home. Electrification for illumination began in cities in the 1880s, displacing kerosene and gas lighting. By the early 1920s, private companies had electrified half of urban America's homes. Modernization brought power tools, heating and cooling appliances, and fuller electrical lighting, making possible renovation of domestic work processes and improving the environmental quality of the home. During the 1920s the basic economic and social processes of modernization were put in place and a substantial percentage of homes were modernized. By 1959, nearly all American households—rural and urban—had been transformed. Scholars also agree on the nature of electrical modernization as a social process. Electrical modernization occurred through private marketplace consumption for all but a few rural and farm Americans. Households chose to acquire electrical goods and services in free markets of competing products offered to them by private American corporations, just as they selected clothes in department stores, cars at dealers' lots, vegetables in grocery stores, and dreams from movies. A feminist historian claims with a hint of exasperation, "All those women actively chose." A historian who examined residential electrification in Chicago argues that "for the most part, consumers used a rational process to decide which products to buy. A comparison of product successes and failures illustrates how city dwellers exercised discretion in making choices from the cornucopia of electrical devices." In brief, scholars explain residential electrical modernization as part of the same phenomenon of consumerism that has typified Western mass production economies since the late nineteenth century.[2]

The thesis that electrical modernization occurred through consumer choice in the private marketplace has two consequences as an explanation of everyday technology. First, it denies that domestic electrical modernization significantly involved collective, public decisions. Historians of electrical technology shunt aside as irrelevant the progressive reform tradition that drew issues of distribution of services by public utilities, electrification, and electrical modernization into its debate over social democracy. They interpret municipal politics of utility regulation as just another venue for struggle within the commercial-civic elite, rather than as a tradition of debate over values between different classes. Since organized politics is the primary American institution for collective, public decision making, the consumerism thesis amounts to a wholesale rejection of the historical role and relevance of political debate to the shaping of American domesticity. We reveal the enormity of this claim when we contemplate the wide range and complexity of political institutions in the United States, including local government and the politics of utility franchises and land use planning, state government and the politics of regulation, and the national government and national mass electoral parties.[3]

Second, the consumerism thesis implicates the rationality with which consumers choose. By denying that consumers choose collectively in a public arena of debate, the idea of consumer rationality is ambiguous. Scholars explain consumer purchase decisions either as private choice reflecting endogenous values or as utilitarian calculation. Absent a public competition of values, value choice may not be choice at all, but value-driven behavior. Choices prescribed by cultures of gender, class, or race can carry such compulsion for individuals as to deprive them of free selection. Behavior can be sociologically functional by reinforcing group identification or by invigorating social positioning, without involving rational deliberation by the consumer. Calculating choice among competing products, as described by microeconomics, is not unambiguously rational. We presume people buy goods and services because they have needs, but modern consumers buy more than they need. In the microeconomic framework, in which households try to maximize their marginal utilities, overconsumption is essentially irrational behavior. Consumers' behavior does not become rational simply because they comparison shop and choose among competing products. (That madmen are methodical and choose among courses of action does not mean they are not mad.) Scholars explain installing electric labor-saving machines in the kitchen basically like buying clothes. We buy the dishwasher, then in a fit of overconsumption we buy an electric knife, can opener, blender, and shredder. A parade of other electric gadgets follows—cocktail mixer, mayonnaise whip, bread maker, knife sharpener. We store most devices at the inconvenient rear of a lower cabinet and use them infrequently, more labor being required to drag them out, set them up, and clean them than they save in food preparation. Still, people never seem to have enough such gadgets for their kitchen, or clothes, or furniture in their house. All commodities become subject to fashion. We consume seemingly irrationally without regard to need and discard goods without regard to remaining usefulness. In the end, supposedly rational, utilitarian behavior paradoxically begets irrational behavior.[4]

The paradox of consumerism reinforces the persuasion that organized politics has been irrelevant to social history. Historians of everyday technology do not deny that political struggles occurred over issues related to consumption, such as the prices of water, gas, and electricity and pure food and drug acts, but they do not see a direct connection between political tradition, political debates, social policy, and household behavior. They describe choice as private, not public; as individually calculating, not collectively rational. For them, choice does not largely take place in public, involve efforts to persuade organized groups to take positions, use a public vocabulary, make arguments open to challenge by others, or endeavor to prescribe social policy for institutions capable of affecting many people.[5]

The consumerism thesis implies that an expanding, conservative capitalism, largely unrestrained by governmental regulation or unfocused by legislatively mandated social policy, deserves credit for domestic electrical modernization. The consumerism thesis thereby denies that the New Deal significantly changed—assuredly it did not revolutionize—American domesticity. Bracketing the New Deal out of the history of modernization means that private industry substantially accomplished domestic electrical modernization in the 1920s, before the New Deal, or created in the decade of the 1920s the pattern of its fulfillment in the economic boom after World War II. Electrical modernization owed no debt to the American reform tradition. According to this conservative interpretation, the New Deal only extended the technological blessings of electricity to socially marginal groups who, for special historical reasons, had not participated in the uplifting forces of the free market. These groups included African-Americans, the urban poor, and farmers. The New Deal did not, therefore, alter the essence of the nation. Private enterprise corporations, driven by the market, shaped the economy. The national government assisted corporations by coordinating market administration, but did not direct the economy toward social goals.[6]

Historians are certain that the adoption of appliances brought significant social change in some homes in the 1920s. They are less sure about the nature of the change. Few scholars think that use of appliances liberated women from home labor as advertisements promised. Historians of women tend to believe that it degraded the upper- or middle-class woman by proletarianizing her: she did servants' work in the home, or made housework into factory production. Labor-saving devices made her labor in the home longer and harder, not easier. If such changes occurred, they would indeed have been revolutionary, because they would shatter the prevailing Victorian rationale of the home and the role of the mother and wife in it.[7]

Did domestic electrical appliances, which consumers bought in a private market uninfluenced by governmental social policy, cause a social revolution in values and behavior in the 1920s? Evidence does not allow us to see either widespread adoption of domestic electric appliances in the 1920s or significant social change due to their adoption. Statistics of adoption of electric refrigerators, ranges, vacuum cleaners, clothes washers, flatirons, and heating pads during the decade demonstrate that private industry put appliances into only a small number of homes. Capitalism drastically skewed the distribution of income, housing quality, and general quality of life in the 1920s. Private sector promotion of appliances did not challenge the highly unequal distribution of wealth. In April 1929, at the end of eight years of expansive prosperity, the majority of electrified homes (81 percent) owned the electric flatiron. Since many of the nation's homes were not electrified, only 60 percent possessed an electric flatiron. Electrified households made the vacuum cleaner the second most widely adopted appliance, but only 39 percent of them possessed one, and only 29 percent of all homes, electrified and not electrified, possessed one. Only 27 percent of electrified homes, 20 percent of all homes, possessed the third most widely adopted device, the clothes washer. The low rates of electric appliance adoption at the end of the 1920s boom mean that less than one in four of all homes owned more than two electric appliances. In every city, in only a "few neighborhoods . . . residents spoke confidently about shaping an environment with the aid of air conditioning, electric lights, and heat. In most other sections of their cities, however, residents continued to watch the price of coal and pass information from one generation to the next about starting a cranking coal stove on chilly mornings." The wondrous commercial vision of domestic electrical technology, a world in which machines and not persons labored, simply could not have been true for the overwhelming majority of American households. Dodsworth's dream was only a fantasy. (See table I.1.)[8]

To deny that a social revolution in the household occurred in the 1920s does not deny that some households adopted appliances, or that some players in the marketplace wanted a revolution to occur, or that popular advertisers puffed mightily to precipitate social change, or that many individuals pined for personal transformation through technology. Undoubtedly, as historians have shown, some manufacturers tried to change household work habits. Many individuals hoped, in an enduringly American way, that electric technology would radically transform their lives. As so often happens in the real world, however, a huge gap separated promise and reality.

We may suspect that a social experience narrowly limited to high-income homes in the 1920s would have a socially conservative meaning, not a progressive meaning. Rather than viewing electricity as a transformative force, these favored Americans might well have employed appliances conservatively to distinguish their class status and to protect and extend their disproportionate share of the nation's social wealth. Social and labor historians have found, looking at the labor role of women in the home, that introduction of electrical technologies reinforced conservative values. For these households, adoption of a full service of electrical devices would not have constituted *modernization.* Electrical labor-saving appliances in the 1920s culminated a century-long embourgeoisment of the home; they did not initiate an era of democratic electrical modernization. Conservative domestic values had great capacity to socialize the new electrical technology, as they were doing in the 1920s and 1930s with the telephone, without significant disruption to domestic habit.[9]

The structural bias in the U.S. economy in the 1920s argues against the thesis that 1920s prosperity planted the seeds of mass electrical modernization after 1945, when boom years returned. Mass electrical modernization after 1945 grew, rather, out of New Deal goals and programs, especially housing programs. New Deal policies sought social modernization of households through electrical modernization of their homes, not status conservation for the well-to-do. Advocates of the rational housekeeping movement early in the century called for social modernization of their homes and used electrical technology for this purpose. They conceived of appliances in the framework of household budgets, so as to transform the technology from simple labor-saving devices into assets that helped families navigate the new industrial economy. Progressive politicians adopted the rational housekeeping project. They proposed to use governmental power to sponsor it for the vast majority of the nation's households unable to buy appliances in the 1920s. Franklin Roosevelt's vision of the home culminated the Progressive reform tradition.

The appropriate historical context for understanding the electrical modernization of American homes is the political history of the nation's housing. The history of the material quality of the nation's dwellings involves the gradual obsolescence of shelter technology as new technologies offered more efficient services than old. It involves racial and class segregation of housing, which affected the housing stock realistically available to different races and economic classes. It involves local and national governmental policies regarding quality of housing. Regional policy debates in southern California and the political and economic history of housing in Riverside, California, typified the coming of electrical modernization to towns and cities around the nation. The New Deal sought a housing revolution—to raise substandard American residences up to minimal standards of physical shelter, to distribute the blessings of electrical modernization to the four-fifths of the nation's households that did not benefit from the domestic electrical affluence of the 1920s, and to modernize the social and moral qualities of the families in those homes. The New Deal sought to make the owner-occupied, electrically modern dwelling a major asset for lifelong security for all families, protecting them from the ragged winds of capitalism's uncertain wage labor market. As a national revolution of social modernization, electrical modernization resulted directly from the New Deal's transformation of the nation's homes.

Appendix

Table I.1.   Appliance Saturation Comparisons, 1922-1960

Appliance Dwellings	April 1922	April 1929	April 1933	April 1940	April 1950	April 1960
Flatiron						
All	26.6	59.9	55.9	66.9	77.9	84.8
Electrified	60.0	81.3	84.6	82.1	81.2	84.8
At risk	60.0	81.3	84.6	82.1	81.2	84.8
Vacuum cleaner						
All	13.5	28.4	31.8	40.5	51.3	69.3
Electrified	30.4	38.6	48.1	49.7	53.5	69.3
At risk	30.4	38.6	48.1	49.7	53.5	69.3
Heating pad						
All	0.8	6.6	9.9	16.0	25.3	34.2
Electrified	1.9	8.99	14.9	19.6	26.4	34.2
At risk	1.9	8.99	14.9	19.6	26.4	34.2
Clothes washer						
All	10.2	20.0	24.3	34.1	48.2	73.1
Electrified	23.0	27.1	36.8	41.8	50.2	73.1
At risk	34.3	38.4	50.7	55.1	62.0	73.1
Refrigerator						
All	0.1	4.6	14.0	40.2	67.1	93.5
Electrified	0.1	6.2	21.2	49.3	69.9	93.5
At risk	0.3	14.1	35.5	70.1	76.1	93.5
Range						
All	0.5	2.2	3.3	6.8	16.1	31.2
Electrified	1.2	3.0	4.9	8.3	16.8	31.2
Radio						
All		33.3	72.2			
Electrified		49.1	108.3			

NOTE: "Saturation" is the number of appliances in stock per one hundred households. Saturation is not applicable as a measure of adoption for range at risk, because I used range adoption to define the extent of modernized dwellings before 1945. "At risk" refers to the class of dwellings that could technologically have served the appliance. A dwelling without electricity is not "at risk" to use electrical appliances and a dwelling with only light circuits is not at risk to use heavy power appliances. I estimated saturation at the end of April to coincide with the decennial census. Floor model vacuum cleaners only; not including hand-held models. Radio saturation estimates refer to year-end, rather than midyear.

SOURCES: I estimated the adoption of household electrical appliances from a model of adoption, rather than generalizing from empirical marketing surveys of adoption. I made this choice for methodological reasons. Constructing a model gives me complete knowledge of the methods involved in estimating adoption, so I know how much confidence to place in my estimates. Also, with a time series model, I can test my projections against the few trustworthy surveys, especially the Bureau of the Census's 1940 survey of household refrigerators. I derived annual sales of appliances from *Electrical World* (established in 1906) and *Electrical Merchandising* (established in 1916), trade journals published by the McGraw Company. The Bureau of the Census also used their data in *Statistical Abstracts* (1963) and *Historical Statistics of the United States* (1976). I obtained annual estimates of the number of households from Patience Lauriat and Paul C. Glick, "Estimates of the Number of Households in the United States, 1900–1958," *Current Population Reports, Population Characteristics,* ser. P-20, no. 92 (Washington, D.C.: Bureau of the Census, 1959). I measured depreciation (i.e., removal of appliances from the stock of appliances in households) empirically by determining the rate of straight line depreciation that would best predict national censuses of appliance stock, such as the U.S. Census's 1940 query on possession of refrigerators. Depreciation estimates are summarized in the table below.

Appliance	Population Service Life (yrs)	Mean Service Life (yrs)	Annual Depreciation Rate (%)
Refrigerator	39	19.5	2.6
Range	35	17.5	2.9
Vacuum cleaner	29	14.5	3.5
Clothes washer	24	12.0	4.2
Heating pads	21	10.5	4.8
Flatirons	14	7.0	7.1

Hence, saturation is derived:

Cumulative sales = Year 1 sales + Year 2 sales . . . + Year × sales [–exports]
Stock = Cumulative sales – Depreciation
Saturation = Stock/Households

OTHER EMPIRICAL SURVEYS: Reports of private marketing studies do not sufficiently describe their methods for me to make confident generalizations on them. Also, nearly all surveys were of special markets, such as a particular city, or the electrified households in an operating utility's service area. Finally, although some marketing surveys asked respondents for income, none looked at housing conditions, which I identify in chapter 1 as a key factor in appliance adoption or housing tenure status of the resident (whether owner or renter), which I discuss as another key factor in chapter 6. I examined the following marketing surveys: Edison Illuminating Companies Survey, 1921–1923, of Selected Wired Residences in Eight Northeastern Cities, reported in *Electrical World* 82 (October 1923): 708–710; New York Edison Appliance Survey, 1925, Manhattan and Bronx Households, reported in "Survey of Appliance and Lighting Load," *Electrical World* 86 (August 22, 1925): 375; Chicago Residential Appliance Ownership, 1926 and 1929, reported in (for 1926) Harold L. Platt, *The Electric City,* table 29, "Household Electrical Appliances in Use in Chicago in 1926," p. 24, and (for 1929) George H. Jones (identified as Power Engineer of the Commonwealth Edison Company of Chicago), "Better Load Factor," *Electrical World* 95 (June 28, 1930): table, "Appliances Used in 5,000 Homes in Chicago," p. 1339; Pittsburgh Appliance Ownership, 1931, reported in table 14, "Consumption by Pittsburgh Families in Three Income Groups, 1931," *Recent Social Trends in the United States,* "Report of the President's Research Committee on Social Trends, " foreword by Herbert Hoover (New York and London: McGraw-Hill, 1933), 2:896; National Summary, Real Property Inventory Urban Places, 1934–1936, and Real Property Inventory Sixty-four Cities, 1934, reported in tables E, L, N, in Peyton Stapp, "Urban Housing: A Summary of Real Property Inventories Conducted as Work Projects, 1934–1936," Works Progress Administration, Division of Social Research (Washington, D.C.: U.S. Government Printing Office, 1938), 17 f.; Percentage of Urban Households Making Installment Purchases of Electric Appliances, 1935, reported in "Expenditures for Electrical Appliances by Workers in 42 Cities," prepared by the Bureau's Cost of Living Division, Faith M. Williams, chief, *Monthly Labor Review* 46 (February 1938): table 2, p. 450 ff.; Pittsburgh Domestic Appliance Ownership Survey, 1944, reported in Tom F. Blackburn, "Survey Reveals Pittsburgh Appliances Possibilities," *Electrical Merchandising* 72 (December 1944): table, "Percent of Families Owning Each Major Appliance," p. 20.

I provide a full account of the sales, stock, and depreciation models and analysis of the empirical surveys in Ronald C. Tobey, "Statistical Supplement to *Technology as Freedom*" (unpublished ms., 1995).

Chapter 1
The Limits of Private Electrical Modernization, 1919–1929

The Perspective of Enterprise

In the 1920s, American electrical utilities completed the final stage of their development. The commercial central station industry had evolved from small, local distribution systems at the turn of the century to regional transmission monopolies by World War I. Holding companies then consolidated regional utilities in the decade before the Great Depression. By 1929, five holding companies controlled 80 percent of the electrical generating capacity of the nation. Electrical operating utilities grew dramatically during the 1920s. The amount of electricity generated by central station utilities rose 228 percent, from 39,519 million kilowatts in 1920 to 90,076 million kilowatts in 1930. Revenues from sales of this electricity grew by 244 percent, from $882 million in 1920 to $2,155 million in 1930. Since the vast majority of ultimate consumers of electricity were households and since domestic consumption of electricity returned a significant percentage of utilities' revenue, observers assumed that utilities as an industry eagerly mass marketed home appliances during the decade to increase domestic consumption of electricity. This was not the case.[1]

Most utilities lacked enthusiasm for the domestic market, because their bottom line showed little profit from it. The industry in fact subsidized much household service—because governments required them to do so. As late as 1930, eight million households, or 40 percent of the nation's private utility domestic customers, did not consume enough electricity to be profitable. The utilities subsidized this service by maintaining higher flat rates to relatively high value domestic users.[2]

The utilities naturally wished to invest their capital in the most profitable projects. In the 1920s, the sale of electricity to industry using electric power motors brought the greatest profit. Between 1923 and 1929, the percentage of total electricity distributed in the United States taken by manufacturers rose from 48.2 to 52.9 percent. Central station electrification of industry brought high returns in two ways. First, many industrial plants and large stores had their own electrical generators and distribution systems. Utilities needed only to convince their management that they could buy central station energy more cheaply than they could generate their own power. The utility then could feed electricity to the industrial plant's electricity system, in some cases requiring installation of couplers to transform AC to DC current. The utilities' industrial campaign met remarkable success. After 1923 the aggregate power generated in the United States by isolated industrial power plants declined. The second reason for the high profit from industrial sales came from the geographical concentration of industrial plant energy consumption. Industrial motors used large amounts of electricity when measured by standard criteria, such as metered connections per mile of distribution line. Other factors also affected the relative profitability of the industrial and the domestic sectors of the business. For instance, domestic consumption's higher ratio of distribution mileage to meters meant greater losses of electricity from distribution lines. More meters brought higher overhead costs for service and management. An analysis conducted in 1923 of residential service in the Middle West revealed that the carrying cost of homes averaged $2 to $2.50 a month, at a time when the average revenue from homes was less than that.[3]

In 1929, domestic customers constituted 82.7 percent of users of central station energy but returned only 29.4 percent of total revenues. Large and small industries, by contrast, constituted 17.3 percent of customers and returned 55.5 percent of total revenues. The 1920s saw tremendous growth in household electrification, but the percentage of total customers comprised by households in 1929 changed little from 1922. Managers of the electric utilities understood their profit situation. As the utilities pulled out of the postwar depression (1920–1921), they looked to industrial electrification and electrical modernization of capital equipment for the profits they needed to attract financing for the increased generating capacity they intended to install. In an editorial of January 1923, *Electrical World,* the major management journal of the industry, pointed to the fact that only one-third of machine horsepower in industry came from electricity. The editors recommended conversion of the remaining two-thirds of industrial horsepower as the outstanding opportunity for the utilities. Projections of future electrical loads pointed to greater increases in industrial power loads than domestic lighting loads. In a set of ten-year projections made in 1924, industrial power clearly ranked as the planning priority, though predicted increases in domestic power sales warranted notice.[4]

An array of problems blocked increased sale of electricity to homes for the utilities. In the early 1920s, utility marketing analysts portrayed American homes as two distinct markets. Home illumination comprised one market for electricity; the other market called for full electrical service. Under public regulation to extend service broadly, utilities had to make capital investment to electrify new houses and to retrofit nonelectrified housing stock with wiring for illumination. Utilities thought households might install one or at most a few small electric appliances on house light lines. Managers drew back, however, from investing in electrifying dwellings for heavy appliances, because heavier appliances required heavier wiring and different neighborhood transformers, with no assurance that the investment would produce significantly greater consumption of electricity. Most utility managers simply did not believe, through the 1920s, that the home heavy appliance market would be sufficiently profitable for them to divert massive capital to it. A marketing study of 584 residential customers conducted by the Philadelphia Electric Company in 1926 demonstrated that the average light customer worked within a rigid budget for electrical service. Though households might be willing to buy appliances up to their budget limits, they resisted raising the level of budgeted expenditures for electrical service. Electrical demand was not elastic: "It would appear that considerable resistance exists to an increase in the annual expenditure even in the face of continual educational effort as to the advantages and economic benefits of a more liberal use of electric service." On the basis of analysis of federal income tax data and utility marketing, another analyst concluded flatly, "The actual demand for electric service will always be a function of the amount of the family budget that can be spent for these domestic requirements."[5]

As a result of the segmentation of the residential market, most utilities refused to build electrical load in the illumination sector that represented four-fifths of their customers. They focused their marketing efforts, instead, on increasing consumption by the few upper-income households who could pay for full electric service. This class represented a large market, no doubt, but not a mass market. A report by *Electrical World* in 1927 testified to this widespread strategy. An industry analyst surveyed 376 large utilities serving an aggregate population of 54,500,000 persons. The analysis demonstrated—in his opinion—that only 28 percent of the utilities promoted "full domestic service," that is, appliances as well as lights, across all their markets. They ignored lower-income households earning $2,000 to $3,000 a year. A review of 1928 revenues from fifty-seven operating utilities led *Electrical World* to conclude that only 10 to 20 percent of these utilities customers were "prospects for complete electric service at indicated competitive rates." The experience of the few utilities that did attempt to market full service indicated that average customers responded to lowered appliance prices and electric rates with increased demand; nonetheless, the overwhelming majority of utilities did not lower prices, refusing to believe that those households had sufficient income to make them worth the investment. Throughout the 1920s, the industry press was filled with self-confirming studies that middle- and lower-income households were not good markets for increased electricity consumption.[6]

For all the claims utilities made in the 1920s of marketing prowess and of the necessity for encouraging diversity of electric demand (for purposes of "load management"), the evidence in their own trade literature testifies that they had little understanding of domestic consumers and marketing. They pigeonholed households in a few large-scale categories. They expressed little appreciation for the individuality of consumer tastes and buying habits. They had little concrete information about how households actually worked inside the home or made buying decisions. Most utilities lacked appreciation for the research on rural, farm, and urban households by women social scientists of the U.S. Department of Agriculture in the 1920s and for the whole range of household management literature by housekeeping reformers. Their ignorance of the home market was not unusual. Telephone companies, for instance, could not initially imagine that households might want to use phones simply for social conversation. As the study by C. F. Lacombe revealed in 1927, most utilities had little understanding of the competitive, mass consumer marketplace.[7]

Some of the utilities' difficulty in assessing the residential market developed because they had no standard accounting methods to analyze the domestic rate structure. They could not determine how to charge the home user of appliances to make a profit. A survey in 1923 of thirty-five midwestern utilities revealed that in small operating utilities, with less than a thousand domestic customers, the utility managers had "almost a total lack of knowledge of what it costs to carry a residential consumer." The domestic rate posed an economic conundrum not solved by the utilities until the early 1930s. On the one hand, the cheap, flat rate enabled the utilities to fulfill their political mandate for universal electrification. On the other hand, the flat rate discouraged consumption of electricity. How did this situation arise? Samuel Insull's Chicago Edison system established the pattern of charging domestic customers by a cheap, flat rate in the 1890s. Insull adopted a two-tier rate that he thought would permit massive residential consumption, though this consumption did not develop as he expected. Ordinary household customers had a flat illumination rate. Large consumers had a second, lower, rate for consumption above a base amount. The two-tier billing structure reflected the utilities' segmented domestic market conception. Shortly before World War I, state regulatory commissions enshrined the flat rate as democratic social policy and thereby threw onto the utilities the burden of justifying a departure from this historic practice. Such justification proved extremely difficult. Not until the early 1930s did the utility industry agree on accounting procedures to determine profit and loss in delivering electrical service to the individual customer.[8]

Theoretically, the flat rate represented the average charge to the individual customer needed to cover capital and operating expenses, proportional to the aggregate ratio of capital and operating expenses for domestic customers as a whole. Being an average charge, domestic customers who consumed high amounts of electricity subsidized domestic customers who consumed low amounts. An analogous situation characterized the telephone industry before

1894. Bell systems charged users a universal flat rate. Only when telephone companies switched to per-message rates could average monthly charges drop sufficiently to make telephones attractive for homes, which used them less than did businesses. Before World War I, the electrical industry could tolerate the economics of the flat rate. Since sales to industry and electric railroads earned most of the utilities' profit, the loss due to subsidization was not great. It certainly did not seem worth the effort to put every domestic customer on a profit basis. During normal growth, the addition of profitable customers balanced the addition of subsidized customers. Subsidized customers had little reason to object. Profitable customers did not use enough kilowatt-hours of electricity monthly to make carrying a subsidized customer burdensome. Across the country, in the 1920s, the domestic flat rate ranged between nine cents and seven cents per kilowatt-hour (kwh). In 1922, a study by the Idaho Power Company demonstrated that to make a profit the company would have to charge 10.5 cents/kwh for the average domestic electric light customer (who used about 21 kilowatt-hours per month [kwh/mo.]). The flat rate did not provide for a decrease in charges as volume of consumption increased, until demand jumped to a higher step. For lower-income households, lack of incentive to increase consumption amounted to disincentive. The utility industry itself felt little motivated to try to change the flat rate structure, as long as economic prosperity continued. As late as 1928, according to an executive of the New York Power and Light Corporation, two of three cities in New York State charged a flat rate that discouraged increased residential consumption of electricity. As a result of this situation, the central station electrical generating industry halfheartedly expressed interest in the domestic market. As the editors of *Electrical World* put it in 1926, "As a matter of fact, frankly admitted, the central-station industry has never actually made serious, intelligent effort to develop the domestic market."[9]

The industry closely watched the Hartford Electric Light Company's experiment with a split rate structure. Before 1922, the company attempted to induce higher domestic consumption of electricity by offering a lower flat rate of 3 cents to 4 cents/kwh for customers with heavier wiring. Only five hundred residences (out of 15,000 served) fitted their homes with heavy wiring capable of taking heavy appliances. Prompted by this failure, in January 1922 the company offered a split schedule, whereby the customer paid 5 cents monthly per 100 square feet of floor area in the home and paid 6 cents/kwh for metered, delivered energy. For domestic customers with light wiring, this split schedule was cheaper than a flat rate of 10 cents/kwh. Over the decade, the company further reduced rates, so that in 1928, residences using over 200 kwh annually paid only 1.5 cents/kwh of delivered energy. By the company's own analysis, the experiment succeeded hugely. In 1921, only 10 percent of the domestic customers used over 480 kwh of energy a year; in 1928, 33.6 percent did.[10]

On the basis of the Hartford experiment and other similar marketing experiments, the utility industry concluded that it had to change the domestic rate structure to reflect the distinction between capital equipment costs and operating costs. Capital investment referred to the expense of extending electrical service to a home, including distribution lines, step-down transformers, light lines, and meters. Operating expenses referred to the costs created by generating the electricity sent over the wires to the residence. If the utility could charge each domestic customer to pay for its capital investment to the residence, then it could encourage all customers to consume more electricity with delivered energy rates cheaper than the existing flat rates. By the early 1930s, utilities were applying to utility commissions for the right to bill a fixed charge to cover capital investment, with a variable electricity rate above that. This split schedule permitted utilities to drop charges as low as 3.5 cents/kwh for delivered energy. As it turned out, the split rate with a lower kilowatt-hour charge returned greater profit to the utilities than the old flat rate, because of economies of scale in central station production of energy.[11]

In the late 1920s, scattered empirical evidence indicated that domestic demand for electricity would increase if prices fell significantly. The evidence convinced some utility managers of the potential of the domestic market. This internal persuasion in the industry never had the opportunity to ripen of its own logic, however; historical events intervened. The onset of the depression changed the context in which utilities thought about and acted in the domestic market. In response to general deflation, regulatory commissions forced domestic rates down. Because of rate experiments in the 1920s, the utilities were ready to respond to the demands of regulatory commissions. Accountants had devised standardized accounting procedures to analyze residential accounts. The new split schedule provided a convenient method for the companies to negotiate rate reductions with the commissions. Without doubt, the pressure of the regulatory commissions accelerated adoption of the new rate and accounting procedures inside the electric industry.[12]

In the economic collapse, the electric utilities lost a huge portion of their industrial market. By 1937 the manufacturing share of distributed electricity had dropped (to 52.3 percent). Who would replace the industrial customer? They could not expect to shift their sales to commercial and retail customers. The depression halted the growth of the commercial market. Nor did electrified mass transportation promise to absorb electricity not sold to manufacturing. The shift of the nation's urban transportation away from electric streetcars in the 1920s accelerated after 1929, so streetcars, once the economic core of the utility business, offered no potential for increased sales. In desperation, the private utilities turned to the only market left—the home. *Electrical World* made the point clearly: "Interest has centered in the home this year. . . . Because of the depression, neither the factory, store nor office has presented a hopeful field for rapid development." Being compelled by the depression to promote the domestic market did not necessarily make the utilities enthusiastic about that market. A positive attitude came later, from the success of the great public power experiment of the 1930s that the utilities had fought successfully in the 1920s: the Tennessee Valley Authority. TVA provided a vast experiment in home electrical modernization. Its extraordinary success in increasing domestic electrical usage among some of the poorest American households in the nation overwhelmingly proved that domestic demand for electricity could be elastic: the lower the price, the more households consumed. "While private utility managers believed in the value of electricity and its promotion, few realized that electricity demand had such a high elasticity. In other words, TVA planners demonstrated that usage could be stimulated dramatically with extremely low rates, which would be justified only if usage actually increased through promotion and appliance saturation." The depression and the TVA committed the private utility industry to the mass domestic market in a way that the prosperity of the booming 1920s could never do.[13]

While utilities approached the home market hesitantly, manufacturers of electric appliances enthusiastically expanded production for the home market in the 1920s. The number of electrical manufacturing establishments increased from 1,333 in 1921 to 1,777 in 1927, and their sales increased from $833 million to $1.6 billion. The increase in manufacturers indicated the entrance into the domestic market of small start-up companies, which might annually build less than a thousand units of an appliance. Large and established corporations also saw opportunity in home sales. General Electric, the nation's largest electrical manufacturer, turned to the residential market to recover from the post–World War I depression, in which G.E. laid off a quarter of its workforce. When Gerard Swope became president of G.E. in 1922, he pushed the company into high-quality appliance lines, starting with refrigerators.[14]

The complications of manufacturers' participation in the residential market, however, constrained its growth. The largest home appliance companies, General Electric and Westinghouse, were deeply involved with the electric power utilities and had to accept the basic segmentation of the residential market as strategized by the utilities. General Electric created the Electric Bond and Share Company in 1905, for instance, to finance expansion of operating utilities, which would purchase electrical equipment from their shareholder, G.E. The issue of the home electrical appliance market in the 1920s is not simply its size and dynamics. It is also the extent to which market categories prescribed by the utilities bound appliance manufacturers. A small historical literature and a few industry aggregate statistics indicate that the manufacturers, like the utilities, did not try to create a mass market for their products in the 1920s. Income segmentation of households raised market barriers for appliance manufacturers as for the utilities. For the appliance manufacturers, as for the utilities, the mass market came in the mid-1930s.[15]

Internal business considerations also limited the interest of large manufacturing corporations in the home market. Domestic appliances represented only one product group in their diversified production. Electrical equipment manufacturers produced for a large market of value-added manufacturers. Home electrical appliance makers took only a small percentage of their production. In 1927, home heating and cooking appliances took only 4 percent of manufacturers' sales; radio equipment, 12 percent. Manufacturers' sales to makers of electrical home appliances totaled only $73 million. The automobile and utility industries, by contrast, took a huge share of manufacturers' sales. Battery sales (9 percent) and generator sales (7 percent) grossed $265 million of revenue. Radio sales greatly exceeded all appliance sales. General Electric and Westinghouse built a wide variety of capital goods for the electric utilities and for other industries, as well as consumer appliances. In the early 1920s, General Electric marketed nearly 400,000 separate catalog items. Home market divisions of these corporations had to compete with other divisions for the corporation's investment capital. G.E.'s board of directors passed on all departmental requests for investment capital exceeding $100,000 for production purposes and $50,000 for research. This scrutiny generated intense interdepartmental competition at budget proposal time, driven by the same profit considerations as intercorporate competition. How did the home market appliance division's gross revenue, return on investment, percentage of profit to sales, and percentage of profit to value added compare to other divisions? The results of this comparison affected the capability and willingness of corporation directors to wage battle in the home marketplace, or to try more ambitiously to break down the utilities' segmentation of the residential market.[16]

Languid price competition among appliance companies is a strong indicator of their lack of interest in breaking down segmentation of the home market. They kept prices high throughout the decade. In 1929, the average price for electric refrigerators advertised in Riverside, California, newspapers was $268, for ranges $111, for washing machines $116, and for radios $116. General Electric, Westinghouse, and Allis-Chambers divided the market and administered prices for industrial electrical equipment in the early 1920s. Despite Gerard Swope's exhortation that price competition in home appliances would benefit his company, manufacturers and retailers did not lower prices of large home appliances rapidly enough in the 1920s to make them affordable to the lower four-fifths of the nation's households. Nor did they have to. Deriving but a small percentage of their income from appliance sales, large diversified companies could afford to keep sales volume low and target households in the top income bracket with high-priced models. The impression is irresistible that the major manufacturers wanted to extend to the new home market the same oligopolistic, administered market structure they had for the market in industrial electrical equipment. General Electric used its patents to control the production and pricing of lightbulbs—by far the largest-grossing product for the home market in the 1920s. Westinghouse, for instance, used G.E. patents to manufacture its bulbs. They did not engage in the severe price cutting that would crush small companies and enlarge their market share at the expense of their large rivals.[17]

Not until the depression did prices of refrigerators, ranges, and washers fall sufficiently to break the dual market barrier of the 1920s. Only when TVA created a prototype mass market did prices fall to the point at which nearly every household, as long as it had some regular income, no matter how small, could buy a major appliance. Industry priced only small appliances—cookers and casseroles, desk fans, heating pads, irons, percolators, and toasters—for the mass market in the 1920s; yet, looking at price changes between 1921 and 1941, only the refrigerator took its largest price drop in the 1920s. Before 1934, few appliance manufacturers priced any models within reach of a true mass market. TVA compelled the large producers, particularly General Electric and Westinghouse, to develop mass market models for it; prices dropped as much as 50 percent below those of 1932. Seven of the eleven leading household appliances took their first or second greatest drop in price after 1932, almost certainly the result of New Deal pressures. At this point, aggregate sales began to soar.[18]

The difficulties for home mechanical refrigeration illustrate the barriers to the domestic market for manufacturers. Engineers did not make key technological inventions until the 1920s. Once manufacturers commercialized these inventions, such as the best refrigerant, electric refrigerators began to flood the market in 1929, just before the depression. Problems of mass marketing of electric refrigerators were, however, just as important as the pace of technical invention in delaying the device's mass adoption. In particular, the manufacturers' acceptance of the utilities' segmentation of the residential market in the 1920s prevented them from trying to develop a truly mass market machine. Before the early 1920s, appliance manufacturers developed industrial and commercial markets for mechanical refrigeration. These markets offered greater profit per refrigerator unit than the home market. Hotels, restaurants, ice cream parlors, and meat and fruit wholesalers were early buyers of mechanical refrigerators. In agriculture in the 1920s, California, Texas, and Florida produce packers built large mechanical precoolers to prepare fresh fruit for long rail journeys to eastern markets by slowly lowering fruit temperature before railcar loading. These commercial and industrial refrigerators were usually of walk-in size and custom designed. Domestic refrigeration represented a significantly different market. Mechanical refrigerators for the home had to be much smaller than commercial refrigerators. In the home, cheap ice dominated refrigeration. In the cities, many households did without any refrigeration at all, preferring to shop as needed for fresh foods rather than storing them. In 1927, only 40 percent of the nation's households had refrigeration (nearly entirely ice refrigeration), and only 17 percent took ice year-round. Home marketing required more than simply sending salesmen out to knock on doors; it required a different product.

The major problem for manufacturers in developing a home refrigerator was lack of standardization of components used in making refrigerators and lack of market standardization in the design and capacity of the refrigerators themselves. Since the industry sold to large commercial and industrial establishments, they designed the motors, compressors, and other equipment to cool large volumes of air. The industry did not standardize fractional horsepower motors for small refrigerators until late in the decade. As late as 1925, motors required higher voltage to operate than many homes could offer. At the 1925 meeting of the National Electric Light Association, "some representatives [of refrigerator and motor manufacturers] said that they had frequently found the supply as low as 70 volts, which, of course, is altogether inadequate for this service, as well as for general service in the home. This was a very general complaint." Motor manufacturers invested in research on fractional horsepower motors reluctantly, because the market for home refrigerators was small. Refrigerator manufacturers similarly had difficulty standardizing the refrigerator itself because the market was so small. For instance, Commonwealth Edison of Chicago undertook a concerted sales campaign in 1923 for home electric refrigerators. The company contracted with a manufacturer for a single small standard box to sell to customers. In 1923 and eleven months of 1924, the giant utility installed only 279 refrigerators. Not until 1926 did the domestic refrigeration market take off, with national sales moving toward several hundred thousand units annually.

The small number of refrigerators sold in the mid-1920s meant that the product had not reached the stage of mass production. In 1925, Frigidaire, the largest manufacturer of refrigerators, had only 35,000 of its machines installed around the country. Kelvinator followed with 26,840 installed. Servel held third place with only 3,500 refrigerators in homes. In 1926, there were ninety-five different makes of home refrigerators on the market, many of them manufactured by companies with annual sales of less than twenty-five units. The distributor-dealers of large manufacturers, such as Kelvinator, Frigidaire, and General Electric, maintained such large repair shops for preservicing the units prior to installation in homes that we cannot call the machines mass produced at all. The low sales volume and the large preinstallation servicing kept prices high. Salesmen reported that potential customers resisted their sales pitch because of the high initial cost of the device. The high price meant that upper-income homes represented the only market for the device.

For prices to drop, manufacturing had to be concentrated in a small number of companies that could build refrigerators in sufficiently high volume to develop effective mass production and to gain economies of scale. Manufacturers had to increase the quality of the machines so that they could move from factory to home directly, without preinstallation services. When this happened, major retailers, such as Sears Roebuck, which did not want to finish manufacturing of low-quality boxes, could market them. At the same time, equipment manufacturers had to develop more efficient motors that worked off low-voltage domestic lines. This conjunction of events occurred in the early 1930s, and prices dropped rapidly. Nonetheless, even as late as 1935, upper- and middle-income families made up the majority of owners. A survey of Austin, Texas, showed that only 15 percent of all households had electric refrigerators but that half of all families with an annual income of $3,000 owned them. A true mass market did not exist until the federal government made refrigerators eligible for Title I insured loans under the National Housing Act and TVA forced manufacturers to build mass market models for the TVA sales programs.[19]

In conclusion, electrical manufacturers did not attempt to break residential market segregation in the decade. Their ties to the utilities effectively bound them to the latter's segmentation of the home market. Even Swope complained that the persistent high price for electricity doomed his ambitions for broadening the domestic market for G.E. during the decade. The depression broke the stranglehold of the utilities' conceptualization of the nation's electrical market. In 1929, electrical manufacturers sold $2.3 billion worth of products; in 1933, they sold only $549 million worth of goods. While general price deflation accounted for some of this decline, decreased sales of their industrial products accounted for most of it. In a long review of the industry in 1935, *Electrical World*'s editors argued that the domestic market represented the only growth market left. New Deal policies had made domestic electrical modernization a national priority. "Electrification is in popular favor. Electrical products and electric service are considered necessary to advance both economic and social standards in this country. Government spending and action are directed toward increased electrification." The electrical market created by the New Deal redirected investment of electrical manufacturing companies and enabled them to work their way toward prosperity.[20]

Enthusiasm of appliance manufacturers for the home market produced an explosion of advertisements for appliances in the mass media. The deluge of advertisement would seem to imply that selling of consumer appliances had no obstacles. Careful study of merchandising in the 1920s shows, to the contrary, that problems in merchandising restrained electrical appliance retailing until the 1930s. The vice president of Commonwealth Edison of Chicago called the distribution of appliances so poor as to constitute a "joke." Three problems were particularly troublesome: the small number of retailers, lack of credit, and the lack of a service industry.[21]

Five classes of retailers sold electrical appliances: the electric utilities, independent appliance specialty stores, hardware stores, department stores, and mail-order houses. The utilities and the mail-order houses used traveling salesmen to supplement walk-in trade. In 1923, electrical utilities sold 31 to 41 percent of total sales (in dollar volume) of electrical appliances, dominating retailing, especially of heavy appliances. Department store and mail-order retailing did not take significant market shares until late in the decade, when consumer advocates and other retailers politically pressured utilities to withdraw from retailing. This means that a seller—the utilities—that had little interest in the home dominated electrical appliance merchandising. Concentration of retailing in a halfhearted retailer throttled sales. Suppliers did not compete in price. Customers found shopping inconvenient. Retailers did not solicit the customer's attention. In contrast, in one of the few cities where the central station utility did not retail appliances, there were two additional classes of retailers—home furnishing stores and electric shops. Department stores had a slightly higher percentage of the trade, but retailing remained decentralized. Retailers competed in prices, a shopper could easily locate a store selling an appliance, and salesmen competed in service to the potential customer.[22]

Retailing did not improve in the next two years. In 1925, *Electrical World* surveyed the selling of electrical appliances in the geographic areas served by 174 operating utilities. Electrical utilities sold 42.5 percent of all electric appliances, in dollar volume, compared to 26.9 percent by electrical dealers (including specialty stores), 15.4 percent by department stores, and 15.2 percent by all other stores. In conclusion, the domination of retailing by the electric utilities in the first half of the 1920s constrained the market for appliances. Even *Electrical World* concluded that electrical modernization of the home would proceed more rapidly if electrical utilities did not dominate appliance merchandising. "If other dealers, both electrical and non electrical, could or would build up their sales volume so as to reduce the power companies' proportionately large share of the total, it would aid materially in a quicker and more complete electrification of the home." Consumers, too, wanted to end the utilities' domination of appliance merchandising. In 1931, Oklahoma and Kansas passed laws prohibiting utilities from selling appliances. With utility merchandising stopped, the number of appliance retailers increased dramatically over the next four years. Sales of appliances increased. In 1930, Oklahoma consumers bought only 2,085 clothes washers; with utilities out, in 1932 they bought 5,487 washers (in the worst year of the depression!), then increased purchases to 8,662 in 1933 and 11,067 in 1934. Sales of all other appliances similarly soared as dealers and merchants invigorated the market.[23]

At the end of the decade, the utilities' domination of retail selling of appliances began to diminish. In 1930, they constituted only 30 percent of national aggregate sales of electric appliances. Observers thought department stores took an increasing share. In 1931, department stores made 24 to 30 percent of retail sales of appliances across the nation. While the number of stores specializing in electric appliances increased in the years 1925 to 1929, the depression reduced their ranks. The decision of Sears Roebuck, of Chicago, in 1931 to offer refrigerators through catalog sales typified the shift in merchandising. The depression rapidly completed this reorganization of the retailing structure of the domestic market for electrical appliances. By the mid-1930s, the utilities no longer dominated retailing and sales of electrical appliances rose dramatically.[24]

The Consumer's Perspective

Powerful restraints reined in consumers' buying of electric appliances in the 1920s. Reduced capability to take on more installment debt, unreliability of the new technology, difficulty in obtaining repair service, incompatible home tenure status, competition from alternative technologies, and preference for services over savings suppressed purchases. Most households bought appliances on installment credit. The amount of credit consumers could acquire and the way they preferred to use it affected what they purchased. Consumers overwhelmingly preferred spending their money on automobiles rather than on household durable goods. Households spent 31 percent of their expenditures on durable goods on automobiles, and only 8 percent on household appliances. The extent of household finances devoted to the automobile dampened purchase of other major goods. Contrast with the 1930s shows the preferences. When hard times reduced the ability of households to buy automobiles, they nonetheless increased their spending on household appliances. The share of household budgets consumed by auto purchases increased only 4 percent in the 1930s over the 1920s. The share of budgets consumed by appliance purchases increased 24 percent. The shift in consumer preferences is more dramatic when stated in dollars. In 1929, of every $100 of consumer debt, consumers spend $47 for automobiles, and only $.91 for home repair and modernization loans. In 1936, they spent $42 for automobiles, and $11 for home repair and modernization loans.[25]

Although appliances were cheaper than automobiles, sales of automobiles soared over appliances. The annual retail sale of autos rose steadily from 1,457,000 cars in 1921 to 4,036,000 in 1929, totaling 26,957,000 vehicles over those years. The cumulative number of autos sold in the 1920s nearly equaled the number of households in 1929 (29,582,000). In nine years, the auto had attained nearly universal adoption. Henry Ford helped the nation to envision a true mass market for the automobile, and in the 1920s automobile manufacturers both created and saturated that market. The contrast with electric home appliances is telling. For every electric dishwasher Americans purchased in 1929, they purchased 336 cars; for every electric desk fan, 6 cars; for every refrigerator, 5 cars. Only the radio surpassed the popularity of the auto in 1929; Americans bought 4,438,000 radios that year. The electrical industry of the 1920s simply failed to grasp the nature of a mass market for their products.[26]

The mass adoption of the radio in the 1920s reveals, as does mass adoption of the automobile, the willingness of households to spend money and, by contrast, their reluctance to spend money on electrical appliances. Commercial radio broadcasting began in 1920. Manufactured radio receivers were widely available by 1922. Montgomery Ward sold its first receiver for $49.50 in its 1922 fall catalog. Radio sets quickly became popular, but not until mid-decade did the radio industry overcome marketing barriers to offer a mass product. Early radios took power from a battery, offering as little as forty hours of reception before the owner had to recharge the battery at a store or utility. Replacement of short-lived vacuum tubes added to inconvenience. Although the radio industry touted its own growth, by the end of 1925, it had placed only 2,850,000 radio sets in American homes, barely 10 percent saturation. The accomplishment is even less impressive when we consider that no division between nonelectrified rural homes and electrified urban homes hobbled marketing of battery-powered radios.

Beginning in late 1925, political, technological, and cultural developments rapidly created a national mass market for radio. After a year of intensely competitive research, in the fall of 1925 ten manufacturers began marketing radio receivers that plugged directly into house current. They built all the components of the radio—receiver, amplifier, tuner, speaker, battery eliminator—into a single cabinet. A year later, RCA, General Electric, and Westinghouse, the major corporations involved in American radio, established the National Broadcasting Company. NBC began the first nationwide continuous programming. In 1927, the federal Radio Act regularized (and thinned the ranks of) the hundreds of independent broadcasting stations, making the airwaves more useful for net-worked broadcasting. Significantly, by explicitly opposing monopoly, the new law indirectly forced RCA to license key patents to competitors, opening up the number of manufacturers of radios, increasing competition, and lowering the costs of radio sets. In just two years, from 1925 to 1927, manufacturers and broadcasters transformed radio, positioning the industry to satisfy a nearly in-satiable demand by American households.

The eagerness with which Americans brought the house current radio into their homes places into perspective their laggard adoption of labor-saving household electric appliances. In the late 1920s, the radio receiver became the most widely adopted electricity-consuming domestic device, after the flatiron and the lightbulb. By 1933, Americans had purchased over 24,400,000 radios, enough for universal adoption by electrified households. The radio consumed enormous amounts of electricity, compared to flatirons and bulbs, and even com-pared to the vacuum cleaners and washing machines used by a minority of homes in 1928. The radio broke the long-standing resistance of domestic consumers to high consumption of electricity. The mass adoption of the very expensive au-tomobile throughout the 1920s and the radio at the end of the decade revealed starkly the consumer choices made by Americans. They chose to modernize transportation and information, but not household labor. The electrical industry caught the comparison. *Electrical World*'s editors scolded their readers: "The more impressive thought is this—that if after all these years a normal household already spends as much for radio as it does for all the benefits of electricity, the electrical industry has not done a selling job of which it can be very proud."[27]

Failings of appliance technology and inadequate repair service also blocked domestic electrical modernization in the 1920s. The technological optimism of advertising did not accurately reflect reality. Lack of standardization meant a consumer could not be sure that she could plug an appliance into her home. Industry standardized plugs and receptacles on the parallel-bladed plug only in the mid-twenties. She could not be sure that wiring and heating element connections were durable, or that she could conveniently make repairs. Major appliances were in their early stages of development with attendant problems of product reliability. An engineer cited as typical a washing machine in which the handle came off, two rivets popped, the motor's torque drove the bracing out of alignment, and the machine worked well only for a month. One service organization, the United Appliance Company and Electric Shop Company, of Jackson, Michigan, kept service records on 450 mechanical refrigerators under its service contracts. Over six years, those 450 refrigerators required a total of 1,440 service calls, an average of 3.2 per machine. Problems included faulty au-tomatic controls, burned out motors, and leaking tanks. The National Electric Light Association calculated that refrigerator service cost as much as $24.39

per year. Detroit Edison Company—a large company serving a large city, admittedly—made 173,928 appliance repair calls in 1923. In August, the company's repair shop made 13,392 repairs on electric iron cords alone. Addressing the Electric Association of Chicago in 1926, Samuel Insull complained, "It is impossible to escape the conclusion that lack of standardization in appliance manufacturing, and the consequent effect upon selling prices, has been a large factor in retarding the use of domestic appliances." Faulty appliances deprived utilities of potential sales of electricity so large that one utility found it economical to establish regular service routes for inspection and maintenance of customers' appliances and to offer the first dollar of repairs free. As late as 1929, the problem of appliance quality remained sufficiently serious that the Association of Edison Illuminating Companies began an inspection and testing program. When utilities were slow to protect consumers from poor merchandise, merchants sometimes stepped in. In 1928, seventeen New York City department stores, in cooperation with insurers and electrical inspectors, organized an inspection program to remove unsafe and poorly manufactured electrical goods from their shelves. Consumers also organized to protect themselves from shoddy manufacturing and lack of standardization. By 1933, forty communities, most in western states, had passed ordinances prohibiting local merchants from selling unsafe appliances, requiring standardization in wiring, and providing for inspection.[28]

Competing technologies and services erected a third major barrier to domestic electrical modernization in the 1920s. Adoption of electric appliances frequently required displacing existing nonelectric appliances, as electric cooking had to replace gas cooking. Despite evidence from home economics studies that cooking costs for gas and electric ranges were roughly equal, or could be made so by careful selection of an efficient electric range, gas ranges overwhelming dominated urban cooking. In 1930, 13.7 million homes used piped gas to cook, and less than a million used electricity to cook. Persistent use of cheap ice refrigeration slowed adoption of electric refrigerators. Once widespread adoption of the domestic mechanical refrigerator began, the ice industry greatly improved ice boxes, intensifying competition. It added, for instance, the finned metal grid for better circulation of cold air and better insulation.[29]

As their incomes rose, households bought services, rather than labor-saving appliances. They ordered industrially canned and bottled foods from stores and prepared foods at delicatessens by telephone, or went out to restaurants instead of preparing food at home. Women went out to beauty parlors, rather than curl their hair at home with electric curling irons. Once bobbed hair became a popular women's hairstyle in the mid-twenties, the sale of electric curling irons declined, since the style required the gas iron available at parlors. In cities and towns, street peddlers sold seasonal fruits and vegetables and meats and fish door to door, thereby making long-term storage of fresh produce unnecessary. Dairies delivered fresh milk products to homes. We can easily imagine that a city household would be reluctant to spend money for a mechanical refrigerator

Plate 2. *Competition for Electrical Refrigerators.* ([Photographer unknown.] "The Meat Wagon." Keystone-Mast Collection. UCR/California Museum of Photography, University of California, Riverside.)

when they had minor year-round cold storage needs. Scholars generally presume that street peddlers disappeared in the 1920s, as Americans bought cars and sped from store to store. This probably did not occur until the 1930s. The business licenses for Riverside, California, through the mid-1920s prove that street peddlers were plentiful and frequent, year-round. (See pl. 2.) As many as four delivery persons and peddlers visited each home every day. Plied from horse-drawn carts and trucks, seasonal fruits appeared at every household's door: Washington navel oranges and grapefruit in the winter, Valencia oranges in the summer, apples from Oregon and Washington in September, apples from southern California mountains in October and November, truck crops from the neighboring arroyos and river bottom all year long. Ice came daily. Laundries made regular pickups and deliveries. In the winter of 1922, police issued forty-seven peddler's licenses, permitting sale of over twenty items, including hats, furs, clothes, raincoats, medicinals, belts, ice, milk, melons, fish, meat, fruit, vegetables, ladies garments, shoes, and walnuts. This situation did not change until the mid-1930s, when the great increase in floating unemployed population and homeless transients, many of whom begged door to door, cast general suspicion on street vendors. At the same time, adoption of refrigerators after 1935 enabled households to dispense with the services of peddlers.[30]

The competition between commercial laundry service and domestic electrical washing machines epitomizes how competition from services dampened consumer demand for electrical appliances. Ownership of home electric clothes washers dramatically increased in the early 1920s. The washing machine apparently had "profound implications for the reorganization of work in the households of the prosperous. Possession of an electric washing machine meant that a 'decent' housewife could do her wash at home." By encouraging women to do laundry in the home themselves, instead of having servants do it or sending it out to commercial laundries, ownership of the home washer dramatically increased the effort, time, and onerousness of laundry duty. These new duties would have ended the Victorian ideal that the bourgeois woman should supervise labor, rather than be a laborer, and use time freed from labor to cultivate the home as a moral setting.[31]

Did a laundry revolution really occur? Statistics on adoption of electric washing machines provide the strongest evidence that it did, but the statistics are misleading. For most of the decade the percentage of electrified homes owning washers increased little. In 1922, 34.3 percent of electrified households had electric washing machines; in 1929, 38.4 percent had them. Between 1921 and 1942, the nation's stock of washers never dramatically and quickly rose so as to indicate a popular revolution in housekeeping. When we look at the percentage of all homes (nonelectrified as well as electrified), the ownership of washers is less impressive. The saturation of all households rose from 10.2 percent in April 1922 to 20 percent in 1929. Four of five American homes did not adopt the electric washing machine in the booming twenties.[32]

Instead of laundering clothes at home, families used wet-wash and dry cleaning services. By the end of the 1920s, nearly two-thirds of households in cities larger than 50,000 persons sent laundry to commercial laundries or to laundresses outside the home. While the ability to send laundry out depended to a certain extent on household income, a study of 12,096 wage-earning families in 1918–1919 showed that 43.4 percent of all families earning less than $900 a year sent laundry out. Isabel Lord, who directed her budgeting textbook toward the small percentage of upper-class families who paid a federal income tax in the early 1920s, assumed they would send laundry out. A 1928 study of 306 families, most of whom were college educated and lived in midwestern small towns, showed that 22 percent of them used commercial laundries or hired laundresses. Detailed study of six of the forty-two cities included in the Bureau of Labor's 1934–1936 household survey confirms the resistance of households to doing their own laundry. Among lower-middle-income households, even in the depression, as many as a quarter to a half of families paid to have their laundry done. In Denver and Los Angeles, over 40 percent of all households paid for laundry service.[33]

When wet laundries opened in a neighborhood, sales of washing machines declined. In Chicago, electric washing machine sales were high during the early 1920s but dropped off at mid-decade after forty-five wet-wash services set up in the city. By 1926, these washes were sending out 350,000 bundles a week, servicing a sizable minority of the city's households. National total receipts for commercial laundering and dry cleaning rose from $362 million in 1925 to $541 million in 1929. Southern appliance dealers long believed that the inexpensive services of African-American laundresses represented a real obstacle to increased sales of electric washers in their region. Phyllis Palmer verified this folk wisdom for one southern city, Jackson, Mississippi, in the early 1930s. She found that 81 percent of all white households in Jackson either had black laundresses in to do laundry or sent out their laundry to black home laundresses or commercial laundries. Half of all white families also paid black housekeepers to iron their laundry. A concerted campaign by laundry owners in 1934 to slow the loss of their business to home electric washing machines produced striking success. Lowering the price of damp wash to forty-nine cents for a fifteen- to twenty-pound bundle brought a 150 percent increase in laundry business in Milwaukee and Oklahoma City, a 100 percent increase in business in Denver, and a 250 percent increase in Kansas City.[34]

Home tenure provided a fourth major constraint on electrical modernization of the household. Until the post–World War I period, most American households did not own their home. Not owning, they did not have the right to renovate the home as needed for electrical modernization. They also would not have the home equity with which to secure modernization loans. Even if they could renovate, they had less interest in doing so than owners. Renters moved more often than owners. Modernization (as by incorporation of an electric range) might encumber the opportunity to move. Mildred Wood, a home economist, reflected this concern in her 1932 discussion of the advantages of owning a home, when she mentioned, as a reason to own rather than rent, that owners could accumulate possessions without having to worry whether they would fit in the next place they lived.[35]

Appliance Sales and Household Formation

Two additional factors limited adoption of appliances during the 1920s: household formation and dwelling technology. Analysis of appliance sales of six electric appliances—flatiron, heating pad, vacuum cleaner, washing machine, range, and refrigerator—shows the influence of household formation. Sales of these appliances did not grow uniformly in the 1920s. In the first half of the decade sales increased rapidly, but sales in the second half of the decade slowed. The slowing is clear in growth rates. Growth rates express more complex demand dynamics than annual sales figures. Sales can increase year to year in absolute numbers, but the rate at which they increase can decline, reflecting some underlying change in demand. In the 1920s, the refrigerator's growth peaked in 1926, when sales were 120 percent greater than the previous year. Range growth peaked in 1926, also, when its sales were 26 percent greater than the previous year's sales. Clothes washer and vacuum cleaner sales growth peaked in 1923, when washers sales were 29 percent greater and vacuum cleaner sales 24 percent greater than the previous year. Heating pad sales growth peaked in 1927, at 71 percent greater than the previous year. Well before the financial crash in fall 1929, electric home appliance sales growth peaked.

The slowing of sales growth coincides with a well-known, national demographic slowdown. In the mid-1920s, the number of marriages, new households, and persons under four years of age began to decline, not to resume an upward trend until the mid-1930s. The growth rate of household formation declined from 2.63 percent in 1921 to 2.02 percent in 1926 and 1.56 percent in 1929. New housing starts in urban areas peaked in 1925 (at 752,000 units) and declined to little more than half that number (400,000 units) in 1929, before the onset of the depression. The growth rates in sales of refrigerators, ranges, vacuum cleaners, and heating pads strongly correlate to growth rates of new households over the years 1921–1941. (Fig. 1.4 illustrates the comparative growth rates for refrigerator sales, households, and housing starts.) After the economic collapse, sales began to rise in 1933. The increase in appliance sales rode the New Deal and the demographic wave upward, following the increase in housing starts and in marriages, new households, and births. These changes in sales rates reflect the significant relationship between the growth in appliance sales and the growth in new households. The stimulation of the economy by the New Deal after mid-1933 increased the nation's capability to form new households. In this way, the appliance sales boom from 1933 to 1941 reflects improving economic conditions resulting from governmental stimulation of consumption.[36]

Normalizing the annual appliance sales against the number of households captures the close relationship between sales and household formation. Normalized data show clearly that the market dynamics of appliance sales in the 1920s were qualitatively different from the 1930s (after 1932). Except for the flatiron and the vacuum cleaner, normalized sales in the 1920s were *lower* than in the 1930s. Some of the normalized sales rates of the 1930s are as high as or higher than the normalized rates of the 1940s and 1950s, the postwar economic boom years. Only flatiron sales grew most rapidly in the 1920s (mean rate = 21.8 per 100 households per year during 1921–1929). Refrigerator sales grew greatest in 1933–1941 (rate = 10.3). Sales of ranges (rate = 11.4), washers (rate = 9.7), vacuum cleaners (rate = 7.2), and heating pads (rate = 4.5) grew most rapidly in 1946–1964. Only the electric range sold (at normalized rates) in postwar years significantly more than before the war, reflecting the significant increase in suburban households who elected to cook with electricity rather than gas and the electrification of the South.[37]

Without knowing the trends of the mean sales growth rates, we cannot interpret the means unambiguously. The unqualified mean rate of sales falling from ten to one million units a year is the same as the mean rate of sales rising from one to ten million units a year, yet no one would say that the averages are the "same." We need to examine the sales trends by direction of change, or vector. Doing so, we see immediately the importance of the 1930s. In terms of the sales growth of the household electric appliances, the decade saw a vector growth in sales rates, while the earlier or later periods saw vector decline in sales rates. Relative to the number of households living in dwellings technologically eligible to employ them, the 1930s were more important for appliance sales than the 1920s or the postwar years. A true mass market in electrical household goods existed for the first time. Sales after the war, from 1946 to 1964, trended downward. In the immediate postwar years, the pent-up demand for appliances expressed itself all at once. The years 1946, 1947, and 1948 experienced spectacular increases in the growth of sales. After a brief lull, in 1950 sales rates rose dramatically for the last time. The outbreak of the Korean War at midyear stimulated a splurge in buying by households fearful that the war would end consumer production, as had World War II. After 1950, growth in sales of appliances never again reached the height of the immediate postwar years. Viewed as a whole, therefore, the period 1945–1964 represented a long-term decline in growth of appliance sales, reflecting the slowing of the postwar baby boom. (See table 1.3.)

Dwelling Fitness for Electrical Modernization

The dwellings in which most households lived also affected their adoption of electric appliances in the 1920s. Electrification did not lead directly to electrical modernization of homes. Because a dwelling had electricity did not mean modernization could proceed simply by plugging in appliances and using them. Conflating electrification with electrical modernization confuses two distinct technological systems. Before federal home improvement programs during the New Deal, wired dwellings differed greatly in their capability to take electric appliances. The number and placement of outlets, the style of receptacles for plugs, and the type, load capacity, and insulation of wiring restricted the number and type of appliances that households could connect to the lines. Heat-producing appliances, such as ranges and ovens, required heavy, insulated wiring. Early refrigerator motors required higher wattage than was normally available to homes. Households could plug a small power appliance into lines, but only if a room had the appropriate receptacle. Until the 1930s, contractors usually did not build dwellings to take a full range of electrical appliances; they wired most dwellings for illumination only. Looking at the bleak prospect for putting significantly more appliances into the substandard American housing stock, the editors of *Electrical Merchandising* put the issue succinctly in 1926. "Some six or seven million new residence customers have been connected up in the United States since the close of [World War I]. These houses have been 'wired for electricity,' so the layman says. Yet every electrical man knows that on the average these homes contain not more than one-quarter to one-half of the wiring equipment which their owners should have installed in justice to themselves and to their families." The vast extent of inadequate residential wiring so alarmed *Electrical Merchandising* that the editors complained in italicized print: *"Electrical articles are the only ones which cannot be taken home and put to use by the purchaser, when, where, and as he pleases!"*[38]

The nation would not easily remedy the material inadequacy of the American dwelling. Despite the new houses built in the housing boom of the 1920s, the electrical industry continued to complain about the substandard electrical infrastructure of the American home well into the next decade. The general manager of the Virginia Electric & Power Company's Electric Department summarized industry opinion in 1933:

> Residential wiring has not kept pace, particularly as regards capacity, with the improvement in utilization devices. Interior wires and convenience outlets of adequate size are not available in any but a small percentage of residences. Many of the present popular appliances require electric currents exceeding the capacity of the common standard convenience outlets and the wires supplying them. Among these appliances the following are mentioned: Automatic flatirons, ironing machines, hot plates, portable ovens, space heaters, small water heaters, sun lamps, etc.[39]

A nation ill-housed did not provide a mass market for an "electrical age."[40]

We can distinguish between four classes of housing from the point of view of electrical service: dwellings with no electricity; dwellings with electricity only for illumination; those with the additional wiring for small appliances; and those fully wired to take stationary heating appliances. These divisions in the housing stock developed historically as builders constructed housing within the regulatory context of municipal building codes. The building codes evolved in response to changing building technologies and housing politics. Local communities around the United States wrote their own building, plumbing, and electrical codes under state enabling legislation. Standards reflected each community's particular environmental hazards, its building history, and the nature of its building stock. Before 1923, cities usually wrote electrical codes only to require electrical illumination and to ensure that electrical wiring, fixtures, and apparatus would not be a fire hazard. Most cities did not require builders to install wiring for electrical appliances. The 1923 electrical code for Bakersfield, California, for instance, required only that ceilings be wired to provide for a minimum number of "lamps" (bulbs). The city legislated that ceiling outlets in living rooms and dining rooms be wired to service at least four forty-watt lightbulbs and bedrooms be wired to supply electricity for at least two forty-watt bulbs. The 1922 electrical code for Pasadena, California, required that each room have a ceiling outlet wired to support at least two forty-watt bulbs. To ensure fire safety, both Bakersfield's and Pasadena's ordinances stipulated that all electrical installations must meet the requirements of the National Electrical Code of the National Board of Fire Underwriters.[41]

The National Electrical Code originated in 1897. A consortium of private manufacturers and insurers, the National Conference on Standard Electrical Rules, wrote the code to reduce fire hazard from early electrical installations and thereby to promote electrification. After disbanding of the conference, the National Fire Protection Association took over the function of testing electrical equipment and revising the code, which it did every two years. Members of the National Fire Protection Association included the American Electric Railway Association, the American Institute of Electrical Engineers, the Association of Edison Illuminating Companies, the National Board of Fire Underwriters, and the National Bureau of Standards (a U.S. government agency). The code had no legal force in itself; it constituted recommendations only. To provide legal force for the National Electrical Code, cities had to incorporate it into municipal ordinances. The 1923 revision of the code was particularly important for domestic modernization, because the association made rules more flexible for plugging in appliances. The 1920 code limited small motors attached to a heavy wire branch circuit to a maximum of 660 watts and limited the number of lamp sockets on a single circuit to sixteen. To meet the code at minimal cost, builders would install only a few illumination outlets (to serve lamp fixtures with multiple sockets), requiring only one circuit. This practice made the safe use of appliances nearly impossible. The 1923 code increased the maximum number of outlets per branch circuit, thereby reducing the cost of wiring while increasing electrical service. In a further effort to make dwellings safe for plugging in appliances, the code provided that circuits for small motor appliances should be of larger wire than lamp circuits and electricity provided through specially designated "convenience outlets." Heavy appliances required a third separate circuit, of still larger wire. The code discouraged use of socket receptacles for appliances, because plugging appliances into lamp sockets could burn out the lamp wiring and start a fire. Some cities did not require convenience outlets; Bakersfield and Pasadena did not, and undoubtedly many dwellings in those cities had no convenience outlets. In such dwellings, households wishing to use an electrical appliance would have to remove a lamp from an outlet and screw in a socket receptacle—a widespread practice around the United States (and still a frequent source of *New Yorker* cartoons). The failure of building or electrical codes to require convenience outlets partially accounts for the finding of a survey in the mid-1920s that the average dwelling in the United States had only three convenience outlets. Since builders frequently installed only a single ceiling outlet per room for a lamp fixture, households tended to fill base outlets, if they had any, with portable lamps, leaving no outlets open for appliances. A few cities took advantage of the code revision to require separate circuits for appliances. Chicago's 1923 electrical code revision required that convenience receptacles for appliance plugs be provided in living rooms, dining rooms, and kitchens. The 1923 version of the National Electrical Code thereby implicitly established categories of building quality in terms of electrical service.[42]

Meeting code requirements for small motor appliances, such as vacuum cleaners and sewing machines, added cost to wiring installation. Installation costs further rose if dwelling owners wanted to use heavy appliances. The code required that heavy heating appliances (such as stoves and water heaters) should be on a separate circuit with larger wire than either illumination or small motor circuits. Heating appliance circuits should also have indicator lamps to indicate whether the appliances were on, switches to shut off electricity to the appliance in an emergency, special grounding, and special fuse boxes. Wiring into kitchens with indoor plumbing required rigid, sealed, metal conduit to protect the heavy wiring from mechanical and water damage. Dwellings electrified for illumination only would not, therefore, have the approved number of circuits, size of wiring, safety devices, or outlets needed for safe use of appliances.[43]

The kind of protection required for wiring also differentiated the housing stock into classes. The National Electrical Code recommended different wiring protection corresponding to three, different, major wiring methods: rigid conduit, flexible conduit, and knob and tube. Rigid conduit involved armoring insulated wiring with rigid metal pipe and sealing it against moisture. Flexible conduit referred to sheathing insulated wiring with helically wound metal stripping. The metal protected wire against mechanical injury but—because the conduit had movable seams—not against water. Knob and tube installation left rubber-insulated wires exposed. Porcelain "knobs" carried wires through the dwelling like tiny power poles. Rigid porcelain tubes or flexible rubber tubes protected wires as they passed through partitions. Many cities, including Bakersfield, Pasadena, Chicago, Denver, and Kansas City, required metal conduit for concealed wiring in large buildings (e.g., office and public buildings and apartment houses with more than six units). Though the municipalities allowed flexible conduit or rigid conduit, metallic conduit was extremely expensive for retrofit installation, because installers had to open walls, ceilings, and floors. The author of one practical treatise on retrofit wiring delicately put it, "It is very difficult . . . to wire an old building throughout with rigid conduit without a great deal of cutting and disfigurement of walls and ceilings." Utilities and builders reluctantly installed more rigid conduit than the minimum required in dwellings, because most households used so little electricity that they gained little profit. Communities with a lot of inexpensive frame housing usually permitted knob and tube installation, because the cost of the housing would not warrant the more expensive methods. Nonetheless, knob and tube wiring for lights only provided minimal electrical service; safe addition of small motor appliances and heavy appliances still required upgrading the wiring. *Electrical World* estimated in 1931 that home owners could raise the average dwelling (of that year) with substandard wiring and fixtures to a "minimum standard" for a cost of $70, including materials, labor, and cost of lighting fixtures. From the point of view of the wiring required for electrical modernization, lights-only wiring was therefore substandard.[44]

I have estimated the changing proportions of the nation's housing stock in the four classes of housing: nonelectrified, "substandard," "standard," and "modern." Substandard dwellings had illumination wiring and minimal illumination only. Standard dwellings had many lights, higher-wattage bulbs, and power wiring for nonheating electrical appliances. Modern dwellings added heavy circuits for heating appliances to the standard wiring. In 1922, 80 percent of the nation's dwellings had no electricity or only substandard wiring. Only 19 percent had standard lights and wiring. By 1932, the situation had improved. Sixty-three percent of dwellings had no electricity or substandard wiring only while 34 percent were in the standard class. (See table 1.1 and pl. 3.) In other words, in the 1920s, nearly two-thirds of the nation's dwellings were *not technologically capable* of being electrically modernized by the simple installation of better illumination and power appliances. Substandard housing alone, among other factors, prevented a household revolution through electrical modernization. By contrast, at the end of the 1930s, two-thirds of all dwellings were technologically capable of being modernized with appliances. The New Deal accomplished this upgrading in the electrical status of the nation's dwellings. (See fig. 1.1.)[45]

In conclusion, underlying social, economic, and demographic constraints on demand limited adoption of electric household appliances in the 1920s. An insufficient number of households adopted appliances to constitute a social revolution, or even a significant social change in the mass of households. The nation's capitalist economy distributed income highly unequally during the decade. Mainly the upper fifth of households, ranked by income, bought appliances. We have no evidence that upper-class women underwent a social revolution—whether liberation or proletarianization—from using the appliances they bought. The evidence indicates that adoption of appliances conservatively reinforced social status and social relationships. Prices remained high during the decade, as utilities and manufacturers sought to satisfy the luxury market. They failed to create a true mass market for the domestic devices. Average households had limited economic capability to adopt appliances, largely because they

Plate 3.   *Substandard Urban Housing.* (Clare L. Brian, photographer. "Urban poverty in Bloomington, c. 1935–1940. ['Sanitation pictures'].") Courtesy of McLean County Historical Society, Bloomington, Illinois.)

had committed their debt to the automobile. Most of their dwellings were not technologically capable of serving multiple minor appliances or heavy appliances. Households did not choose to invest money in upgrading their dwellings' electrical wiring, undoubtedly because most households rented. Growth in aggregate demand for household appliances slowed in the latter half of the 1920s, as household formation declined and the number of new houses being built also declined. For a mass market in domestic electric appliances to exist, the nation had fundamentally to restructure the economy of its homes. The New Deal did.

Appendix

Table 1.1.   Electrical Technology Classes of Urban and Rural Housing

Dwellings		Percent of Total Occupied Dwellings in Technological Class			
Class Description	U.S. Census Category	1922	1932	1942	1952
No electricity	Urban and rural, incl. farm	57.6	31.7	16.3	4.3
Substandard, lights only	Urban only	23.1	31.1	21.6	1.0
Standard, *add* small power and small heating	Urban and rural, incl. farm	18.8	34.1	52.7	73.7
Modern, *add* heavy heating	Urban only	0.7	4.1	11.5	23.9

Definitions

Dwellings with no electricity: Urban and rural dwellings with no electrical service. This category includes dwellings that the 1933–1936 real property inventories and the 1940 and 1950 censuses identified as dilapidated and providing inadequate physical shelter.

Substandard dwellings: Substandard urban dwellings as a percentage of all occupied dwellings. The substandard dwelling has only wiring for illumination. Because of the light wiring, households could not install additional outlets for power appliances (directly off the illumination circuit). Frequently, a single 40- or 50-watt lightbulb illuminated each room. This category also includes all urban dwellings, even when the state of their electrical service is unknown, identified by the census with substandard plumbing, defined consistently by the real estate inventories and national censuses to be lack of private toilets or lack of indoor toilets (for urban dwellings only) and lack of running hot water. The assumption is that dwellings with substandard plumbing are unlikely to have more than substandard electrical service.

Standard dwellings: Urban dwellings with wiring for illumination, a branch circuit for convenience outlets, and more than average number (3.4 in 1924) of convenience outlets, and all rural and farm dwellings with electricity. Urban standard structures were usually not wired for heating appliances, such as the range and water heater. Urban dwellings had private plumbing and running hot water. I class farm dwellings as standard if they had electricity, regardless of the state of their toilets, because farm structures were usually wired for power at the same time they were wired for lights. Farmers frequently took electrical service, since it enhanced farm productivity, before they built indoor toilets.

Modern dwellings: Urban dwellings with electric ranges. Dwellings have standard light wiring and above standard high conduit, permitting installation of a large number of outlets, especially in the kitchen. In the absence of national statistics of the number of urban dwellings with heavy wiring, I have used the estimated stock of domestic electric ranges as an indicator of dwellings with heavy wiring. Given that builders did not, as a matter of course, install heavy conduit branch circuits in new housing until after 1945, it is likely that most civilian housing before 1942 received such wiring by retrofit when the dwelling owner wished to install a heavy appliance. As such, the percentage of dwellings with such wiring is probably the same as the percentage of dwellings with installed electric ranges. After 1945, the range becomes a less reliable indicator of the presence of heavy wiring, because contractors built most new dwellings ready for heavy appliances. If a dwelling did not have a range, it may have had an electric water heater or air conditioner.

Methodology

Dwellings without electricity and standard dwellings determined by linear estimation from cross-sectional surveys and decennial census statistics from the U.S. Bureau of the Census. Modern dwellings determined by national stock of electric ranges, as explained above. Substandard dwellings determined by subtracting the estimated number of non-electrified, standard, and modernized dwellings from the total number of occupied dwellings. Although the procedure for determining the percent of substandard dwellings is indirect, its result is close to Edith Wood's survey of the nation's housing. Edith Elmer Wood, a housing reformer, estimated that in 1930, 34 percent of the nation's urban dwellings were substandard; this compares to my estimate of 31.7 percent in 1932. (I calculated the unitary urban substandard dwelling statistic from Wood's data in Edith Elmer Wood, *Recent Trends in American Housing* [New York: Macmillan, 1931], 40.) I do not distinguish between standard and superior farm dwellings. Most farms (87 percent) were electrified after REA electrification began, when federal intervention increased the wiring standards. In addition, most farmers intended to put heavy motors or farm electrical equipment on the lines that required heavy branch wiring. Wiring costs would quadruple ($100–$200) the cost of retrofit wiring of urban dwellings ($26–$50) at this time. See, for example, J. C. Damon, "Lower Cost Wiring," *Electrical World* 105 (September 14, 1935): 32, for wiring costs of a typical urban house. For these reasons, when farms were electrified, they usually were given power wiring (60-amp. capacity). See Donald S. Stophlet and Tom F. Blackburn, "Selling Appliances on New Rural Lines— 2 Reports," *Electrical Merchandising* 61 (May 1939): 8 f.

Because independent estimations were made for the different classes of dwellings in table 1.1 and because of rounding in chain calculations, the columns do not cumulate to 100 (percent). A full account of the housing model is provided in Ronald C. Tobey, "Statistical Supplement to *Technology as Freedom*" (unpublished ms., 1995).

Table 1.2. National Price Drops for Eleven Appliances, 1926–1939

Appliance	Year of Greatest Drop	First Drop (%)	Year of Second Greatest Drop	Second Drop (%)
Vacuum cleaner	1932	20.0	1927	19.7
Cooker	1939	33.3	1929	25.0
Fan	1932	33.3	1933	28.3
Heating pad	1937	36.8	1931	33.9
Flatiron	1932	17.2	1937	12.6
Percolator	1928	45.3	1936	44.1
Radio	1930	34.9	1931	28.6
Range	1930	9.3	1934	8.4
Refrigerator	1932	24.4	1933	12.8
Toaster	1931	27.3	1932	19.3
Washer	1932	30.6	1931	19.7

SOURCE: Percentage changes in price calculated from average national retail prices in "10 Years Sales and Retail Value of Electrical Merchandise [1926–1935]," *Electrical Merchandising* 55 (January 1936): 2–5; "10 Years Sales and Retail Value of Electrical Merchandise [1930–1939]," ibid., 63 (January 1945): 8–9. Data for each appliance include number of units sold and aggregate retail value. Unit price determined as aggregate retail value divided by number of retail units sold.

Table 1.3.   Trends of Annual Normalized Sales, 1921–1964

Appliance	1921-1929	1933-1941	1946-1964	(1921-1964)
Refrigerator	+ 0.643	**+ 0.702**	- 0.330	+ 0.161
Range	+ 0.199	**+ 0.767**	- 0.004	+ 0.299
Clothes washer	- 0.242	**+ 0.026**	- 0.272	+ 0.068
Vacuum cleaner	- 0.241	**+ 0.358**	- 0.128	+ 0.021
Flatiron	- 2.239	**+ 0.505**	- 0.564	- 0.163
Heating pad	+ 0.236	**+ 0.258**	- 0.030	+ 0.083

INTERPRETATION: Data represent the annual trend, determined by regression, of sales of appliances per one hundred households living in dwellings capable of servicing them. The trend figures should be read comparatively; that is, "compared to the refrigerator upward trend in sales of 1921–1929 of + 0.643, the upward trend of refrigerator sales in the years 1933–1941 was greater (+ 0.702)."

SOURCE: See Introduction, table I.1.

Figure 1.1. Dwellings Ineligible for Electrical Modernization. 1920–1954

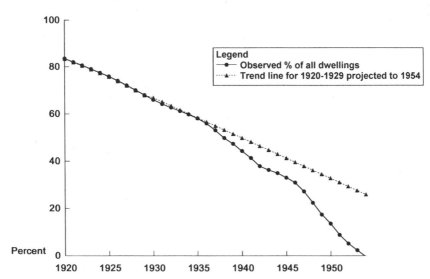

SOURCE: See Introduction, table I.1.

INTERPRETATION: The trend line after 1932 projects the decline of ineligibility of dwellings for electrical modernization by the rates of private modernization through 1929. The observed line begins in 1935. The difference between the projection of the private trend line and the observed line estimates the impact of New Deal housing programs.

Figure 1.2. Heavy Electrical Appliances Annual Sales, 1919–1965

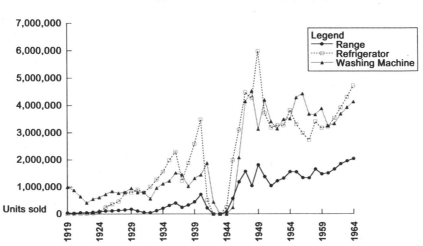

SOURCE: See Introduction, table I.1.

Figure 1.3.   *Small Electrical Appliances Annual Sales, 1919–1965*

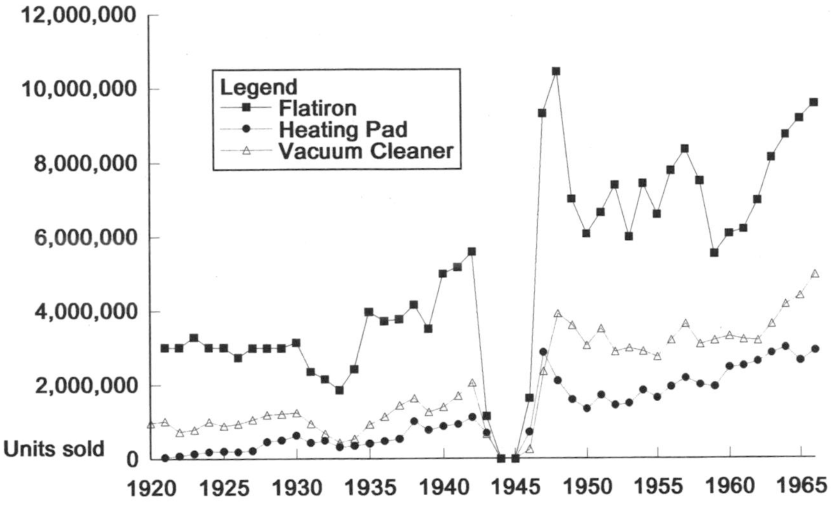

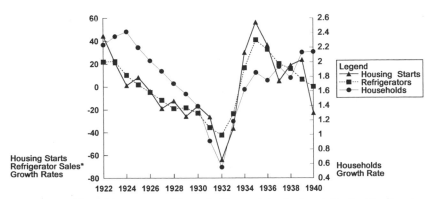

SOURCE: See Introduction, table I.1.

Figure 1.4.   *Comparative Growth Rates, 1922–1940*

SOURCE: For refrigerators and households, see introduction, table I.1. For housing starts, see Series N 157, "New Housing Units Started, by Ownership, Type of Structure, Location, and Construction Cost: 1889–1970," U. S. Bureau of the Census, *Historical Statistics of the United States, Colonial Times to 1970, Bicentennial Edition, Part 1* (Washington, D.C., 1976), 2: 639.

NOTE: Refrigerator rate is 3-year moving average of sales growth rate; $r = \mathrm{LN}$ $(p2/p1)/t*100$.

Chapter 2
The Reform Tradition

Rates and the Failure of Private
Electrical Modernization

The Reformers' Charge

For progressive reformers, there was no mystery in the failure of private utilities to bring electrical modernization to the majority of American homes in the 1920s. The utilities charged too much for electricity. Sen. George W. Norris of Nebraska, leader of the public power movement in Congress, put it simply: only when electricity was cheap "would the modern home contain all the appliances necessary to do most of the work and drudgery now done by hand." Reformers divided between two basic strategies to lower electric rates, regulation and public ownership. They trod both paths before 1914, but their efforts remained with municipal and state governments. In 1913, San Francisco's plan to dam the Hetch Hetchy Valley in Yosemite National Park ignited the issue of regulation versus ownership at the national level. Controversy flowed over national utility politics for the next two decades. And it was from this controversy that Franklin Roosevelt gained his political ideology regarding electrical modernization of the home.[1]

Major issues of electric utility regulation that dominated the 1920s appeared earlier in the progressive struggle to reform railroads. In Wisconsin and California, reform legislation brought water, gas, telephone, and electric companies, as public utilities, within the same framework as the railroads. Reformers could easily redirect issues and analyses from one utility to another. As Robert M. La Follette fought railroad rates, so he fought electric rates. He argued that lowering electric rates increased the sale of electricity. Even with increased taxation due to a progressive income tax and fair valuation of property, greater sales resulted in greater after-tax profits. "After two years of careful investigation, the Railroad Commission, after improving the quality of service, reduced the maximum price of electricity in the city of Madison [in 1910] from sixteen cents to fourteen cents/kwhr/mo, and adjusted the other rates on a lower basis. The result was that the sales of electricity increased 16 percent." California similarly reduced electric rates. Its commission lowered household rates from ten cents to eight cents in northern California and from ten cents to seven cents in southern California. In response, the utilities improved and expanded their service. The commission compelled companies to keep accurate books by a methodology it mandated, and it inspected their books. The new regulations took inflated values out of companies. They could lower rates and still make a fair profit, because they did not have to cover bloated capitalization.[2]

Commissions regulated service as well as rates. What "service" ought to include depended on the reform camp with which a progressive identified. The individualist progressives said that service must be judged against the "interest of the public"—a narrowly legalistic interpretation of the contractual responsibilities of utility corporations as defined in their charters. At this simplest level, service only obligated a utility to deliver its commodity or technological service safely and at the mandated level. California progressives considered public safety the most important service consideration. A generation of train wrecks and of street railways without crossing guards made safety a highly charged local issue. New York's progressive Republican governor, Charles Evans Hughes, spoke of service in this sense in 1907 when he called for enforcement of "adequate service" from the state's public service corporations, "which they are bound by their charters to render." Closely related to this idea of service was the expectation of responsiveness by the company to consumer complaint. Since individual consumers could not force utilities to amend their service through the marketplace (there were no competing companies for the consumers to take their business to), the state had to ensure a minimum level of service to the customer.[3]

Other reformers expanded the concept of service to include substantive contribution to the public good. In New York, William Randolph Hearst forcefully put this idea in front of voters by advocating the public ownership of utilities. The utility should deliver a social benefit—what a later generation might call "quality of life." As a congressman (representing a Tammany district in New York City), as a mayoralty candidate in New York City, and as the Democratic party opponent of Charles Evans Hughes for the governorship of New York in the 1906 election, Hearst broadcast this view to the New York voters in his own newspapers. Clearly opposed to this concept of utility service, Governor Hughes told the Republican Club of New York in 1908, "Our government is based upon the principles of individualism and not upon those of socialism. . . . It was founded to attain the aims of liberty, of liberty under law, but wherein each individual for the development and the exercise of his individual powers might have the freest [sic] opportunity consistent with the equal rights of others."[4]

Utilities responded to reformers with three claims. Domestic electric rates fell steadily after the turn of the century, and utilities lowered rates as much as costs would permit, continually passing efficiencies to the consumer. Rates also had to cover the total cost of providing electrical service, including attracting new private investment capital. They denied that state franchises obligated utilities to provide a social service. Regarding the first thesis, the utilities were correct: rates generally fell. National average prices of residential electricity fell from 10.9 cents/kwh in 1907 to 5.8 cents/kwh in 1937.[5]

Analysis of the decline in electric rates shows how the utilities could claim to have lowered rates, and how reformers could find the extent of lowered rates inadequate. An operating utility builds its generating capacity to serve all its customers at once, that is, to supply electricity to all connected electrical devices at peak demand. In normal circumstances, consumers (residential, industrial, commercial, and transportation) do not use all devices at once, so the average demand for electricity is less than the peak-load capacity. In 1938, for instance, average load was only 35 percent of peak capacity. Utilities tied the capitalization and finance of building generating capacity to the normal load. The normal load paid the bill. The utility need not make major additional capital expenditures to meet load added to the normal load, as long as additional load did not rise above the peak load. Meeting additional load could simply be a matter of fuel costs—firing up another generator at the steam plant. Marginal demand (i.e., demand above normal load) did not cost the utility as much to meet as normal demand, because normal demand paid for all the generating capability; hence added load brought greater profit. Utilities had a built-in incentive, therefore, to encourage consumers to use additional electricity by lowering the cost of that electricity when their demand rose above the average.[6]

From early days in the industry, the utilities had a graduated-scale pricing system. They priced electricity in blocks or steps of consumption, with higher blocks of usage carrying lower rates. All domestic customers paid a flat rate for the lowest block, and most consumers did not use enough electricity to jump to a higher block. Consumers who used enough electricity to obtain the lower rate for higher blocks would lower their overall average rate. Average rates could also reduce the mean consumption of a group of customers. In a group of ten homes, for instance, two households might increase their consumption to higher steps with lower rates. Their lower average rates would lower the rate of all ten consumers averaged as a group. Not until we break out the distribution of consumption do we see that eight of the ten homes were still paying the high base rate and had not increased their consumption at all. The utilities could say, accurately, that the average cost of electricity for all consumers had declined. The reformers could claim, accurately, that the cost for most consumers had not declined.[7]

For reformers, the cost structure of residential electricity raised a serious conundrum. Graduated schedules provided declining prices for electricity, apparently a good thing for everybody, but they carried a built-in bias against households consuming the least electricity. Such households may not necessarily have been low-income households. In the early years of electrification, before electrical appliances were widely available, all households, no matter how well-off, would be consuming little electricity. After 1919, however, when appliances made modernization possible, the industry's pricing schedules worked against the electrical modernization of lower-income households and households in technologically inadequate dwellings. Even setting aside the cost of the appliances and of rewiring a dwelling, the initial block of electricity was expensive. A household had to consume a lot of electricity to get into the sliding-scale range. The pricing structure of electricity before 1933 worked against electrical modernization for the mass of American households. From the reformers' point of view, the households who would benefit most by modernization were least able to jump out of the high base block. To the extent that the pricing structure of electricity reflected the technology and corporate organization of the central station electrical utility, the progressive reformer could say that the very structure of the private electrical utility made electrification possible but worked against electrical modernization.

The simplest regulative reform turned out to be impossible. Why not reduce the rates for upper blocks of consumption less and reduce the base rate more? Reformers did not expect this strategy to work. Utilities would not lower general domestic rates, because domestic rates subsidized industrial rates. Utilities charged industries far less (per kilowatt-hour) than domestic consumers. They did so because industrial plants and other large consumers, such as hotels and department stores, could threaten to withdraw from central station service and install a small generating plant for their own, in-house power. They could reverse the process of central station electrification that brought the utilities easy money.

For progressives, a rate structure that assigned the highest rates to ordinary households prevented a social revolution in the American standard of living. Here is H. S. Rauschenbush and Harry W. Laidler's indictment, published by the *New Republic* in 1928:

> The power industry has for some years had a startling differential rate structure, favoring the power consumers over the domestic light consumers.
>
> This is a form of social control which the industry has the power to exert. When a rate structure is built on high domestic rates, when the benefits of the industry go mainly to the large power consumers, something is being done to determine the standard of living of the people. Reversibly, when a rate structure is built on low domestic rates, when the greater electrification of various forms of domestic toil are encouraged, something else and different is being done to the living standards and culture of a people. This is especially true of the farms. When light and power reach them, they are different places, for work, for men and women to live in, than when light and power are absent or may be obtained at a rate they do not feel they can afford.
>
> For those interested in the development of a homogeneous civilization in this country, in a natural and easy growth rather than in a development proceeding by a series of explosions caused by a head-on collision of different racial and cul-

tural heritages, the development of power on a large scale and its long distance transmission have been of immense importance. These reformers expect the rebirth of small towns, not located as before, of necessity, on a watercourse or at a waterfalls, but wherever the soil, timber and other mineral resources are best, drawing their power by wire, able at last to exist economically independent of the great industrial centers which have, in the main, put the small towns and the economic independence and cultural unity they were developing, out of competition.[8]

The first reason, then, for the peculiar price schedule of the electric utilities: their social vision of America differed fundamentally from the progressives' vision. The progressive vision as represented by Rauschenbush and Laidler, of socially modernized American homes, with electricity lifting the standard of living of small towns and farms, of the dispersion of industry out of the industrial centers, of social harmony for a heterogeneous population, found a responsive audience in the newly elected governor of New York, Franklin Roosevelt, who made it his own.

The second reason reformers found for utility resistance to subsidizing modernization of the lower block of domestic consumption related to holding companies, which created a vast debt in their consolidation of the industry. Their debt to capitalization ratio (including bonds and stock in the debt) exceeded that of American industries generally. In 1927, the utilities held $51 of debt in bonds for every $100 of investor shares and funded debt. Manufacturing corporations averaged only $13.4 per $100 of capitalization. Corporations had to pay this debt. Court decisions regarding rates required that return on investment be paid to investors at the next quarter of the corporate year. Utilities could not forgo profit now for greater profit a few years later. This restriction prevented utilities from using profits to lower rates to consumers. Utility reformers asserted, however, that holding companies created much of their debt fraudulently to fatten banks and a few directors' purses. Consumers should not pay false debt. Fighting for public electric power at Muscle Shoals, George Norris charged in 1925 that electric rates were high, because rates paid not only for electric current but also for "premiums on watered stock, profits on fictitious values." Holding companies also extracted huge fees for management services from the operating utilities, thereby raising the operating costs of the industry. Reformers thought the service fees far exceeded the value of the management advice rendered. The fees virtually constituted extortion. They bloated operating expenses of the utilities, expenses that utilities met with higher domestic rates.[9]

The rise of the holding company in the electrical industry in the 1920s effectively neutralized the power of the state regulatory commissions. Operating electrical companies (the companies that built and managed the electrical generating plant and the distribution lines) before World War I were local and regional, given corporate charters by their host states for operations inside state boundaries. Consequently, state commissions could effectively regulate operating utilities (given sufficient political will). Holding companies, by contrast, were often interstate. Frequently, the holding company was headquartered out-side the state where it conducted most of its operations. For example, the hold-ing company that owned Southern Sierras Power Company, a private utility op-erating out of Riverside, California, was headquartered in Denver, Colorado. Since a regulatory commission of one state could not open the books of a hold-ing company in another state, the holding company could effectively hide the financial details of the operations of its group of utilities and thereby deny the commission the information needed to determine whether local rates were fair. Clearly, only national-level regulation could reach the holding company.[10]

At every turn, private utilities thwarted the progressive reformers' efforts to obtain social benefits through regulation. In addition, the conservative side of the progressive ideology, stressing individualism and competition, made it dif-ficult to stretch the justification of reform enough to include the social welfare of the household. Some influential progressives believed the time had come to have publicly owned power and avoid the problem of regulation altogether.

The Public Power Movement

Until 1913, the movement for public power did not have a unified national lead-ership. The sentiment for municipal ownership developed locally, and only at the local level did voters have an opportunity to vote directly on public power questions, as when a ballot proposition called for municipal purchase of a pri-vate utility. Municipalities sponsored electrification as a last resort when local markets or local capital failed to attract private investors. Many reformers turned to municipal ownership well before it became a last resort, however, because it held the promise of lower electric rates. By 1913, these pressing problems led reformers to establish 1,833 municipally owned electric systems around the na-tion. After 1913, the movement jumped to the federal level. Municipalities be-gan to reach across state boundaries, which required the concurrence of the fed-eral government and therefore involved Congress. The effort of the City of San Francisco to dam the Hetch Hetchy Valley in Yosemite National Park set off the controversy that drew federal involvement. The city sought legislation in 1913 to permit it to dam the valley to impound drinking water and to generate hy-droelectricity. Pacific Gas and Electric Company, in northern California, opposed the legislation, because it would strengthen San Francisco's municipally owned electric utility and weaken the private utility's chances of bringing the bay city back into the private sphere. Los Angeles substantially repeated this episode in the 1920s, when the city sponsored the Boulder Canyon project, to provide wa-ter and power to southern California's municipally owned utilities. Again, the private power interests, principally Southern California Edison, vigorously op-posed the project.[11]

Five hydropower projects shaped public power policy at the national level from 1913 to 1928: Hetch Hetchy Valley, Great Falls on the Potomac, Muscle Shoals on the Tennessee, Boulder Canyon on the Colorado, and the St. Lawrence

River. Muscle Shoals eventually led to the New Deal's great public power experiment in regional development, the Tennessee Valley Authority. Boulder
Canyon led to the pathbreaking public–private power partnership for southern
California's regional industrialization. At the end of the 1920s, congressional
investigations of the electric "Power Trust" (dominated by General Electric companies) led to a demand for a federal policy on the holding company. This demand did not culminate in a national power policy, but it set the stage for the
public power reforms and policies of the New Deal. In Hetch Hetchy, Great Falls,
and Muscle Shoals, Senator Norris led the progressive forces of the Senate toward publicly owned power. In Boulder Canyon, he joined California's Sen.
Hiram Johnson. Muscle Shoals cut the political edge in public power questions
through the entire decade of the 1920s and later became the nucleus for TVA.
In the Muscle Shoals fight, Norris developed the social benefit argument for public ownership.

In World War I, the national government built two nitrate plants at Muscle
Shoals, Alabama, on the Tennessee River. The plants used electricity to remove
nitrogen from the air for the purpose of making gunpowder. At the end of the
war, Congress had to decide how to dispose of the plants. Despite the attraction
of the site, no industry stepped forward with a plan to lease, purchase, or use it,
perhaps because of the postwar depression. A bill to have the United States operate the second nitrate plant passed the Senate in May 1920 but failed in the
House of Representatives. No consensus existed on the disposal of Muscle
Shoals. In 1921, Henry Ford broke the stalemate with an offer to purchase and
develop the plants. He also set up a new stalemate. His bid called for the United
States to sell the site at a price much lower than its cost of construction, and at
a price that did not reflect its productive value. The Senate sent Ford's offer to
its Agriculture and Forestry Committee, because it considered the potential agricultural value of Muscle Shoals greater than its usefulness for defense. Norris,
chair of the committee, took responsibility for evaluating the offer from America's great automobile manufacturer. The more Norris reflected, the more he convinced himself of its inadequacy and of the importance of maintaining public
ownership of Muscle Shoals. Because of the initial publicity surrounding Ford's
offer and of the mythic reputation of the man himself, the issue of Muscle Shoals'
disposition dominated the public power debate in the 1920s.

Boulder Canyon created another controversy. Los Angeles's effort to build a
dam at Boulder Canyon brought the municipal power movement to the national
level, because Congress had constitutional authority over the nation's naviga-
ble rivers. As with San Francisco's earlier project at Hetch Hetchy, Boulder
Canyon dam would support the growth of a major city. The Los Angeles project
also focused national debate on public power for the benefit of households. Senator Johnson introduced the Colorado River project in the Senate in 1924. Norris
strongly supported it. Norris's biographer, Richard Lowitt, says that this project
excited Norris more than Muscle Shoals did. Both were similar and would further the cause of public power. But Boulder Canyon was more dramatic, with

bigger players. Los Angeles played a big stakes game with political cunning. The booming city provided more muscle for public power than had any of Muscle Shoals' sponsors.[12]

The political rhetoric of the public power movement differed significantly from that of regulatory reform. Public power advocates denied the efficacy of rate regulation by itself to secure the public good out of privately owned utilities. They denied that electric power ought to be privately owned in the first place. Norris, who led the Senate fight that transformed Muscle Shoals into the TVA program in 1933, put the matter bluntly: "Every stream in the United States which flows from the mountains through the meadows to the sea has the possibility of producing electricity for cheap power and cheap lighting, to be carried into the homes and businesses and industry of the American people. This natural resource was given by an all-wise Creator to his people and not to organizations of greed."[13]

David E. Lilienthal, who administered the Tennessee Valley Authority, succeeded Senator Norris in the mid-1930s as the leading ideologist of public power. Lilienthal's *TVA: Democracy on the March* (1944) represented the most popular expression of the public power ideology. A Harvard Law School graduate of 1923 who studied under Felix Frankfurter, Lilienthal practiced law in Chicago, specializing in labor law, and edited a public utilities review. In 1931, Governor Philip La Follette of Wisconsin appointed Lilienthal to the Wisconsin Public Service Commission. Here Lilienthal developed his national reputation as a progressive regulator that prompted Frankfurter to recommend to Roosevelt his appointment to the TVA. Lilienthal's participation on the Wisconsin board gave him personal contact with the Wisconsin progressive tradition that had developed the social benefit concept of utility service. He would in turn bring this ideal to the TVA. Lilienthal's vision combined the Enlightenment belief that material progress brought moral progress with the American progressive's faith in the power of government to change society for the better through law. Lilienthal believed that improvement of the physical conditions of life enhanced persons' spiritual and moral lives. Material abundance makes "men's lives richer, fuller, more 'human.'" That "extreme poverty is an evil" does not necessarily imply that "a high material standard of living" is good of itself. Material abundance is good, because it gives persons the opportunity to exercise choice:

> A Tennessee Valley farm wife who now has an electric pump that brings water into her kitchen may . . . be more generous of spirit, less selfish, than when she was forced to carry her water from the spring day after day. A once destitute sharecropper who now has an interesting factory job at good wages and lives in a comfortable house in town may . . . be more tolerant, more rational, more thoughtful of others, more active in community concerns.[14]

The TVA's great purpose was social modernization. Electrical modernization brought the material means for "greater individual and spiritual growth."

For Lilienthal, material technology enabled individuals to escape the material and cultural constraints of the past. It placed them in the position of being able rationally to reform their social relations and to choose to develop their individual potentialities and desires. The purpose of electrical modernization was to provide a sufficiently abundant material life that "individual personality can flourish."[15]

For a public power advocate such as Lilienthal, the enabling framework of public power provided the distinctive New Deal contribution to social modernization. The TVA did not command "social planning" as the fascist governments of Europe had in the 1930s, compelling "complete reconstitution of our social system." The TVA "planned," argued Lilienthal, in that it brought to individuals the resources—primarily cheap electricity—they could use, if they chose, to develop themselves, their homes, and their enterprises.[16]

Residual populism provided one source for this public power ideology of electrical modernization as social modernization. Populists did not focus on consumer interests and did not put forward a household ideology, but they remained an influential political force in scattered agricultural regions. In Norris's senatorial district, populism counted many voters in the 1880s and 1890s, and populist sentiment remained strong through the 1920s. Norris's political career made him a lonely Republican in an area long dominated by the Democratic party or by local fusion politics between the populist remnant and the Democratic party. Norris could not have stayed in office had he played the stand-pat Republican. Publicly owned electrical systems were more popular in Nebraska than in any other state. When the number of municipal electrical systems peaked nationally in 1923 at 3,083 systems, Nebraska peaked three years later at 282 systems. Norris's national leadership of public power, therefore, stood on a local populist base.[17]

Private industry constituted an ironic source of the vision of social revolution through electricity. Enterprises promoted an inherently conservative vision of electrical modernization, by prescribing appliances to preserve a bourgeois style of life. Reformers could, however, cut and paste images of machines being used in the home into an ideology of social revolution. Reformers needed an instrument and an occasion to do this. Muscle Shoals and, later, TVA provided both. A fanfare of publicity accompanied Henry Ford's bid in 1921 to purchase Muscle Shoals. Ford voiced the ethos of private capitalism that combined individual profit with social benefits from private investment. Fordism brought the social blessings of technology to the ordinary man. In rhetorical promotion of his Muscle Shoals bid, Ford and his spokesmen did not directly emphasize electrical modernization of the home. They proposed the social modernization of the Tennessee and Mississippi River valleys through cheap electricity for industry and urban development. While on a personal tour of Muscle Shoals, in late 1921, Ford excited reporters with his vision of a linear city running seventy-five miles along the river, with cheap electricity powering industry and illuminating homes. Ford's ideas ignited a year of real estate speculation that ultimately rebounded negatively against the new city concept, but also revealed how widely the general public believed in Ford personally. He would use the electricity of Muscle Shoals to create a social transformation of the Tennessee River region as profound as the national transformation brought by his inexpensive mass-produced automobiles. Few Americans would deny, especially in the 1920s, that the automobile revolutionized American life. Newspapers, many owned by the electric utilities, trumpeted Ford's potent mystique. Ford's "millennial imagery" stimulated rural America to envision electricity transforming their lives. It beguiled even Franklin Roosevelt. Years later, as a new president embarking on the visionary program of TVA, Roosevelt invited Ford to visit him at Warm Springs, Georgia, to talk over plans of rural modernization through electricity.[18]

Ford's Muscle Shoals proposal promised to be a public relations steamroller, flattening the public power movement. It ignited a fight for cultural symbols. In the advertising age, mass symbolism could win the hearts and minds of voting consumers. The private advertising during the 1920s of household appliances implicitly made social claims. It reinforced a socially conservative, upper-income vision of American domestic life. It focused on the materially comfortable suburban family with a housewife performing housekeeping chores, who wished to use appliances to replace servants or to lighten her own labor. The imagery symbolized the notion that domestic electricity would better enable upper-class households to maintain the lifestyle they already enjoyed. Ads emphasized the connection between the affluent consumer and the private market and subliminally worked against cooperative housekeeping arrangements. They did not suggest that women could use the time saved in housekeeping to enter the wage labor force. They did not suggest that if consumers wanted to use these new gadgets, they might lobby regulatory commissions to lower electric rates. Private advertising represented one facet of a multimedia political campaign waged by an electrical industry unified in trade associations. Through these organizations, utilities, manufacturers, retailers, and holding companies denied the claims of municipal power advocates, deflected criticism of pyramiding holding companies, and masked economic fraud, in order to minimize criticism of U.S. Senate committees investigating the power trust. Advertising was just one battlefield for the struggle between private utilities and public power over the nation's social agenda.[19]

As a leading advocate of public power, Senator Norris had to defuse the political threat of Ford's proposal for private development of Muscle Shoals by convincing voters that public development would bring greater social benefits. Ford promised interclass mobility for farmers and rural workers, industrialization of the countryside, modernization of personal health, and revitalization of community relations. To counter this vision, Norris argued that only public power necessarily led to social modernization. Forgoing profit transferred the benefit of public power to households through lower rates. Utility rates tied together consumer, utility, and government interests in electricity. Public power advocates detached Ford's powerful imagery from private enterprise and attached it to public control of electrical modernization through public ownership. Norris contended that if Henry Ford got control of Muscle Shoals, its benefits would flow to a private corporation, rather than to the public. Private utilities would put Muscle Shoals' power rates high, because of the necessity to pay for their watered stock and for the propaganda with which they deceived the public. Only public ownership would guarantee a new "Electrical Age."[20]

The rational housekeeping movement provided a third source of the ideology of social modernization through electricity. Calling for electrical modernization to reorganize the family in the name of freedom for all its members, the movement had the potential to provide a powerful moral theme to the politics of public electrical power. By the early 1920s, rational housekeepers fastened on electrical modernization as the key to household reform. Nearly all public power advocates illustrated the social possibilities of electricity with the example of social modernization of the home. The rational housekeepers' call for transformation of the home moved electrical modernization beyond the Progressive Era's simple focus on efficiency in housework. They emphasized a new conception of the household economy as based on assets, rather than simply wages or salary. Assets protected family economic security against the vicissitudes of the wage labor market. Assets also made possible social transformation of family relations. When adopted by New Deal policy makers, the conception of electrical technology as assets for the home distinguished the public power vision of the New Deal. The rational housekeeping movement did not propose that its program be accomplished by governmental action, but the public power movement did.

Major figures of Roosevelt's New Deal electrical policies, such as Morris Cooke of the Rural Electrification Administration (REA) and David Lilienthal, directly drew on the rational housekeeping movement. Cooke, a mechanical engineer who directed Philadelphia's Public Works Department, earned a national reputation as a progressive when he forced the Philadelphia Electric Company to reduce rates. Though not trained in electrical engineering, Cooke's reputation enticed Gov. Gifford Pinchot to appoint him as chair of the Giant Power Survey of Pennsylvania in 1923. Influenced by the Regional Planning Association, Pinchot hoped electricity would make possible revitalization of country life, including community and family, as well as industry. Despite their efforts, the Pennsylvania state legislature failed to pass Pinchot's Giant Power proposal. After a stint in private consulting, Cooke accepted Governor Roosevelt's appointment in 1931 to the New York State Power Authority, with which Roosevelt hoped to develop rural power in upstate New York. Cooke synthesized the rational housekeeping movement, with its emphasis on transformation of the household, and the progressive power movement. In his edited anthology, *Giant Power* (1925), he and his contributing authors systematically developed an alternative economic and social organization for regional electric systems to the "Super Power" arrangements being created at that time by the rapid consolidation of private electric utilities by holding companies.[21]

In his contribution to *Giant Power,* Pinchot expressed the basic assumption of the public power movement, that electricity would transform society as fundamentally as had the steam engine in the industrial revolution. "The change from muscle, wind and water to steam as a source of energy was an epochal change. The change from steam to electricity which is now upon us will not be less so." Pinchot explained that because steam power had to be used at the site of its generation, it forced the geographic concentration of industry and the enlargement of central cities. Urban concentration led to "a decline in country life, the decay of many small communities, and the weakening of family ties." Since electrical power could be distributed and used miles from its site of generation, electricity would make possible "the decentralization of industry, the restoration of country life, and the upbuilding of the small communities and of the family. In this hope of the future lies the possibility of new freedom and the great spiritual enrichment of individual life." President Roosevelt repeated this argument ten years later when justifying his New Deal electrical programs.[22]

To discuss the possible effects of electricity on the home and family for his volume, Cooke turned to prominent writers in the rational housekeeping movement. Both Martha Bensley Bruère, associate editor of *Survey Graphic,* and Mary Pattison emphasized that electric home appliances would greatly reduce labor and drudgery in housework. Both envisioned that they would bring about radical transformation. Bruère thought distribution of electricity to rural communities would have dual effects. Women could use electric appliances to reduce the time required to accomplish their housework. Electricity would also allow manufacturing industries to locate in rural areas. With freedom from housework, women would have leisure; they could enter the labor force and earn money. Following a reference to the radical feminist Charlotte Perkins Gilman, Bruère envisioned electricity enabling women to leave their limiting roles as housewives, earn money, and develop their personalities. Then they could return to their families on the new basis of "life born of her own wider participation in it." Pattison thought that full development of women and children required a total transformation of the home. "There must be some big fundamental changes in this home of ours if it would be the social unit it gives promise of being." Though she thought of the transformation in terms of modeling homemaking labor on the factory, this analogy represented only the limited range of social alternatives the Progressive Era gave her. In her vision, electrical modernization would sever the home from its past and enable it to transform itself. Electrical modernization was not social conservation; it was social modernization. Electrical modernization radically transformed consanguineous relations. Each member of the family could have control over her own destiny and could have the health, wealth, and opportunity to fulfill her own individual potentiality inside and outside the home. The new era should be one of "domestic independence."[23]

Bruère's and Pattison's themes expressed broad currents in the rational housekeeping movement, shared by the movement's popular literature: Helen

Campbell's *Household Economics,* Isabel Curtis's *The Making of a Housewife,*
Lucy Salmon's *Progress in the Household,* Bertha Richardson's *The Woman Who
Spends,* Georgie Child's *The Efficient Kitchen,* Mary Pattison's *The Principles
of Domestic Engineering,* Christine Frederick's *Household Engineering,* and
Lillian Gilbreth's *The Homemaker and Her Job.* The desire to make the new
electrical household technologies into assets for effective freedom for family
members appears in three major homemaking concerns: the functional architecture of the dwelling, the labor of housekeeping tasks, and the expenditure of
money. The movement's program started with the architectural redesign of the
house. The shift from farm to city had given rooms new functions. Farm kitchens
of the past were large for good reasons, but the kitchen of the urban house needed
to be small and compact. "We can foresee the time when . . . the equipment necessary to feed a family shall be beautiful in form and portable in simplicity, when
the odors of fat and steam shall have vanished and the cook's apron shall have
become a forgotten weapon." To replace the rambling farmhouse and the Victorian mansion, rational housekeepers promoted the "bungalow." The bungalow synthesized English and American nineteenth-century cottage architecture,
Arts and Crafts design, and standardized tract housing. Books on bungalow architecture stressed the virtues of necessity. Houses were smaller because high
costs drove conventional housing beyond the reach of the middle-income household; but, architects said, smaller was better anyway. In the search for ways to
economize housing construction, "standardization" produced not only cheaper
but better houses. To save space, cabinetry should be "built-in." As Robert Jones
explained, writing for the New York-based Small House Service Bureau of the
American Institute of Architects, kitchens should be "efficient" and convenient.
He meant by this, *very* small. Rational housekeepers did not disagree. Georgie
Child went so far as to recommend, for servantless homes, the "kitchenette,"
seven by eleven feet.[24]

The labor program of the rational homemaking movement centered on the
reorganization of housekeeping tasks on principles of industrial efficiency. Eventually, Frederick Taylor's scientific management, which became popular among
progressives after the Eastern Rate Case of 1907, provided the form in which
the rational housekeepers articulated their scientific analysis of housework. Marion Talbot and Sophonisba Breckinridge's *The Modern Household,* Child's *The
Efficient Kitchen,* Pattison's *Principles of Domestic Engineering,* Frederick's
Household Engineering, Martha Breùere's *Increasing Home Efficiency,* and
Gilbreth's *The Homemaker,* all popular and much referenced texts, espoused Taylorism. Scientific management provided analytical techniques and a useful model
for the organization of housework. Taylorism research required time and motion studies to determine the most efficient means of performing tasks and reorganization of the administration of the work environment. The main thrust of
Taylorism was reform of work organization, not the reassignment of work to
machines. Following Taylor, reformers organized housework generally on the
principles of specialization and standardization of function. Housewives should

perform housework in areas architecturally designed for a specific category of tasks.[25]

As oil, gas, and electric stoves and furnaces replaced coal stoves and heaters (at the end of the century), airborne soot decreased and housecleaning became less burdensome. Meal preparation and laundry now took the most time and effort. Women used to do laundry in the kitchen, because the kitchen stove provided the hot water used in washing. With centralized, hot water service, however, pipes could deliver the hot water to a separate laundry area, permitting the removal of clothes washing from the kitchen. The kitchen and the laundry thereby became the two major work centers in the house. So separated, kitchen cabinetry could be designed and appliances grouped for ease and efficiency of the housewife working in the center. These were the keys to increasing labor efficiency: "This principle of arranging and grouping equipment to meet the actual order of work is the basis of kitchen efficiency."[26]

The rational homemaking movement produced instructional manuals on keeping household budgets to explain how consumption and appropriation of household technology should take place within the new world of salaries and mass markets. Making a household economically viable over the long run and maintaining a healthy standard of living necessitated control over the expenditure of money. Control was crucial. Frederick stated, "The health of the family, its education, its savings, are determined, not by the amount of . . . income, but by the distribution, or the spending of that income." As a program of reform, rational homemaking came down to the handling of family finances. Industrialists defined efficiency in accounting terms: less input, more output—measured and counted. Reformers expected the same efficiency at home. "It is clearly evident that domestic economy, or household management, is very largely a matter of money and money's worth." Budgeting, and the full accounting apparatus it implied, provided the basis for comparing expenditure of money, time, and effort toward one purchase with the money, time, and effort toward another purchase. This was the only means by which the household could know that they were getting the most for each dollar spent. The budget texts taught mastery of commodity capitalism and consumerism.[27]

Beneath the text of the budget manuals lay a radical subtext—reformation of social relations between household members. In terms of what feminists proposed to do, an agenda of household politics took precedence over consumer decisions. If the wage earner of the household refused to participate in budget management, then all other planning for the household fell apart. It would not do for the wage earner to hand over a portion of the wage income as an allowance for the housewife's household expenses. An allowance was fatal to the concept of the household as a unit of planning. The allowance was, Frederick said, "unbusinesslike, and makes impossible the satisfactory carrying out of any uniform 'budget' plan of expenditures for the whole family." It simply did not work: "Nothing is done as it should be done." No man was "serene and steady" in the confidence that an allowance provided adequately for the family's living. But the main failure of the allowance system was moral. It denied the housewife equality with the male wage earner. It denied the marriage partnership. It denied self-respect to the housewife.[28]

Faithfully carried out, a budget mapped a household's passage through life. To set up a budget, a family first decided on its largest goals—its life projects. The budget transformed all sources of income and savings into household community property, symbolizing and implementing cooperative living, directed toward the project. The budget became an intellectual technology to enable the household to transcend the salary or the wage. Dependence on the weekly paycheck put life in a precarious position. The household lived from paycheck to paycheck without being able to transform income into assets of any kind. If a family saved income, or invested it in education, or spent it on permanent improvements to the home, they transformed income into assets. Assets reflected a life plan. Assets secured future income, as, for example, by enhancing the future earning capabilities of family members. Security represented freedom. The budget, mundane as it may seem, exemplified a technology that brought effective freedom. For this reason, Child insisted that all income, "whether it is salary or dividends, an unlooked-for windfall, or merely a birthday present," must be deposited in a common bank account and managed through the household ledger. Isabel Lord took income accounting one step further, including labor income. Labor income always represented the substitution of family labor for paid services and consequently had a monetary value that the budget should include.[29]

The budget made adults equal partners, gave children dignity, and enabled their real participation in the household. "If marriage is a full partnership, then husband and wife are contributing alike to the family resources. They decide together on the best use of each division as seems best." It transformed self-sacrifice into savings that another person's extravagance would not fritter away. It became the mechanism by which all members of the household participated in defining goals for the family. It ensured that the family financial program incorporated each family member's personal goals. As a cooperative group based on the budget, the family could foster "the greatest individual development." For Gilbreth, the heart of "scientific management" was "personnel supervision." Each member of the family had a role to perform for the household. Behind her personnel chart of functions and jobs, of staff levels, of lines of authority, which made a household look as complicated as the Pennsylvania Railroad, there was a tacit agreement by all the household members. This agreement was Gilbreth's goal. Gilbreth desired, as nearly all the rational homemakers desired, the moral renovation of the social relations of the household. Without a cooperative budget, family life became "humiliating" and "demoralizing." By "demoralizing," Lord did not mean discouraging or fatiguing; she meant stripping family members of moral relations, literally *un-moralizing* them. For rational homemakers, the budget was a Lockean contract as a liberal community. All social, labor, and property relations rose out of it. Economics flowed from a political agreement. This agreement provided the moral foundation for a prescriptive program of fulfillment for the family, both as individuals and as members of the household community. It provided the moral basis for reform of household relations. Toward this goal, technology—whether budgets, or smaller kitchens, or vacuum cleaners—was an instrument. Pointedly, the household budget was the *only* instrument for the urban household to provide equality and dignity for all household members.[30]

The goals of social equality and full development of individual potential defined rational homemaking as social modernization. The writers of the rational homemaking movement saw the issue clearly: "The whole family must plan together: No other question is so important to the happiness of the home as the mutual understanding of finances by all members of the family.... [T]he ideals, standards and plans must be equally shared by both husband and wife, and understood by the children, in order to have happy united 'pulling' toward a definite aim." The long-term security of the family, attainment of a measure of independence from the week-to-week vagaries of wage labor or salary, in a word, effective freedom, required social modernization.[31]

Enter, Franklin Roosevelt

Before the Great Depression became the nation's ranking problem, many liberals and many of Franklin Roosevelt's advisers considered public electric power to be the most important political issue. Norris said that public power "is one of the greatest issues presented to the American people in the last century." Liberal magazines, such as the *New Republic,* pressed hydroelectric power as the most urgent issue before New York State, before its governor, and before the American people. The American Academy of Political and Social Science, representing the nation's scholars, declared that "one of the most important economic and political questions before the country . . . is the relations between our public utility companies and the public." The nation's philosopher of progressivism, John Dewey, identified public power as "the most weighty single issue in the political field." According to Felix Frankfurter, who became one of Roosevelt's chief advisers on regulation of public utilities, "Hydroelectric power raises without a doubt the most far-reaching social and economic issues before the American people, certainly for the next decade." Roosevelt, too, believed this. During his two terms as governor of New York, he made electric power his chief issue in campaigns for election and in his unending row with the Republican-dominated legislature.[32]

Martin Sklar's analysis of the trust issue enables us to categorize power issues, from regulation of utility holding companies to public ownership, in the liberal tradition of the Progressive Era. Sklar distinguishes between three progressive ideological orientations toward trusts. The "statist-tending" orientation, with Theodore Roosevelt as its symbolic spokesman, called for state direction of large corporations, compelling them to serve public policies, such as promotion of equality of wealth. Publicly owned corporations were compatible with this orientation, because public ownership involved society using the state to wring public benefit out of the corporate form of economic organization. The "regulatory corporate" orientation, represented by Woodrow Wilson, accepted the existence of corporations, but not their direction by the state. This centrist ideology called for governmental regulation, but not administration, of corporate capital. The "minimalist regulatory" orientation, associated with William Howard Taft, sought to preserve the private property contract in capitalism in its strongest form by reducing governmental regulation of corporations to the lowest level compatible with simply preventing the existence of monopolies. Positions on the power issue coincided with this larger topology. Each played in presidential politics. Business or stalwart or conservative Republican, progressive or insurgent republican, and new freedom democrat considered themselves progressives. The business Republicans, from the smoking barbecue of President Ulysses Grant's administration to the new era of Harding-Coolidge-Hoover, spoke for the loosely fettered freedom of the private enterprise corporation in the marketplace. The gentlemen of this orientation tended large financial corporations, drove the cartelization of American manufacturing and finance after 1893, and concentrated the electrical industry in the 1920s into holding-company pyramids of power. The well-known private power industrialist, Martin Insull, an early associate of Thomas Edison, typified the business Republican. Insull built the central station industry in Chicago and the Midwest. In 1929, he controlled the third largest electric utility holding company in the nation. The crash of Insull's empire in 1932, amid corruption and his flight to Europe to escape prosecution, became a key event building public support for Franklin Roosevelt's efforts the following year to control holding companies. New freedom Democrats, led by Woodrow Wilson, called for the dismemberment, rather than the regulated existence, of the holding companies. During World War I, when governmental boards controlled the wartime economy, Wilsonian democracy espoused national planning, without public ownership, to replace the marketplace in the development of national resources and natural monopolies, such as utilities.[33]

Theodore Roosevelt led the progressive Republicans' strenuous struggle to subdue the cartels. Roosevelt's appointed chief of the Division of Forestry of the Department of Agriculture, Gifford Pinchot, became a leading spokesman for progressivism and won the governorship of Pennsylvania in the 1920s on the issue of controlling the private utilities. The left wing of the progressive Republicans, including Sen. George Norris, called for public ownership of electrical power. Both Pinchot and Norris would be important sources of inspiration and counsel for Franklin Roosevelt when he was governor. The important contribution made by Sklar's classification of progressives is to place public ownership of utilities in the same category as the statist regulation of private utilities. Public ownership was not, as Gov. Charles Evans Hughes inflammatorily charged, a socialist program outside progressivism. Socialists, such as the famous General Electric scientist, Charles Steinmetz, audibly sounded their note in the potpourri of American political opinion. Socialism as a tradition of collectivist social theory hostile to capitalism did not, however, significantly motivate the leading statist progressives. They approached public ownership as an expedient in their political fight with utilities, or as a special case of natural monopoly, rather than out of Marxist doctrine. Through Sklar's classification, we can see an unbroken tradition of ideological orientation toward society, the state, and corporations from T. R. through FDR. Though a member of the Democratic party, who served in the Navy Department in World War I under Woodrow Wilson, Franklin Roosevelt came near the end of this line of "statist-tending" liberals.[34]

The new freedom of Wilson and the new nationalism of Theodore Roosevelt both inspired Franklin Roosevelt. Biographers agree that Theodore Roosevelt's vigorous advocacy of natural resource conservation and the outdoor life decisively shaped FDR's views. FDR listened to Theodore Roosevelt's lieutenants, such as Pinchot. FDR also served as assistant secretary of the navy during World War I. The national planning of the War Industries Board and other boards favorably and strongly impressed the young public servant. As governor of New York, Roosevelt wanted to put planning for New York on a regional basis. Through this political practice ran sotto voce an interest in regional planning as advocated by urban planners in the City Beautiful movement and later in the American Planning movement. Historians see in these political experiences the source of President Roosevelt's support of national planning in solving the problems of the Great Depression, which he likened to a war. When tested with the political litmus of ideological purity, Roosevelt's amalgamation of eclectic views and political experience therefore lacks consistency. Roosevelt looks like a man without a coherent vision, an opportunist "guided" only by political pragmatism—another president in the line of American presidents who saved the nation by eschewing doctrinal rigidity and pragmatically serving the Union and its conservative middle.

In the 1920s, the kaleidoscope of political ideologies and the contest of competitive economic interests produced pure stalemate in the electrical power industry. New era Republican presidents did not want to control the holding companies. Deprived of executive power, reform in both political parties halted. The Federal Power Act of 1920, which mandated the Federal Commission to regulate all stream-produced electrical power in the nation, ostensibly gave the commission the authority to deal with domestic rates. However, commissioners appointed by the Republican presidents did not invoke powers at their command. The failure of the Federal Power Commission to act, and the refusals of Harding, Coolidge, and Hoover to press for change in the act, pushed energy politics down to the state level. Divided government locked electric power politics into ineffectualness. States could not regulate the holding companies, even if they wanted; the federal government would not, even though it could. Stalemate did not disrupt the status quo, of course, so industrialists supported no action, when their internal divisions prevented support for a new policy direction.

Traditional political language, from the era of Theodore Roosevelt and Woodrow Wilson, available for public discourse on energy and electricity policy, bore little relation to government and industry administrative struggles. Politicians' electoral rhetoric winged higher and higher on thermal currents of frustration. This was the political situation when Franklin Roosevelt became governor of New York in 1929.[35]

Roosevelt's ignorance of economics initially limited his capability to participate in the progressive reform tradition on electric power. Walter Lippmann lacked confidence that Governor Roosevelt mentally grasped the problems he addressed when he picked up the policies of his popular predecessor, Al Smith. Roosevelt's lack of academic knowledge of economics occasionally astounded his early advisers. When bleak depression settled over the nation in late 1930 and 1931, for instance, Roosevelt seemed unresponsive to innovative economists who argued for federal deficit spending to stimulate consumer spending. Instead, Roosevelt talked about balancing the federal budget as late as 1932.[36]

Two qualities enabled Roosevelt to overcome his limitations in a way that Herbert Hoover, the pertinent historical contrast, could not overcome his. Roosevelt responded with compassion to individual suffering. He thought in terms of anecdotes of real persons, rather than abstractly, as did Hoover. Knowledge of suffering reinforced his pragmatism and experimental attitude. He relinquished doctrines when they did not lead to solutions, solutions defined as improvement of individual lives. Roosevelt willingly, even studiously, learned about what he did not know. As governor, he diligently studied electric power issues. Frank Freidel, one of his biographers, claimed that "there was no other area, even that of agriculture, in which Roosevelt undertook such intensive study." He used his expert advisers not only for advice but also as teachers. They proposed books and articles for him to read and prepared explanatory issue papers. They introduced him to new authorities, with whom he conversed late at night at the governor's mansion in Albany (until Ray Moley, his political chief of staff, broke meetings off so visitors could take the last train back to New York City). His "Brain Trust" gave him so much "'homework'" in 1932, that Roosevelt virtually "'went to school.'" Egotism did not drive his confidence that he would be president and egotism did not lead to inflexibility. As a result, Roosevelt's views evolved continually after 1928. He grew toward the presidency.[37]

Different approaches to the presidency of Roosevelt produce different impressions of the president's vision and pragmatism. Looking backward from today, from the perspective of institutions created in the 1930s toward their organic origins in legislation, we must puzzle our way through thickets of New Deal bureaucratic power struggles amid local and national politics. So viewed, we glimpse President Roosevelt's electric power "policy" as disconnected legislative initiatives, addressing different economic and political problems. So viewed, our impression would be of politics that failed, without our quite knowing what failed, of fragments without our having seen the fabric. Yet, approaching Roosevelt's presidency historically, by tracing his path forward from public service in the Wilson administration and two terms as governor of New York, we see his social vision of America raveling itself together with the different threads of electrical power issues. If the carpenters of congressional politics failed to build every pillar and post of Roosevelt's hopes into the house of the New Deal, his vision yet provided architectural sketches for major achievements of the 1930s.

During his two terms as governor of New York, FDR developed the vision and policies for electrical power that he would implement in the nation during the New Deal. He began his governorship in 1929 wearing the mantle of Al Smith's hydroelectric power proposals and left the governorship in 1933 with a new vision he would unveil to the nation in the TVA. In his four terms as governor (1919–1929), Al Smith wrested important, progressive victories out of an unremittingly hostile Republican legislature, including the reorganization of the executive branch and the state's budgeting arrangements. The legislature did not put hydroelectric power among Smith's victories. Smith favored retaining public ownership and development of the valuable hydroelectric sites in New York (which had the third most sites among the states). The Republican legislature refused to agree with this program and kept regulatory power over electric rates in the Public Service Commission. This tactic favored the private companies, because endless court cases restrained the rate-setting effectiveness of the commission. In response, Smith proposed establishment of a new commission with authority to negotiate construction of power facilities on the St. Lawrence and to control the bookkeeping methodologies involved in establishing rates.[38]

Governor Roosevelt reintroduced Smith's St. Lawrence River proposal in 1929. The proposal failed. In the ensuing struggle with the legislature, Roosevelt's electricity program moved left. He endorsed the possibility of public distribution of electricity. He favored providing authority to New York communities to own their local electric utilities. Some of this shift came in the political dialectic. When Roosevelt began to win his battle over the Republican legislature, the private utilities countered by merging. The bank of J. P. Morgan arranged the merger of New York's three largest power utilities. Combined into one corporation, there would be no competition in bidding to distribute publicly generated power. The state would finance and build generating stations, saving the utilities the trouble. Then the utilities, organized into a cartel, would distribute and sell the electricity at a high price, taking large profits. It seemed a clever move. The move forced Roosevelt to threaten the industry with public distribution of power, in part as a ploy to get the regulatory powers of an electric commission sufficiently strong that it could keep down the rates that the cartel would, presumably, charge. The utilities were ready for this countermove, too. Court cases established that the utilities could use "replacement cost" as the basis for determining fair profits and rates. This rule permitted the utilities to bloat their capitalization, because the costs of electric plants in the future would be higher (if only because of general inflation). Roosevelt in turn pushed for statutory determination of "cash cost" as the basis for determining profit and rates. Profit ought to be determined on the basis of the actual cash capitalization made by the companies in building their electrical plants and distribution system. This, after all, was the real debt being paid. Court permission to base profit on future replacement costs meant that companies could calculate profit on fictitious sums they had not really spent. Rates were correspondingly higher.[39]

During the twists and turns of this political dialectic, it did not occur to Roosevelt to drop the issue and find something else on which to build his political reputation. With it, he had little to lose and much to gain at the polls. As an issue, hydroelectric power transcended upstate New York parochialism and reached out to all middle-class Republicans. High New York electricity rates irritated middle-class New Yorkers. Roosevelt hoped to use the issue of high rates, and his program to lower them with stronger regulation of power, to pry some upstate voters out of the Republican bailiwick.[40]

To transform irritation over high electric rates into votes, Roosevelt had to explain his program to upstate Republicans. This would not be easy. Upstate newspapers were uniformly Republican and hostile. Roosevelt's behind-the-scenes organizer and strategist in New York City, Louis Howe, resurrected the New York State Democratic Committee and began a mailing campaign. But selective mailing was not mass mailing, and Roosevelt's message seldom reached Republican voters without being accompanied by contradictory Republican editorials. Roosevelt sagaciously turned to the new medium of radio, which had been widely adopted only in 1928, when it could operate off house current. In 1929, FDR broadcast his first radio report, paid by the state democratic committee, to New York voters, evaluating the legislative session then ending. He resorted to radio broadcasts frequently thereafter. By 1930, listener response proved he had leaped over the editorial wall raised by Republican newspapers. By 1933, he was an accomplished radio orator and had transformed his New York governorship "fireside talks" into major ideological instruments in the nation as a whole.

Roosevelt's fireside chats and his campaign speeches in 1928, 1930, and 1932 fill in the detail of his vision for electricity. In his address accepting the Democratic nomination for governor, Roosevelt made public ownership the first of four issues on which he intended to base his campaign. (The other issues were the inefficiency of the justice system, the lack of progress of New York agriculture, and reform of local government.) Recent technological advances made electric power more important for homes than it had been before World War I. As a resource now crucial to progress in the home, the public's interest in it had to be protected. He called for a constitutional law to keep New York State-owned hydroelectric sites in state ownership. He labeled as theft the effort of private utilities to obtain fifty-year, free leases of public hydroelectric sites.[41]

In his inaugural address, Roosevelt opened a second theme. Despite the "great change of economic conditions in regard to the use of power," there had not been commensurate progress in domestic and rural power use. Private utilities charged consumers too much, prohibiting full utilization of electricity in homes.

He developed this theme more fully in 1930. The claim reflected reality. Electrification had not brought social modernization, despite the promises of private industry.[42] Roosevelt laid out the history of electrical diffusion, basically correctly, in a campaign speech in Syracuse, New York, in October 1930:

> We all know that the great magic of electricity was originally used for lighting purposes only. It then spread to the factory for industrial uses. Now, however, the time has come when electricity should be carried right into our very homes so as to lighten the drudgery of housekeeping. You and I know that scores of electrically operated household appliances have been invented. Of course, the housewives of the State cannot enjoy these new inventions as long as the rates for current continue to run as high as they now do.[43]

He compared rates in New York to those in Ontario, Canada, where the provincial government generated and distributed electricity. In Canada, an electrically modernized house (with electric lights, cooking, refrigeration, ironing, toasting, vacuum cleaning, radio, washing machine, fan, waffle irons, chafing dish, and other appliances—following Roosevelt's language) cost only $3.40 a month in energy charges. But it would cost $25.63 in Westchester County, $19.95 in New York City, and $13.50 in Rochester.[44]

In the 1920s, the private utilities preferred selling to industry over selling to the consumer. Franklin Roosevelt, like many other progressive leaders, believed that utilities should serve the home owner first. "I have stressed the fact that the home user is one to be given first consideration, because today the small home owners and storekeepers are carrying a relatively far greater burden [in the rate structure] than the industry." The 1931 St. Lawrence River hydroelectric power bill reflected Roosevelt's priorities: "The primary purpose . . . is the benefit of the people of the State as a whole, and particularly the domestic and rural consumers of the State so that the houses and farms of the State may receive cheap electricity." Of secondary importance was "the furnishing of cheaper electricity to factories and industrial establishments." He carried these priorities into the New Deal.[45]

Chapter 3
Homes or Industry?

The Modernization Debate in the 1920s

"Ten thousand towns from Albany to San Diego"

California's public power movement and Los Angeles's drive to develop the Colorado River forced the issue of who gets cheap electricity to the center of 1920s politics. Socialists and progressives sought state ownership of all electric power in California. Republicans, representing the bourgeois elites, rejected state ownership and promoted development of new sources of hydroelectricity, especially the Colorado River. Neither group stated the issue in either/or terms, but their debate portrayed public power as a means to obtain cheap electricity to modernize homes and Colorado River development as a means to obtain cheap electricity to industrialize southern California. Riverside, California, typified thousands of towns and cities around the nation that wrestled with electrical power issues raised by regional metropolitanization. For fifty years, the city followed its own destiny. Its Anglo bourgeoisie played the "city growth game," building wealth through local property ownership. They promoted city growth and increased land values through city services financed by municipal debt. Los Angeles's industrial development eventually conflicted with the ambitions of its smaller neighbors. Manufacturing and commercial elites of the central metropolis encroached on local elites based on land wealth. Urban visions of an industrial future clashed with suburban and agricultural reality.[1]

Riverside's deliberation over electrical modernization policy more realistically reflected middle America in "one of the eras of greatest rapidity of change in the history of human institutions" than Robert Lynd and Helen Merrell Lynd's familiar Middletown. The Lynds deliberately selected Muncie, Indiana, to exclude considerations of race in American life. They wanted their subject city to have "a small Negro and foreign-born population," though they realized that "a homogeneous, native-born population . . . is unusual in an American industrial city." Their selection permitted them to focus on cultural change, without paying attention to racial change. By "cultural change," the Lynds meant primarily changes affecting the division between the wage-earning class and the property-owning bourgeoisie. For the Lynds, class structured Middletown sociology. "The mere fact of being born upon one or the other side of the watershed roughly formed by these two groups," they claimed, "is the most significant single cultural factor tending to influence what one does all day long throughout one's life." Their study revealed little about central social changes of twentieth-century America due to nationalization of the "race question." By changing the issues of distributive justice and housing, race relations profoundly affected the role of politics in the social construction of residential electrical modernization. The history of southern California's policy debates and the effect of policies on Riverside neighborhoods show how race as well as class affected whose homes were electrically modernized and when.[2]

Riverside sprawled across forty square miles in 1920. Its 4,900 families lived in about 4,500 dwellings. Of its population of 19,539 persons, 505 were African-American, about 100 were permanent Chinese residents, about 600 were Japanese, and more than 1,000 were Mexican immigrants. The city reigned as the capital of California's navel orange industry. Introduced in Riverside in 1875, the Washington navel orange created the vast southern California citrus industry. In Riverside, horticulturists rapidly planted sixteen thousand acres of citrus trees into an urban republic of ten-acre groves. The Southern Pacific and Santa Fe railways shipped navel oranges eastward to the nation's cities and returned with parlor cars full of tourists. Citrus agriculture supported extensive manufacturing. In 1920, sixty industrial establishments in Riverside manufactured foundry products, fruit boxes, citrus machinery, and printed publications. In city center, Mission and Spanish revival architectural styles expressed the Anglo elite's cultural power. Around the business district, their residential neighborhoods strode a brief distance toward the orange groves in the familiar marching grid of American urban plans.[3]

Behind the gracious suburban living depicted on colorful orange crate labels, Riverside exemplified the hard-edged political economy of urban capitalism. Private property required—the white bourgeois elite believed—racial segregation and control of wage laborers. The citrus industry depended after World War I on a captive Mexican labor force. Twenty-three citrus packing houses employed over twelve hundred packers, and eight hundred grove owners employed one thousand pickers. Some Mexican workers lived in the half-dozen citrus labor camps in the city, but most of them lived in colonies adjacent to Riverside, as they did at other citrus cities. The image of white southern California as the greatest civic achievement of the English-speaking people, vigorously promoted in the first third of the century by the region's Anglo boosters, also required that

African-Americans and Asians be sequestered out of Anglo sight. Although non-white Riversiders comprised a small percentage of the city's total population, the city's neighborhood geography reflected Anglo civic leaders' preoccupation with race. They carefully concentrated nonwhite minority households in segregated residential districts. The bourgeoisie did not exempt the residence of white laborers from its control. They based manufacturing industrialization on the open shop. They vigilantly guarded against any form of social life among wage earners that might incubate class consciousness. White working-class homes dispersed themselves among bourgeois homes in Mile Square, where the elite's families could know their laboring neighbors. Each laborer's home isolated itself in its southern California garden, as if the atomization of landscape would thwart the collectivization of consciousness that led to labor unions.[4]

Riverside's Anglo bourgeoisie sorted Riversiders into eleven distinct neighborhoods—Mile Square, Old East Side, South East Side, North East Side, Expansion, Wood Streets, Country Club, Arlington, Casa Blanca, Government Tract, and Groves.[5] (See fig. 3.1.) Ten of the neighborhoods (excluding Groves) fall into three familiar qualitative classes. Country Club and Wood Streets were "upper class"; Mile Square, South East Side, Expansion, and Tract were "middle class"; Old East Side, North East Side, Casa Blanca, and Arlington were "laboring class." Casa Blanca and Old East Side were segregated for nonwhite minorities. (See table 3.1.) Although each neighborhood had a dominant class character, all-white neighborhoods, except Country Club, were economically integrated. In Country Club, expensive houses on large lots preserved the hilltops and arroyo slopes for the city's wealthiest families. The dominance of renting and high rooming rates reinforced economic integration in the city's white neighborhoods. (See table 3.2.) In 1923, 47 percent of Mile Square dwellings rented to roomers, slightly above the citywide average, 43 percent. The shifting fortunes of skilled white laborers also affected neighborhood composition. Prosperity in the 1920s advanced some skilled laborers into the middle class as contractors; with hard times in the depression, many dropped back to working-class lives. The depression eroded the economic position of Wood Streets' skilled blue-collar households, for example. Skilled blue-collar workers' residence declined from a high of 22 percent in the 1920s to 14 percent in 1936–1940. The industrial boom of the war and postwar economy returned skilled industrial workers to their earlier share of the district's households. These sprints and slides along the ladder of social mobility circulated households in and out of the neighborhoods, reinforcing economic integration.[6]

Until the population boom after 1950, Mile Square contained most of the city's homes. Over a quarter of all households in Riverside between 1921 and 1950 lived in the historical central district. Middle-class households numerically dominated the neighborhood. Nearly half of Mile Square's heads of household held low-paying white-collar jobs, such as store clerk, salesman, and assistant manager, or skilled labor jobs, such as carpenter. The district rigidly excluded nonwhite families. Only a half of 1 percent of all households in the district were Mexican or

Asian. The common experience for Anglos of living in Mile Square undoubtedly accounts for Riverside's reputation as a white, middle-class community.[7]

Segregation restricted African-American and Asian residents to the Old East Side and Mexican residents to the Old East Side and Casa Blanca. Segregated employment relegated minority workers to manual and casual labor. Old East Side and Casa Blanca did not have a significant number of middle-class households, in contrast to white laboring-class neighborhoods, North East Side, South East Side, and Arlington. (See table 3.3.) Until 1948, white Riversiders used the city government's zoning power to suppress population growth in minority neighborhoods. By prohibiting construction of apartment houses and division of single-family dwellings into apartments, zoning regulations inhibited increase in households. Inhibiting growth is not the same, however, as preventing growth. Riverside's two Mexican communities accommodated the tremendous Mexican immigration of the 1920s through overcrowding. The African-American community similarly accommodated the doubling of Old East Side's African-American population during World War II. Overcrowding rapidly reduced the proportion of quality housing in Old East Side for everyone.[8]

Casa Blanca originated in the nineteenth century as a small settlement of Mexican citrus workers in the middle of the groves, isolated from the rest of the city. Most of the wage earners in the village of several hundred residents were unskilled, casual laborers. In the years 1921–1925, 86 percent of Casa Blanca's heads of household reported unskilled labor as the highest occupational level they reached, and all others reported their jobs as semiskilled labor. During the navel harvest season—December through March—migrant Mexican laborers doubled the village population, causing a deterioration of the already poor living conditions of its residents. The prosperity of the 1920s barely seeped into Casa Blanca. In 1926–1930, the percentage of unskilled laborers in the neighborhood's labor force dropped to 78 percent, 7 percent of workers claimed skilled labor jobs, and two businessmen made their appearance in the little village. The depression struck Casa Blanca's Hispanic households hard. It wiped out their meager occupational gains in the late 1920s. In 1936–1940, the percentage of unskilled laborers in Casa Blanca rose to 83 percent. The prosperity during World War II and the subsequent postwar industrial boom finally trickled down to minority households. During the war, village population increased, thereby increasing the Spanish-speaking market. Nine percent of the heads of household reported their occupations as dealers and growers. The proportion of skilled laborers rose from 2 percent in 1936–1940 to 11 percent during the war. The proportion of unskilled laborers declined to 69 percent. They carried most wartime occupational gains into the postwar civilian economy. The percentage of unskilled workers remained at 69 percent, and the proportion of skilled workers slipped only slightly to 8 percent.

In the segregated neighborhoods, the continual deterioration of dwellings from overcrowding worked against electrical modernization. The depression also knocked many households down the social ladder. Electrical modernization of the dwellings and social modernization of the homes of the overwhelming majority of Riverside's Mexican and African-American families therefore required destruction of the local bourgeoisie's power over housing and employment. The war indirectly weakened the bourgeoisie's local power by opening employment in defense industries and by general diffusion of economic prosperity. Better incomes could not directly guarantee better homes, however, until the U.S. Supreme Court prohibited state enforcement of restrictive real estate covenants in *Shelley v. Kraemer* in 1948. Housing modernization for minority Riversiders awaited a fundamental change in the nation's philosophy of race.

Housing modernization for many white labor families waited a return of economic prosperity after the depression. Several neighborhoods tell this story. Heavy industrialization came to North East Side after the war. A large aluminum fabrication plant located in North East Side, increasing the need for blue-collar housing. The new industrial plants shifted the labor force in North East Side dramatically. During the war, 17.5 percent of the zone's labor force was unskilled and 29.8 percent was skilled; in 1946–1950, the percentage of unskilled dropped to 7 percent and the percentage of skilled workers rose to 34.9 percent. As the blue-collar middle class increased, professional and business families withdrew. In 1936–1940, the upper class comprised 21 percent of the neighborhood's households; during the war, this proportion dropped to 16 percent; during 1946–1950, it dropped to 12 percent. Their houses became available to laboring-class families who were moving up.[9]

The Supreme Court's decision in *Shelley v. Kraemer* in 1948 and the City of Riverside's decision to rezone the North East Side to multiple-family housing opened the neighborhood to African-American and Mexican families. From 1921 to 1940, not a single Hispanic name appears in the North East Side, while in the adjacent neighborhood of Old East Side, the Hispanic population grew rapidly. In 1921–1925, 20 percent of Old East Side households were Hispanic; in 1926–1930, 22 percent were Hispanic; in 1931–1935, 33 percent; and in 1936–1940, 38 percent. Only one Hispanic household, representing less than 1 percent of the city's Hispanic population, lived within North East Side during World War II. Movement to North East Side finally began after the war. By 1950, 4 percent of its households were Hispanic. After the desegregation decision of 1954, *Brown v. Board of Education,* the Hispanic and African-American proportions of North East Side's population increased rapidly, completing the movement that began in 1948.[10]

The sprawling citrus-growing district, Groves, and part of Expansion and Tract supported two lifestyles—"small grower" and "planter." Most orange growers owned only five to ten acres of land, lived on their land, and marketed their fruit through the California Fruit Growers Exchange (today called Sunkist Growers, Inc.). They lived a suburban, not farming, lifestyle. The small growers supplied the initial capital to carry citrus growing through the five to seven years from planting to first crop. The California Fruit Growers Exchange managed their groves and marketed their harvests. In 1921–1925, 79 percent of

Groves' heads of household described their occupation as citrus farmer or businessman. No one in Groves identified himself as a professional. After 1925, residential development crept into Groves along the main boulevards. Many newcomers retained citrus, while pursuing other occupations, with marketing associations doing their "farming." During World War II, the army took Groves land for military camps. After the war, aerospace manufacturing plants located there. The percentage of Groves residents identifying themselves as farmers or dealers declined steadily: 62 percent in 1925–1930; 54 percent in 1931–1935; 49 percent in 1936–1940; 40 percent during World War II; 34 percent in 1946–1950. Despite the decline, citrus culture remained a popular lifestyle and provided supplemental income for white families.

Planters owned hundreds of acres, employed their own professional managers for their citrus groves, and usually did not belong to the small grower associations. The planter social style came to Riverside shortly after an English investment syndicate bought over five thousand acres for citrus cultivation in 1889. The development of the English navel district placed English names on Riverside's map and popularized English sports, such as polo. Planters might gain their income from pursuits other than citrus but owned groves as part of the style of the local social elite. For example, William Porter, who owned a large Spanish revival home, La Atalaya (The Watchtower), surrounded by acres of orange trees, was chief executive of Southern Sierras Power Company. Some planters lived in exclusive residential districts, which I call collectively "Country Club," after the Victoria Club located by the Tequesquite Arroyo. Seventy percent of heads of household in Country Club reported high white-collar occupations, with 40 to 50 percent of the district's households reporting themselves as businessmen or citrus farmers. S. C. Evans, one of the city's earliest and largest landowners, developed Indian Hill, a discrete neighborhood in Country Club, by subdividing eight acres into large lots. Evans required buyers of the lots to agree to build homes costing at least $3,500, with architectural designs approved personally by him. Country Club and Groves held, as neighborhoods, the city's highest percentage of white-collar occupations. These households were the wealthiest in the city.[11]

Evans also developed the village of Arlington, a distinct city subcenter at the southern end of his landholdings, five miles from Mile Square. In 1888, the new Riverside and Arlington Railroad, a street railway, connected Mile Square to Arlington. Evans planned Arlington as a shopping and community center. The village undoubtedly looked much like the small farm service communities that dotted America's Midwest where many of the city's founders originated. Arlington supported a small middle class of business proprietors, proportionally 23 percent of the neighborhood's households, near the citywide average. Over half of the district's households were working class. Over the entire period 1921–1950, 34 percent of heads of household held semiskilled and unskilled jobs and 19 percent held skilled jobs. Arlington was open to Hispanic residence, unlike other Anglo neighborhoods. Although Hispanic upward social mobility was rare, the percentage of Hispanic households in Arlington climbed through the 1920s and early 1930s to 7 percent by 1935. After 1935, through the end of archival records in 1950, the percentage of Hispanic households in Arlington declined below 4 percent. The association of the decline with the depression suggests that the neighborhood became less affordable. Two Mexican-American workers, Ignacio Diaz and Alfonso Machado, illustrate the hope for prosperous blue-collar homes in Arlington. Diaz, a meat cutter, began working for an A. M. Lewis Company store in 1929. He commuted five miles to the store's downtown Riverside location from his home on Merickel Street. Fifty-one years old in 1940, Diaz owned his home, where he and his wife raised eleven children. Machado worked as a machinist for the Food Machinery Corporation (FMC), a maker of citrus packing machinery, which had a large manufacturing plant near the railroad tracks in Old East Side. Machado also owned a home on Merickel Street, where he and his wife raised three children. He had worked for FMC for seven years by 1940. If they did not own cars, Diaz and Machado could have commuted to work on the street railway that ran between the suburban center and the city center until the late 1930s.[12]

Tract slices east-west through the center of Riverside. Tract's development largely paralleled that of the Groves district until 1947. In 1921–1925, 51 percent of Tract's households reported themselves as citrus farmers or businessmen. They scattered their homes on large lots throughout the district in the 1920s. A developer of 1922 advertised half-acre lots ("small ranches"), protected by race and building restrictions. The chamber of commerce's effort to stimulate manufacturing in Riverside in the early 1920s led the city to create an industrial zone at the eastern end of Tract near the Sante Fe railroad's Pachappa Station. The city hoped developers would build low-cost housing near the zone as Tract's first industrial labor neighborhood. Few dwellings rose before the depression devastated the housing market. The percentage of skilled blue-collar workers in the district actually declined from 29 percent of households in 1921–1925 to 23 percent of households in 1926–1930. Semiskilled and unskilled workers' households increased from 3 to 7 percent at the same time. Tract shifted to a blue-collar occupational profile during the Second World War. The proportion of semiskilled labor households leaped from 10 percent in 1936–1940 to 23 percent during the war. After the war, the proportion of all blue-collar households rose to 45 percent, up from 41 percent in 1936–1940. The proportion of households in citrus farming and business families declined from 25 percent in 1936–1940 to 23 percent in 1946–1950. Developers built the city's first mass tract development in "Levittown" style, using a few basic architectural designs for its sixty homes, in Tract in 1947. An electronics manufacturing plant and aircraft fuselage factory located at the western end of the district. Investors built blue-collar housing subdivisions around these plants. Federal Housing Administration (FHA) guidelines for subdivisions reinforced the homogeneous class ownership of homes, sealing Tract's destiny as a middle-class district of white, skilled, blue-collar workers and their families. In 1946–1950, less than 3 percent of the city's Mexican population lived in Tract.[13]

Large-scale housing development reinforced in a rush the economic segregation of the city's neighborhoods that began piecemeal after 1941. The class integration that had characterized Mile Square from the 1880s to late 1930s ended quickly. More of the city's wealthy families withdrew to enclaves like Country Club. Mass housing projects offered hundred of houses at similar prices, appealing to a single class of families. The white working class became segmented, with skilled and union labor entering middle-class life in mass tract housing designed for them and priced to their pocketbooks. White unskilled laborers remained in older neighborhoods, such as North East Side, being rezoned from single-family residences to multifamily homes. Simultaneously, racial residential segregation began to break apart. In North East Side, white unskilled workers competed for rental housing, often through conflict, with African-American and Mexican-American families released in 1948 from their ghettos to search for decent homes.

Homes Before Electrical Modernization

Riverside's utility department inventoried electrical devices in the city's 4,338 electrified homes in 1921–1923. The survey gives a detailed picture of homes before electrical modernization. The average Riverside home had only fifteen lightbulbs in 1921–1923, close to California's and the nation's averages. These bulbs undoubtedly drew fifty watts of electricity or less, in line with national averages. National surveys by the electrical industry in the years 1923–1924 found that the average home had 21.7 lightbulbs. In California, the average residence in a "substantial town" had 15.9 bulbs. Before modernization, the number of lightbulbs in a home indicated the number of rooms. Research on Hamilton, Ontario, has shown conclusively that the number of rooms reflected the value of the home and the income of the household. Through this connection, the number of lights indexed the socioeconomic ranking of the home. The neighborhoods of Riverside's racial poor had the fewest lights, and the Country Club homes of the commercial-civic elite shone brightly from their hilltops. (See pl. 4.) In Casa Blanca, no dwelling had more than eighteen lightbulbs, and nearly half had no more than six. In Old East Side, 93 percent of dwellings had fewer than eighteen lightbulbs and over 29 percent of homes had no more than six. In Country Club, 62 percent of homes had more than thirty-two lightbulbs. (See table 3.4.)[14]

Besides the electric iron, owned by 82 percent of electrified households, only a minor kitchen appliance, such as the toaster or waffle iron, appeared in more than 22 percent of homes. In other words, only one in five households had an iron plus another appliance. Only one in five dwellings had the vacuum cleaner and just one in ten had the electric washing machine. Casa Blanca's seventy households did not own a single vacuum cleaner or washing machine. In Old East Side, only a little better off, a few African-American homes sampled the new labor-saving technology. In the 403 dwellings in Old East Side in 1922

Plate 4.   *The 1920s: The Homes of the Elite Shone Brightly from Their Hilltops.*
([Photographer unknown.] "Hammond Residence at Night, Victoria Hill, Riverside,
California, c. 1928/1929." Riverside Municipal Museum.)

(many of which white families occupied, since only about a hundred African-
American families lived in Riverside at this time), the city's appliance inven-
tory reported twenty-three vacuum cleaners and thirty washing machines.
African-American families must have owned some of these machines. In his
Riverside personals column for the *California Eagle,* southern California's
African-American newspaper, Reverend H. H. Williamson reported in Decem-
ber 1922 that Julian H. L. Williamson (presumably his son) had "accepted the
Agnew Agency of the following electrical goods[:] Royal, Premier and Eureka
Vacuum Cleaners. Electric Washing Machine and other electrical supplies." For
African-American families who could not afford to buy the new appliances, Julian Williamson "has bought two standard Vacuum Cleaners which he has for
rent. The Vacuum does more good than all carpeting [carpet beating] in the
world."[15] We do not know how Julian Williamson's business fared. We can imagine sales in the Old East Side's minority communities were not great. Few
African-American homes or Hispanic households consumed enough electricity in the 1920s to have used electric appliances.

Until their first leap in electricity consumption in 1928, when the average
upper- and middle-class household adopted the plug-in radio, Riverside's homes

used little electricity. The meager increase in average consumption from 1921 to 1927 implies that few appliances were added after the 1921–1923 inventory. During the drought of 1923–1924, when civic leaders appealed for a reduction in electricity consumption, average usage actually dropped. Except for the mansions of Country Club, all homes in all neighborhoods used close to the same amount of electricity monthly, from 15.9 kwh/mo. in poor Casa Blanca to 19.3 kwh/mo. in upper-class Wood Streets. That white middle-class homes used little more electricity than the city's humblest households starkly reveals the absence of electrical appliances. The mansions of Country Club stood aside from this pattern, consuming an average of 30.8 kwh/mo. (See table 3.5.) Differences in dwelling size accounted for differences in electrical usage, even for Country Club homes. At decade's end, over half of the city's households possessed only lights and a flatiron.[16] (See table 3.6 for the fall appliance inventory.)

Introduction of the electric refrigerator did not significantly change usage. In the years 1926–1930, only 4 percent of Riverside's households had an electric refrigerator. (See chapter 6, table 6.5 for related data.) Fourteen percent of the households of professionals, citrus farmers, and business proprietors adopted the refrigerator, the only significant adoption for any class of homes in the 1920s. In Riverside, these occupational groups constituted the city's bourgeoisie and comprised 21.5 percent of all households. They are the only group in which a majority owned the houses they lived in. They constituted the restricted market for electric appliances—the "20 percent" identified by *Electrical World*—that the private power utilities targeted in the 1920s.[17]

The low level of electrical consumption before 1928 means that households had not electrically modernized, but it does not indicate what other domestic technologies they had or whether these technologies were modern or antiquated. Most Riverside homes installed gas cooking technology after the turn of the century and gas heating technology in the decade of the First World War. In 1910, there were 1,970 gas meters installed in the city (and 2,706 electric light meters), for both residential and business use of gas. Judging from the timing of ads for gas furnaces, Riversiders did not widely use gas for house heating until the decade of the First World War. Until then, they used oil stoves for cooking and oil and coal furnaces for central heating. Wood stoves remained common in 1900, and oil furnaces were common through the 1920s. Gas furnaces significantly improved the quality of life, because coal was dirty to handle and there were frequent complaints about smoke. In 1920, there were 3,747 gas meters in the city. Since there were 4,338 dwellings with lights in 1921, we may assume that about 85 percent of them had piped gas. Homes without piped gas were probably isolated in the citrus groves and minority neighborhoods.[18]

Although households used gas for cooking, this does not mean that they cooked with modernized technology. In the 1930s, most installed gas stoves were so antiquated that modern electrical ranges took a significant share of the home cooking market for the first time. In 1930, most gas ranges did not have oven heat controls; baking was a risky culinary adventure. Most first-generation gas

ranges also lacked insulation, which would have made Riverside's kitchens un-
bearable in the region's hot summers. Urging Riversiders to buy major electric
appliances, a 1935 advertisement by the City Light Department recited a litany
of miseries associated with first-generation gas ranges: "Electricity can be safely
used by automatic appliances such as a range, water heater or refrigerator over
a long period of time. There is no need to clean or adjust burners and there is
no pilot light to blow out. The heat in an electric oven does not warm the kitchen
in the summer and there are no fumes in winter when the house is closed up
tight." In summary, by the First World War, most Riverside families had
equipped their homes with illuminating, heating, and cooking technologies developed by the 1880s and widely adopted in the nation's cities by the end of the
century. Except for poorer households and labor camps, Riversiders enjoyed the
basic utilities Victorians believed necessary for domestic comfort. Yet the average home almost certainly did not have the latest models of these technologies.[19]

Public Electricity for Homes

To meet the needs of the million new residents who moved to southern California in the 1920s, the City of Los Angeles, the surrounding smaller municipalities, private electric utilities, and private water companies competed for the
West's scarce water, power, and land resources. Their struggle escalated up
the staircase of governmental jurisdictions to involve other southwestern states,
the federal government, and Mexico. Southern California, Nevada, and Arizona
fought in Congress for the waters and hydroelectric potential of the lower Colorado. Arizona hoped to develop irrigation agriculture in its central valley and
anticipated vast growth for Phoenix. The federal government provided a forum
for this political and economic contest. Federal bureaucracies with their own
interests entered into negotiations as independent parties. Constitutional powers to regulate interstate rivers and to negotiate with foreign nations meant that
Congress and the State Department had to act. The Department of Interior's Bureau of Reclamation, devoted to western land development through irrigation,
had its own political constituency and its own mission.[20]

Competing growth policies framed the hunt for water and power resources.
After World War I, Los Angeles's civic government and private organizations
began an industrialization campaign. Although the opening of the Panama Canal
promised cheap water transportation to eastern markets, Los Angeles nonetheless suffered competitive disadvantages as a location for traditional manufacturing. Lack of local markets, distance from most raw materials, and lack of a
skilled labor force made southern California unattractive for export-oriented
heavy industries. To compensate, the progressive oligarchy of the West's biggest
city followed a Southern industrialization strategy. They sought to lure industries from the East and Midwest, as the Southern states would a decade later in
a better-known campaign, by promises of cheaper labor, the open shop, cheap
water and power, and municipal subsidization. Industrialization clashed with

the 1920s agenda of California's social progressives, who wished to utilize state powers to obtain a higher standard of living for California's burgeoning homes.[21]

The political struggle enflamed debate and brought repeated balloting. Did California want to bring private electrical utilities under public ownership of the state to provide cheap electricity for homes? Would southern California's cities join a consortium to develop cheap public power and water for industrial modernization? Firmly in control of city government and dominating civic forums, Riverside's bourgeoisie chose, as did civic-commercial elites around the country in the 1920s, cheap power for industry rather than cheap power for homes. They valued manufacturing and an industrial labor force more than improved quality of worker home life. The social organization of the city, typical of the region, supported the politics of these important decisions by preventing opponents from mounting successful opposition. Racial residential segregation divided white and nonwhite laborers. Segmentation of the labor force accomplished the same end. Only white laborers could hold industrial jobs. Mexican laborers were relegated to agricultural and casual labor. African-Americans could not even work in agriculture and patched together livelihoods at domestic service and manual labor. Nineteenth-century Chinese exclusion acts reduced the Chinese laborer's presence. California's alien land law of 1913, which prohibited Asian aliens from owning land, forced the Japanese to the margins of California corporate agriculture. High rates of residential mobility among laborers, racial segregation, the weakness of unions, and the lack of organized political parties at the local level made it difficult for the working classes to participate in the political and civic life of the city, where they might otherwise have used governmental power to address their needs.[22]

Riverside owned its electrical utility, distributing power it purchased wholesale from Southern California Edison. Municipal ownership did not make Riverside's social and political history of electrical modernization atypical. It ensured only that Riverside would debate the issues more frequently than communities where private utilities distributed power and state commissions governed rates. Electrical power development and the extension of the benefits of electricity to homes and industry raised persisting and overarching issues of social, economic, and political policy for most of the regions in the nation. All classes and civic groups participated in the vigorous debates over policy. The American middle class is thought to have had little interest in politics after 1920: "The middle class displayed a . . . lack of concern about public affairs in general." Riverside demonstrates how mistaken that impression is.[23]

By 1921, the struggle contained its major actors. To the west: the City of Los Angeles, with its capable and expansive municipal Bureau of Water Works and Bureau of Power and Light, the Los Angeles Chamber of Commerce, and the Southern California Edison Company. To the east: the City of Riverside, owning its municipal electricity system, the Southern Sierras Power Company, a private utility operating out of the city, the Riverside Chamber of Commerce, and private water and land development companies. Both Riverside's and Los

Angeles's public power advocates allied with the progressive reform movement. In Congress, Senators Hiram Johnson and George Norris and Representative Phil Swing carried the legislative fight for southern California's claim on the Colorado.

Before the race to the Colorado River erupted in June 1921, Riverside city leaders cooperated with other municipalities that owned their own electric systems, including the City of Los Angeles, to develop new public sources of electric power. Unless they met the rapidly growing need for electricity, popular support for municipal ownership would diminish. New sources would also lessen municipal dependency on private power suppliers. The City of Los Angeles bought Southern California Edison's distribution lines in 1922, after nearly a decade of opposition from the private utility's allies. Even before it took over the lines, however, the engineers of the Bureau of Power and Light realized that the capacity of the city's San Francisquito Canyon generators would be inadequate to meet anticipated demand. Other cities found themselves in the same situation as the region's population boom of the 1920s got under way. In January 1921, meeting in Sacramento, city representatives from around the state organized the California League of Municipalities, with Dr. Horace Porter, mayor of Riverside, chairing the organizing committee. Porter would be one of the state leaders of organized California municipalities throughout the year.[24]

Porter, who held a doctorate in Divinity, ministered to Riverside's First Congregational Church, the church of the civic elite. Following service in Alabama, he became associate pastor of the Plymouth Congregational Church in Brooklyn, New York, under Dr. Lyman Abbott, a leader in the Social Gospel movement. He arrived in Riverside in 1900, bringing the Social Gospel with him. City voters elected him mayor of Riverside for two two-year terms, beginning in 1918. Until mid-decade, Porter took an active role in California's public power movement.[25]

In February 1921, the League of Municipalities proposed that southern California's cities cooperatively develop the remaining hydroelectric sites wholly located within California. The state could issue bonds through the municipalities for construction work. The region's small municipalities had limited financial capability to carry bonded indebtedness and counted on the aid of giant Los Angeles. The completion of the Owens Valley aqueduct in 1913 provided Los Angeles with adequate water but not hydroelectric power. The city's holdings in the Owens Valley did not provide hydroelectric potential, because they were in the valley floor. Hydroelectricity generation required a mountain site above the valley. Not owning this site, in August 1920, the city council directed the city to obtain electricity from Colorado River development.[26]

What Los Angeles gave, Los Angeles could take away. In spring 1921, Los Angeles acted, quite unexpectedly in the view of its municipal allies, as if it wanted to monopolize all the power and water resources available to southern California. Los Angeles's large ambitions needed resources owned in Riverside. The Southern Sierras Power Company owned the important Owens River mountain hydroelectric site. It was "the principal private developer" in the Owens River and Valley areas, self-consciously driving up speculative land values that Los Angeles wanted to buy. Riverside politicians took prominent roles in the public power movement. The city's well-organized civic elites packed influence in state agriculture. Finally, power lines and aqueducts from the Colorado River had their most convenient routes across Riverside County. The Los Angeles Bureau of Power and Light boldly struck for Riverside's resources. In 1920, the City of Los Angeles filed suit against Southern Sierras Power, seeking to acquire through condemnation its Owens River gorge property. This struggle between Los Angeles and Southern Sierras lasted over a decade. Los Angeles's suit to obtain the Southern Sierras Power property was part of a scheme to control over twenty hydroelectric sites on the Kings and Kern rivers in Northern California. In May 1921, in a second move, Los Angeles filed with the Federal Power Commission to develop by itself the hydroelectric power of the Colorado River.[27]

The legal suit concerned Riverside's business leaders more than Los Angeles's application for the Colorado River. Los Angeles sued to obtain the Owens River site as one aspect of its visionary plan to shift its economy from agriculture and service to industry. The new generation of electrically powered machine tools required a virtually inexhaustible supply of electricity. The web of this municipal ambition caught Southern Sierras Power Company, because its Owens River gorge property was the most powerful resource wholly within California desired by Los Angeles. The Owens River had the theoretical potential of 90,000 horsepower of hydroelectricity, not insignificant even when compared to the 500,000 horsepower the city wanted to produce at Boulder Canyon on the Colorado. In its simplest form, then, the effort of Los Angeles to secure the Owens River gorge site pitted the industrial interests of Los Angeles against the urban agricultural interests of Riverside and the suburban and rural farming interests represented by Southern Sierras.[28]

Besides blocking Los Angeles's municipal expansion eastward, Southern Sierras Power Company also blocked the expansion of Los Angeles's bitter, private rival, the Southern California Edison Company, which served the rest of Los Angeles County and Orange County. Edison epitomized the suburban supplier, serving homes and electric streetcar companies. After World War I, Edison regularly raised some of its capital for expansion from its customers. It initiated the customer stock ownership plan during World War I to raise capital for expansion, but the company soon realized the plan brought political benefits. As the struggle over Los Angeles's municipalization of its electrical supply heated up, Edison built up customer stock ownership to defend itself against municipal takeover, assuming that customers who owned stock would be less likely to vote against their own private ownership of the company. By 1928, nearly 118,000 stock owners, one in six households in Edison's service territory, held company shares, making the company partially, if not completely, independent of the Los Angeles elite and the capital it controlled. Southern California Edison owned hydroelectric sites in the central California mountains and steam plants on the coast; in self-defense, it sought to develop Colorado River power sources. Every hydroelectric site monopolized by Los Angeles's Bureau of Power and Light meant one less site for Edison and imperiled Edison's capability to expand. Southern California Edison filed an application to build at Glen Canyon on the river, following Los Angeles's filing within days.[29]

With giant public power and giant private power slugging it out over the Colorado, smaller cities outside Los Angeles reorganized themselves to plan development of their own hydroelectricity. The *Riverside Enterprise* succinctly summarized the opinion of Los Angeles's neighbors: "The smaller cities must move quickly if they are to secure any hydroelectric rights in Southern California, the declaration having been made that Los Angeles has established large plans in connection with its Owens river project and has made extensive filings on the Colorado river for power purposes." Reacting to Los Angeles's moves, public power advocates sought to place all hydroelectric sites in California under state ownership. In summer 1921, the small cities drafted a proposition for the November 1922 ballot to amend the state constitution to create the California Water and Power Board. The board would have bonding authority to raise capital funds and authority to contract with municipalities and legal rural districts (such as irrigation districts) to build hydroelectric generating facilities for them. In addition, the state board could assist municipalities in buying private distribution systems within their jurisdiction. Ominously, from the point of view of private utilities, the board would have the power of eminent domain to purchase through condemnation the power and water resources of private companies. The committee fashioned the proposed water and power board after the public power administration of Ontario, Canada. It cited the example of Ontario's publicly owned electric utility as evidence that public ownership could supply cheaper energy for domestic electrical modernization—the same example that New York Governor Franklin Roosevelt would later use in his struggle over the development of Niagara River and St. Lawrence River hydropower. The association named Horace Porter to be secretary of the executive board, which also included representatives from Modesto, Sacramento, Alameda, Berkeley, Coulusa, and Santa Clara. Dr. J. L. Haynes, a prominent progressive reformer, represented Los Angeles as a private individual. Rudolph Spreckels represented San Francisco.[30]

The proposed power act epitomized the social and political goals of the progressive movement's public power wing. Porter argued that public power would reduce electricity rates. He justified public ownership in the same language as Senator Norris did on the other side of the country: "The mechanical revolution which the world is undergoing calls for cheap power and a good living wage." In a public debate in 1922, Porter focused the issue of state ownership on the cost and standard of living: "Our prosperity must be built on cheap water and power. Without it the farmer cannot flourish, and industry, business and domestic life cannot be conducted in the most economical manner." At the time

of the formation of the power act's campaign committee, Porter's public statement justifying the proposition pointed to the central theme of the progressive
movement: private monopolies taking excessive profits deprived the general public of the blessings of the new technology.

> The water and hydroelectric power in the public domain of our mountains should
> remain in the public control. We believe the people in the farm districts, the peo-
> ple of the cities, and the manufacturing interests can get light and power at lower
> rates by public ownership than by any other system. We believe that those who
> own and control the water conservation and hydroelectric power will own and con-
> trol the state. We believe that the people themselves should be the owners and con-
> trollers.[31]

As a political tactic, organizers of the measure hoped that the proposed State
Water and Power Act would preempt the City of Los Angeles's grab at hydroelectric sites around the state. Nonetheless, not all cities living in Los Angeles's
shadow perceived the politics that way. Long Beach thought that Los Angeles
would dominate the board and twist its broad powers to its own ends. Since the
board would be constitutionally beholden to no other authority, it would effectively make Los Angeles's municipal water and power bureaus into supergov-
ernments all on their own.[32]

The State Water and Power Proposition appeared on the November 1922 state
general ballot—its first of three appearances. It failed to receive the needed two-
thirds majority of votes to pass—the first of three defeats. After 1922, progressives formed a new campaign organization, the California State Water and Power
League. In November 1924, California progressives tied the proposed act to the
presidential campaign of Robert La Follette. Voters defeated it, along with La
Follette. The final defeat came in November 1926.[33]

By the November 1924 election, political conflict over the development of
the Colorado River replaced debate over the State Water and Power Proposition. The development of the Colorado River rearranged the political alliances
associated with the power act. The League of Municipalities strongly favored
the power act; private electric companies and the land development industry and
private mutual water companies, especially of southern California, opposed it.
After some delay, the league decided to support the federal development of the
Colorado River through the sale of electricity generated at the proposed Boulder Canyon high dam to both municipal and private customers. This position
allied the league with the private utilities and private land developers. Colorado
River development also shifted the issues of the debate. The broadest issue remained in both controversies how to obtain a high quality of life, defined as an
electrical standard of living, but the strategy of reaching that goal changed as
the politics moved from one controversy to the other. Advocates for the water
and power acts, such as Horace Porter, stressed the need to lower electric rates
to home users, so that they could afford to use more electricity for labor-saving

devices and for lights. In the campaign for the Colorado River development, advocates emphasized obtaining a better standard of electrical living indirectly through economic and population growth of California, made possible by cheap electricity for industrialization. Henry Ford used this argument to justify his ownership of Muscle Shoals. The distinction between these positions was not subtle. The power act would take economic power away from the private utilities and place it in the hands of the state; the Colorado River development would increase the power of private land and real estate industries by opening more southern California and Arizona lands to development.[34]

Electricity for Industrialization

The recession following World War I stimulated the Riverside Chamber of Commerce to search for industry, joining other southern California communities looking for a new base for their local economies. In January 1922, the chamber of commerce created a special industrial committee, whose members included George Parker (of the Parker-Stebler Box Company, originating company of the Food Machinery Corporation). In mid-1923, private businessmen around the state created the California Development Association to coordinate national marketing of California sites for industrialization and to bring together governmental officials and private business organizations, such as chambers of commerce. Behind the scenes, Los Angeles's oligarchy sponsored this campaign for new industry. In a shift away from their land development strategy for accumulating wealth, they looked to future fortunes in industry.

Riverside's chamber perceived big local benefits from industrial enterprises. At a chamber forum in June 1923, Fred Stebler, of the Parker-Stebler Box Company, presented evidence that local industrial employees spent 90 percent of their pay inside the city. Wage earners, he told the civic leaders and businessmen, were "the lifeblood of the community"—a novel idea for his audience with a small producer ideology. His message enticed Riverside. Investigation uncovered several matters, however. First, manufacturing companies were more likely to come to Riverside from Los Angeles and Orange County than from the Midwest or eastern United States. Second, Los Angeles's chamber of commerce already campaigned nationwide to recruit industry for itself and all of southern California, including Riverside. As it turned out, Riverside did not face the issue of whether to industrialize or remain agricultural. Los Angeles's push for industrialization would inevitably involve the entire region. A. G. Arnold, the assistant secretary of the L.A. chamber, explained to Riverside in June 1923 that no city in southern California could go it alone in industrialization, not even Los Angeles. Industrialization required regional cooperation, because only the region had the resources to compete against New England, New York, or the upper Midwest. To industrialize itself, Los Angeles had to industrialize the region. Riverside had only to decide whether to join willingly. If it willingly invested local capital, it would have more control over local destiny than if it opposed industrialization. The *Riverside Enterprise* called Arnold's address "remarkable" and reprinted it.[35]

Failure to industrialize would bring disastrous consequences. Explaining the Los Angeles Chamber of Commerce's position, Arnold claimed that southern California needed to industrialize to cope with the fundamental and assured fact about its future: population diversity. The Pacific Coast was "more or less the last outpost of the white race," but "within the span of our lifetime," he predicted, a tidal wave of nonwhite peoples would fill the region. Cities as large as those on the Atlantic Coast would exist from Mexico to Canada. No region would be exempt from the onrush. Southern California confronted a simple question: Would the region achieve its population growth in a way that maintained its quality of life and so that the new arrivals would also enjoy "a contented and rounded out existence"? Or would quality of life disintegrate, communities rupture into conflict, and the destiny of the region drift as institutions deadlocked between competing special interests? If southern California were to shape its own destiny, Arnold asserted, referring to the white business elites currently in control, then all its communities must cooperate. Riverside (or any other citrus city) might stand aside from the move toward regional industrialization, but, he implied, the flood of humanity would inundate it also. Standing aside would destroy the quality of life of the region.[36]

Without industry, southern California could not accommodate the inevitable emigration of nonwhite peoples. Agriculture alone did not provide sufficient employment. Industry must balance agriculture. Arnold elaborated a development strategy that would be employed in Mississippi a decade later and promoted by TVA liberals for the entire South. Low-skill, low-wage agriculture and industries had to be replaced with skilled, higher-wage industries. Without regular industrial employment at reasonable wages, laborers could not buy land and houses, they could not pay taxes, and they could not buy the material things that "are vital to humanity." Southern California could not continue to progress simply by endless subdivision of its land and furnishing a horticultural Eden where the rich retired. Arnold put his message to city beautiful Riverside bluntly. Riverside and Redlands in the citrus belt, Santa Barbara on the coast, and all other rigidly defended bastions of the rich were not visions of southern California's future; they were visions of its past. If southern California's white elite wished to preserve its future, it had to create a big enough future to give the American promise to all the nonwhite peoples coming into it. Arnold did not elaborate in graphic detail what would happen if the region did not adequately industrialize, but the horrors seemed obvious. Resistance to a multiracial future would invoke the nightmare of the industrialized Midwest and East. Riversiders since the 1880s had known what shape this nightmare took: unionized labor and the end of the open shop, periodic massive unemployment, a huge propertyless laboring class, squalid cities unrelieved by climate or gardenesque landscape, political deadlock, the old white elites without influence, racial conflict, social disorder. He concluded with a plea for economic progress for all races:

Is it not then a laudable ambition for Southern California to send forth to the world still another principle, still another indication of our spirit and of our progress— that of the guarantee of a job and a happy home for the red-blooded Americans who have in their heart the desire to live here. Thus will Southern California become not only the "white spot," but the "red, white and blue spot" of the United States—the home of the contented American.[37]

To implement its industrialization strategy, the Los Angeles Chamber of Commerce in 1923 funded a three-year, $100,000 campaign to bring industry to southern California. Los Angeles clearly had taken the lead. The Los Angeles plan, calling for an industrial basis for multiracial economic progress and social order, represented a different racial vision than southern California's founding racial vision. The Anglo elite proposed a social compact with the nonwhite immigrants. Play the game our way, don't unionize; we'll guarantee you industrial employment providing a comfortable standard of living. Did Riverside and other communities of the citrus belt want to become parties to the compact? For a few years, Riverside moved to the affirmative. The Riverside Chamber of Commerce decided to study the question. It hired a specialist from the Los Angeles Chamber of Commerce to survey "the potential and industrial resources of Riverside county." The survey not surprisingly demonstrated that Riverside had a bright future as a manufacturing center. Access to southern California markets and to Pacific trade, good rail transportation to the rest of the United States, an open shop labor force, developable land, many raw materials for manufacturing, and a pleasant climate gave Riverside, along with other southern California communities, advantages for industrial location. The likelihood of southern California's development of the Colorado River promised abundant, cheap electrical energy for the factories. Southern California could become a smokeless Pittsburgh.[38]

Local businessmen pressed for establishment of an industrial district in the city, to be served by rail transportation, where manufacturers could build plants, carefully zoned apart from residential areas. After community discussion, the chamber of commerce adopted a plan in October 1924 to establish an industrial district along the Santa Fe Railway line, and build nearby residential neighborhoods for the laborers, "with streets, sidewalks, and other improvements." Financial credit would be established to build apartment complexes for laboring families. They dedicated funds received from the sale of residential lots to subsidize the building of factories. The city platted the industrial zone several miles south of the central residential area of the city, near Pachappa Station in Government Tract. As further encouragement, the city utilities board lowered the electrical rate for manufacturers.[39]

Results from the industrialization campaign came slowly. A steady parade of spokesmen for industrialization pumped up the city's enthusiasm for its new future and assured them that major new manufacturers would soon locate there. Speakers from the California Development Association, the Los Angeles Chamber of Commerce, and the Boston Chamber of Commerce trooped into the city, stayed at the Mission Inn, boosted the industrial potential of the area, and then moved on to the next southern California city in the civic speaking circuit. In 1927, businessmen formed a regional council of the California Development Association. Self-conscious identification of local and regional industrial interest came in 1927, when the Riverside Chamber of Commerce agreed to support the effort of the Los Angeles Chamber of Commerce to lobby the U.S. Census to report its 1930 census of manufactures for the Los Angeles metropolitan area, in addition to separate reports for each of the region's cities. It was a large conceptual step for Riverside to take. The city momentarily repressed fears of being lost in the ambition of Los Angeles, "the big brother to the west."[40]

Defining Quality of Life

In late 1924, five governmental representatives from southern California, appointed as a committee by the Colorado River Aqueduct Association, drafted legislation for the California State Legislature to create a special regional water district for the appropriation and distribution of Colorado River water. The committee included William B. Mathews, chief legal counsel to the Los Angeles Public Service Department, Riverside Mayor S. C. Evans, Jr., F. W. McNabb, mayor of San Bernardino, O. E. Gunther, chairman of the Board of Supervisors of Orange County, and James H. Howard, Pasadena city attorney. Although politicians still had to work out important details, such as representation of unincorporated areas of the region's counties, planners expected the new district to include twenty-five municipalities in southern California and to provide water only for domestic and industrial uses, excluding water for irrigation. At the same time, California state engineers, working in cooperation with William Mulholland, the Los Angeles water department engineer, and engineers of other regional governments, surveyed for possible routes and reservoirs between the river and the inland communities the district would serve. The creation of the Metropolitan Water District (MWD) represented another step in Los Angeles's bold efforts to unify southern California as a region around itself. The MWD cooperated with the concurrent effort to obtain electricity for homes and industry from a dam at Boulder Canyon and the campaign to industrialize the regional economy. The debate in Riverside stimulated by the MWD continued earlier debates over electrical modernization and industrialization. It addressed quality of life issues closely linked to electrical modernization. The election on joining the MWD in 1931 culminated a decade of community debate over how to modernize the city.[41]

Mayor Evans discovered, as had Mayor Porter in pushing the state power and water acts of 1922 and 1924, that executive initiative did not always lead to business consensus. Besides being one of the region's big land developers, Evans served at different times as vice president, president, and executive director of the Boulder Dam Association, a regional lobbying group, and as a member of the Southern California Aqueduct Association. Evans tried to forestall opponents of the MWD with the argument that Riverside should keep open its option to join the district until it was clear whether the city would need its water to grow. The Riverside business and civic community could not, however, see that Riverside had much interest in a metropolitan water district. Riverside fought for a generation to obtain its own water supply by wresting artesian water away from its neighbor, the City and County of San Bernardino. With local water supply guaranteed, most Riverside leaders did not feel compelled to grant to the City of Los Angeles the enormous power it would obtain under the Metropolitan Water District bill being considered by the state assembly in 1925. Consequently, as it had opposed the state power and water acts, so the Riverside Chamber of Commerce, to Mayor Evans's chagrin, opposed passage of the MWD bill. This position lined up with the opposition the chamber of commerce expressed, under the leadership of the Southern Sierras Power Company, to relinquish any local resources to Los Angeles. By the proposed calculus for representation on the MWD board, the City of Los Angeles would have a majority by one. Cities the size of Riverside would have no more representatives than small villages. Controlling the board, the City of Los Angeles would have enormous powers, including the right of eminent domain, the right to make property assessments independently of counties, and the right to set tax rates for the aqueduct. In the case of conflicting assessments, the MWD's assessment would prevail. The board could issue bonds without submitting them to voters. Once a city joined the district, it could withdraw only with permission of the board. The MWD would be the true regional governing body of the region's key natural resource.[42]

Riverside's unwillingness to join the regional venture notwithstanding, the Colorado River Aqueduct Association progressed rapidly in settling details of water appropriation and selection of the delivery routes. In early April 1926, construction work on the 260-mile aqueduct began. Initiation of actual construction, with a projected cost of a third of a billion dollars, revealed southern California's political hubris. The U.S. Congress had not yet approved the legislation—the so-called Swing-Johnson bills—to build Boulder Dam. The date for legal formation of the Metropolitan Water District, 1927, came and went, Riverside debated, Los Angeles pressured. Los Angeles Chamber of Commerce officials toured the inland valleys, appearing before local chambers and service clubs, such as the Lions. A publicity campaign promulgated Mulholland's basic message about water ("if you don't get it, you won't need it"). Advocates and opponents argued at innumerable civic forums.

Population growth defined the most important issues in the question of joining the Metropolitan Water District. Participants discussed taxation, the cost of joining, and possible domination by huge Los Angeles often, but framed these issues in growth expectations. Growth had been the issue since formation of the water district in 1925. The Riverside City Council sent a representative to the organizing meetings, with one councilman explaining, "If Riverside is to grow and develop its surrounding territory, plans must be made for future water development." Six years later, when the city finally faced a vote on joining, growth remained the issue. Summarizing discussion at one of several public meetings called by the city council to discuss the question in 1931, the *Riverside Enterprise* reported, "Development of Community Termed Issue." But growth was a complicated issue. "Growth" really referred to three definable subissues. Was population growth inevitable? Would population growth change the character of the community? Who would benefit from growth?[43]

Most residents expected considerable population growth for the city. They had witnessed the previous decade's increase of nonwhite population into the city and had acted—as in the industrialization policy—on it. Many accepted a version of the growth argument presented by the Los Angeles Chamber of Commerce: lack of water would not stop migration (which not subtly contradicted Mulholland's dictim). The president of the MWD stated, "Tremendous increase in population [is] certain to come to this section." The region must find water for it. The mayor of Riverside echoed this sentiment: "Riverside is bound to grow and she must have domestic water." The choice facing the city was not whether to grow. The choice was, growth without water and hence "economic ruin" or growth with water and hence prosperity.[44]

Proponents of joining the MWD wanted increase of population with a high standard of living. Population growth with new industries and lovely homes and lush gardens would require new sources of water. A long-term resident and land developer, Dr. Joseph Jarvis, put the issue in these terms:

> If the City of Riverside is to continue to grow and maintain its place among the principal cities of California, an active prosperous business center, sought after by those seeking homes because of its beauty as a city; a city of orchards and gardens; a clean, wholesome, beautiful city; offering to both the homeseeker and the tourist the best there is, in moral, educational and recreational facilities, it will before many years have passed be necessary for Riverside to add to its water supply an amount far greater than it can possibly hope to obtain from the present source of supply.[45]

Jarvis hoped for an upper-class city. He knew his audience would compare Riverside to eastern and midwestern U.S. industrial cities, while forgetting Riverside's own barrio and ghetto. They hoped Riverside, as a garden suburb, would not have huge slums like New York or crowded ethnic blocs like Chicago. Riverside did not have miles of poorly maintained row houses, crowded with working-class wage-earners. Riverside wanted to be the kind of city that people from other cities visited on their vacations. Prosperity lay behind the social and personal health of the civic social morality that made Riverside a desirable community in which to live. Without additional water, Riverside could not be an upper-class city.

Would population increase change the character of the city? The Los Angeles Chamber of Commerce confronted Riverside with this issue when it asked for support for regional industrialization. Industrialization would shift the city's population profile. The proportion of residential owners of land as a capital asset would decrease and the proportion of blue-collar laborers, many renting their homes, would increase. Many laborers would not be white. The industrialization campaign implicitly called for abrogation of California's agricultural settlement before World War I, restricting nonwhite workers to agricultural labor with regulated wages and reserving industrial labor in a competitive wage labor market for whites. For a while in the 1920s, a multiracial, blue-collar future appeared not to frighten Riverside's Anglo elite. Perhaps they thought the city would evolve slowly toward that future, with plenty of time for them to retain control of the social order. The MWD raised this issue also. Southern California needed the MWD, because the region inevitably faced heavy population growth and the concomitant growth of a multiracial manufacturing labor force serving the vigorous industrialization. What made the issue of joining the MWD so passionately controversial was the shock of realization. The future was close and coming all at once. Realization enflamed the debate over the extent of the groundwater supply on which Riverside and other citrus cities depended.

Proponents believed that the city's own well water would accommodate significant growth for only four to five years, ten years at most. Their presumption precipitated debate among water experts and engineers over the rate at which the Santa Ana River basin's groundwater supply was falling. "The best Federal authority," Walter C. Mendenhall, "agreed upon the permanency of the water supply in the area east of the Bunkerhill dykes from which Riverside receives its water." Contrarily, A. L. Sonderegger, "eminent hydraulic engineer," stated, "The Santa Ana basin has been exhausted. There is no more material amount of water for appropriation in this basin." A host of popular conjectures and impressions seconded the opinions of experts. Some users were pumping well waters from lower depths than twenty years ago; others thought basin water was even increasing.[46]

The third issue concerned who would benefit from joining or remaining outside the Metropolitan Water District. The debate split—by no means neatly—the elected politicians and land development businesses interested in long-term city growth away from the Southern Sierras Power Company, the Riverside Water Company, and the agricultural interests, whose assets the district endangered. The cost of joining seemed great to opponents, because joining would lead to loss of local economic power, put pressure on irrigation water resources, and threaten to limit horticulture in the city. Proponents expected to amortize the cost of building the water delivery system over a future of increasing wealth and power, the cost becoming more bearable year by year. Opponents feared they would have to amortize the cost against decreasing future assets, making the burden progressively heavier. The eminent domain issue particularly frightened owners of local water resources. MWD district directors had requested from the state legislature the power of eminent domain over local water supplies. If granted, the MWD would have the power to condemn the mutual water companies that had been the basis of citrus horticulture around southern California.

The MWD withdrew its request for this authority to placate Riverside's agricultural interests, but citrus growers remained suspicious that, were they to join the water district, the huge organization might return to rapacious empire building.[47]

On March 31, 1931, 52 percent of Riverside voters voted against joining the district. Riverside became the first inland community to break ranks with Los Angeles, but by the end of the summer neighboring San Bernardino and Colton also voted to withdraw from the district. The City of Los Angeles submitted to its voters a $200 million bond issue to build the aqueduct, which passed by six to one. Riverside's refusal to join the Metropolitan Water District represented a victory of local capital and agricultural interests. A majority of voters rejected the aggressive, regionalizing capitalists of Los Angeles, who needed to subsume the assets of many Southland communities to build their industrial metropolis. The vote also defeated a regional compact that welcomed immigrant minorities and would build for them the steady industrial employment they needed to afford a decent life. Not coincidentally, southern California pressed at this time for a repatriation program to return Mexican nationals to Mexico. Depressed industry did not need nonwhite labor. Riverside's local capitalists enjoyed their victory only briefly. The Metropolitan Water District became the region's most powerful water broker. The depression threatened to ruin the community's land-based capitalism. In the 1930s, Riverside's elites lost much of their power to determine the quality of life in their city.[48]

Appendix

Figure 3.1.   Riverside, California Neighborhoods, 1921–1950

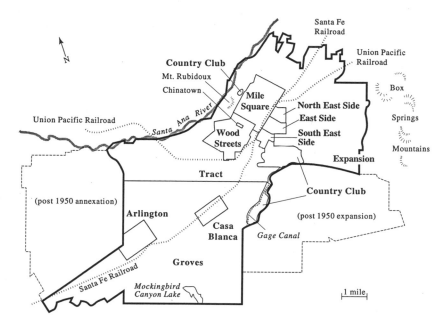

Table 3.1. Qualitative Grouping of Riverside Occupations, 1921–1950 (excluding Citrus Farming)

"Class"	Typical Occupations	Neighborhood	Neighborhood Occupational Composition		
			Professionals, businessmen (%)	Low white-collar and skilled laborers (%)	Semi-skilled and unskilled laborers (%)
Upper class (Bourgeoisie)	Professional, business proprietor, corporate officer, district manager	Country Club, Wood Streets	20.2	32.7	16.1
Middle class	Assistant manager, clerk, craftsman-contractor, industrial foreman insurance agent, salesman	Mile Square, South East Side, Expansion, Tract	7.5	44.8	26.9
Laboring class	Auto mechanic, dressmaker, driver, machinist, packer, picker, road worker, servant, wood chopper	Old East Side, North East Side, Casa Blanca, Arlington	3.95	27.6	40.8
Nonwhite classes	[African-American, Hispanic, Asian workers in laboring-class occupations]	Old East Side, Casa Blanca	1.4	15.8	74.9

SOURCE: Riverside Sample Data.

NOTE: The occupational hierarchy follows Alba M. Edwards, "A Social-Economic Grouping of the Gainful Workers of the United States," *Journal of the American Statistical Association* 28 (December 1933): 377–387. The Edwards scale differs from the scale used by Stephen Thernstrom, *The Other Bostonians,* primarily by breaking Thernstrom's Group 1 into two groups, professionals and businessmen. In the table above, our "upper class" is virtually equivalent to Thernstrom's Group 1. Our "middle class" combines Edwards's scale groups 2 and 3 and many occupations from group 4. Our "middle class" therefore combines Thernstrom's low white-collar with some skilled blue-collar occupations. The use of the status ranking, in addition to an occupational ranking, is justified by the clearly distinguished neighborhood occupational profiles. The occupation distributions for each class do not add to 100 percent, because some occupations, such as citrus growing, are excluded.

Table 3.2.   Home Tenure Characteristics of Riverside's Neighborhoods, 1921–1950

Community	Resident owner (%)	Duration of Tenure (mean years)		
		Owners and renters	Owners	Renters
Mile Square	22.4	1.9	5.3	1.1
Old East Side	32.9	3.2	6.2	1.6
North East Side	31.3	2.4	4.9	1.3
South East Side	32.6	2.3	4.5	1.1
Expansion	45.5	2.7	4.3	1.9
Country Club	59.4	4.5	5.9	2.2
Wood Streets	41.1	3.2	5.7	1.5
Casa Blanca	45.0	4.7	7.1	2.7
Arlington	36.6	2.3	4.1	1.2
Groves	55.0	3.1	4.6	1.2
Tract	50.9	2.9	4.5	1.3
Citywide	38.6	2.68	4.9	1.3

SOURCE: Riverside Sample Data.

N = 8,774 cases of residential tenure and status; Pearson chi-square = o.o.

Table 3.3.   Occupational Characteristics of Riverside Neighborhoods, 1921–1950

Community	Proportion of Heads of Household by Highest Occupation Held (%)					
	Profes- sionals	Growers, business persons	Clerks, insurance agents	Skilled laborers, industrial foremen	Semi- skilled laborers	Unskilled laborers
Mile Square	9.5	20.4	28.4	19.2	16.9	5.6
Old East Side	2.8	5.0	8.4	14.5	22.9	46.4
North East Side	4.3	13.0	15.5	29.8	25.5	11.8
South East Side	7.0	18.9	21.7	19.6	24.5	8.4
Expansion	5.1	20.8	16.8	27.8	21.7	7.8
Country Club	26.4	40.0	15.2	6.4	8.0	4.0
Wood Streets	13.9	22.1	27.9	15.8	16.8	3.4
Casa Blanca	0.0	10.9	1.6	7.0	13.3	67.2
Arlington	8.7	23.6	13.5	20.0	20.7	13.5
Groves	4.6	37.0	15.0	19.2	13.7	10.4
Tract	8.2	23.6	21.9	23.8	16.5	6.1
Citywide	8.2	23.0	20.2	19.9	17.7	10.9

SOURCE: Riverside Sample Data.

N = 4,089 cases of identified occupations; Pearson chi-square = o.o.

Table 3.4. *Riverside Neighborhoods, Light Groupings, 1921–1923*

Neighborhoods	1-6 lights (%)	7-18 lights (%)	19-31 lights (%)	32-100 lights (%)
Mile Square	9.4	62.0	21.6	6.9
Old East Side	29.4	63.4	5.2	2.0
North East Side	16.9	72.1	10.7	1.1
South East Side	11.9	73.0	15.1	0.0
Expansion	22.3	59.6	14.2	3.8
Country Club	2.9	11.8	23.5	61.8
Wood Streets	8.0	50.0	34.1	8.0
Casa Blanca	48.6	51.4	0.0	0.0
Arlington	13.9	70.8	11.6	3.7
Groves	12.1	55.6	21.8	10.5
Tract	17.6	63.5	13.9	4.9
Citywide	14.0	61.8	18.3	5.9

SOURCE: Riverside Appliance Inventory.

NOTE: Groupings explain 81.4 percent of the variation in the number of lights. Eta-squared = .81, probability > .01.

Table 3.5.   Social Characteristics of Riverside Neighborhoods, 1921–1950

Community	Mean Electrical Consumption, 1921-1950 (kwh/mo)	Ethnic Proportion: Hispanic	Ethnic Proportion: Asian
Mile Square	67.9	0.4	0.1
Old East Side	35.9	30.0	1.4
North East Side	54.9	0.8	0.0
South East Side	63.3	2.1	0.6
Expansion	75.3	1.4	0.4
Country Club	190.4	0.4	0.0
Wood Streets	72.8	1.1	0.0
Casa Blanca	32.1	59.5	3.6
Arlington	53.5	2.9	0.0
Groves	112.4	3.7	0.6
Tract	76.5	1.3	0.0
Citywide	75.9	4.4	0.3

SOURCE: Riverside Sample Data.

Hispanic and Asian identity established by classification of names. Of a pool of over three hundred Riverside African-American surnames from the 1910 federal census schedules and the local columns of the *California Eagle* from 1916 to 1922, we identified in sample data as probable African-Americans only twenty-three individuals and as certain African-Americans (100 percent name match and residence in Old East Side) only six individuals. This number of individuals was too small for statistical analysis.

Table 3.6. *Appliance Inventory of Electrified Residences, Riverside, 1922*

Appliance	Residences with Device	Percent	Mean	Standard Deviation	Total Devices*
Lights	4,338	100.0	15.1	11.6	65,671
Irons	3,554	81.9	0.9	0.5	3,714
Telephone	2,158	49.7	0.5	0.0	2,158
Minor kitchen	955	22.0	0.3	0.5	1,092
Vacuum cleaner	817	18.8	0.2	0.4	820
Washing machine	455	10.5	0.1	0.3	460
Space heaters	257	5.9	0.1	0.3	287
Major kitchen	160	3.7	0.0	0.2	166
Fans	120	2.8	0.0	0.2	139
Tools	79	1.8	0.0	0.4	129
Sewing machine	62	1.4	0.1	0.1	62
Personal	52	1.2	0.0	0.1	56
Water heater	5	0.1	0.0	0.0	6

SOURCE: Riverside Appliance Inventory.

*Total appliances in some categories are more than the number of residences with the appliance, because some residences had more than one such appliance.

Chapter 4
The New Deal in
Electrical Modernization

Public Enframing

We stand on the concrete pad for a new house we are to build. We survey the landscape. We might be in New Jersey, and view the straggling border of a green field against a pine wood. We might be in southern California, and view the golden dust and crackling grass of the heated summer being plotted for a vast tract. Surveyor's flags dance in the breeze, signaling an abstract geometry soon to be scraped and pushed into reality by graders and bulldozers. We enact an American ritual. The empty land and the limitless horizon become a place. Governments plan and enable, industry plans and speculates. Developers name streets and subdivisions. Contractors construct mass housing seriatim, trench and string utilities. Local government will draw ward lines. A school board will devise elementary school districts.

As we stand on the pad, carpenters raise the stick walls of two-by-fours around us and install roof trusses above. Roofers close the space with plywood sheets, asphalt paper, and shingles. Perhaps we chose the floor plan from the developer's models, or sketched it with an architect, or ordered it from a magazine and customized it to fit our special dream. This floor plan marks out the paths we will take from now on, from the baby's room to the kitchen, from the master bedroom to the living room. Now the floor plan materializes: the faint must of curing concrete, the sweet aroma of sawdust, the sharp ping of hammered nails and thup-thup of pneumatic staplers, the rasping of a saw cutting plaster drywall. Cladding blocks old views to the outside. The boxed spaces of windows and doors enframe new views.

Winston Churchill said, borrowing from John Ruskin, "First we shape our buildings, and then our buildings shape us." This is true of so much, not just of buildings. It is true of politics. In the 1930s, the United States built the national politics of housing around itself. Circumstance and politicians' visions shaped this new housing policy on two design axes: publicly regulated or owned electric power and adequate, fully modern homes for all families. Whereas the national political landscape had previously contained no structure of federal power policy or federal housing policy, the New Deal of Franklin Delano Roosevelt built these policies up around the nation's electorate. Americans had previously fought the old politics of electric power regulation and housing regulation largely at the state and local levels. Distinct political and governmental jurisdictions separated political issues as effectively as fencing and entailment divided agricultural fields. Reformers had not connected hydroelectric power regulation and all its issues, from the problem of determining fair residential electric rates to the question of who should own and develop hydroelectric sites to the problem of ensuring potable water and sanitary tenements, of regulating housing density, of the adequate supply of low-density housing, or of zoning industry out of residential neighborhoods. The New Deal brought power regulation and housing reform into national politics and national policy, linking them into a single, complicated issue of American housing. Progressive dreams in an era of economic crisis returned Americans to the new world of state regulation. Roosevelt reshaped those dreams into a unified vision of the planned improvement, support, and regulation of American homes. The New Deal constituted a political enclosure movement; jurisdictional fences dividing issues came down. New political institutions and new bureaucracies rose like the new houses in which the electorate would live.

Within the New Deal national political framework, most American families modernized their homes with electricity. Federal electrical modernization programs publicly enframed their conception and effort. New ideologies and political issues and the new fabric of political history of the 1930s through which Americans wove their lives became the foundations, stick walls, and plaster drywall, as it were, of their new houses. Electrical modernization did not arrive as prophesied in the gospels of corporate capitalism. Technological utopias of the electrically modern house, secreted from the hearts of the individual consumer, did not drive the market of modernization in the 1930s. That scenario lay behind the nation, fragmented and ruined, now almost an archaeological relic, graded over by the New Deal.[1]

Based on his experience as governor, Roosevelt believed that only a fundamentally new social arrangement centered on full utilization of electricity could bring a higher quality of life to American families. Fully matured and bound together by his central belief, Roosevelt's vision had the following major components.

> Economic improvement required that the operation of the marketplace
> be supplemented by vigorous, broad governmental planning.

Governmental planning had to apply to geographic-economic regions, superseding jurisdictional divisions of the states and local government.

Partial redistribution of the American population and industries would be needed, from large cities into regions where planning would address all the needs of farm and village families—employment, health, housing conditions, and social welfare. The notion of resettlement reflected Roosevelt's antiurban bias.

Full electrical modernization of households defined the standard for quality of life, no matter where the households resided.

Electrical modernization of farm productive processes, within the framework of planned production and marketing, would lower farm costs and return farms to prosperity.

Electricity must be affordable to all households in quantities required for electrical modernization. Publicly owned and private utilities, lightened of their false capitalization by public regulation and the breakup of holding companies, would provide inexpensive electricity.

Cheap electricity would make the redistribution of population and industry possible, because it could be transmitted long distances and sold at near cost to rural consumers.

Roosevelt realized his vision most fully in the Tennessee River valley, in the South, and in rural electrification, but he self-consciously applied it to cities elsewhere, large and small. The focus of his political opponents on governmental planning obscured the place of electricity at the center of the vision. Planning arose as an instrument, not an end, during Roosevelt's governorship. His original, enduring, and consistent intent was to improve the everyday lives of individuals through electricity. He had been interested in regional planning for social improvement for over thirty years. In a speech in 1931, FDR spoke of the influence of City Beautiful movement planning for Chicago, which came to him through his uncle, Frederic A. Delano, a Chicago railroad executive and civic leader. The vision defined a goal, not a program. Roosevelt did not present programmatic details of electrical reform to voters in their choice of governor in 1930 or president in 1932. He offered them a social destination and a strategy to guide their travel arrangements.[2]

Roosevelt did not borrow his vision from private industry's notion of better living through electricity. In Roosevelt's vision, electrical modernization transformed lives. The private utilities desired *electrical* modernization; FDR desired electrical *modernization.* He wanted the *social modernization* of the American home. In 1934, Roosevelt used cheap electric power as a major campaign issue in his support of his party's congressional candidates. Following his campaigning in the Northwest in the summer of 1934, *Business Week* paraphrased the president's vision for its audience: "The supply of cheap power at many points throughout the nation is intended to underlie new social development." He saw electricity as the best technology to obtain social modernization. Social modernization as transformation of the home was a politically defined vision, the domestic microcosm in the macrocosm of the national body politic. A progressive politician in his heart, Roosevelt believed in the political process as a rational means for collective choice of social policy and in the capability of rationally directed governmental action to improve the lives of the masses. The electrical utilities targeted the few consumers already modernized, whose privileged modernity had sprung from the crippled magic of the marketplace, seeking to shift their energy source, as from coal to electricity, or enhance their experience of being modern. Roosevelt focused on the great majority of households who were not modernized, for whom electrical modernization would bring a qualitative change in lifestyle. The electric utilities looked to the one-fifth of the American homes with some share of electrical modernization and said they had done everything they could. Roosevelt looked to the four-fifths of the homes the utilities claimed were incapable of modernization and said everything remained to be done.[3]

Roosevelt wove the theme of domestic electrical modernization as social modernization into speeches and extemporaneous remarks during his presidency. Little of his public conversation with the American people remains part of today's collective political memory. To understand the full force of FDR's progressive vision, we need more than references to his speeches in footnotes. For this reason, I quote a few addresses at length. He was the author of the speeches, not in the sense of privately penning each word, but by placing them in the public discourse of politics. That his political advisers may have drafted his speeches does not lessen their importance for indicating his vision. The advisers wrote to fit his vision, and he often rewrote to cast phrasing in his own voice.

Progressive social modernization meant more than the material improvement of lives. It meant also the moral improvement of life, as a matter of social justice, through technology. Roosevelt provided no greater personal testimony to this progressive vision than his emotional reaction to the poverty of Tupelo, Mississippi. He visited Tupelo during the 1932 presidential campaign and again the following year. He blanched at the poverty of this village, lacking electricity, sewers, and other urban services. Tupelo was the first town to sign a contract with the Tennessee Valley Authority for cheap electricity. The community's rehabilitation became a New Deal showcase. Roosevelt revisited the hamlet in 1934. His extemporaneous comments at that visit reveal the human dimension of his vision of social progress through technology. (See pl. 5.) In the quotation below, he associates transformation of persons from despair to a higher moral state in words quietly resonating with the salvationist themes of the nation's Christian culture ("hope," "something in people's faces," "determination," "knowledge"), with governmental planning and public ownership of electricity (TVA), with personal technology ("refrigerators," "cooking stove," "dozens of things," "gadgets"), with a new definition of household standard of living ("necessities"). He situated this

Plate 5. *President Roosevelt Speaks of Hope Through Electrical Technology in Tupelo, Mississippi, November 18, 1934.* ([Amateur photographer.] "Tupelo, Miss., Nov. 18, 1934, Roosevelt Day." Lee County Public Library, Tupelo, Mississippi.)

vision of just technology in a new civitas ("our American life"), which collapsed the conventional distinctions of local village, state, and nation as effectively as when he spoke over the radio directly to voters. He may have calculated the occasion—he was a master politician—but he did not feign his vision.

> What I saw on those [earlier] trips, what I saw of human beings, made the tears come to my eyes. The great outstanding thing to me for these past three days has been the change in the looks on people's faces. It has not been only a physical thing. It has not been the contrast between what was actually a scarcity of raiment or a lack of food two years ago and better clothing and more food today. Rather it is something in people's faces. I think you understand what I mean. There was not much hope in those days. And yet today I see not only hope, but I see determination and a knowledge that all is well within the country, and that we are coming back. And there is another side of it [TVA]. I have forgotten the exact figures and I cannot find them here in this voluminous report at this moment, but the number of new refrigerators that have been put in, for example, means something beside just plain dollars and cents. It means a greater human happiness. The introduction of electric cook stoves and all the other dozens of things which, when I was in the Navy, we used to call 'gadgets,' is improving human life. They are things not especially new so far as invention is concerned, but more and more are they considered necessities in our American life in every part of the country.[4]

Plate 6.   *Treadle Machine: The Unelectrified Life in the Rural South.* ([Photographer
unknown.] "Woman at sewing machine, Gee's Bend, Alabama." Farm Security
Administration Photograph, c. 1938–1940, from the Library of Congress. Courtesy
of Birmingham Public Library, Department of Archives and Manuscripts.)

At a press conference in November 1934, Roosevelt again explained the goals
of TVA in terms of the transformation of human life. Electrical modernization
would change the nature of the citizenship. (See pl. 6.) His conversation with
reporters tied social modernization (from "rural" "mountaineer" to a "different
type of citizen") to the American ideal of equality of opportunity ("they never
had a chance") to better homes ("the houses in which they lived").

> [Electric] Power is really a secondary matter. What we are doing there is taking
> a watershed with about three and a half million people in it, almost all of them
> rural, and we are trying to make a different type of citizen out of them from what
> they would be under their present conditions. Now, that applies not only to the
> mountaineers—we all know about them—but it applies to the people around
> Muscle Shoals. Do you remember that drive over to Wheeler dam the other day?
> You went through a county of Alabama where the standards of education are lower
> than almost any other county in the United States, and yet that is within twenty
> miles of Muscle Shoals Dam. They have never had a chance. All you had to do
> was to look at the houses in which they lived.[5]

In an address in fall 1936, Roosevelt described the effect of electricity as a
"social revolution," using a phrase Morris Cooke embedded in the progressive

lexicon. As had Gifford Pinchot, Roosevelt compared the dramatic changes due to electricity to those due to the steam engine, a century and a half earlier. He linked the steam engine to a revolution in industry, but he linked electricity to a "social revolution," which "sound and courageous public policy" could accomplish. "It is not irrational to believe that in our command over electrical energy a corresponding industrial and social revolution is potential, and that it may already be underway without our perceiving it."[6]

The Housing Crisis Cometh

Before the New Deal, progressives did not link housing reform to reform of the electric industry or holding company regulation. Housing politics did not have a clear arena at the national level, while the electrical struggles did. Except for a brief episode concerning defense worker housing in World War I, the federal government had no experience with housing. During the New Deal, advocates of housing reform criticized the federal government for lacking a unified housing policy that linked reconstruction of the mortgage financing and banking industry, national regulation of the private housing market, and public housing. Indeed, the New Deal never included housing legislation that unified most aspects of the nation's varied housing problems in the way that the Agricultural Adjustment Act or the National Industrial Recovery Act addressed agriculture and business. The shotgun pattern of housing initiatives did not contradict the idea that the first New Deal saved capitalism without reforming it. Some New Deal housing policies, such as the Federal Housing Administration's racial loaning policies, became the not entirely inadvertent origins of pernicious features of today's problematic American urbanism. The lack of an architectonic national housing policy does not mean, however, that New Deal programs did not address piecemeal many of the social objectives housing reformers desired. Federal housing programs recast the localized housing industry into a highly structured, uniform market, which the U.S. government underwrote. They extended private home ownership to the majority of households. They effectively imposed national standards of building design and shelter quality. They extended the blessings of electrical modernization to the majority of homes. They made public housing a federal responsibility. They made mass tract suburban communities comfortable and healthful for an enlarged middle class. In a word, the programs effectively *nationalized* housing—even though they did not "nationalize" housing in the sense desired by many housing reformers. Housing legislation and housing programs represented Roosevelt's core philosophical vision of the home. We look to Roosevelt himself for the unification of electrical policy, housing reform, and social modernization. Though the housing programs (except for public and subsidized housing) had a conservative tone, benefiting the middle class and a private housing industry and reinforcing their bourgeois vision of society, this conservatism did not reflect FDR's own vision.[7]

When governor of New York, Roosevelt signed several laws concerning better housing and delivered one radio address on the subject, but clearly he did not rank housing as important as electrical modernization. His attitude reflected the national mood before his presidency. Concern over the lack of minimal quality shelter and the costs of home owning erupted and subsided mainly at local levels. The saga of tenement reform in New York City after the exposure of unsanitary and overcrowded immigrant tenements in the 1880s, philanthropic apartment projects in Chicago for black residents in the 1920s, and the fitful efforts of companies to house their workers in company towns, such as Pullman, Illinois, are well-known episodes in American history. Nevertheless, measured against the total housing stock of the nation, they constituted meager and inadequate efforts to increase the number of better dwellings. We understand the erratic behavior of the speculative housing market, which passed through numerous boom and bust cycles—Los Angeles in the 1880s and 1920s, Florida in the 1920s, for instance—as a patchwork of colorful episodes for which there is no single coherent national historic narrative. The situation changed little in the 1920s. In 1926, the Supreme Court decision *Euclid v. Ambler Board of Realty* upheld residential zoning as a legitimate extension of the police power, not requiring compensation to landowners whose development rights zoning had restricted. The model uniform zoning law for states, written by the U.S. Department of Commerce, prompted some national uniformity to municipal regulation of land use, and, thereby, standards for houses, when the states enacted zoning laws at the end of the decade. In 1932, as a last-ditch effort to stem the onrushing depression, President Herbert Hoover obtained passage of the National Reconstruction Corporation, which provided aid for mortgage lenders. It offered too little, too late. Until the reforms of the 1930s, most of the nation's families lived in minimally regulated dwellings. A vast, private, highly speculative construction industry, composed of small and middle-sized construction companies, decentralized at the local level, guided by minimal building codes, constructed their homes. The story of American housing took place at local communities and in local economies.[8]

Home financing instruments—construction loans, builder mortgages, first and second home owner mortgages—originated locally, regulated only loosely by state usury laws that usually capped interest rates on mortgages. At the end of the 1920s, home owner first mortgages ranged from 5 to 9 percent interest, with the normal being 6 percent. This is a wide range of variation in rates; nine basis points is 80 percent higher than five basis points. Terms of loans similarly varied widely. Insurance companies and building and loan associations occasionally offered first mortgage loans with fifteen-year payback periods. Other insurance companies and deposit banks offered first mortgages with terms as short as one to three years.[9]

Governments regulated home construction less than the lending industry. City and county construction standards primarily concerned building densities and connection to municipal services. Standards seldom included quality-of-life criteria, such as landscape, sunlight, and square footage of floor space. Standards for electricity, gas, and plumbing seldom reflected the most advanced technology available. Architects, builders, and brokerages operated locally. Speculative construction could embody minimal standards, because the housing shortage ensured sale. Custom-built homes were subject only to agreement between the parties. While some national market constraints existed (for instance, building supplies existed partially within a national market), in the absence of national housing corporations, contracts varied widely for similar dwellings on similarly priced land in different regions of the nation. Housing built on speculation sold at prices determined by local supply and demand.

Finally, property taxes varied considerably across the country. In the absence of income taxes, the property tax carried most of the public tax burden and, consequently, was high. In 1928, in cities of over 30,000 persons, the property tax contributed 64 percent of total revenue receipts. In Arkansas (1923–1925), property taxes took an average of 17.1 percent of net rental income (before taxes). In South Dakota (1922–1926), property taxes took 29.9 percent of net rental income. In Washington State (1924–1926), they took 31.7 percent. Locale to locale, variation could be much greater. In Montrose, Colorado, property taxes on residential properties took 52 percent of net rent, and in sections of central Iowa, they took 41.8 percent of net rental income. Such heavy property taxes naturally led to high rates of delinquent taxes. These rates, too, varied widely. Delinquency rates in North Carolina averaged 9.3 percent of the gross tax levy (1928), but Cook County, Illinois (Chicago, 1927), suffered at 37.1 percent.[10]

The housing market did not encourage home ownership. Ownership took a large share of income. Owning cost more than renting. Regionalization of housing markets frequently meant that home owners lost equity when moving from one region to another. In 1930, two-thirds of American urban households could not afford to buy homes on the market that year. Only 47.8 percent of American households owned their homes. When the market did encourage home owning, it was not always a good deal for the household. Lack of rental housing in many areas of the country meant that families had little choice of whether to rent or buy, so we cannot assume that houses being purchased were of higher quality than rented quarters. Many families unwillingly owned their homes. Landlords forced them to purchase substandard dwellings after government removed World War I rent controls after 1919. Forced ownership of substandard homes scandalized postwar Philadelphia. The numbers point clearly to the fragility of home ownership at the opening of the depression. Indeed, "in 1933, 49 percent of the $20 billion home mortgage debt was in default. The monthly rate of foreclosures was approximately 26,000—an average of 1,000 per day." In its first year of operation, the Home Owners' Loan Corporation received applications for loans on approximately 40 percent of all nonfarm residential properties (appraised at less than $20,000 and having one to four dwelling units).[11]

The lending industry in collapse, nearly half of the nation's urban home owners in foreclosure and facing eviction: *now* the nation had a housing crisis.

Home Ownership for a "Settled Place of Abode"

At the outset of his presidency, Franklin Roosevelt ranked inadequate home ownership as the leading threat to the social contract between the government and the
people and inadequate "security of the home" as the leading social problem of
the American people. He linked home quality to home ownership, setting aside
renting as a viable means of obtaining security. In 1934, addressing Congress with
a review of the first year of his presidency, Roosevelt stated his vision unequiv-
ocally: "Among our objectives I place the security of the men, women and children of the Nation first. This security for the individual and for the family concerns itself primarily with three factors. People want decent homes to live in."[12]

He expressed the philosophy behind home ownership in September 1932 in
the famous Commonwealth Club speech in San Francisco. Adolf Berle wrote
the speech, with the assistance of Rexford Tugwell. In his book, *The Democratic
Roosevelt,* Tugwell recalled that Roosevelt had not seen the speech before delivering it and did not have time to revise—his usual practice. In the speech,
Roosevelt argued that industrialization and urbanization changed the economic
order of the nation in a way that threatened the social compact between the people and their government. Until the great corporations concentrated economic
power in themselves at the turn of the century, an open frontier, abundant cheap
farmland, and plentiful industrial work for wage laborers enabled every person
to work and to accumulate property. The recent concentration of economic
wealth and power into a corporate oligarchy changed that situation; the mass of
individuals could no longer accumulate property. In this new situation, the national government had to intervene in the economy to make it possible for individuals to accumulate savings and property on which to live when they could
not labor.[13]

The speech previewed the New Deal's massive intervention in the economy.
Roosevelt's notion of a new social compact between the people and their government describes the rationale by which he sent the national government into
the economy to save American homes and to broaden home ownership. The frontier was no longer available for social modernization. The national government
needed to create a new setting and new processes for social modernization. In
other addresses, he tied this rationale to home ownership. In the new economic
order of great corporations, most persons could not own a small business. The
major form of property ownership would therefore have to be home ownership.
When underwritten by the national government, home ownership represented
asset savings on which everyone could draw when they could no longer work.
In the new economic order, Americans had somehow to obtain, or be given, economic security where they lived, in homes they owned in long-term residency.
Home ownership would be an asset for social modernization. In the Commonwealth speech, Roosevelt pledged the national government to play a major role
in generating this progress.

By making home ownership and the material rehabilitation of American dwellings integral components of social modernization for the mass of Americans, Roosevelt transformed a previously conservative philosophy into a progressive philosophy. Since the mid-nineteenth century, the home ownership ideology had supported social conservatism. Not surprisingly, Herbert Hoover spoke for the conservative vision of home ownership. In a 1923 pamphlet on home ownership, prepared under his direction as head of the Department of Commerce, Hoover saw the conservative vision of the home owning creed in terms of creating sentiment for individualistic capitalism. "A husband and wife who own their home are more apt to save. They have an interest in the advancement of a social system that permits the individual to store up the fruits of his labor." For Hoover, home ownership made less government, not more, possible.[14]

Unfortunately for social conservatives, home ownership had not advanced significantly from 1900 to 1920. It increased only slightly during the 1920s housing boom. By the end of the 1920s, many home owners could not pay property taxes or meet mortgage obligations. Members of the real estate and mortgage banking industries noted these problems, prompting Hoover to call another of his well-known presidential conferences. Failure of the system of home ownership imperiled a major foundation of social conservatism. The President's Conference on Home Building and Home Ownership of 1930 studied every aspect of home ownership in the 1920s. Especially important, the conference recommended putting the nation's mortgage system on the long-term mortgage. Roosevelt's new FHA adopted this recommendation in 1934.

Conference panels also expressed concern about the high rates of residential mobility they perceived around the nation which economists and sociologists believed harmed the body politic. In the tradition of Lockean liberalism, property ownership anchored citizenship and civil order. As America passed from its Jeffersonian republic of rural landowners to an urbanized society of renters, Hooverians feared that civic order would disappear. Eva Whiting White stated the problem clearly: "Those conditions which give every evidence of causing lowered vitality and lack of ambition, which put a premium on vice and crime, and challenge our civic life, [should] be replaced by such a development of city planning, zoning, and housing that the next generation shall have, to the full, opportunities for constructive home influences and normal community life."[15]

FDR's conservative family culture heavily steeped his views in the home owning ideology. In the depression his personal solicitude for desperate American families transformed home owning from a conservative basis of social stability to a progressive basis for social justice. A passionate, anecdotal vision of health, security, and physical comfort in modernized homes empowered Roosevelt's commitment to the ideal of social justice. He preached to the American people that they had a right to health and security in their own home, conceived as a dwelling of long-term residence, meeting minimum standards of physical shelter and hygiene, and fulfilling an electrical standard of living. To speak of home owning as a "right" shifted the meaning of home owning. In the conservative

Jeffersonian philosophy, the rights of local property ownership justified restriction of national governmental power. In the progressive Rooseveltian philosophy, the right of local property ownership justified enlarging national governmental power. That the American people had a right to a secure and materially comfortable standard of living meant that the national government had to guarantee it. In supporting the National Housing Act, the president reviewed the goals of the New Deal, emphasizing the importance of the security of home: "These three great objectives—the security of the home, the security of livelihood, and the security of social insurance—are, it seems to me, a minimum of the promise that we can offer to the American people. They constitute a right which belongs to every individual and every family willing to work. They are the essential fulfillment of measures already taken toward relief, recovery, and reconstruction."[16]

Besides residential security, Roosevelt also spoke about residential stability— the idea that families would remain in their homes for long tenures. The mythos by which Roosevelt understood the historic situation the nation occupied in the 1930s directly implied the need for residential stability. He made permanent residential tenure a policy goal for farmers. He injected residential stability as an implicit element of the quality of life and social justice that the New Deal's urban programs sought. Reviewing the New Deal in June 1934, Roosevelt emphasized that Americans had to obtain better lives where they currently lived. Reconstructing American society involved creating the conditions to make possible residential longevity in the same home. "When land failed, our ancestors moved on to better land. It was always possible to push back the frontier, but the frontier has now disappeared. Our task involves the making of a better living out of the lands that we have." The National Housing Act would stimulate private lending for modernization of homes and building new homes with "the ultimate objective of making it possible for American families to live as Americans should." The Resettlement Program, which Rexford Tugwell promoted, approached residential stability in a roundabout way. Tugwell proposed to resettle poor farm families from submarginal land to better land where they could profitably pursue agriculture and where the future would include generations of farm families making a satisfactory livelihood. Uprooting and resettlement by a regimented society were not the purpose or spirit of the Resettlement Administration; the program sought intergenerational residential stability on productive land. Roosevelt explicitly stated the goal of long-term residential stability on the farm in a message to Congress in 1937 on farm tenancy. Roosevelt worried that "many tenants change farms every two or three years, and apparently one out of three changes farms every year. The agricultural ladder, for these American citizens, has become a treadmill."[17]

When Roosevelt wished to remind his audience of the full horror of the depression, he painted the picture of homeless, unemployed persons, in which he emphasized the supreme importance of a stable home by its loss, as in a campaign speech of 1936: "I need not remind the young people of this country of the black future which lay ahead of them in those days. That was the era of the wanderer—boys and girls who had grown tired of living on the vanishing savings of their parents, and who had set out on the highways in all directions to look for work which they could not find." In a radio address, commitment to a home of long residency appeared in a discussion of children. Americans had to measure their democracy against the needs of children. A child "should live in a home where he will find warmth and food and shelter." Especially, the government should not let the poverty of parents deprive the children of "a settled place of abode or normal community relationships."[18]

As European nations moved toward war, Roosevelt returned to his Commonwealth Club campaign speech to reiterate the theme that democratic society could not exist without economic security, including home ownership. Historical events turned the barrel of the social kaleidoscope, and the familiar elements of the mosaic at which the president looked fell into a new picture. Now he could see clearly that a stable home provided more than normal community relations that were every American's birthright. The stable, secure home made possible a democratic citizenship. "If by democratic methods people get a government strong enough to protect them from fear and starvation, their democracy succeeds; but if they do not, they grow impatient." Democracy required a government strong enough to provide security, including home ownership.[19]

European war finally erupted in September 1939. Invasions and combat inevitably destroyed homes and displaced vast populations. Roosevelt's fear for the security and stability of the home deepened, and called up his most emotional statement of his social vision. Against the background of a new war in Europe, he urged support of the Community Chest campaign in a radio talk. He placed himself with his audience, sitting around the radio. The comfort of their home should evoke their sympathy for those without such comfort. "It is [for] the survival of the old spirit that the home must be guaranteed. For the family still remains the basis of society as we know it, and it must be preserved as an institution if our democracy is to be perpetuated. If we lose the home we are in grave risk of undermining all those other elements of stability and strength which contribute to the well-being of our national life."[20]

The New Deal in Housing

New Deal housing programs intervened in the housing market through financial intermediaries. The national government did not deal directly with households and did not directly impose national regulations and standardization on the private housing market; the powerful real estate industry opposed nationalization in this sense. Influenced by the bankers, the New Deal sought primarily to save the structure of mortgage banking, that is, housing sector capitalism itself. The New Deal slighted—though it did not ignore—urban housing. The Public Works Administration (PWA), established by Title II of the National Industrial Recovery Act, built 21,800 dwellings in fifty-one public housing projects, under the directorship of Harold Ickes. The PWA acted in the name of unemployment relief. Its housing projects did not significantly meet the national need for low-income housing. The Wagner-Steagall Act of 1937 elevated slum clearance and public housing to the level of national policies, but Congress limited the act's effectiveness before 1942 by refusing to increase appropriations to the Federal Housing Administration. The National Housing Act of 1934, which established the Federal Housing Administration, had the greatest effect on the nation's housing but focused this impact outside central cities onto suburbs. These priorities partly reflected President Roosevelt's own commitment to capitalism and his preference for country over city.[21]

Historians identify eight major programs directly related to housing. Hoover created three of them in the last year of his presidency, in last-ditch efforts to induce recovery. The Reconstruction Finance Corporation (RFC) had the broadest mandate to inject capital into the economy, but its administrators frittered away their opportunity and scandalized the Hoover presidency by saving a few banks whose directors were associates of RFC directors. The New Deal, typically, invigorated these Hooverian programs, transforming them into potent instruments of massive, national relief and recovery. The eight major housing programs were:

1. Federal Home Loan Bank System (1932)—purchased mortgages from banks to stimulate home loans;

2. Reconstruction Finance Corporation (1932)—issued bonds to banks as the basis for banks to make mortgages;

3. Home Owner's Loan Corporation (HOLC) (1932; ceased taking loans in 1936)—refinanced home mortgages;

4. Farm Credit Administration (1934) and Farm Security Administration (1937);

5. National Housing Act (1934)—loans for modernization of existing housing, including appliance purchase, and for construction;

6. Reconstruction Finance Corporation's Mortgage Company (1935)—purchased FHA mortgages on individual homes and on large housing projects;

7. Wagner-Steagall Housing Act (1937)—established United States Housing Authority to loan housing construction funds to states and other governmental subdivisions for publicly owned and rent-subsidized housing projects;

8. Reconstruction Finance Corporation's Federal National Mortgage Association (1938)—bought mortgages on new homes and large housing projects and authorized after World War II to purchase Veterans Administration home loans.[22]

Several programs targeted specific clients for loans: the Electric Home and Farm Authority (1933); the Federal Credit Union Section of the Farm Credit

Administration (1934), which acted within the Federal Credit Union Act of 1934; the Disaster Loan Corporation (1937), administered under the Reconstruction Finance Corporation; and the Rural Rehabilitation Division of the Farm Security Administration of the Department of Agriculture.[23]

By supporting the housing financing structure, the federal government did more than simply "save capitalism." It made the national government the guarantor of local property, thereby establishing a structure that could revolutionize local property relations. FDR did not utilize the new structure. Out of political expediency, he refused to interfere with local custom. He would not jeopardize his political coalition built on Southern Democrats and burgeoning urban Democratic electoral machines by attacking race and class relations—the heart of local custom. Nonetheless, he put in place the nationalized property structure that his successors could use to fulfill his vision of social modernization. This perspective on the ambiguous nature of the New Deal accomplishment in housing parallels other Rooseveltian jousts with reality politics. For instance, Roosevelt's eight appointments to the U.S. Supreme Court provided the progressive shift that led to the civil rights decisions of the 1950s and 1960. When national leaders finally decided to modernize the nation's racial relations, the instruments by which they could modernize those relations in terms of housing were already in place.[24]

Roosevelt signed the National Housing Act on June 27, 1934, nearly a year after the landmark legislation of the "Hundred Days." For many historians, the political path of the statute's enactment implied inadvertency, rather than design. Marriner Eccles, a Utah banker in the Treasury Department who drafted the proposal, recalled that FDR's "decision to initiate a housing program was reached by a back door approach." Since many of the nation's unemployed were construction workers during 1933, Roosevelt's advisers frequently discussed proposals for housing programs to relieve unemployment and stimulate economic growth. To focus the discussion, in 1933, the president established the Emergency Committee on Housing to prepare a housing proposal. The committee included Harry Hopkins, Henry Wallace, Frances Perkins, Rexford Tugwell, and Averell Harriman. Before the committee could make a formal proposal to the president, in December 1933, the Federal Home Loan Bank Board appeared before the National Emergency Council (a coordinating group to advise FDR) and requested a $2 billion loan for the Home Owners Loan Corporation. The request came long after the New Deal programs were already spending billions of dollars and criticisms of government diseconomy pricked Roosevelt's desire for limited federal expenditures (he had spoken conservatively about balancing the federal budget during the 1932 campaign). When informed of the request, Roosevelt supposedly protested more lending. "Some one present suggested that a new housing program was at least a partial answer to the President's question." The royal outburst initiated the train of discussion among the advisers that eventually led to the National Housing Act.[25]

The president's Emergency Committee on Housing moved slowly to develop ideas. In early 1934, the president appointed Marriner Eccles to the National Emergency Council, representing the Treasury Department. Eccles took discussion of a housing proposal out of the hands of the Emergency Committee on Housing, by persuading the National Emergency Council to appoint a subcommittee on housing, with himself as chair. He gathered a technical advisory group of his own choosing. This group, which included General Motors Company's consumer credit administrator, came up with the idea of FHA insurance. Eccles drafted the National Housing Act.[26]

By mid-August 1934, the new national office of the Federal Housing Administration and its field offices were taking applications. The act provided federal insurance for lenders for two types of loans, home modernization (Title I) and home purchase mortgage (Title II). Only home owners could apply (through a lending institution) for modernization loans. Regulations limited Title I loans to a maximum of $2,000 with a maximum payback period of five years. The law restricted the loans to rehabilitation of the physical dwelling. Congress amended the act in May 1935, to permit the purchase of detachable equipment (such as refrigerators); this amendment was in effect until April 1936. Lending institutions, such as commercial banks, savings and loans, credit unions, and industrial lenders (e.g., the Morris Plan), began to participate in the modernization insurance and offered loans to home owners. The Federal Housing Administration insured participating lenders to a maximum of 20 percent of their dollar volume in modernization loans; that is, the agency would reimburse lenders for defaulted notes to a limit of 20 percent of the gross outstanding loan amount. In exchange for this protection, the agency limited the lender to charging 5 percent interest per year on the loan.[27]

The government did not compel participation in the housing insurance program. By the end of 1934, 11,945 lending institutions, including 10,029 banks, had joined. In the first three years of the program, 6,433 commercial banks made National Housing Act Title I loans. While these are large numbers, most financial institutions initially stayed outside the program. Joseph Coppock, who studied the program for the National Bureau of Economic Research at the end of the decade, thought the major reason was simply that the requirements of the plan limited its desirability. Restriction of loans to home owners disqualified clientele of credit unions and financial companies, most of whom were wageearning renters. Many financial institutions were already in the consumer loan business, for instance, appliance retailers and electric utilities, and did not want the 5 percent interest cap.[28]

As a result of the requirements for loans and the low initial institutional participation, the total volume of FHA loans (over 1,400,000 loans in the three years 1934–1937) represented only a small percentage of the total mortgage and modernization loans extended by all lending institutions. Conventional wisdom diminishes the importance of the FHA loans in promoting recovery or improving the nation's housing stock prior to 1946. Discounting the plan's impact is easy to do only if one compares the volume of loans and mortgages to the nation's total. From other perspectives, the plan had a sizable and significant impact. First, not all households could qualify for the loans—only home owners. The program targeted urban (and suburban) dwellings, not farms; farmers had their own farm security and improvement programs. As a consequence, we measure home modernization loans against the 11,413,000 owner-occupied homes, not against the nation's total, farm and nonfarm, housing stock of 34,855,000 dwellings (1940 census statistics). From this point of view, about one in eight eligible households took loans in the first three years of the program. At a rate of one in eight, nearly every urban family would personally know another family who took a federally insured loan, even if they themselves did not. The program had high social visibility.[29]

The National Housing Act's modernization program had a significant impact on the nation's housing in another way. The president, his team, and Congress intended the act to draw commercial banks into making consumer loans. Banks largely avoided the small consumer loan business in the 1920s and 1930s, as other credit agencies sprang up to fuel consumerism. Federal Housing Administrator Steward G. McDonald testified in March 1938 before a congressional subcommittee that "the big thing" about the program was "to educate the banks to do this kind of business." The program met this goal. With the federal government assuming much of the risk in consumer home loans, banks could set up consumer loan departments, learn the nature of the market, establish in-house expertise in judging applicants, and obtain experience in making the loans. How much more enticing could the free market be made? Short-term installment loans made by commercial banks stood at $44 million in 1934 and jumped to $258 million in 1937. In 1934, commercial banks extended only 1 percent of the short-term installment debt to consumers; in 1937, they extended 3 percent; in 1941, 8 percent. For comparison, observe that the percentage of total installment loans extended by small loan companies fell from 6 percent in 1934 to 5 percent in 1941, and the percentage of total installment loans extended as sales credit by retailers rose from 30 percent in 1934 only to 38 percent in 1941. Commercial banks clearly were the dynamic sector of this industry.[30]

How much home improvement did the modernization loans accomplish? The average amount for modernization loans for additions, alterations, and repairs to dwellings was $385. The average amount of a loan spent on buying an appliance was $220. The average amount from a loan spent on rehabilitation would pay, for example, for the installation of heavy wiring and some architectural alteration to a kitchen. The average appliance purchase note barely exceeded the cost of a refrigerator. Nearly half of home owners used Title I loans for kitchen modernization. An analysis in April 1937 of 23,000 claims for Title I insurance by the FHA showed that 40.8 percent of Title I loans were for purchases of refrigerators (and 11.4 percent for washing machines). In Electric Home and Farm Authority contracts, refrigerators represented 49.9 percent of the appliances purchased in the same years. For the Rural Electrification Administration, refrigerators made up 47.3 percent.[31]

Over the long haul, the National Housing Act's impact on housing transcended the home improvement of millions of dwellings spread across the map of the United States. The federal government effectively nationalized housing, even though the FHA strenuously denied that it sought to impose national housing standards or override local conditions. The administration's technical bulletin on the principles of small housing construction stated clearly that the FHA "has consistently sought to avoid the standardization which is threatened by the use of [stock or prepared] plans on a national scale. It has emphasized its disapproval of such standardization through insistence upon the localization of its architectural and other professional service by builders and owners of low-priced dwellings." Despite this avowal, FHA policies created a nationally uniform set of expectations about housing design. They set into place a uniform set of criteria for the appraisal and evaluation of housing. They nationalized the rules for capital investment in housing. Federal reconstruction of housing capitalism and FHA standardization of dwelling appraisal separated housing in the 1930s from housing in the 1920s.[32]

FHA policies deliberately promoted electrical modernization. We see self-consciousness in policy changes in the first few years of FHA activity. Initially, it did not include electrical service or indoor toilets in its minimal property standards. The reason for their omission is unclear, but the agency quickly corrected itself. Both the appraiser's underwriting manual and the agency's publications required electrical and indoor toilet services for FHA insurance. The technical bulletin on planning small houses explained the necessity for electricity in terms of electrical modernization, rather than illumination. "Electric wiring, while not stated in Circular No. 2 as an essential requirement for a minimum house, is nevertheless included, because of its great utility in improving comfort and simplifying household operations, and also because of its availability and economy in most communities." Significantly, the FHA required convenience outlets for portable power appliances, as well as outlets for illumination. "The use of an ample number of double convenience outlets is to be recommended so that movable lamps and appliances may be utilized rather than permanently placed fixtures, permitting a system of great flexibility." The technical bulletin outlined the standards of the National Electrical Code (without mentioning the code by name). The agency required that the smallest, single-family detached dwelling specified under FHA standards should have two circuits rather than a single circuit—one for lights and one for power. Recommendations for outlets included two separate outlets for the kitchen, one for the refrigerator and one for appliances to be used on counters. The FHA underwriting manual enforced the new electrical standards—along with other national standards. The agency detailed minimal standards for new dwellings it insured and referenced the National Electrical Code of the Fire Underwriters of the United States. It required its inspectors to check buildings under construction for four electrical mandates. These requirements include that "the feeders, switches, and panels [are] of sufficient size to fulfill the requirements to which they are put, without the overloading of circuit or switch capacities, and [that] they conform to the Underwriters' Code and local ordinances"; that "power circuits [are] provided where needed, and [are] separate from light circuits", and that "there [are] a sufficient number of fixtures and outlets to distribute illumination properly and . . . fixtures [are] of suitable design and construction." The FHA thereby made the National Electrical Code the national standard and provided it with federal subsidy.[33]

Riverside approved the effect of standardizing endorsed by the FHA early in the agency's history. FHA standards effectively guaranteed the value of property and the security of the lending institutions, not simply by warranting the loans against default, but by enforcing standards of material quality of secured properties. The FHA announced its first building standards at the end of 1937, after three years of federal administrative experience with local building practices. "These new standards . . . represent a powerful blow to cheap and shoddy construction and the use of inferior materials, and assure the home seeker full value from his investment and a home that will stand up in future years and represent value commensurate with its cost." The ordinary home seeker knew so little about construction technique, design, and material qualities that she could not protect herself against inferior or fraudulent practices. With the new FHA standards, she did not need to know, "because the FHA will protect." Surely, every prospective property owner got the implication. The invisible hand of the local marketplace and its small capitalist entrepreneurs did not protect the value of locally owned property. The visible hand of the national government did. FHA inspectors visited building sites three times during construction. One visit came after the installation of electrical (and heating and plumbing) systems, to ensure they met FHA standards. By 1945, a popular book on the future of American housing could take federal standardization for granted: "Today, FHA-insured mortgages and their various equivalents have been so standardized as far as technical requirements are concerned that the chances of getting a jerry-built house are slim."[34]

Constance Perin obtained strong evidence of the national uniformity that resulted from the FHA and other federal programs in a set of interviews she conducted in the mid-1970s in Philadelphia and Houston, a generation after FHA established standard appraisal guidelines. Philadelphia adopted land use zoning in the late 1920s, while Houston notoriously has none, leaving land use to the marketplace (and real estate covenants associated with deeds). It would be difficult to imagine more dissimilar land use regulatory environments. Nonetheless, Perin discovered the same patterns of residential, commercial, and industrial land separation and the same appraisal standards of housing by all the professionals involved in the housing market, including appraisers, sales agents, and attorneys. Perin writes, "I asked [interviewees] whether the Federal Housing Administration in Houston ever did battle with the national regulations of the F.H.A. in order to preserve some regional distinctions, whatever they might be in the way of neighborhood layout or housing styles: ' . . . I think [one interviewee responded] the F.H.A.'s been instrumental, having been here so many years that our [federal] patterns and [federal] forms for subdivisions and all were followed by local attorneys.'" FHA national guidelines on building materials, architectural design, and site location for insurable housing were used in Houston by the lending industry even when the specific lender did not intend to apply for FHA mortgage insurance. One Houston appraiser called the FHA guidelines the "Bible."[35]

The FHA implemented standards when the program originated in the mid-1930s. The agency imposed minimum standards for planning, construction, and acceptability of housing on the whole nation. It established twenty-one districts for regional administration of its programs. Central FHA administration did not permit the district offices to suspend national standards, but they did permit them to impose additional standards to meet local needs.[36]

New Deal housing programs cumulatively reshaped the quality and size of the nation's housing stock and the structure of the real estate market. They created the housing patterns that became the national norm after 1945. They placed federal policy behind the geographic shift of the nation's residential communities from the city to the suburb. FHA lending policies effectively locked suburban land use into large subdivision planning. By slighting inner-city urban renewal and favoring large subdivision suburban development, the New Deal programs forced mass housing on to the cheapest land by means that promised efficiencies of scale, thereby significantly lowering the cost of resident owner housing. Together with the long-term self-amortizing mortgage, the cheap price of mass tract housing made possible the democratic diffusion of home ownership, one of Roosevelt's fundamental values and an underlying goal of the New Deal. As corporate home building companies increased their percentage of private housing starts, New Deal agencies effectively came to regulate the nation's housing real estate industry. By providing the basis for democratic home ownership, in large detached suburban dwellings, New Deal programs effectively created the national mass market for electrical modernization of the home. In conclusion, by 1941, New Deal housing programs had established the basis and regulatory arena for the postwar housing boom. In Roosevelt's language, the New Deal had successfully established the basis for the democratic social modernization in the home. When the post–World War II housing boom took off within the New Deal framework, the national construction industry required less than ten years to modernize the material home life of most Americans.[37]

The New Deal in Electrical Modernization

Electrification programs reinforced housing programs. The largest social objective of the housing as well as the electrification programs had been to improve the quality of life for the majority of American households, who lived in dilapidated or substandard dwellings. Roosevelt spoke of the need for new and rehabilitated housing to provide families with the electrical standard of living.

The progressive political tradition envisioned electrical modernization as a major element of the social modernization of the American home. The president wanted the New Deal to break the cycle whereby high private utility rates and high appliance prices prevented mass electrical modernization. Such a policy would create the market that would make lower prices profitable: "The broader the base of consumers of a product that is now classed as a necessity, the lower would be its costs and the greater its stability. A great many years ago Dr. Steinmetz observed that electricity is expensive because it is not widely used, and at the same time it is not widely used because it is expensive. . . . There is a vicious cycle which must be broken, and a wise public policy will break it." Even the private utilities, against whom Franklin Roosevelt fought his entire political career, recognized the central significance of Roosevelt's vision. Writing about the recently increased residential market for the sale of electricity from privately owned public utilities, *Electrical World* in 1935 obliquely expressed the new understanding: "The household use of electricity has been so small, however, and the appeal of modern electrical appliances has become so strong and public interest has been so increased as a result of the wide publicity that has grown out of President Roosevelt's enthusiasm for the social benefits that come from electricity in the home that the domestic market has offered immediately possibilities for load building."[38]

Two major electrification programs directly furthered this social objective: the Tennessee Valley Act of 1933 and the Rural Electrification Administration, established by executive order in 1935 (and the subsequent Rural Electrification Act of 1936, which made the REA a permanently and separately funded agency). TVA initially benefited small towns and farms in TVA service areas; eventually, TVA became an instrument of a broader transformation of Southern society. After presentation of the National Emergency Council's *Report on Economic Conditions of the South* in July 1938, Roosevelt's conception of TVA shifted. Removing Southern poverty required more than just cheap electricity. Low-wage industries and unmechanized agriculture lay behind the low standard of living in the South. The traditional Southern industrialization strategy of attracting industries by low wages and low costs had not transformed Southern society as a whole. The region needed high-skill jobs to bring higher wages. Higher wages would force Southern industries to be efficient and capable of competing with their Northern counterparts. Cheap electricity and electrical modernization of home, farm, and industry could help if they created skilled manufacturing industries and growth of cities.[39]

Rural Electric benefited rural households everywhere in the country. Historians generally represent TVA and Rural Electric as the only major New Deal electrification programs, or simply as programs to provide rural households the electrical benefits already available to city households. TVA and REA accomplished these program objectives, but both also had a significantly larger political objective, which included urban as well as rural households. TVA and REA sought by demonstration, competition, and administrative compulsion to force private utilities, which provided most Americans with their electricity, to extend electrical modernization to the four-fifths of the nation's households that were still unmodernized.[40]

Roosevelt's vision did not limit electrical modernization to the rural areas of the nation. TVA and Rural Electric achieved stunning successes, but these should not obscure the effort made by other programs to bring electrical modernization to the nation's cities and large towns. These programs are well known:

1. National Housing Act Title I home rehabilitation loans (1934), providing for electric wiring upgrade and retrofit.

2. National Housing Act Title I loans for purchase of major, home electric appliances (1935–1938).[41]

3. Federal Housing Administration electrical wiring standards in the building codes required for homes to qualify for FHA mortgage insurance.

4. TVA as a "yardstick" in forcing neighboring private power utilities to lower domestic rates. Despite criticisms that no one could give the yardstick idea precise legal meaning, TVA did force down rates by Southern utility companies, for instance, the rates of the Commonwealth and Southern, headed by Wendell Willkie.

5. Electric Home and Farm Authority (established by presidential authority, December 1933). The EHFA assisted TVA in marketing electric appliances to the TVA service area and planned cooperative marketing with private appliance manufacturers. Manufacturers would provide their dealers in the TVA service region with special models of their appliances for sale at lower prices. Households would receive special low rates from the Tennessee Valley Authority or private utilities participating in the plan. Banks would finance the appliance purchases with low rate loans that the EHFA would in effect guarantee with a loan from the Reconstruction Finance Corporation. Administrators intended to demonstrate that even poor households would buy appliances if their prices and the cost of electricity were cheap enough. In August 1935, the administration transferred the EHFA to the Rural Electrification Administration, where it could reach more households with its services. "By 1938 the Electric Home and Farm Authority, a subsidiary of the Reconstruction Finance Corporation, had purchased over 100,000 installment contracts from over 2,500 dealers, spending $15.5 million in thirty-three states."[42]

6. Farm Security Administration (1937–1946). Henry A. Wallace, Secretary of Agriculture, under authority of the Bankhead-Jones Farm Tenancy Act of 1937, created the FSA to assist tenant farmers and poor farmers to purchase land, improve farms, and recover from natural disasters. From 1937 to 1946, the FSA made 893,000 rehabilitation

loans, assisted 187,272 cases of debt adjustment between farmers and their creditors, resettled 15,000 farmers in 164 projects, and operated 95 camps for 75,000 migrant laborers.[43]

7. Public Utilities Holding Company Act (1935). This act broke up and regulated holding companies by requiring them to register with the Securities and Exchange Commission (established in 1934) and giving the Federal Power Commission (established in 1920 in the Federal Water Power Act) and the Federal Trade Commission (established in 1914) the authority to regulate interstate shipments of electricity and gas. Although historians generally characterize the PUHCA as a progressive effort at busting corrupt monopolies, the president himself linked the act to the problem of providing lower electric rates and the benefits of electricity to the consumer and to other measures to provide lower electricity rates. According to Ralph De Bedts, a recent historian of the Securities and Exchange Commission, Roosevelt believed "the holding companies . . . were directly and indirectly responsible for boosting rates. Their greed made rate reductions impossible."[44]

8. Public Works Administration loans to municipalities for building public electric systems. By 1935, the PWA had financed 274 public power systems to compete with private electric power. The purpose was to enable municipalities to obtain lower rates.[45]

9. "Seven Little TVAs." In June 1937, Roosevelt asked Congress to duplicate the TVA in seven other major rivers around the nation, including drainage basin systems of the Great Lakes and the Ohio River, the Tennessee and Cumberland regions, the Missouri and Red rivers, the Arkansas and Red rivers and the Rio Grande, the Colorado River, the Columbia River, and the drainage basins of the rivers flowing into the Pacific south of the California-Oregon border. Senator Norris, who had introduced the original TVA bill in 1933, introduced a bill to accomplish the president's objectives. Progressives hoped to duplicate the success of the Tennessee Valley Act around the United States. This vision of superfederalism died quickly, but its demise did not end the New Deal effort to replicate the TVA. Scaled-down, multipurpose, flood control and power projects, drawing political support from regional needs, succeeded in accomplishing electrical modernization, even if this was not their primary purpose. These projects included the Bonneville Power Act of 1937 that built Grand Coulee dam on the Columbia River in eastern Washington; the Santee-Cooper Hydro Project in South Carolina, and the Loop River Public Power District in Nebraska. Even shorn of TVA's social objectives, these projects served the progressive principle of providing yardsticks to determine the fairness of private power generation in the regions. The post–New Deal dam building era began with the emergency needs of the Second World

War and the Korean War. After the war, President Truman made a last, unsuccessful, effort to revive FDR's plan for more TVAs.[46]

10. The Electric Home and Farm Authority (1933), the Federal Credit Union Section of the Farm Credit Administration (1934), which acted within the Federal Credit Union Act 1934, the Disaster Loan Corporation (1937), administered under the Reconstruction Finance Corporation, and the Rural Rehabilitation Division of the Farm Security Administration of the Department of Agriculture offered smaller and more specifically targeted loan programs.[47]

Expansion of private consumer credit to low-income households represented a major New Deal commitment. The Roosevelt administration recognized that, short of outright public subsidization of home modernization, enabling households to obtain credit to modernize themselves represented the most effective tool for breaking down the private utilities' segmented market for modernization. Before passage of the National Housing Act, one of the major constraints on appliance sales, according to electrical industry analysis, had been lack of credit to appliance dealers to finance their long-term loans to customers. Title I removed the "bottleneck" that had impeded passage of credit from large capital lenders, such as the utilities and automobile finance companies, to the dealers. Title I shifted the burden of credit risk from the dealers (whose credit ratings the depression hurt) to the ultimate customers. With the federal government insuring the loans to the customer, the dealer merely acted as a conduit for financing paper. With the risk removed, large lenders were willing to lend to the merchandisers. Large industry credit houses, such as General Motors Acceptance Corporation, General Electric Contracts Corporation, and Morris Plan Bank, and the half-dozen largest commercial banks in the country jumped into appliance lending. Some of these lenders took over the billing and collecting of installment payments for the dealers, substantially relieving them of expensive overhead. Once Title I brought these large credit houses into the appliance credit business, they did not leave. Even when the special provision for Title I insurance on major appliances expired in 1938, the large lenders remained in place, preventing the expiration of this Title I program from undermining the national boom in appliance sales.[48]

The federal government also liberalized installment credit terms, lengthening the average payback period for consumer durables loans from twelve months in 1929 to twenty-two months in 1938. Lengthening the payback period permitted persons with lower monthly incomes to purchase on the installment plan and thereby enlarged the market for electrical modernization.[49]

Joseph Coppock wrote in 1940 of the FHA and Electric Home and Farm Authority, "Their importance does not arise from the volume of instalment financing which they have directly facilitated, but from the impetus they have given to a wider use of instalment financing, and the influence they have exerted on instalment financing practices in general." The National Housing Act's Title I brought commercial banks into consumer installment financing, an area in which they had been unwilling previously to make significant ventures. The federal government forced the liberalization of credit terms, capped interest on loans at a low rate, and generally made consumer loans sufficiently risk-free and enticing that most banks for the first time set up consumer loan departments. Government encouragement of home modernization through guaranteeing bank loans for this purpose represented, in the view of another contemporary observer, "one of the most notable developments in the field of instalment financing during the recovery period." Twenty-five years later, Thomas Juster could write, in his extensive assessment of consumer credit, "The most striking development during this depression decade was the huge expansion of commercial bank participation in the consumer instalment credit market after 1935." Bank holdings of credit paper for automobiles and other consumer durable goods rose 50 percent per year from 1934 to 1941.[50]

The 1935–1936 Works Progress Administration survey of the budgets of 60,000 families revealed how deeply into the nation's lower income groups these programs expanded short-term consumer credit. Among households with less than $500 income for the year (the lower 16 percent of the nation's families), 15 percent carried installment debt (excluding mortgages). This compared to 32 percent of families with incomes above $1,750 a year (who comprised the upper 24 percent of the nation's families) carrying installment debt. In this survey, the average urban family income was about $1,500 for the survey year. That households with less than $500 income for the year could make installment payments showed that in principle households at all income and wealth levels were capable of participating as consumers in a mass consumption economy. The most immediate effect of liberalization of credit was the national adoption of the electric refrigerator. Nearly all households purchased refrigerators on installment plans. By spring 1940, over 44 percent of the nation's households possessed a refrigerator.[51]

The National Housing Act changed the relationship between the home buyer's mortgage and electrical modernization, providing the basis for what became called, after 1944, the "complete home program." Before 1935, contractors did not design or build houses to support the electrical standard of living. They built many houses as starters or shells, into which the home owner would bring amenities, appliances, and utilities, as desired. They could sell such dwellings at a lower price. In other words, the home owner would have to acquire the "electric standard of living" through piecemeal retrofit. This practice constituted a major constraint on private sector electrical modernization during the 1920s. The private sector sought to overcome this restraint by a variety of merchandising experiments in the early 1930s. Eventually, the industry came to the opinion that the only way to electrically modernize dwellings, at a standard of complete electrical service with a full set of electrical utilities and devices, would be to sell all electrical appliances to the home owner as an ensemble under one contract, including installation. Home buyers could then finance the contract by installment payments over a three- to five-year term, so that monthly payments would be low enough to be affordable. Electrical industry spokesmen proposed that the appliance ensemble be bundled with the home mortgage. The marketing strategy was, as the industry came to understand it, to sell the home, not the appliances.

The electrical industry saw several benefits in the plan to merchandise all electric appliances together with unitary financing through the mortgage. First, the plan reduced the overhead costs of multiple, individual sales of appliances and their installation. Second, utilities could tie appliance ensembles to split rate schedules, since the customer's total electric demand would qualify them for promotional rates. Third, the larger companies in the industry controlled quality of home construction and utility and appliance installation. Earl Whitehorne, assistant vice president of McGraw-Hill Publishing Company, which published *Electrical World* and *Business Week,* editorially argued to the electrical industry in 1930 that speculative home contractors, who built 65 percent of the nation's housing, were the root of the problem. They built to sell quickly, which meant selling at an unreasonably low price and required that they keep appliance installation to a minimum. The implication seemed clear. Until the industry brought the speculative home builder under control and under standards, the complete electric home had little future. The electrical industry needed regulations to compel this segment of the construction industry to meet its needs. "The fact that electrical men have always been accustomed to sell appliances one at a time to families in old homes has built up an obstructing tradition. The sound suggestion that a complete equipment of all the economically desirable major appliances might just as well be installed, built into all new houses when they are constructed and financed under the original mortgage, has had to fight this precedent." These arguments eventually persuaded the industry. In 1932, the Commercial Section of the National Electrical Light Association—a trade association of electrical manufacturers—voted to promote the complete electrical home plan. Their timing could not have been worse, of course. Selling appliances by selling homes would hardly save the electrical industry during the depths of the depression.[52]

What the electrical industry could not do, the national government could. The FHA implemented some reforms of the national electrical and home construction industries. Title I of the National Housing Act put the power of federal guarantee behind the strategy of complete electrical modernization of the home, paid off by installment loans of low cost. Ten years later, the FHA and the Veterans Administration housing program tied complete electrical modernization to the amortized mortgage, thereby bringing down the level payment cost of the electrical service, utilities, and appliances. Although Congress did not renew the home appliance provision of the FHA in 1938, the Veteran's Act (G.I. Bill of Rights) in the summer of 1944 built a version of it into the veteran's home loan provisions. Also in 1944, the FHA adopted the policy that, if local custom permitted it, regional FHA offices would approve mortgage loans that extended the mortgage to major appliances, such as ranges, refrigerators, water heaters, and hot air heaters. The "local custom" option gave the impression that the decision really rested on local lending practices or on state law (which defined the parts of a dwelling as real or personal property), but in effect the FHA nationalized policy. Borrowers and lenders seeking FHA-insured loans would lobby state legislatures to revise "fixture laws," which defined what parts of a dwelling were security for a real estate mortgage. The FHA forced liberalization of these fixture laws by permitting the definition of permanent fixtures to a dwelling in terms of the intent covering a fixture or appliance, rather than its physical connection to a house. When seller and buyer agreed that a vacuum cleaner was a permanent fixture of a house, then, for FHA purposes, the vacuum cleaner was fixed to the house, regardless of whether it was physically attached to the dwelling. The standard FHA commitment form (FHA Form 2007), used by all regional offices, provided printed spaces for the inclusion of electrical appliances for purchase through the mortgage. Possibility constituted invitation, and the invitation stimulated political pressure for national conformity. States quickly expanded the list of electric appliances that could be brought under a home mortgage as a part of a dwelling. In 1944, home owners could buy ranges, for instance, under mortgages in forty-two states, refrigerators in forty-one states, dishwashers in forty, garbage disposals in thirty-four, and automatic cycle washers in eighteen.[53]

In 1945, private electrical utilities, commercial banks, and savings and loans associations rapidly adopted FHA and VA style mortgage lending plans. Home buyers would buy long-term mortgages, paying less for a house, on a monthly basis, than they would pay for rent. From the beginning, they would have an electrical standard of living. Consolidated Edison of New York, for instance, adopted a "completed home" plan in 1945. The company projected that 90,000 one- and two-family dwellings would be built in New York City and Westchester County by 1954. "Defining the 'Completed Home,'" Mr. Schofield [Consolidated Edison general sales manager] said it must be well built, good looking, well planned and convenient to care for, be easy to operate, economical to maintain and be financed by the lending institutions as one transaction, including all essential operating equipment." Operating equipment included ventilation and exhaust fans, sink with disposal unit and dishwasher, automatic refrigerator, range with oven control, full automatic washer, automatic freezing unit, ironer, bathroom heater, built-in water connection and electric outlets in garage, automatic garage door lock, automatic opening garage doors, clothes dryer, and combination heating, cooling, and water heating. The National Life Insurance Company, of Montpellier, Vermont, adopted a similar program. National Life Insurance was the first insurance company to lend under the FHA program and became the first insurance company to offer the "Packaged House," financing all electrical appliances as well as the real estate itself. FHA policies made single-lender amortized loans for equipment as well as a house of so little risk that even conservative lenders, such as an old line life insurance company, would enter the market.[54]

We do not have statistics to indicate what percentage of new housing after 1945 represented the ideal "complete packaged home" and what percentage represented "starter homes." FHA historical statistics from 1945 to 1962 do not include the percentage of FHA-insured homes in which electrical appliances and home "operating equipment" were part of the value of the sale transaction. It is likely that immediately after the war most houses did not come fully loaded with complete electrical devices. The immediate postwar housing shortage and the political call for inexpensive houses for returning veterans probably compelled most contractors to build dwellings with the minimum equipment, so that the selling price could be low. Until housing floor size began to increase in the early 1950s, therefore, new houses probably had attached electric technologies offered among utilities (e.g., ambient heating, water heating, ventilation fans, garbage disposal, range), but not a full range of appliances, built in and included in the value mortgaged under FHA or VA contracts. FHA statistics after 1962 show that sellers included the range (electric or gas), garbage disposal, and ventilator fans in home sales, but not the refrigerator, clothes washer, and clothes dryer. Since households had widely adopted the latter appliances by 1947, when the new housing boom began, builders probably found that buyers intended to bring these appliances, which they already owned, to their new houses; therefore their inclusion in the "completed home" would not offer a marketing advantage.[55]

TVA's Lessons about Electrical Mass Consumerism

The social experiment of the Tennessee Valley Authority had broad meaning for the nation's electrical future. Fulfilling the ideology of the public power movement, the TVA proved that electrical modernization could bring social modernization to the poorest Americans. Specifically referencing the Electric Home and Farm Authority plan that David Lilienthal proposed to the National Electric Light Association in December 1933, *Business Week* summarized the TVA challenge to its business readers in these words: "TVA believes that the manufacturers and power utilities can afford 'to gamble for volume,' hopes that the financing experiment will encourage private capital to back similar programs in other parts of the country, [and] stimulate the use of electrical appliances everywhere."

The TVA's success proved several points for private industry. It proved that even households with extremely low ability to pay could modernize their homes and their lives. Private utilities could profit from mass social modernization. Social modernization could come for the mass of households, who had low incomes, before they had accumulated the savings needed to buy appliances and modernize their homes by cash purchase. The TVA sought to disprove the assumptions underlying the private electric industry's strategy of domestic electrification in the 1920s, according to which the utilities and manufacturers segmented the home electrical market by income. The electrical industry targeted the highest income households, constituting about one-fifth of all families, to receive the benefits of appliances. Electricity did not bring social modernization to these well-to-do households, however, because they were already socially modernized.[56]

Years of public-private power debate had well-rehearsed ideological arguments about the first lesson that Lilienthal proposed TVA would prove. *Business Week* voiced the private business point of view, when it initially objected to TVA on the grounds that its service region already had enough electric power. There was no genuine demand remaining unfilled: "Existing systems already provide more [electric power] than the market can use for years to come." Low, government-subsidized rates would only drive private power out of business; they would not sell more electricity or increase purchase of appliances. The private utilities argued that "low rates and low-priced products will not sell themselves." The industry could not get households to adopt electrical appliances simply by forcing down electric rates and prices for appliances; therefore, no sound economic reason existed for government to lower rates through regulation. Supporting the private utility thesis, a report from the U.S. Chamber of Commerce in 1934 concluded that "electrification is not entirely a matter of rates."[57]

TVA announced the Electric Home and Farm Authority plan for cooperative marketing of electric appliances in December 1933. The agency's directors wanted EHFA to prove that consumers would buy appliances and increase consumption of electricity if both were cheap enough. The experiment intrigued *Business Week,* but it remained unconvinced. "Are they [private manufacturers and dealers of appliances] facing a new era in electrical appliance buying or just a chance to burn their fingers in pulling T.V.A.'s kilowatts out of the fire?" Electrical appliance purchases could only be produced, as a 1933 editorial in *Electrical World* put the matter, by "extraordinary efforts to mold public opinion and thus create consumer demand." As free market enterprises, the utilities and electrical manufacturing industry thought they did this best and wanted the government to leave them alone to do it. The economic way of stating this thesis is to say that, according to industry, demand for electricity modernization was inelastic.[58]

Public power advocates denied the industry thesis. David Lilienthal explained the public power philosophy for the readers of *Electrical World*. Electrical modernization was not simply desirable, but socially necessary. It was the key to social modernization for disadvantaged Americans—to "lightening their burdens, increasing their incomes and making for a richer and better life," in Lilienthal's words. To accomplish electrical modernization, "our entire rate structure must be reexamined and drastically revised" and prices for heavy electric appliances reduced. When the market met these conditions, electrical modernization would occur. The market needed no special advertising, no extraordinarily arduous molding of opinion, to convince households to take advantage of the devices and the cheap electricity rates. Economically, if rates were low enough and if households could purchase appliances at sufficiently low credit terms, "the bulk of our people literally cannot afford *not* to own and use such appliances." Electrical modernization was not about consumption of goods and services; it was about capitalizing the household with assets that more than paid for themselves. The utilities had failed to understand this point. They had conceived of the market for electric devices in terms of the one-fifth of American households that were already modernized, for whom the electrical labor-saving devices were conveniences, but not necessities. Companies did not have to stimulate and mold consumer demand for electrical appliances. If prices were low enough, Americans would seek out electrical appliances to accomplish social modernization. For four-fifths of American households, whose need for social modernization private sector capitalism ignored in the 1920s, electrical modernization meant the full realization of the social potential of the household in all its relationships— labor, emotional, child rearing—for producing individuals with the health, intelligence, personality, and family support to fulfill their unique potentialities. For public power advocates, such as Lilienthal, electrical modernization, defined as social modernization, represented the long-sought goal of the industrial revolution and the development of social liberalism that accompanied it.[59]

If Lilienthal was right, demand for electricity was elastic. Even the most impoverished households, with almost no money to buy electricity or installment contracts for appliances, would use more and more electricity. If the industry was right, they would not. Once the national government started TVA, and resisting it any longer was futile, *Electrical World* welcomed TVA for this reason. It would test the fundamental issue that private and public power advocates had contested for a generation. Within a year, TVA returned an answer. The public power advocates were right. *Electrical Merchandising* (sister publication to *Electrical World*) followed the experiment attentively and in 1935 printed a decisive journalistic review of TVA. The *Electrical Merchandising* reporter, Laurence Wray, examined particularly the work of the Electric Home and Farm Authority within the TVA service area. "The first question that comes to the mind is whether the EH&FA . . . program produced the results that were anticipated. We can answer that definitely: It has produced results already and with the growing interest and impetus that attaches to the movement, it is producing greater results every day." The detractors' "current sneer" had been that the impoverished farmers and rural residents of the TVA service areas had too little purchasing power to buy the subsidized electricity brought to them or to avail themselves even of cheap, governmental credit. "'What are these poor farmers going to use for money when they do have electricity?' has been the current sneer. Rates couldn't be low enough and appliances cheap enough to make buyers out of natives who were burning oil for light, pumping water from a well, washing clothes over a piece of corrugated tin, and frying their razorback over a wood stove." Wray illustrated the dramatic upswelling of consumer demand by the story of Lauderdale, Alabama, near Muscle Shoals. Within sixty days of receiving electricity, 175 households of Lauderdale bought on cheap government credit 135 radios, 29 refrigerators, 14 ranges, 5 water heaters, 16 washing machines, and 27 water pumps, at a total cost of $39,083. Just as pointedly, an examination of the records of the Tennessee Power Company—an operating subsidiary of the Commonwealth and Southern holding company headed by Wendell Willkie—showed that many of its customers bought TVA model appliances. Sixty-five percent of purchasing households had annual incomes of $1,500 or less. Private lending agencies had turned down loans for 30 percent of them before they got government credit. Wray cited a Commonwealth and Southern spokesman as saying that TVA "had been invaluable in waking utility men generally into some realization of the enormous potentialities of the domestic electrical markets."[60]

Similarly dramatic progress in electrical modernization occurred in Tupelo, Mississippi. Tupelo symbolized TVA's electrical modernization philosophy. Congressman John Rankin, who sponsored Norris's TVA bill in the House, claimed Tupelo as hometown. President Roosevelt had a personal interest in the community. "This little town of less than 10,000 people—if you take in the surrounding countryside—became the guinea pig for one of the most far-reaching experiments in the production, distribution and use of electrical power." Tupelo voted to contract with TVA for power generated at the new Wilson Dam. In response to lower prices (which dropped to one to three cents/kwh within one year), customers added over 500 refrigerators, 150 ranges, and 75 water heaters. In three years, the eight appliance dealers in Tupelo sold over $500,000 worth of appliances. The editors of *Electrical Merchandising* feared—without a hint of coyness—that in reporting the spectacular TVA success their industry readers might think they were advocating TVA. "Here we'd like to pause a minute and explain that there is no intention in this article of proving that TVA, as a governmental agency, has been responsible for the remarkable showing in appliance distribution and saturation."[61]

Electrical World, also writing in 1935, credited to TVA the lesson they learned, that low rates would lead to mass domestic electric consumerism. Addressing the utility industry's new interest in the residential market, *Electrical World* admitted:

> The goal should not be the complete electric equipment of a few million homes, but the large proportion of [the entire nation]. There was encouraging evidence this year that this new concept of universal use is dawning. The spirit of large scale selling is beginning to be seen. [It] has come, out of the competitive pressure for lower rates, that has sprung from the TVA "yardstick" program. It has taken the form of reducing rates, of making it easier for the customer to purchase appliances and the intensifying of selling appliances.

As the Electric Home and Farm Authority plan had gotten under way, *Business Week,* unable to hold back its own excitement, anticipated what success might mean: "A revolution in the appliance and power industries." The resistance of utilities in the 1920s to marketing electric heating to the mass market crumbled in the face of evidence from the TVA that even the poorest household would buy electric ranges and use them with increasing demand for electricity. "The old prejudice against the cooking load is crumbling fast under the urge of necessity. The development of the TVA models was a powerful impulse, but the need for load is the driving force."[62]

In 1934, *Business Week* took advantage of a small episode to draw the lesson and preach it to the business community. Lilienthal had rejected a manufacturer's proposed "TVA model" of a refrigerator, to be sold under the EHFA program. The price was low, but not low enough. To which *Business Week* responded: "This industry [the appliance industry], paralleling the development of the automobile industry, has skimmed the top markets, realizes that hereafter volume must be gained in the lower income brackets. . . . What Lilienthal is asking is not just a good, plain, refrigerator to use in a great social experiment, but a new base price for the industry—and another Ford to break with tradition, and make it possible." General Electric took up the challenge and tried to make itself into the "Ford" of refrigerators. Following TVA specifications, General Electric in 1934 designed a low-price refrigerator for the mass market. At the time, the lowest-priced, nationally available refrigerator was a Sears Roebuck four-cubic-foot model, selling for $94.50. General Electric's model was to sell for the "revolutionary" price of $74.50. G.E.'s competitor, Westinghouse, subsequently followed TVA design specifications to manufacture an electric range to sell for $61.25, less than half its previously cheapest model. Reporting on G.E.'s plunge into the mass market, *Business Week* editorialized:

> What GE has done is to create a Model T for the great mass market which will buy plain refrigeration just as it bought plain transportation. With some 5 million electric refrigerators sold, the Model T approach seems necessary. The easy, luxury market may be approaching saturation, may eventually depend (like automobiles, again) on replacement sales, but the balance of the 20 million wired homes in the country as yet unrefrigerated electrically makes a far bigger market.[63]

T. K. Quinn, vice president of General Electric, acknowledged that TVA had demonstrated that the electrical industry could create a mass market by lowering electric rates and selling appliances in low-cost installment plans. The industry was not locked into an upper-income market composed of a small minority of the nation's households: "The prices of energy and of appliances are not too high from the profit and loss standpoint of the producers. But they are too high in relation to the overwhelming minority of the pocketbooks of the country. Fortunately, there is a way out. The payments per unit of electricity may be lowered easily enough if we can only produce and sell more current. We can sell more current if the payments for current and appliances are lowered." Would this strategy work? No doubt, Quinn said. TVA had demonstrated that it would.

"The plan is not brand new. It has been successfully worked, in somewhat different from, by several companies, with beneficial results. It is an important part of the promotional plans of the Electric Home and Farm Authority in the Tennessee Valley."[64]

TVA's second lesson taught private utilities and manufacturers that they could profit from sponsoring social modernization of the poorest households. Social modernization did not have to be charity. No doubt, high-income households offered the possibility of higher-profit sales than lower-income households calculated on a per unit or per household basis; but TVA proved to the private sector that aggressive marketing of the implements of social modernization to the lowest-income households could be profitable. The lesson applied equally to poorer rural nonfarm households, farmers, and urban homes. The impending competition of TVA forced Wendell Willkie, manager of Commonwealth and Southern Corporation, to implement the "Objective Rate Plan" in 1933, which sought to encourage the private utility's domestic customers to consume more through lower rates. It was a scheme whereby "the company could not lose." First quarter 1935 earnings of electrical appliance manufacturers and other consumer businesses also proved the point; they rose dramatically over earnings the previous year. This increase in earnings reflected the first foray by companies, such as General Electric, into the middle- and lower-income mass market. General Electric's earnings rose to their highest since 1931. By 1939, in spectacular success, the Rural Electrification Administration had brought electricity to 25 percent of the nation's rural residents and transformed rural areas into markets for private manufacturers. Private merchandisers came to the opinion that the nation's rural areas were an electrical market larger, in some comparative ways, than the nation's cities. Because the cost of living was less in rural communities than in cities, rural households had a greater percentage of their income to spend on electrical modernization than urban households of equal income. Rural electric users wanted tools for production, not gadgets. The private sector had difficulty understanding the thesis of public power advocates, such as Lilienthal, that urban households would "produce," not consume, with electric appliances. They had no similar difficulty in understanding the attraction of appliances for rural households. Though it might slow adoption of electrical tools, farm tenancy did not stand in the way of electrical modernization of production for farmers. Tenants needed to increase production as much as owners, though they might not have as much capital to do so. Moreover, the cooperatives did not monopolize selling appliances to rural areas. The REA invigorated the economy of central town merchants and dealers, thereby strengthening the private sector economy, an ironic result of the public power movement.[65]

The federal government similarly created and underwrote a commercial market of low-income urban consumers. Since 1933, one of the major recovery efforts by the New Deal had been to stimulate urban consumer demand. Agreeing with the consensus of private economists on appropriate strategies to counter business cycle depressions, Roosevelt supported large debt-financed public works as a means of putting idle investment money to work, of increasing and stabilizing employment, and, thereby, of indirectly stimulating consumer demand. The TVA, the REA, and the other New Deal electrical programs separated out and promoted the electrical marketplace as a leading effort to prime the pump of consumerism. The electrical marketplace was more, of course, than simply one sector of consumer demand. It was a part of the progressives' ideology of electricity. It opened the door for private electrical industry to fulfill its part in bringing social modernization to the nation's households whom they had neglected in the 1920s. The electrical industry now looked forward to selling in it. In 1939, households making less than $25 a week in income represented sixty million Americans. The private sector had largely ignored them; yet they constituted, *Electrical Merchandising* reported, "the greatest untapped market" remaining to the nation's utilities and appliance manufacturers. One study of the "living habits" of lower-income households in a small city showed they could spend up to $63 a year on appliances, which could represent a lot of small appliances, if bought on installment plans. Willkie grudgingly admitted that the TVA proved that a utility could even take a loss on cheap credit, extended to customers for purchasing appliances, and make up the profit on the increased sale of electricity.[66]

An economic success, the TVA became a political success. Having succeeded economically in helping the TVA service region, TVA had the political muscle to compel the private utilities to lower their rates. TVA's yardstick rapped Wendell Willkie's knuckles hard. He acknowledged that private power utilities would lose to the government if they did not reduce rates. The testimony of Roosevelt's future presidential adversary is telling on the importance of TVA:

> Recognition is spreading throughout the power industry that a solution of the present economic problem of electric public utilities is to build up domestic load. Political attacks all center on the cost of electricity to the home. The federal "yardstick" experiments and municipal elections are all focused upon the rate for electric service to the householder, and that is what the voter has in mind when he goes to the polls. The fairest answer and the surest defense against competitive government power projects, therefore, are for privately operated power systems to so increase their household use of electricity that domestic rates may be reduced to the point where the differential between the cost of service for private companies and government operations becomes so inconsequential that it will no longer constitute a political factor.[67]

TVA's third lesson concerned consumer credit, modernization, and the production of wealth. If households could get credit, they could buy the technology for electrical modernization before they had saved out of current income the money needed to buy things. Modernization created wealth, rather than wealth being prerequisite for modernization. The New Deal changed the old way of thinking for society as a whole. The old way of thinking about consumption had been "savings-based consumption." The new way of thinking about consumption was "debt-based consumption." In the old way of thinking, a household worked, saved money out of current earnings until it had accumulated enough to buy something, then bought that object, subsequently consuming its services, while beginning a new cycle of savings for its replacement. In the new way of thinking, a household took credit (more if it was working, but at least some even if it was not), used the credit to buy technologies, and paid off the debt through savings or income earned while using them. Industries borrowed money to buy capital assets to make things to sell to earn income, then used the future income to pay off the loans—pay as you go. Households could and would do the same, whether buying a car, a radio, a vacuum cleaner, or a refrigerator. This had been the philosophy behind the New Deal's effort to increase consumer credit by guaranteeing private bank loans to "credit worthy" customers. TVA demonstrated that this principle could be extended even to poor households, which banks would not previously have thought of as "credit worthy."

The changed way of thinking about consumption and credit appeared in industry publications. An appliance merchant explained to *Electrical Merchandising*'s readers the new meaning of installment credit for consumption purchases. There were two kinds of "consumption" purchases, he wrote: those that "finance themselves" and those that do not. Electric appliances financed themselves, because they generated a stream of savings, out of which households could make their installment payments. This was the financial meaning of electrical modernization. "Automobiles, radios, and many other products create convenience, pleasure and many other use advantages, but are unable to create use savings. Home appliances, on the other hand, provide added comfort while at the same time, create these use savings which make them, wholly or in part, self-financing to the point where they constitute no drain on the family purse." To say that electric home appliances would finance themselves was to say exactly what Lilienthal had said. Consumers would buy appliances, if prices were within reach, simply because they could not afford not to. The technology of electrical modernization was an asset that raised families to a higher plane of economic security. Social modernization through electrical modernization paid for itself, because it enabled the household to realize its full potential to participate in and contribute to society.[68]

Chapter 5
The New Deal Saves the Home, 1933–1949

Local Property in Crisis

The Great Depression began the transformation of the American home. Over two decades, seismic changes rolled under the foundations of American domesticity: economic collapse, the New Deal, threats from socialism and communism in America and from fascism in Europe, the Second World War and federal economic controls, the postwar political struggle over rent control, subsidized housing, urban redevelopment, racial desegregation. These challenges to the American system did not destroy private real estate in the United States, but they transformed it. They led to federal policies that severely limited the power of local property capitalism to control the local social order. A generation of Rooseveltian legislative programs politically enfranchised local non-propertied groups, bringing them into the civic community, and corroded the iron grip of white property owners over the fate of nonwhite property and propertyless citizens. Roosevelt's appointees to the U.S. Supreme Court shifted the nation's high court toward active protection of civil rights, divorcing civil rights from property rights. Federal money and regulation intruded into local affairs, and federal bureaucrats shared power with local property owners. In the South, federal programs created a new liberal elite who used administrative authority to challenge the entrenched county elite that had held power since the end of the nineteenth century.

Housing finance and housing quality became key arenas in which federal administrative power challenged the power of local property elites. Over the course of the 1930s and 1940s, the federal government regulated, at one time or another, the housing of nearly every group of Americans—home owners, home renters, apartment renters, agricultural laborers, armed forces personnel. On many crucial issues of local life, regional federal administrators made decisions previously made by the chamber of commerce, savings and loan association directors, and other boards of local capitalists. The new class of governmental administrators set up the potential for conflict between local and nonlocal social values. Local bourgeois elites and national democratic elites fought over what neighborhoods families could live in, what public schools their children could attend, what kinds of dwellings they could own or rent, what material quality of life they would enjoy in their homes, what employment opportunities they would have, and how much wealth they could accumulate. In the midst of this conflict over distributive justice, and because of it, electrical modernization, as an instrument of social modernization, came to the majority of America's homes.[1]

The New Deal focused its reorganization of the relations between property and social order on the home. First it saved home ownership, but rescuing home owners was only half of the New Deal's program for the American home. For the American people to enjoy the "more abundant life" that Roosevelt promised in 1936, the federal government had greatly to enhance the material quality of their home life. Roosevelt defined the minimal standard of living for all Americans, whether they owned property or not, in terms of the electrically modern home. In the progressive vision of public power that he shared, electrical modernization led to social modernization. Democratic home ownership emerged as the cornerstone of social stability, as well as a major benefit of the welfare state. Riversiders paid rapt attention to federal efforts to save and modernize the American home. Successive New Deal programs and, later, wartime programs addressed the housing needs of one group after another: urban home owners, family farms, transients, agricultural laborers, the urban poor, soldiers, veterans. Riverside came to understand that the meaning of property ownership had profoundly changed, and with it the locus of power in the community. The power of local landlords over tenant households and in civic real estate institutions ebbed as home owning came to dominate community residency.

Home owning collapsed quickly in the depression. By early 1933, a significant minority of home owners did not have enough money to continue to own their homes. Rising tax delinquencies signaled the social dimensions of the problem. Riverside tax delinquencies soared in 1932 and 1933, even though the city had cut tax rates annually since 1927. For fiscal year 1932–1933, the city lowered its tax rate 7 percent and in the following year another 10 percent. Taxpayers failed to pay 15 percent of their 1931–1932 property taxes; the following year, delinquent taxes rose to 22.4 percent. Rural areas of the county had the highest tax delinquencies, undoubtedly reflecting the economic difficulties of agriculture and the inability of property owners of unimproved land to pay taxes on land that produced no income. The county tax assessor believed that tax delinquencies for the City of Riverside in 1933 were half the countywide rate, that is, perhaps 11 percent. The tax delinquency rate for the county would remain high, at 18.5 percent, after the spring 1935 tax payment deadline. The city followed with a delinquency rate of 8 percent. Other governmental jurisdictions around California shared Riverside's problem of tax delinquencies. Political pressure on the California state legislature brought passage of a tax leniency act in April 18, 1933, declaring a sixty-day moratorium on tax collection.[2]

The inability of home buyers to pay on their mortgages signaled the collapse of home ownership. Relief from foreclosure sales by lenders soon followed the tax leniency act. The California state legislature intervened again with a law to protect home owning constituents from their creditors. Resident owners of single-family dwellings could not have their property sold for failure to make mortgage payments through the remainder of the year. Later the legislature extended the moratorium on foreclosure through 1937.[3]

The new president, inaugurated on March 4, 1933, turned his attention at once to the home ownership emergency. Riverside—in step with the rest of the nation—had believed for two generations that home owning meant security for the family. The singular strength of that article of faith magnified the impact of the collapse of home ownership on the local consciousness. Regular Republican as Riverside's civic elite may have been, staunch in their support of Herbert Hoover's candidacy, they gave the new president loyal and hopeful support. "The Republicans, who now become the party of the minority, are pledged to abstain from obstructive tactics and to use their voice and power only for the purpose of constructive criticism. . . . The Republican party rendered great service to the nation by its support of the hand of Woodrow Wilson during war time. The same degree of support is due to Franklin D. Roosevelt during this new national emergency."[4]

Riversiders audibly sighed with relief when the new Democracy party president made home owner rescue a first priority. The *Riverside Enterprise* ran a banner headline across seven of eight columns on Friday morning, April 14, 1933: "Roosevelt Asks Home Mortgage Relief." The owner of the newspaper took the left sidebar on the front page to write in his own words, again with extensive quoting, the drama of saving the nation's distressed home buyers. "His purpose [is] to have the general Government interfere where home ownership is about to be lost." "Ultimately three-fourths of the nation's home owners may get relief." With a single piece of legislation, the national government reorganized the hierarchy of real property. For the half century of Riverside's municipal existence, local property owners and mortgage holders existed in a web of local property relations. Local landowners and developers, local banks and mutual savings institutions, a local secondary mortgage market, local real estate industry with local realtors, administering local racial and class rules to persons they usually personally knew—all this had been destroyed by the depression. Now the president of the United States proposed to "save" local property owners by having them deal directly with the U.S. government, bypassing the local real estate institutions. The newly established Home Owners Loan Corporation would take defaulted mortgages from banks and other holders of the loans, refinance the loans on fifteen-year terms, and reinforce the capital of the loan institutions with 4 percent government bonds.

Newspapers initially estimated that three-fourths of mortgaged home buyers would refinance their loans. In one stroke, responsibility for the security of home ownership shifted from the local community to the national government.[5]

Riverside newspapers followed the HOLC legislation and the president's announcements with an attention that undoubtedly reflected the interests of its readers. One local newspaper reprinted in full the president's address to Congress requesting the legislation. It quoted, rather than summarized, federal officials' explanations of how the new agency would work. We cannot doubt the agreement that the president's words received in Riverside. After fifty years of reciting the local ideology of home ownership, Republican Riversiders now found their words repeated back to them by the Democratic president. The policy of Riverside had become the policy of the nation: "Implicit in the legislation which I am suggesting to you, is a declaration of national policy. This policy is that the broad interest of the nation requires that special safeguards should be thrown around home ownership as a guaranty of social and economic stability, and that to protect home owners from inequitable enforced liquidation, in a time of general distress, is a proper concern of the Government."[6]

It reflected the new order of the civic universe that the *Riverside Enterprise* reported when the Los Angeles regional federal administrator of the HOLC traveled to and from Washington, D.C. In the mid-1920s, no editor could conceive that his local newspaper would pay as much attention to the comings-and-goings of federal bureaucrats as to local civic leaders and elected government officials. When HOLC bureaucrats explained how they would administer the act, the newspapers reported verbatim. When federal administrators turned to radio broadcasts to inform Americans of the new relief program, the paper reported the event as news. The newspapers accorded the opening of HOLC offices, their patronage by local home owners, changes in regional and local personnel, these and all the mundane events of an administrative bureaucracy, all the attention traditionally devoted to local civic notables, their business enterprises, and their personal and social lives.[7]

In five months of administration of the HOLC act in 1933, nearly 1,200 Riverside County mortgaged home buyers applied to the agency for refinancing of their loans. These were separate from farm mortgage refinancing loans under the Farm Credit Administration. Nearly 300 of the HOLC applications, averaging $2,000, were from the city of Riverside. In 1934, Riverside home buyers filed 837 more refinancing loan applications. The number of refinancing applications may seem low, but their impact diffused throughout the community, for mortgages or investment certificates based on them were sold by loan institutions to investors. Local investors, whose financial position was at stake with the mortgagee, probably held many of the troubled mortgages. Although some home buyers eventually defaulted on their new governmental loans or were unable to pay taxes, by the end of the HOLC's emergency program, Americans widely agreed that the national government had saved the nation's system of private home property.[8]

Riverside hoped that the HOLC would not only bail out beleaguered home buyers and the financial institutions dependent on their repayment of loans but would also revive the home building and real estate industry. Congress did not design the HOLC for that purpose, however. The *Riverside Enterprise* remarked soulfully, "Some of the bright hopes that were built around this play are beginning to fade." Riverside listened closely, therefore, to rumors in fall 1933 that the president wanted additional home legislation to extend home ownership more broadly in the nation and revive the home building and real estate industries through federal housing programs. When two different federal programs emerged from the executive branch in spring 1934, again, the Riverside newspaper heralded the news in huge banners across seven columns of the front page. One bill created an urban redevelopment program under the Federal Emergency Relief Administration, administered by Harry Hopkins. Absorbing unemployed laborers and artisans in the building trades, the program would demolish "useless and unsanitary" buildings, replacing them with clean and neat, if unostentatious, housing. The other program, the National Housing Act, would create the Federal Housing Administration to extend home ownership. The *Riverside Enterprise* reprinted the complete text of Roosevelt's May 14, 1934, message to Congress urging passage of the National Housing Act. From Riverside's point of view, the president had no choice but to revive the building industry and home owning. Riverside again approved.[9]

As in the creation of the Home Owners Loan Corporation a year earlier, Riverside understood that the National Housing Act turned the world of property upside down. Until 1933, private property and home ownership had been the basis for the Lockean contract that created and guaranteed social order and legitimated and restrained government. Savings banks and commercial banks linked the local bourgeoisie who invested and the middle and working classes who saved. When savers bought a home, they ensnared themselves in a web of contractual relations. Housing tied together the local status order. The quality and location of a family's house depended on their income and simultaneously determined and announced social status. Debt contracts bound the mortgaging household to the financial institutions presided over by the elite of local capital. Maintenance of local property values, of personal wealth in real estate, required placing trust in the local businessmen. If the trust failed, local government provided police and courts to enforce contracts. Interlocking directorates with other private businesses, elected government, and civic associations wove the influence of the elites into a seamless fabric of power that maintained the local hierarchy of class and status. The New Deal housing legislation reversed the relationship. Through the HOLC and the National Housing Act, the national government guaranteed the capitalist system of private property based on the home and guaranteed individual homes themselves. The *Riverside Enterprise* thought the emergency demanded the action. "We think the President is amply justified in taking the Government into what has hitherto been private business. There is apparently no other way to get the action needed." Other communities shared Riverside's perception of a Copernican revolution, in which the federal sun displaced the local community at the center of the universe. When the Lynds returned to "Middletown" to report on its experience in the depression and the New Deal, they observed that "with the injection of Federal planning into the local scene, [Middletown] began to move in a non-Euclidean world in which the old civic axioms were suspended."[10]

State-sponsored Consumerism in the Home

The National Recovery Act hit Riverside in the summer of 1933 like a grass fire in a Santa Ana wind. Hugh S. Johnson, director of the National Recovery Act's administration, initiated a nationwide public relations campaign to win support for a blanket code, with a minimum labor work week and wage, to supplement the specific industry codes that his office was then negotiating in the basic industries. The "Blue Eagle" emblem symbolized compliance with the general code. At the same time, the NRA campaign sought to increase consumer spending and revive business. Much consumption naturally related to living in homes. The NRA thereby became the first federal program to promote self-consciously the electrical standard of living. Riverside's businessmen of course approved of an increase in consumer spending. The chamber of commerce urged support; it coincided with the spending message the chamber had promoted since 1930. Riverside was not just a center of citrus agriculture; it was also a commercial and shopping center. Store owners numerically dominated the business community, and they responded enthusiastically to the NRA program to increase spending. The NRA campaign in August and September 1934 included obtaining pledges of cooperation from businesses and households. In Riverside, NRA canvassers reached 733 businesses and obtained 637 pledges, for which the businesses received a Blue Eagle emblem, signifying compliance with the act's codes regarding business hours and wages. Businesses added 263 employees under NRA pressure. Nine teams, each administered by a "campaign major," canvassed households. They walked the city streets, going house to house to obtain pledges to cooperate with the president's recovery program. By mid-September, campaign teams returned exactly 4,951 household pledges. In other words, an official delegate of the federal government had approached nearly two of three the community's households and personally asked them to participate in the recovery program. We do not have information about which households the teams overlooked or did not wish to pledge, but we may reasonably assume that surveyors reached the entire white and English-speaking city.[11]

Product and business advertisements in the city's newspapers jumped quickly into the spirit of the NRA program. (See figs. 5.1–5.5 following this chapter.) A local hardware store, Franzen's, carried a quarter-page advertisement on August 1, 1933, with the NRA emblem figuring large to announce, "We Deem It An Honor . . . To Be the First in Riverside to Receive the Official Emblem and

Sanction of Compliance with Our President's Recovery Program." A few days later, a half-page ad, sponsored by dozens of businesses and stores, announced their support of the National Recovery Act. A huge photograph of President Roosevelt, his eyes looking directly toward the reader, occupied the top of the ad. The caption announced that the forty-four businesses, most of their owners no doubt proud to be Republicans and believers in President Hoover's voluntarist vision of America, were "supporting our president in his national recovery program." Still another advertisement commanded sternly, "Gen. Johnson says, 'Buy Now!'"[12]

The National Recovery Act provided a new context for buying appliances. In the 1920s, advertisers conservatively pitched electrical appliances as labor-saving devices for the housewife. The NRA directed its "buy now" campaign specifically at the housewife, but few persons wanted to save labor now. They wanted to labor—for pay. So a new theme appeared beside the old: buying an appliance was not only good for you, but good for your community. One newspaper quoted Hugh Johnson as saying, "'the housewives of the country, the purchasing agents who spent 85 percent of the family income, will realize that now is the time to buy, not only to save money but also because every dollar spent now is helping to keep the wage-earner in her family on a payroll. For four years the American consumer has been skimping, putting off buying more than bare necessities until "better times." Better times are here.'"[13]

Frigidaire, maker of refrigerators, "adopted the N.R.A. code 100 percent" and displayed the NRA eagle in its advertisements. Other manufacturers similarly identified their products with the NRA in their advertisements, for example, Leonard electric refrigerators and Apex electric washers. As a major industry of a new technology, the electrical appliance industry naturally tried to put itself at the center of the national recovery effort. In 1934, the Riverside municipal light department cooperated with the appliance industry to sponsor southern California's first all-electric cooking show. Besides the cooking demonstration by a well-known chef, manufacturers exhibited electric ranges, refrigerators, and other kitchen appliances. The city utility offered to wire in and install electric ranges free of charge to the customer, including retrofit with conduit cable. Few Riverside households used electric ranges, but the utility department promoted the electric range as part of the all-electric kitchen. Kitchen modernization would be a major promotional theme of the National Housing Act Title I loan program, just beginning in summer 1934. Riverside housewives thronged to the cooking show. The chamber of commerce repeated it in October, and in December the City Light Department sponsored electric range cooking demonstrations in the Better Homes Exhibit in the basement of the City Hall, as part of the FHA home modernization campaign. Three years later, the city offered a lower, incentive electric rate for consumers who installed an electrical range or water heater.[14]

The local newspapers editorially endorsed the NRA's buy-now program with philosophical rumination. The *Riverside Enterprise* ran four editorials in as many months supporting the NRA and explaining what was at stake in the campaign.

The NRA created a new arrangement for the universe of American business. State-coordinated consumerism and state-regulated business cooperation were probably not temporary, the newspaper editor believed, even if the NRA itself might have a brief life. The era of competitive, laissez-faire capitalism seemed past; without cooperation and control of business, the economy might "crack up." The *Enterprise* must have taken a long, deep breath and sighed before saying it, but the Riverside voice for conservative Republicanism now thought only government could provide the control needed for economic progress. The state would now be a central part of everyday community life:

> The time has come when industry must have intelligent correlation and control, or crack up. The more of this control industry can provide for itself, the better. But industry is only a part of community life. A part cannot dominate the whole. Government, which alone can profess to represent society as a whole, necessarily has the last word. Wherefore, just as we must have more order in business in order to survive, we must have less political confusion in Government—more science, more responsibility, more statesmanship.[15]

That Riverside, which suffered the effects of the depression less than many other cities, embraced the New Deal shows just how deeply the depression frightened the local bourgeoisie in 1932 and 1933. The nation had lost, or "liquidated," as newspaper columnists like to say, so much property and the depression imperiled so much more, that the real fear of losing it all made FDR's vision pragmatically acceptable. One editorial, positioned like an advertisement in the *Enterprise,* explained the lesson of the depression. The government needed to intervene to save property itself: "It is one of the chief aims of the N.R.A. to restore value to the common things of life . . . a man's labor . . . a manufacturer's product . . . a citizen's property. The Government is trying to make everything worth something again."[16]

The Electrical Standard
for Housing

Expensive homes with the new technology of the 1920s automatically downgraded the older housing stock. Technological obsolescence and building depreciation occurred, as with any asset, because of product innovation that shifted market values away from older products as well as wear and tear on the dwelling. The nation's housing boom of the 1920s thereby fragmented the housing stock into different technological classes. Technological differentiation crowded a higher percentage of Riversiders, white and nonwhite, into inadequate dwellings and intensified racial residential segregation. Well-to-do white families, representing a small percentage of all households, moved to new and technologically modern dwellings, or upgraded the technology of their present home, leaving older dwellings to the less-well-off. When the building boom began in 1922, local realtors estimated that 90 percent of the new dwellings were being custom built by local families who expected to move to them. Custom and speculation houses tended to be expensive; in 1924, the average single-family detached dwelling cost $3,000 to build, as estimated on permits. In 1926, the average cost of over four hundred new residences had risen to $4,500. While the average building cost reached a peak in 1926, new dwellings averaged above $3,000 through the decade.[17]

Builders and the real estate industry paid little attention to technologically antiquated dwellings until the boom collapsed; then they looked around for work other than new housing construction. Perception is a matter of interest. Until the collapse of the building boom, the construction and real estate industries had far less money to make in fixing up older housing than in building new housing; when their interest shifted, they perceived the inadequate housing as a new market to keep themselves in business. Their situation was analogous to that of American's private electrical utilities. During the 1920s, utilities made their big money in industrial electrical modernization. Not until the depression destroyed the industrial market did the private utilities turn in earnest to the home market. With the building and real estate industries, perception of the home market preceded the stock market crash and the onset of the depression in mid-1930. This is because the building boom of the decade locally peaked in 1928, then rapidly faded. Its collapse by itself shoved the nation closer to the depression.

In August 1929, the *Riverside Enterprise* carried its first building trade article on modernization, claiming that "25 Per Cent of Riverside's Homes Need Modernization." Electrical modernization featured prominently in the local home industry's promotion, with two ads on a modernization theme page promoting electrical modernizing and an editorial advertisement urging homeowners to modernize. A local real estate investment company urged home owners to take loans to modernize, promising that "the security is good because modernization adds much to property values."[18]

When the depression arrived in full force, the construction and building industries suffered deeply with a dramatic decline in business and massive worker layoffs. The industries desperately tried to stimulate modernization business for themselves. Advertising of modernization services emphasized that when a home owner modernized her dwelling, the community would gain by employing workers and buying building materials locally. One ad explained: "Buy your building materials and other supplies from local dealers; Do your building, remodeling, repair work, painting, etc., now—give employment to your neighbor now. The Riverside Chamber of Commerce and the Riverside Building Trades Council advocate the employment of hour labor and local help."[19]

To stimulate home owners' interest in modernizing their homes, the Riverside Chamber of Commerce organized a modern home exhibition in the Municipal Auditorium for October 1931. Local builders, retailers, and suppliers in the home modernization and remodeling industry rented space to exhibit their products and services. The chamber individually invited prominent citizens from the region to attend and the public entered free. The First Annual Building Materials and Home Furnishings Style Show was a huge hit. All seventy-three available booths rented out and Riversiders toured the weeklong show in large numbers. A few months later, in another effort to stimulate building business, the chamber sponsored a "small house contest." To enter the contest, individuals would submit rough plans for a small house, and a committee would select six plans as winners. The prize included professional redrawing of the plans by architects and all materials needed for building the dwellings supplied at cost by local suppliers. On March 5, 1933, a day after President Roosevelt's inauguration, a final and pathetically desperate local civic advertisement appeared in the newspapers to urge home owners to modernize their way out of the depression. The advertisement for the "Spend An Extra Dollar Campaign" spanned two full pages, naively bordered by a band of swastikas. A photograph of a suited middle-aged gentleman, with right hand raised as if to take an oath, dominated the advertisement. The huge caption read: "1933 Depends on Me." The text of the advertisement solemnly declared that 6,080 of Riverside's 8,388 homes were obsolete and needed repairs and modernization. The last decade's advances in "electrical, plumbing, heating, and cooking equipment, refrigeration, insulation, ventilation, air conditioning, bathrooms, and decoration" made obsolete 90 percent of the 2,937 homes built before the decade began. If owners modernized all these obsolete homes, the ad promised, prosperity would be around the corner.[20]

Of course, neither breast beating nor boosterism nor commanding authority would avail. The economy by then was mired too deeply in the depression for wishful thinking to succeed. Except for a very few homes built by wealthy families, home building and modernization were dead in the nation, dead in Riverside. The depression marketplace framed the housing industry's perception of the need for home modernization and shaped the housing industry's solution for filling that need. Precisely because the marketplace was in depression, the problem of technologically out-of-date housing was beyond local redemption. If home building and home modernization were to prime the pump of consumption and raise prosperity, households would have to spend more than "an extra dollar." The federal government would have to spend extra billions of dollars in construction and modernization. Home buying would also have to come within the reach of the average family. Renters do not fix up the dwellings they live in. President Hoover tried to address this need. His housing conference in fall 1931 studied the problem of broadening home ownership and stimulating the home industries. A variety of measures, similar to measures that Franklin Roosevelt's administration sponsored in 1933 and 1934, were recommended. The conference culminated a half century of home ownership ideology and represented the last expression of the notion that private capital was largely capable of resolving the crisis and rescuing the American dream.[21]

Home modernization emerged in 1934 as a major priority of the New Deal. The Home Owners Loan Corporation began accepting applications for modernization in September 1934. Title I loans of the National Housing Act financed modernization. Riverside welcomed the news that the HOLC would give modernization loans. "Riverside Home Owners File Applications for Loans Tuesday," the *Daily Press* announced, personalizing the news. Riversiders had waited long enough for this assistance to appreciate that "every effort will be made by the corporation to eliminate red tape and simplify procedure up to the limit imposed by law and good sense."[22]

The National Housing Act of June 1934 fulfilled the long-anticipated promise of home modernization. Indeed, in initial local coverage of the Federal Housing Administration, the newspaper characterized the National Housing Act in terms exclusively of home modernization, neglecting to mention its title to broaden home ownership. Speaking of the FHA's appointed director, one article said, "Moffett's job is to sell the landlord the idea that his house is not in shape, that it should be made more pleasing to the eye or more commodious, and that he should go to his bank or building and loan association and borrow enough money, with Government guarantee, to do it." Editorial support for Title I clattered out of the Linotype machines. In August 1934, the *Riverside Enterprise* described the program as having "considerable promise." By September, anticipation had raised the stakes. Verging on belief, the paper reported that "some hail the new housing act as providing a method of ending the depression."[23]

To assist implementation of Title I of the National Housing Act, in fall 1934 Riverside surveyed its housing conditions. Around the nation, federal agencies similarly surveyed social and housing conditions of other cities, to assist formation of policy and administration of relief projects. In 1933, the federal and state emergency relief administrations conducted numerous house-to-house surveys of social conditions. The Department of Commerce conducted a similar survey of housing conditions in over seventy major cities to determine the need for electrical and gas modernization. The department intended to assist private industry in developing new markets and thereby, it was hoped, stimulate business recovery. In the late spring, as the National Housing Act made its way through Congress, the Riverside Chamber of Commerce's Building Trades Committee discussed the usefulness of a housing survey, and in July approached the new Federal Housing Administration to request a survey. A few months later, the chamber sponsored the "Better Housing Campaign," to link a survey of housing conditions to local builders, with a similar hope of stimulating the modernization business. California's State Emergency Relief Administration agreed to pay forty canvassers, to be trained and managed by the local office of the Federal Housing Administration. The canvassers would go house to house, survey the dwelling, noting needed repairs and modernization. They would distribute information about Title I home modernization loans, up to a maximum of $2,000 per dwelling. Pledge cards requested owners to commit to modernize their home. Households mailed the pledge cards to a "clearinghouse." Lumber companies and local building businesses paid the budget of the clearinghouse, which distributed to the businesses information about which owners wished to modernize. Coordinated with the housing survey in November 1934, the chamber sponsored "before and after" exhibits of bathrooms, roofs, and other possible modernization projects in the basement of the City Hall. A more extensive exhibit replaced the basement exhibit in March 1935. In January 1935, builders rehabilitated a "run-down residence" into "one of the classiest small homes in the city" as a modernization demonstration for public viewing.

The Better Housing Campaign attracted enormous publicity within the city. It is difficult to conceive that any permanent resident did not know that the federal government surveyed dwellings to prepare for a national program to repair, rehabilitate, and modernize homes. The morning newspaper alone carried over twenty-five news stories and editorials covering the survey and the Better Housing Campaign. Although I could not locate visitor statistics for the City Hall building exhibition in place from November to March, a later exhibition attracted 2,845 registered visitors between March and September 1935—surely testimony to the popular consciousness of the campaign. The house-to-house survey conducted by forty State Emergency Relief Administration (SERA) paid canvassers in November and December 1934 visited nearly ten thousand dwellings, interviewed residents, filled out questionnaires, and personally acquainted Riverside's citizens with the federal program. Since the campaign resurveyed some homes for verification, program representatives visited some households as many as three times (including a business follow-up). So much personal visitation occurred that the police warned households of con men fraudulently representing themselves as part of the government's program. An advertising campaign by banks, loan finance companies, the building trades, and the building supply industry offered to facilitate federal loans for the home owner or landlord. Official proclamations by the mayor and city council and informational meetings at numerous civic clubs and trade associations accompanied the campaign. Radio news reinforced local campaign news and movie news clips of national aspects of the modernization campaign gave Riversiders a sense of their participation in a nationwide movement. Obviously, a plethora of advertising did not guarantee that the federal program impinged on the consciousness of each Riversider; the wish may be mother of the deed, but it is not the deed. Nonetheless, coupled with the door-to-door survey, we should have little doubt that nearly everyone, including East Side residents, knew of it.[24]

Electrical modernization played a major role in home modernization. The need for electrical modernization of dwellings made obsolete by electrical technology of the 1920s had been a prominent theme of the modernization campaign when it was started by industry in 1929. After the FHA campaign of 1934 got under way, a more systematic education of the home owning public began. Householders had to understand that electrical modernization involved more than simply buying an appliance, a higher wattage lightbulb, or an additional lamp. It required more than the increased consumption promoted by the National Recovery Act. Electrical modernization usually required rewiring dwellings, reconfiguring rooms, and by reconfiguring them, changing the architectural arrangement of living and working in the house. Electrical modernization was not piecemeal; it led to the whole renovation of the home to bring the quality of living in it up to the electrical standard. Obviously, such extensive renovation required an FHA Title I loan. (See figs. 5.6–5.8 following this chapter.) Advice given in 1936 in a full page of advertisements typified electricity's Great Instauration:

> Electric wiring in the home has undergone many changes in recent years. The wider use of electrical appliances of all kinds had made provision for adequate outlets important; planning placement of the large pieces of furniture before wiring facilitates a good arrangement of these conveniences. New types of nonmetallic sheathed cable make for greater safety in interior wiring, and the use of a circuit breaker instead of a fuse box makes this safety device more convenient. Wiring supplies should bear tags or imprints signifying the approval of the Underwriting laboratories, to assure the best operation and greater safety.[25]

Riverside's municipally owned electrical utility assisted the education, emphasizing the extent of inadequate or faulty wiring strung around the city. Installing a new underground distribution system in the central business district, the city light department discovered that many businesses had defective entrance switches, inadequate fuse protection, and other defects in their wiring systems. The light and water department displayed a traveling exhibit on faulty wiring, put together by national underwriting laboratories, in its main office. Familiar electrical devices could be dangerous. "First to meet the eye of many Riversiders who have visited the display during the past two days is an inexpensive radio which caused its own destruction and other damage when it caught on fire because of inadequate insulation." "'Even the hook-up of electric clocks can prove dangerous, though they draw a very small current,' declared C. G. Dahlfren, business agent of the city light department."[26]

For several years, Congress added temporary provisions to the National Housing Act providing for purchase of large electrical appliances through Title I loans. The government promoted refrigerators as especially important. The national advertising campaigns for refrigerators in the 1930s defended the appliance as a way to save money and promote health. Refrigerators permitted longer-term storage of food and thereby promoted more efficient food management. At the same time, colder food storage decreased the risk of food poisoning. Private industry attributed the dramatic drop in food poisonings in the 1930s to the mass adoption of mechanical home refrigerators. The Title I appliance loans also benefited renters. Since new refrigerator models did not require remodeling of the dwelling itself (which only owners could have done), the legislation permitted renters to take out loans for the purchase of the appliances. With refrigerators selling as low as $100 and three-year Title I loans available at 5 percent interest and no down payment, households could buy a refrigerator for as little as $3 to $5 a month—little more than the cost of ice. This plan placed mechanical refrigeration—the key to modernization of the kitchen and food management—within the reach of nearly all Americans.[27]

Although Riverside's construction and real estate industry enthusiastically promoted the FHA Title I modernization loans and Title II mortgage loans, Riversiders initially took out FHA loans slowly. From 1934 through March 1939, homeowners in Riverside took out 171 FHA-insured loans. Of that total, they took 159 loans in 1938, seventy-three for new dwellings, eighty-six for modernization. The mortgage loans constituted only 35 percent of the 207 permits issued in 1938 for new dwellings, and the eighty-six modernization loans accounted for only 9 percent of the permits for alterations to existing dwellings. Other southern California cities did better in 1938. In Alhambra, Bakersfield, San Gabriel, and Whittier in the second quarter of 1938, the FHA insured all new buildings; in San Bernardino in the same quarter, the FHA insured 54 percent. Ever mindful of Riverside's position in southern California's municipal growth competition, the Riverside *Daily Press* editorially scolded the city for failing to take advantage of the FHA programs and urged greater participation. By 1941, the last prewar year of unrestricted building, Riverside had finally caught on to the FHA. Of the 260 permits issued in 1941 for new dwellings, 246 were FHA-insured loans.[28]

Labor Housing

The role of organizers from the Communist party of the United States and the rapid escalation toward violence in labor's confrontation with capital proved to California's bourgeoisie the fragility and volatility of the state's traditional labor system in cities and in agriculture. Many observers thought that better housing for harvest laborers would defuse radicalism. So the state's agricultural interests turned to the housing ideology that had served them so well since the turn of the century. Southern California's citrus industry implemented the family labor system and built family labor housing at the time of the First World War. Led by the California Fruit Growers Exchange, the American Latin League (a regional organization of large agricultural growers lobbying for Mexican labor), and the influential large citrus ranches, such as Limoneira in Santa Paula, the citrus industry created a system of residential villages to attract a permanent Mexican labor force and to dampen the discontent that had attracted Industrial Workers of the World organizers during the war. By the early 1920s, citrus-affiliated Mexican villages dotted the Southland, housing perhaps a quarter of the industry's residential laborers and their families. The policy worked. When unionization and political radicalism finally reached the citrus industry in the mid-1930s, the housed laborers formed the core of citrus workers who broke the orange pickers strike of 1936. Together with the unified social support of the region's white communities and the usual exercise of police power, the family labor system squashed a burgeoning movement toward collectivization of citrus labor.[29]

Other sectors of California's agriculture did not follow citrus in creating a family labor system housed in permanent, high-quality planned villages. A 1919 state law requiring minimum standards of sanitation and shelter failed to persuade large commodity growers to provide adequate housing for their harvest laborers. Labor camps in the Central Valley and the Sacramento Valley in the 1930s usually offered the attractions of overcrowded urban slums, as John Steinbeck described in *Grapes of Wrath.* The underfunded California Department of Immigration and Housing, responsible for inspecting camps, could not force their improvement. As the labor violence escalated in the decade, growers themselves and civic leaders affiliated with agriculture increasingly suggested that it was time for the state's agriculture to take seriously the problems of harvest labor housing.

New Deal federal funds offered the opportunity to build the needed camps. Accounts of local governmental, grower, and federal politics and programs on behalf of labor housing flooded the state's newspapers after 1934. The labor camps in the San Joaquin Valley and Sacramento Valley, where California's labor and agricultural capital struggled most violently, generated the greatest interest in newspapers and magazine stories. Riverside focused its attention on nearby Coachella Valley, a big producer of lettuce and other table vegetables, grapefruit, and dates. Housing conditions in the valley appalled state investigators. A survey of the living conditions of 137 families by the SERA reported, for example, twenty-one persons living in four rooms and at another location eight persons living in one room, "disreputable and unsanitary hovels." In fall 1934, growers and local politicians organized themselves to apply for federal work relief funds to build labor housing. They desired "centralized settlements of several units, each building providing living quarters for possible seven families." When the citrus industry began building labor housing in 1919, they referred to the "American standard" of quality needed to attract residential Mexican labor. In the 1930s, the New Deal rephrased this standard with an electrical standard of living. "'These buildings would be constructed in a group and would be heated from a central heating unit, would be equipped with electrical refrigeration and would be constructed of permanent materials such as concrete.'" The organizers did not disguise their political motives. "This seems an ideal solution to the poor housing conditions of the Coachella and Imperial valleys of which radical agitators have created such a furor throughout the country." As with the family labor system in citrus, the plan involved housing primarily the core of year-round resident laborers, providing separate camps for harvest pickers. Within several years, project design had expanded to provide quarters for 206 families, with sanitation and water facilities nearby capable of temporarily supporting two to three times that number of harvest laborers. As finally built, the largest housing units were twenty-two-by-twenty-two feet, with two bedrooms, a screened porch, a bathroom, a shower, a kitchen, running hot water provided by a kerosene heater, and a "cozy" living room.[30]

From the perspective of growers and federal administrators, the new housing met project goals. Laborers relocated to it from unsanitary camps elsewhere in the valley. To qualify for a dwelling, workers had to document their permanent employment around the valleys. Permanent residents received medical exams and basic medical care to prevent spread of diseases. Some measures of success were less tangible than the residents' improved physical and medical health. Riverside's press editorially informed its readers of what it hoped families would get out of living in public housing projects, undoubtedly including the local farm laborers' camp. Referring to the residents: "They had come to like community living. 'We've learned to live and work together, and we have become accustomed to facing problems together and helping one another in time of stress,' wrote one tenant. Thus a new and unexpected result comes from the housing drive of the thirties, not merely a change in the manner of housing, but a change in the social habits and thinking of the occupants themselves."[31]

Defense Housing

Construction of defense housing during World War II continued the expansion of the national government's role in local housing economies and reinforced the new top-down structure of the national housing economy. Private, nondefense housing construction ceased after April 1942. Defense housing referred to more than housing for uniformed military personnel. It included housing for civilian workers drawn to one of the national "Defense Housing Areas" where extensive military production occurred. It could include housing built by local private contractors, which met certain criteria, as well as federal project housing by the Works Progress Administration and the armed services. The federal government regulated the production and use of war materials and stipulated design, quality, and materials standards. The wartime revival of local building economies, like the home building revival under the National Housing Act a few years earlier, symbolized state-administered and state-guaranteed home life. During the war, national symbols associated with the federal government clustered reassuringly around patriotic and socially conservative themes.

The federal defense housing program began in 1940 when Congress, at the request of the National Defense Commission, appropriated $100 million for construction of military housing at key defense areas. With March Field—a World War I vintage army air base—just east of the city limits, Riverside expected the government to require the city to provide about five hundred additional dwellings for military personnel. Local real estate spokespersons thought that regional city cooperation could meet the burden. The thought of providing merely five hundred additional houses for the war represented the last vestige of innocence about the scope of the impending war economy. Besides basing the headquarters of the army air force's Southwest District (encompassing California, Nevada, Arizona, New Mexico, Texas, and Oklahoma) at March Field, the war brought an antiaircraft training camp and a quartermaster depot. To accommodate the thousands of military personnel stationed at these three army posts, the War Production Board designated Riverside a "Defense Housing Area." Local contractors could build housing after approval by the Federal Housing Administration, which managed the War Production Board's permit process in southern California. Housing had to meet social criteria, such as being available for rent or purchase at no more than 20 percent of the income of the average worker in the nearby defense industry.[32]

Half of the new defense houses had to be for rental, rather than purchase. In addition, the army requested that the city provide eight hundred rooms to rent to army personnel at the quartermaster depot. To facilitate creation of rooms for rent, the Federal Housing Administration provided loans to convert single-family dwellings to duplexes or triplexes. The district administrator for the Federal Housing Administration told city leaders that "increased interest has developed in the program for remodeling or converting of existing properties, particularly where a large, single family residence exists in a well-located, desirable, mature residential district. Often such properties are ideal for conversion into duplex or triplex units for rental to war workers." The magnitude of the federal government's thinking soon became apparent. It wanted 125 single-family dwellings converted to multiple living units. In instances in which the government put up the funds for conversion, the power of landlords to control tenant selection would pass to the government, which would take a seven-year lease on the property (making mortgage payments, paying taxes, and maintaining the dwellings). To facilitate conversions and construction of new apartment houses, the city council rezoned portions of the city. The federal government imposed building standards on the housing; the electrical standard of living again represented a national norm. For one project of twenty duplexes, for instance, "each unit is to be provided with a spacious kitchen, with an abundance of cabinet storage space, tiled drain boards, large closets, tiled bathroom floors, built-in tile tubs, and oil heating. All units will be rented unfurnished. Electric refrigerators can be secured under the builders' priorities, for tenants who desire to purchase them."[33]

The forced introduction of mass rental housing into Riverside effectively ended a civic debate over the acceptability of rental housing that had begun in the late 1930s. The city's passed its first substantial rezoning from single-family residential to multifamily apartment and duplexes in 1939 for a few blocks of Mile Square. The city drew rezoning boundaries precisely. Propertied Riverside did not want multiple-family dwellings to enable racial integration or increase nonwhite populations. Renting houses permitted property owners to get around the restrictive real estate covenants that enforced racial segregation. In 1930, in an argument in favor of citywide zoning for classes of housing, Riverside Planning Commissioner Henry Coil had warned that deterioration of resident owner housing would undermine the power of property ownership to organize local society. While Coil's argument did not convince civic leaders in favor of master plan zoning, the Planning Commission had been reasonably successful on a case-by-case basis in preventing apartment houses from significantly displacing single-family dwellings as the city's main living arrangement. Now emergency needs of the war and the power of the national government, as expressed through the army, the War Production Board, and the Federal Housing Administration, ended the power of local property to control social life. The federal government pointedly and carefully did not interfere with local racial segregation, but the white community clearly understood that the suspension of local authority by federal power constituted a threat to local arrangements. The Riverside *Daily Press* editorially expressed the underlying racial fear behind residential segregation on several occasions. The context for the editorials was not explicitly the intrusion of rental housing, but the general advancement of African-American civil rights around the nation beginning in the late 1930s, which threatened the spatial separation of black and white communities. In 1937, the editor discussed a recent publication by a University of California professor which argued that the higher reproductive rate of African-Americans might lead to the "crowding out [of] the white population." "Race mixture" was a "grave question that cannot be sidestepped." A few years later, the editor again addressed the problem of "amalgamation," this time through a discussion of an editorial in an Alabama newspaper in favor of segregation. The *Daily Press* hoped time, not demagoguery, would solve the problems of race relations. Then the editorial stated, while ambiguously eliding the distinction between its own views and those of the Alabama newspaper, "Without segregation, it is stressed [in the Alabama newspaper editorial], there would be a tendency toward amalgamation, and that is something which races of different types have fought against from the earliest Eolithic period."[34]

Postwar Housing

Following the war, the nation experienced a severe housing shortage. The federal government capped defense and veterans house prices at $10,000, which unintentionally restricted construction sharply because of shortages of building materials and postwar price inflation. Truman also continued federal wartime controls, which prohibited nondefense housing construction, through 1946, thereby exacerbating the shortage of conventional housing for hundreds of thousands of American households who were civilians during the war. Even before the war, the real estate industry believed that a shortage in some kinds of housing, especially single-family detached dwellings, existed. This shortage had partly justified the federal public housing programs established under the Wagner Housing Act in 1937 and linked to slum clearance. The economic growth during the war and family formation after the war exacerbated the shortage. The California state legislature asked the federal government in 1946 for funds for 250,000 statewide housing units, and estimated the following year that California needed over 700,000 new housing units. The federal government's housing expediter estimated in 1946 that the nation needed 2,515,000 new housing units (houses and apartments) for veteran and nonveteran families. Only 700,000 were built in 1946, thereby ensuring that the housing shortage continued into 1947. The head of the local chamber of commerce estimated Riverside's shortage at 3,500 houses.[35]

The United States was not the only nation to experience a severe housing shortage. Housing shortages characterized Western economies for years following the war, placing housing programs high on the agenda of national politics. The war destroyed or damaged nearly one-third of Great Britain's houses, and that nation needed 4,000,000 new housing units. In France, nearly 2,000,000 citizens lived in barracks, and the national government estimated the housing need at 2,000,000 units. The Netherlands needed 400,000. In Italy, combat damaged some 6,800,000 residential rooms, 2,000,000 beyond repair. In defeated Germany, the situation was desperately worse. Although the United States did not suffer housing destruction from bombing and shelling during the war, it nonetheless started out the war with a greater housing need than many European countries, because during the 1930s it had not built the public housing common in Europe. Undoubtedly, the nation did not have the capability to solve its immediate postwar housing problem quickly. The number of houses needed in 1946 exceeded the total number of housing units started from 1940 through 1945.[36]

Short-term factors exacerbated the immediate postwar housing shortage. Price ceilings discouraged developers, builders faced shortages of building materials, union hiring halls were short of construction labor. Everyone expected relief as the nation's economy returned to normalcy. The building industry geared up, and the crisis slowly abated. In late 1948, Riverside city officials reported that the housing shortage had ended. Nonetheless, one analyst predicted that the nation would not return to complete "normalcy" until 1956.[37]

One short-term factor in the housing shortage, wartime rent control, ironically dragged on for years. The federal Office of Price Administration imposed rent control on rental housing, hotels, and rooming houses in 302 national "defense areas," including Riverside, on April 28, 1942. Rent control administration offices opened in cities around the country. In October, the federal government extended rent controls to virtually every city in the nation. Wartime controls initially lapsed on July 1, 1946, and landlords raised rents, frequently 50 to 100 percent over wartime rates. Across the nation, renters stormed municipal legislatures, which began, with questionable legal authority, to reimpose ceilings. Congress then again authorized federal rent controls, reimposed by a new bureaucracy. Subsequent rent control relaxation came slowly, amid a protracted, five-year political brawl between landlord and tenant organizations, with landlords threatening to withdraw rental property from the market, or mass evictions, or to cease signing rental contracts. The long duration of the controls naturally angered landlords after the war, since postwar inflation affected the cost basis of maintaining rental properties. As long as the housing shortage persisted, however, the Democratic president knew that complete decontrol of rents would subject millions of Americans to dramatic increases in housing costs, and the Democratic party would feel the voter reaction. In 1949, Congress passed authority to states, and states passed authority to municipalities (the "local option rule"), to decide the question of whether to impose ceilings on rents. In Riverside, local rent control politics began in earnest in the summer of 1949. Land-lords swiftly won the battle, and on November 16, 1949, rent control ended in the city. But the end of rent control did not mean the end of federal policy en-framing local real estate property, as the struggle over desegregation soon proved.[38]

A Dry Storm

The historic American order of state, in which the nation built itself from the bottom up on the foundation of locally owned property, collapsed in the de-pression. To save the state, the New Deal inverted the historic relationships be-tween state, property, and social order. FDR hoped that socially modernized home life would rejuvenate local communities. Out of vital and healthy com-munities would flow social commitment to American democratic political in-stitutions. Roosevelt adapted the traditional Jeffersonian vision to an industrial urban society in his famous Commonwealth Club speech in 1932, but changed how the Jeffersonian vision worked. For Jeffersonians, localism was inherently stable and constrained the national government to performing its limited role. For Roosevelt, localism and local property relations were not inherently stable and required underwriting by the national government.[39]

The New Deal's reframing of local property constituted the American polity's second "property revolution." The first property revolution involved the rise of the corporation at the end of the nineteenth century. The corporation brought vastly increased size and capitalization of business enterprises. Ownership (in shares) became separated from management. Small business ownership in commerce and agriculture became less important in the American economy. In the early twentieth century, the corporation came to control a large percentage of the nation's industrial and financial wealth. Corporations integrated indus-tries, such as oil, steel, and automobiles, eliminating competition. Administered markets replaced the competitive proprietary capitalism of small, owner-managed, local businesses that typified private American enterprise through the mid-nineteenth century. The rise of the corporation and American society's accommodation to it dominated politics from the Grangers of the 1870s to the New Deal in the 1930s.[40]

Despite the concentration of wealth in corporations, local society remained largely tied to the order of locally owned property. Absentee landlords and cap-italists seldom interfered with the local mores of "settled life" whose mainte-nance commanded fierce commitment from the resident bourgeoisie. Owners of small, local properties controlled local social relations, politics, and civic life and ruled local custom. A chain of circulating local capital bound together land-lords and land developers, owners of commercial real estate, small business-men, and the professional class who served them. They comprised the group whom Robert Lynd and Helen Lynd called the "Business Class," who supplied "the multitude of non-material institutional activities such as 'credit,' 'legal contract,' 'education,' 'sale for a price,' 'management,' and 'city government' by which Middletown people negotiate with each other in converting the narrowly specialized product of their workaday lives into a 'comfortable evening at home.'" Locally owned wealth centered on land values. Land values aligned home owners, many of whom owned no other real property, with the interest of the local bourgeoisie. Because changes in the racial and class composition of a community might—some property owners feared—dramatically change property values, local custom revolved around racial and class relations. This combination of property and custom gave local society its peculiar sense of finality, in which "the mere fact" of being born into either the working class or the business class "is the most significant single cultural factor tending to influence what one does all day long throughout one's life." A series of classic expositions described local community life in the 1920s, 1930s, and 1940s, including the Lynds' *Middletown* (1929) and *Middletown in Transition* (1937), John Dollard's *Caste and Class in a Southern Town* (1937), Lloyd Warner's "Yankee City" studies of Newburyport, Massachusetts, beginning with *The Social Life of a Modern Community* (1941), and James West's *Plainville, U.S.A.* (1945).[41]

The New Deal gave federal institutions power over local institutions of capital, but Roosevelt chose not to use that power to disturb local custom. The creation of a new relationship of power and the absence of exercise of this power in the 1930s made the new local-federal relation seem unreal. The barometric pressure had fallen, the wind had shifted, but the storm had not arrived. The air felt charged with electricity, but no lightning flashed. Returning with their research team to Middletown, the Lynds noted that in 1935, Middletown's values had not changed from 1925. "Those members of the research staff who had expected to find sharp differences in group alignments within the city, in ways of thinking, or feeling, or carrying on the multifarious daily necessities of life, found little to support their hypotheses. Middletown is overwhelmingly living by the values by which it lived in 1925." The Lynds ascribed the lack of change to cultural lag—"the thick blubber of custom that envelops the city's life." They did not see the true reason for the continuance of local custom: simply that the federal government did not use its new power for another decade.[42]

Appendix

Figures 5.1–5.8.   Advertisements of the New Deal Programs in Home Modernization

Supporting Our President In His

NATIONAL RECOVERY PROGRAM

The Following Firms
Have Adopted
Uniform
Store Hours

STORES WILL BE OPEN FROM

8:30 A. M. to 5:30 P. M.

EACH DAY INCLUDING SATURDAY

Franzen's	Coldren's Electric Shop	Riverside Furniture Co.
Montgomery Ward & Co.	Electric Supply Co.—W.V. Pittman	Riverside Hardware Co.
J. C. Penney & Co.	Ark Housefurnishing Co.	F. W. Twogood—Jewelry
Allen & Kearne	Golden Rule Furniture Co.	Matthews Paint Co.
Reynolds	Binford Furniture Store	Clinton L. Fanton-Radio
Schacker's	Huffman & Karmann—Furniture	B.-K. Radio Co.
H. F. Grout & Co.	Schwartz Bros. Furniture Store	Riverside Baking Co.
Tiernan-Sanders Co.	Page Furniture Co.	Radio Equipment Co.
Morgan Typewriter Co.	Salt Lake Transfer & Storage Co.	A. R. Coffin—Shoes
Burroughs Adding Machine Co.	J. C. Smith's Hardware Store	Oaks Shoe Store
Mott's Cycle & Supply Co.	R. J. Welch—Luggage—Tires	The 8th St. Store—Shoes
B. J. Starkweather—Sport Goods	Frank S. Fisher—Jeweler	Stoner's Quality Shoe Store
Harrah's Clothing Store	Chas. E. Goldsmith-Jeweler	Riverside Hardware Co.
McGrath-Olson	H. C. Schultz—Jeweler	Adamson Studio
Stockwell & Binney	Hinckley's-Ladies Ready-to-Wear	Rubidoux Photo Studio
Buchanan's—Women's Wear	Umholtz Music Co.	Caldwell Kodak Service
Mission Dress Shop	Gurr-Smith Radio Co.	Sears Roebuck & Co.
Riddick Dry Goods Co.	Rouses	

NRA MEMBER U.S.

WE DO OUR PART

We Deem It An Honor....

To Be the First in Riverside to Receive the Official Emblem and Sanction of Compliance with Our President's Recovery Program

FRANZEN'S

Loans to Repair and Modernize Your Property

Under the new National Housing Act, in cooperation with the Federal Housing Administration, Bank of America announces that it is prepared to receive applications for loans of from $100.00 to $2000.00 to be used for alterations, repairs, and improvements on real property.

This step is in conformity with Bank of America's established policy of making loans to aid employment and stimulate the entire building industry. Under the provisions of the new housing act the modernization of homes, farm buildings, and business properties may be undertaken.

Applications for loans may be filed at any one of Bank of America's 417 branches in 249 California communities.

FREE INFORMATION

ON THE

Federal Home Modernization Plan

Please print or write plainly.

Please send me your pamphlet explaining the home modernization plan.

I am interested in the type of home improvement checked below:

☐ Roofing	☐ Painting
☐ Plumbing	☐ Redecorating
☐ Electrical Work	☐ Plastering
☐ Additional Rooms	☐ Cement Work
☐ Heating	☐ Garage

Or...

Name..

Address.......................................

Address your letter to:

Home Renovation Editor,

Chapter 6
Political Paths to Electrical Modernization

Charles Wetherell, coauthor

The Leap to Modernization

Three times between the end of World War I and the Korean War, the national government changed the domestic lives of Americans by shifting the nation's political economy. On each occasion, the government enabled Americans to transform their material lives with electricity. In 1927, as part of Secretary of Commerce Hoover's progressive adjustment of the nation to the corporate economy, the federal government passed the Radio Act, which regulated the broadcast industry, greatly encouraged its nationalization, changed the nature of programming, and stimulated the mass adoption of the plug-in radio. Mass adoption of the radio convinced Americans of the value of greatly increasing their consumption of electrical energy. Energy budgets became elastic. In 1935, as part of the New Deal in electricity, the national government subsidized refrigerator ownership through Title I of the National Housing Act and other programs, especially the TVA and rural electrification. New Deal public power advocates considered refrigerator adoption to be central to social modernization of the home. In World War II and the postwar years, in part to democratize electrical modernization, the national government restructured the nation's economy through Keynesian fiscal policy, democratized home ownership, and reduced racial restraints on minority housing markets.

Riverside households revealed the effect of federal policy shifts. They leaped, rather than leaned, into electrical modernization. In mid-1928, the average Riverside home bought a radio, doubling its electricity consumption while reconstructing family life around the home's new hearth. In 1937, they

156

bought refrigerators, doubling consumption again and reorganizing home labor around the kitchen, as the rational housekeeping movement had prescribed. During the last year of the World War II, they cashed in on wartime prosperity and increased their electrical service a third time. These quantum jumps in electrical consumption occurred against the backdrop of very little domestic use of electricity. In the early 1920s, the nation's average household consumed barely 30 kwh monthly. A generation later, in 1950, the majority of the nation's households employed modernized electrical services, using more than 150 kwh monthly. Most households enjoyed radios, refrigerators, several labor-saving appliances, and high-wattage lamps. Their lifestyles fulfilled the progressive political vision of mass electrical modernization. Households of differing economic class, social status, and race jumped to new electrical lifestyles at different times, following socially and politically distinct paths to new lifestyles. All of them, however, modernized electrically in the same way. They dramatically shifted their domestic lifestyles around adoption of new electrical services.[1]

Scholars have not observed that households leaped in steps into electrical modernization, because they commonly use the Bureau of the Census's time series data on residential consumption of electricity (see fig. 6.1). The series imply a smoothly rising curve of national domestic usage of electricity, with no boundaries intuitively corresponding to conventional historical periodization. This national consumption pattern is particularly meaningful for economists. They see it as evidence for the hypothesis that increases in consumption relate to increases in income, which also occur—in aggregate time series—incrementally. Despite its plausibility, the conventional interpretation of the Census Bureau's historical series is wrong. Individual households increased electrical consumption by jumping from level to level, rather than by making incremental increases. Riverside's annual consumption from 1921 to 1950 reveals the pattern (see fig. 6.2). That the national incremental curve is continuous and smooth does not imply that the "average" household used electricity differently from those in Riverside. Rather, the smooth appearance of the national curve is an artifact of averaging many step-jumps distributed over time. Calculating a population mean masks discontinuity in the historical time series by confounding a few dwellings that increase their consumption with the many dwellings that do not.[2]

Using a structured random sample of Riverside's households and their electrical consumption from 1921 to 1950, we are able to avoid the mistake of inferring individual behavior from aggregate data by examining individual-level data directly. Three residences illustrate the qualitative nature of increases in electricity consumption from July 1921 to December 1950. (See figs. 6.3a–c.) The steps and plateaus are obvious in each dwelling. We also notice differences between dwellings in the seasonal usage of electricity. The light cycle drives the consumption of all dwellings. Electricity usage is greater in the winter because more lights are on and for a longer time than in the summer. Other devices reinforce this seasonality. People are indoors more in the winter, so they listened to the radio, for instance, more at that time. The electrical consumption histories of these three dwellings illustrate, almost as Platonic models, the stepped increase in consumption.[3]

Consumers normally used electricity within a stable consumption horizon. They increased their consumption by qualitative changes of lifestyle. Federal policy removed barriers or raised floors for new levels of consumption. By suddenly removing the social constraints that confined household demand, or by erecting a new scaffolding for greater home spending, social policies empowered families to jump to new lifestyles. Each style required different amounts of electricity. From monthly consumption of electricity, we can easily detect what standard of electrical living a household enjoyed and when it changed electrical styles. We distinguish three floors of consumption (see table 6.1 and fig. 6.2). Use of lights determined the first floor. All electrified dwellings had lights. In Riverside, the lights floor represented minimal use of electricity and required about one forty-watt bulb for every room, or about 11 kwh/mo. The electric flatiron found nearly universal adoption as the only electrical appliance in many homes. Adoption of the radio drew household consumption up to a second floor of consumption. The house-current radio, whose mass adoption began in 1928, required another 7 kwh/mo. of electricity and added an hour a day of electrical illumination. To be using a radio, therefore, a household had to consume a floor of 23.5 kwh/mo. Use of a refrigerator required another 22 kwh/mo., creating a third floor of 45 kwh/mo. Consumption at a fourth floor involved use of an electric cooking range or water heater, and falls outside the period covered by Riverside data. Use of a cooking range required at least 123 kwh/mo. and thereby raised the cooking range floor up to 168 kwh/mo. exceeding the city-wide average usage from 1944 to 1950. Households adopted the water heater, the next appliance to be widely added to the household inventory, after 1950. The water heater also falls outside the period covered by the Riverside data. The average electric water heater consumed 334 kwh/mo. of electricity; except for a few dwellings in Riverside's Country Club neighborhood, no Riverside dwellings consumed at the floor of 457 kwh/mo. required to have an electric water heater.[4]

The picture of stepped consumption changes how we must interpret the lives of families living in electrified homes. The purchase of the radio changed family lifestyle. The shift from seasonal ice refrigeration, or no refrigeration at all, to mechanical refrigeration represented an equally important shift in food management. Meter readings are not final evidence of lifestyle projects, but other circumstantial evidence supports the inference of projects. Since the distinctive consumption plateaus reflect the classes of housing quality, lifestyle reorganization involved renovation of the dwelling, or a move to a dwelling with higher electrical technology capability. Stepped consumption plots a distinct chronology linking households to municipal policy and the New Deal.

The Radio Jump

The timing of the first jump to a higher level of electricity consumption—1928—tells us what did *not* stimulate the jump, as well as what did. By a process of chronological elimination, we can confidently infer that labor-saving appliances did not cause consumers to break with their established electrical frugality. Manufacturers introduced the electric washing machine and the vacuum cleaner earlier in the decade, but few consumers adopted them. Their mass adoption would not have required households to use as much electricity as registered by the eruption in electricity consumption in 1928. The refrigerator's widespread acceptance did not come until the 1930s. Given the electricity requirements of different appliances, we can be certain that radio adoption increased demand from 1927 to 1929. The radio consumed so much more electricity than average consumption earlier, that it broke the "inelasticity" of consumer energy budgets that utilities believed prohibited a mass market in electrical appliances. (See pl. 7.)

The radio did not cause a revolution in household *labor.* The radio did not save labor in an ordinary sense; rather, it changed consumer's values by providing information and entertainment. The importance of mass adoption of the radio was cultural. National programming by the Columbia Broadcasting System eroded parochial and ethnic values by diffusing mass culture. Market forces in the 1920s bypassed labor processes in most American homes, instead intensifying mass consumerism.[5]

Electrical modernization in neighborhoods and classes reflected the political power of households. The multiple graph of neighborhood electrical consumption, 1921–1950, shows the distinctive timing of each district's individual leap to the lifestyles represented by the radio and refrigerator (see fig. 6.4). Upper-class homes in Country Club and upper-middle-class homes in Wood Streets adopted radios earliest. The seventy-six Country Club owner-resident homes in our sample in 1929 used enough electricity for all of them—not simply the average of the neighborhood—to have radios. Although renting households lagged behind owner homes, even in Country Club, the forty renter households sampled in Riverside's two posh neighborhoods also used enough electricity in 1930 to put the average renting household on the radio floor. In middle-class Mile Square and South East Side, the average household obtained the radio in 1927; in middle-class Expansion and Tract, in 1928. In Mile Square, Expansion, and Tract, home owners obtained the radio in 1927, a year before renting households. In South East Side, renters obtained the radio the same year, 1927, as owners. By 1930, 44 percent of households in middle-class neighborhoods listened to their own radios. In Riverside's minority neighborhoods, poverty and occupational backsliding during the depression delayed adoption of the radio until well after its adoption in white neighborhoods. By 1930, only 26 percent of Old East Side households had the radio. The average household of Old East Side and Casa Blanca did not have a radio until after 1935, eight years after the

Plate 7.   *Jumps in Electrical Consumption — The Radio.* ([Photographer unknown.]
"Woman Sitting on Couch." Keystone-Mast Collection. UCR/California Museum of
Photography, University of California, Riverside.)

average Mile Square home. In the 1936–1940 period, only 41 percent of households in Casa Blanca could have used a radio. Old East Side was slightly better off. For the same period, 57 percent of its homes had the radio.

   Proponents of the home owning ideology during the 1920s claimed that
owner-occupied homes were of higher quality than rented homes. Resident owners took better care of their property and invested in it. The benefits of home

ownership emerged as one of the major conclusions of President Hoover's 1931 conference on home owning. New Deal housing planners shared the conservatives' faith in home ownership and built the nation's housing programs around the objective of shifting households from renting to owning. The Riverside electrical data allows us to test the belief that the dwellings of resident owners were of higher material quality than those of renters.

Renting and home owning households shared similar levels of electrical consumption from 1921 to mid-1928 (see fig. 6.6). The radio created the decisive difference in consumption in 1928, when households who owned their homes jumped to a new level of consumption with the radio, leaving the renters a full year behind. After the jump, owners led renters in consumption in nearly all aspects of their householding through 1950. The distinction between owning and renting households allows us to disaggregate the jump to the radio. Owner-occupied households in middle-class neighborhoods, representing a minority of households, adopted the radio in 1927. Renter households adopted it in 1928 and, representing the majority of homes, moved the average adoption of owners and renters into mid-1928. Adoption of the house-current radio raised owners to a higher level of electrical consumption. This greater consumption by home owners than renters, once they both bought radios, indicates either that owners bought bigger radios (with more vacuum tubes, thus drawing more electricity) or that they used them more. In the first years of the plug-in radio, the difference between owners and renters in radio adoption was significant primarily at the opposite ends of the income scale. More home owning professionals than renting professionals owned the radio. Among unskilled labor households, more renters—interestingly—than owners adopted. (See tables 6.2, 6.3.) Differences in income did not necessarily cause the differences between owner and renter adoption. The majority of Riverside's (and the nation's) households rented in the 1920s. Even among the upper class, nearly 40 percent of households rented, so many renters had the money to buy a radio at the same time owners did. Since nearly 40 percent of renters also moved to a new consumption level shortly after settling in a new residence, many renters apparently waited until they had moved to buy a radio.

The Refrigerator Jump

In no neighborhood, except Country Club, did more than 11 percent of households have a refrigerator before the 1930s. In Country Club, 43 percent of households had a refrigerator, and 12 percent had an electric range or water heater (and several appeared to have both) in the years 1926–1930. High-income occupations explain the concentration of heavy appliances in Country Club. Professionals, citrus farmers, and business proprietors, the major residential groups of Country Club, owned 75 percent of the city's refrigerators and 92 percent of the city's ranges. Among the rest of the city's occupational groups, only the households of low white-collar workers had significant ownership of refrigerators. Low white-collar households owned 12.5 percent of the refrigerators in Riverside homes. Sixty-nine percent of refrigerators and 93 percent of ranges and water heaters were in owner resident homes. In Old East Side, where nearly all African-American and a third of Mexican Riversiders lived, no households at all used refrigerators until the 1930s. In Casa Blanca, only 4.5 percent of households had refrigerators in 1926–1930. The households of M. Martinez and M. Torres successively rented a dwelling owned by the absentee landlord, Josephine Pretti, possibly a widow. Pretti installed a refrigerator in December 1929, for the use of her tenants, just before the Martinez family moved in. The Martinez family lived in the rental until February 1930, when the Torres family replaced them, renting the dwelling until April 1931. Later Pretti herself lived in the house for several years. It is possible that she originally installed the refrigerator with the intent of using it herself, but found her move-in delayed. These Casa Blanca households were among the few Mexican families to enjoy mechanical refrigeration in these years. (See tables 6.4, 6.5.)

Riverside's professionals, citrus growers, and business proprietors constituted 21.5 percent of the city's households, confirming *Electrical World*'s judgment that private industry reached only the luxury market. The decisive importance of home owning in adopting the refrigerator in the years 1926–1930 reinforces the luxury status of the refrigerator. Among professional households, 27 percent of owner resident homes had the refrigerator, but only 3 percent of renters also did. This distinction persisted into the worst years of the depression, 1931–1935. Then, more than half of owner resident professional homes, but less than a third of renters, utilized mechanical cold. In Riverside, as in the rest of the nation, the private marketplace had not established a mass market for domestic electric appliances in the 1920s.[6]

Mass adoption of the refrigerator stimulated the second jump in electrical living in the mid-1930s. (See pl. 8.) Historians largely interpret refrigerator adoption in microeconomic terms. Following economists, they see refrigerator buyers as responding to the rapid drop in refrigerator prices in the decade. This explanation is insufficient. The New Deal's restructuring of the market for appliances and national and local subsidization of refrigerator purchases made refrigerators a mass—rather than luxury—appliance. The middle-class market became the crucial market for the industry in the depression, because many upper-class homes had already acquired their appliances. The working classes did not have the income—as the industry then priced the market— to buy appliances. In industry's eyes, this left the middle class. In Riverside, the middle class of clerks, office managers, salesmen, skilled craftsmen, and industrial foremen constituted 39 percent of the city's households in the years 1931–1935. Their inability to buy refrigerators without governmental assistance is clear. Only 24 percent of low white-collar households and only 15 percent of skilled blue-collar households had refrigerators in these five years. Households of semiskilled and unskilled laborers filled one-fourth of Riverside's homes. Only 16.5 percent of semiskilled households and only 7 percent

Plate 8. *Jumps in Electrical Consumption—The Refrigerator.* ([Photographer unknown.] "Mother Ironing." Keystone-Mast Collection. UCR/California Museum of Photography, University of California, Riverside.)

of unskilled households owned refrigerators. The Real Property Inventory of 1934 confirms these statistics. Surveyors found that 16 percent of dwellings in San Diego and 17.6 percent of dwellings in Sacramento had refrigerators. (Riverside was not surveyed.) An estimated 23 percent of households in Riverside had refrigerators (in 1934). Clearly, private market forces, unaided by governmental policy, had not been able to make the technology for domestic electrical modernization available to over three-fourths of the nation's households.

Households of Riverside's middle-class and white working-class neighbor-hoods upgraded their homes to the electrical standard after 1934 by adopting the refrigerator, home modernization, and better lighting through New Deal pro-grams. National Housing Act Title I loans for home modernization accounted for much of the home improvement reflected in the increase in electricity con-sumption at mid-decade. From 1934 to mid-1938, Riverside County took a to-tal of 2,971 Title I modernization loans (in contrast to only 193 Title II mort-gage loans). Since 37 percent of the county's population lived in the city, about one thousand Riverside households, or one in five owner-occupied homes, took Title I loans. The federal policy connecting home modernization with home own-ership proved crucial in moving middle-class households to electrical and social modernization. Home owners and home renters adopted the refrigerator at sig-nificantly different rates. In 1936–1940, 88 percent of home owning professional households possessed the refrigerator, while only 64 percent of renting profes-sional households did. In the same years, among middle-class blue-collar fam-ilies, 65 percent of owner-occupied homes owned refrigerators, but only 49 per-cent of renters also did.[7]

In 1932, Riverside's utilities board lowered its basic residential electric rate from eight to five cents per kwh for the first 100 kwh/mo. The board also es-tablished incentive rates, setting the rate for the next block of 400 kwh/mo. at only 4.5 cents/kwh/mo. The city continued to lower incentive rates in the decade, often by half a cent per kwh. In 1935, the basic residential rate stood at 5 cents/kwh for the first 45 kwh/mo., 2.5 cents/kwh for the next 110 kwh/mo., and 1.5 cents/kwh for all electricity over 155 kwh/mo. The city hoped lower rates would encourage Riversiders to buy refrigerators, water heaters, and ranges. The strategy worked. In the fiscal year, July 1, 1934–June 30, 1935, the River-side light department sold 144 electric ranges and 200 electric refrigerators. These figures did not include sales from Riverside's private businesses, also try-ing to sell these large appliances. The combination of federal promotion and subsidy of heavy electrical appliances, through Title I loans, incentive rates that lowered electricity charges for heavy appliances by 69 percent from their rates in 1929, and depression prices for the appliances themselves, lowered further by promotional campaigns by the city's light department, brought full electri-cal modernization within reach of Riverside's middle-class families for the first time. The city more slowly reduced the basic rate for consumers who used less than 45 kwh/mo., reflecting the middle-class political base of the city govern-ment. Los Angeles, which had encouraged industrialization and establishment of a comfortable lifestyle for the laboring class in the 1920s based on cheap publicly owned electricity, had by comparison the lowest rates for consumers of all classes of any city in the state. They set rates low, in part, to encourage consumption of surplus Boulder Dam power, whose sale paid for the dam. In Riverside's middle-class neighborhoods, ownership of refrigerators jumped from fewer than one in five households in 1931–1935 to more than one in two households in 1936–1940.

Labor neighborhoods did not catch up to middle-class neighborhoods in refrigerator ownership in the 1930s. Nonetheless, both the middle class and the working class benefited from New Deal policies. The benefit is clear from a comparative analysis of refrigerator buying over two periods, 1931–1935 and 1936–1940. In the first half of the decade, 40 percent of upper-class households (professionals, citrus farmers, and business proprietors) had refrigerators; but only 20 percent of middle-class households (clerks, salesmen, skilled craftsmen, and industrial foremen) and only 8 percent of working-class households (semiskilled workers and unskilled laborers) owned refrigerators. In the second half of the decade, when New Deal policies had taken effect, the percentage of upper-class households owning refrigerators doubled; by contrast, middle-class households increased their ownership rate by 220 percent and working-class households with refrigerators quadrupled. By 1940, 63 percent of middle-class households and 40 percent of working-class households owned refrigerators. We see hints of the results of the New Deal policy when we open up the broad class categories to look at more limited occupational groups. The incidence of refrigerator ownership among households of unskilled laborers rose more than the rates of skilled and semiskilled workers. Casual laborers increased their rate of refrigerator ownership by 285 percent over the earlier period (1931–1935). This increase undoubtedly sprang from the restoration of income by New Deal programs and by federal incentives to commercial loan institutions to extend credit to low-income groups. The assistance is especially evident when viewed from a neighborhood perspective. In 1931–1935, less than one in ten households in labor-class neighborhoods owned the refrigerator; in 1936–1940, one in three did. Riverside's working-class families led insecure lives in these years, typified by frequent changes of jobs, unemployment, and changes of residence. That they were able to benefit from the programs reveals the extent to which public policy opened the marketplace beyond its narrow boundaries of the 1920s.[8]

In conclusion, Riverside's utility billings reveal a structured adoption of the refrigerator rather than a simple diffusion of the device down the income scale. Mass ownership began with the middle class rather than the bourgeoisie. This pattern contrasts with the adoption of the telephone. Phone service spread through the nation's households in classical fashion—top down from high-status, high-income groups to urban blue-collar households. Housing tenure and dwelling condition affected telephone adoption far less than appliance adoption. New Deal promotion of the refrigerator and local municipal politics extended the mass benefit of the device to the middle class. Then during the slow climb out of the depression after 1935, in the context of New Deal recovery programs, the average white working-class household brought the refrigerator into their homes. Riverside's neighborhoods show the unfortunate failure of New Deal programs to address minority problems. In 1936–1940, only 16 percent of households in Old East Side and only 7 percent of households in Casa Blanca used refrigerators.[9]

Wartime and Postwar Prosperity

The final consumption horizon emerged, ironically, in World War II. Nondefense housing construction and production of civilian commodities, including electrical appliances, came to a virtual halt. Commercial manufacturers of electrical appliances converted to war production, and the federal government seized most of the unsold inventory for military use. Workers saved increased earnings obtained from war work, investing much of it in war bonds. The expansion of ownership of major consumer goods, including electric appliances, supposedly halted. What explains the timing of Riverside's final leap to modernization? Two factors seemed to be at work. Wartime overcrowding increased consumption of electricity for illumination, without, however, necessarily advancing social modernization. The city's whole population increased 50 percent in the 1940s, much of the increase coming during the war. The number of African-Americans doubled during the war years. Between 1942 and 1947, residential building stock increased little. Many dwellings held double households, and many more households took in transient boarders. Owners converted single-family dwellings to multiple apartments, without adding additional meters. Even if households did not augment or upgrade their appliances during the war, increased household size and doubling households per dwelling would have raised electricity consumption because the existing appliance stock got more use. Radio listening increased, thereby increasing the evening use of lights. Federal policy permitted some home renovation in designated defense areas around the nation, including Riverside, to increase the stock of multiple housing for war workers and military personnel. Responding to federal pleas, many Riverside home owners apparently converted their single-family dwellings into apartments. The city council made these conversions possible in 1939, when it approved an apartment and duplex housing zone within Mile Square.[10]

Social modernization due to the war also promoted electrical modernization. Owners of apartments designated for defense workers could apply for refrigerators. It is possible that some of Old East Side's African-American homes, like others around the nation, took advantage of this opportunity, because the federal government avoided room assignments for African-American service men and women outside segregated districts. Also, African-Americans left the South for employment in Northern industrial cities. Many of them earned enough money to enjoy a better material quality of life than they previously had in their rural Southern homes. Minority soldiers sent some of their duty pay back home. During the war, 40 percent of Old East Side's homes and 29 percent of Casa Blanca's homes used enough electricity to have refrigerators. Possibly, some African-American homes without official defense apartments could obtain refrigerators in the gray market of yard sales, from secondhand stores, and by importing from other areas of the nation. Women's work in the defense industries expanded women's social expectations. We can reasonably assume that advances in home modernization, including electrical modernization, accompanied these strides in social modernization.[11]

When President Truman released the economy from wartime controls in 1947, he did not rely solely on private market forces to bring prosperity. He revived the New Deal goal of housing modernization both to stimulate the economy and to achieve a New Deal social goal. New Deal social policies and goals enframed the postwar housing boom. The housing boom became one of the principal engines of postwar prosperity. The residential electric billings in the Riverside municipal archives end in 1950, so they catch just the beginning of this great postwar housing modernization. Many Riverside dwellings greatly increased their electrical consumption in the late 1940s. In this context, the increase in consumption undoubtedly represented new consumption processes, not simply intensification of old. Indeed, most minority Riverside homes did not purchase the refrigerator until the years 1944 through 1950. The disproportionate representation of racial minorities in the class of unskilled labor certainly suppressed the rate of refrigerator ownership among unskilled laborers generally. Why did the households of nonwhite unskilled laborers not buy into modernization earlier, at the same time as white laborers? The answer lies in the New Deal's strategy of tying home modernization and social modernization to the owner-occupied home. This strategy tied modernization to the order of local property. In Riverside, as well as elsewhere in the nation, local property owners used their power to maintain a racially segregated social order and to prevent an increase of dwelling stock available to minorities. Segregation systematically degraded minority housing through overcrowding and materially impoverished the lives of nonwhite households. Some minority families certainly had enough income to afford higher rents or higher mortgages but were denied access through local segregation to better housing on which to spend their money. Undoubtedly, minority home owners had to use much of the money that might otherwise go toward electrical modernization to cope with increased occupancy of their dwellings. Electrical modernization required an electrical infrastructure above the standard of electrification that private utilities put into homes from 1882 to 1929. Local racism thereby tied social modernization for racial and ethnic minorities to civil freedom. Most minority households would not be free to use the new technology until the nation destroyed the racism of local property after 1948.

Historians do not doubt that the 1940s and the 1950s produced the greatest improvement in the standard of living of the nation's minority households in this century. Riverside's minority homes reflected this improvement. In 1946–1950, 70 percent of homes in Old East Side and 68 percent of homes in Casa Blanca obtained refrigerators. Eighty-seven percent of semiskilled laborers' households and 82 percent of unskilled laborers' households had refrigerators by 1950. Ranges and water heaters now appeared in significant numbers of homes. Although the 2.4 percent of Old East Side and 3.7 percent of Casa Blanca homes to have ranges or water heaters in 1946–1950 were far below the 56 percent of Country Club's homes to own them, it is significant that *any* of the minority neighborhood's families used these expensive devices.

Strategies for Economic Security

Riversiders—owners and renters alike—moved often. Over the thirty years from 1921 to 1950, the average household stayed in a home only 2.7 years—4.9 years for resident home owners and 1.3 years for renters. These tenure patterns affected household passage to electrical modernization. In another publication, we have placed this remarkably short residential tenure in historical perspective. Americans historically have had high rates of residential mobility. Using the Riverside utility billing data, we demonstrated that the high rates of the nineteenth century continued in the twentieth century through the Second World War. Only after 1945 did mobility rates slow. This finding confounds both scholarly and popular expectations. Scholars had presumed that nineteenth-century rates slowed down earlier, after 1920, once the nation had completed its shift from a rural to an urban society. Popular opinion assumed (contrary to scholars) that geographic mobility rose above historical levels after World War II. The Riverside utility billings prove just the reverse.[12]

Did household social and economic characteristics, the quality of housing, and residential mobility affect one another? The data provide two answers to this question. The largest answer is that residential tenures were brief, regardless of household characteristics. Three factors taken together—whether a household owned the home in which they lived, in which of the eleven neighborhoods they made their home, and the occupation of the head of household—explain less than 20 percent of the length of residential tenures over the decades from 1921 to 1950.[13] This finding means that the policies of Riverside's elite did not create brief residential tenures as a basic social phenomenon. We cannot infer from the finding, however, that the social policies of the property-owning bourgeoisie had no influence at all on residential mobility. Elite policies determined destinations of residential mobility inside the city and kept out or pushed out minorities of color from the city.

Local policies also modified the brevity of residential tenure of households at the top and bottom of Riverside's social hierarchy by influencing tenure status, social status, and material affluence. Tenure status—home owning or renting—made the greatest difference. Home owners lived in their homes for an average of five years, whereas renters lived in their homes for barely a year; indeed, the majority of renters lived in their homes for *less* than a year. Socioeconomic status, as indexed by occupational grouping, also differentiated length of residence. Owning and renting households of workers in high white-collar occupations had the longest residential tenure, averaging sixty-three months. The households of semiskilled laborers had the shortest tenure, only twenty-six months on average. Leaving aside renters, high white-collar home owners pushed that occupational group's tenure rate up further, to 7.2 years.

As an indicator of social status, residential location links to occupation in influencing length of tenure. (See table 6.6.) Households in the richest and poorest neighborhoods in Riverside had the longest tenures. The city's elite in Country Club (owners and renters together) lived an average of fifty-four months in their homes, and the poor Hispanic families in Casa Blanca lived an average of fifty-six months in their homes. High white-collar households and the households of racial minorities also differed widely from Riverside's norm. High white-collar households were the *only* occupational group a majority of whom owned their homes. Fifty-eight percent of high white-collar households owned the homes in which they lived; the next highest home owning group, households of skilled workers, owned at the rate of 47.3 percent. As a neighborhood, Casa Blanca also had a high home ownership rate—45 percent of households owned their own homes (above the city's average of 38.6 percent). These groups, including Old East Side, lived the longest in their homes. Figure 6.6 dramatically illustrates the close coincidence of the residential stability of Country Club and Casa Blanca, in comparison with Mile Square, which solidly represented the tendencies of the middle class.[14]

Finally, a third variable—level of material affluence—affected the time a household stayed in a home. We can associate levels of material affluence with the four floors of electricity consumption: (1) households who limited electricity consumption to lights and an iron, (2) households who also owned the radio but whose electricity consumption went no higher, (3) households who owned refrigerators, and (4) households with other heavy appliances besides refrigerators. Each group lived in their homes for significantly different lengths of time. As households consumed more, they lived in their homes longer. Households with only lights and an iron lived the briefest time in their homes; they had a median survival time of less than three fourths of a year. At the other end of the scale of affluence, households with refrigerators and other heavy appliances lived the longest time in their homes, with a median survival time of 3.14 years. (See table 6.7.)

Differences in electrical status related to social and occupational differences between different groups. Groups, such as professionals, with long home tenures, lived even longer in their homes when they had a refrigerator or other heavy appliances. Groups with shorter tenures, such as unskilled laborers, stayed longer when they owned heavy appliances, but not as long as professionals. Possession of only lights and an iron, or only a radio, had the opposite effect: it shortened the time a household lived in its home. From these relationships we infer that possession of appliances did not establish basic patterns of tenure, but modified them. The split between the effects of lights, iron, and radio, on the one hand, and refrigerators and other heavy appliances, on the other, suggests that the difference between brief tenures and longer tenures was more than simply a matter of degree. Households who lived only briefly in a home had even briefer tenures when they did not raise their level of material affluence by purchase of heavy appliances during their stay. Possession of lights or a radio only did not cause them to move sooner; rather, lack of heavy appliances enabled them to move sooner. The contrast is between two different ways of living: moving often and accumulating few heavy appliances, and moving less often while accumulating heavy appliances. (See table 6.8.)

The two different lifestyles reflected different life plans for obtaining economic security. Following one plan, families sought economic security primarily through accumulation of assets, including heavy appliances. Asset security refers to investments that return a stream of income or a stream of cost-savings. In a small producer ideology, real property holdings constituted the preferred capital asset. Farmers who owned their land, proprietors of small businesses, and landlords, for instance, obtained the income on which they lived from owning real property assets. With the rise of salaried white-collar occupations in the twentieth century, education and vocational training also constituted assets. The education of physicians and lawyers, for instance, is an asset that returns a stream of income. Professionals maintain and upgrade their educational asset by ongoing education. Insurance and pensions represented another asset intended to provide a flow of income when illness or death ended the wage earner's ability to work.

Following the other plan, workers sought economic security primarily by wage labor. Until the New Deal, semiskilled and unskilled wage earners lived off their labor and owned few assets. They received income only as they worked. Laborers secured their stream of income by moving around to find jobs or higher wages, thereby reducing their time of unemployment. Asset security and wage security were obviously not exclusive. Wage earners tried to accumulate assets, such as savings and insurance, that could replace income when they were unemployed. From this point of view, maintaining networks with kin on whom they could depend when wages dried up also represented asset building. Home ownership did not necessarily increase economic security for wage laborers. If home buying or home owning reduced their mobility to find jobs, then it was undesirable. The bourgeoisie may have depended on rents or interest from investments, but most also had to work to maintain those investments, though managing investments did not constitute wage labor. Undoubtedly, few depended on rents exclusively for their income. The distinction between asset security and wage security was therefore a matter of emphasis. Most of the wage earner's security of livelihood depended on wage labor income, supplemented by asset income, and most of the bourgeoisie's security of livelihood depended on investment assets, maintained by active management or professional practice, that is, salary and fees. Riverside's high white-collar households derived a significant part of their income from property assets, such as productive agricultural land, residential rental properties, shares in packing house cooperatives, and retail businesses. Ownership of local real property assets restricted the bourgeoisie's residential mobility. Since maintenance of the stream of income required asset management, heads of household had to live in Riverside. Home ownership and living for a long time in one home maximized the purchasing power of income by reducing debt payment.

The most important factor shaping the length of residential tenure—wage-based economic security—resulted from the nation's industrial commitment to a wage labor system. Obtaining a regular wage income compelled wage laborers to move frequently in response to national wage labor markets. Skilled craftsmen and semiskilled workers migrated to places where economic activity generated demand for their labor. Gladys Palmer's survey of labor mobility in Los Angeles and five other cities during the 1940s, conducted for the Social Science Research Council, provides broad evidence of a relationship between wage earning and mobility. Palmer and her associates interviewed 2,001 men and women over fourteen years of age working at a cross section of occupations in Los Angeles in 1951, obtaining detailed employment records for the previous ten years on each worker. Twenty-seven percent of the workers had worked for only one employer in the decade; half of the workers had worked for two or more employers. Men and women held virtually the same average number of jobs—3.2 for men, 3 for women. Professionals and other salaried workers had the fewest jobs—2.9. Wage laborers held the most—3.9. Male operatives held an average 3.7 jobs. The researchers found similar patterns in five other cities (San Francisco, Chicago, Philadelphia, Saint Paul, New Haven).[15]

Other social science surveys support this assessment of labor mobility. In their classic community study of Middletown in the 1920s, the Lynds observed, somewhat impressionistically, that unemployment drove working-class migration. To a lesser extent, it also drove residential mobility. Six of 122 interviewed families had moved to cheaper housing when the wage earner became unemployed. Reviewing three decades of labor mobility studies in the mid-1950s, Herbert Parnes concluded that the wage earner's age, business employment practices, governmental policies and business prosperity, and wage levels were among the major reasons that laborers changed jobs. The age of the laborer is clearly associated with how often she or he changes jobs and whether wages or assets predominantly influence the decision. While young, laborers have little vestment in their jobs. The pull of higher wages at a different job or the push of being fired or furloughed motivates the young laborer to move to another industry or another part of the country. Laborers change jobs less often as they get older. Older laborers build up a high level of assets that constrain their willingness to leave for another job, even if wages were to be higher, or to leave a community if laid off. Their seniority in employment reduces their chances of layoff and increases the likelihood that they will be rehired when the employer's business picks up. When unemployed, they have well-established networks of family and friends on whom to call if they need emergency income or other kinds of help. Social science researchers also found that friends provide most information about new jobs, so an older worker would be reluctant to leave an area where a coterie of friends provided the greatest likelihood of learning about new jobs. Level of material assets increases with age. Older workers are more likely to be buying their homes or automobiles that make them reluctant to leave a job or migrate to another area. Parnes cites a study of Saint Paul workers in 1941–1942, in which home ownership restrained workers' desire to move more strongly than any other variable. Interviewers of New Haven manual workers found that home owners required promises of greater wage increases than renters to leave a current job.[16]

The Social Science Research Council measured the extent to which New Deal policies affected labor mobility. Researchers expected to find that work relief programs, unemployment compensation, social security, and survivors' benefits, for instance, increased labor mobility by releasing workers from direct dependence on employers. While surveys did find that governmental programs generally encouraged mobility, they did not do so greatly. By far the greatest impact came indirectly through governmental stimulation of economic prosperity. Laborers who changed a job voluntarily, including a geographic move, did so in response to job opportunity. Business activity and economic prosperity created job opportunities. Since federal governmental stimulus during World War II and in the welfare state after 1945 directly affected the general economic prosperity, social science researchers believe that national governmental policies had the greatest positive influence on labor mobility. Researchers concluded, albeit tentatively, that during times of economic prosperity, desire for higher wages and general economic improvement primarily stimulated voluntary job changes and migration in pursuit of a new job. Laborers perceived steadiness of employment to be a major element of "general economic improvement." A second, large, indirect effect of governmental policies concerned governmental support for home ownership. Governmental policies shifted the nation from renting to home owning. By encouraging laborers to own their homes, the government restrained their willingness to migrate in response to labor opportunity, as the Saint Paul survey demonstrated.[17]

A final characteristic of labor mobility is important. Researchers found that when laborers changed jobs, the greatest percentage of them also made as many other changes as possible at the same time: they changed jobs, changed employers, and changed industries. In other words, when laborers changed jobs in the 1940s, they were likely also to change other major home and work arrangements. These studies do not indicate whether laborers changed residence as part of changing their work life, but our study of residential mobility makes it likely they did so. The extremely brief residential tenures for renters, who made the majority of job changes (accounting for three-fourths of job changes in the study of Saint Paul workers in 1941–1942), make it probable that change of residence came within a few months of a job change. We found that nearly 40 percent of renters who changed their level of electrical consumption did so in the first decile of their residence. This finding reinforces the association between job change and changing residence. Since laborers made most voluntary job changes to better wages or to increase steadiness of employment, most of them experienced an improvement in their income because of changing jobs. They probably spent that increased income in improving their standard of electrical living when setting up a new home.[18]

Social science survey research about labor mobility in the 1940s reveals the manner in which federal government policies shifted laborers from a wage strategy to an asset strategy that previously only the bourgeoisie enjoyed. One major governmental policy, home ownership, powerfully affected wage earners' lifestyles. Besides constraining mobility, home ownership tied the wage earner to federal policies supporting electrical modernization of the home. Buying the panoply of electrical appliances for the home further reduced labor mobility by increasing material assets. As the home ownership rate increased after 1945, the nation's mobility rate declined. The impact of home ownership on mobility was not a unique phenomenon but indicated the general shift of the nation's labor force to greater asset accumulation to lessen their dependence on wage income.

In conclusion, Riverside's high rate of residential mobility before 1945 was an environment, not a structural variable. The wage labor system created this environment by compelling wage laborers to move frequently to secure their wage income. They did not restrain their accumulation of material goods because they had a low income, but to minimize interference with their capability to move often. The radio may have facilitated moving by providing information about job opportunities. The automobile assisted a wage strategy. Automobiles increased wage laborers' geographic mobility to find jobs. In contrast, the refrigerator restricted wage mobility. Wage laborers would resist buying it until they were able to pursue an asset strategy. Refrigerators provided the first demonstration of the benefit of building electrical assets into the home. Refrigerators had been the key to reorganization of the kitchen, the central recommendation of the rational housekeeping movement and a central component of the New Deal vision of social modernization. Refrigerators generated cost savings through long-term storage of food, buying in bulk, and retarding spoilage. Storage of food reduced market shopping trips and decreased household dependence on street peddlers, who were disappearing in a decade increasingly suspicious of strangers. A wider inventory of fresh foods increased the household's ability to prepare healthy meals. Households that moved frequently would not have had the time to accumulate enough cost savings through use of a refrigerator to repay the cost of buying and owning one. Economists' studies of the cost savings of mechanical refrigeration reinforce this notion that households needed long-term tenure to accumulate savings from mechanical refrigerators. A home economists' study cited in a 1935 article in *Electrical Merchandising,* for instance, assumed that the families owning the refrigerators lived at least a year in the same home to generate cost savings.[19]

Riverside's ethnic minorities lived in one place for a long time to increase their asset security. Segregation partly dictated their choice of an asset security strategy. Anglo racism all over California restricted the wage labor market for Riverside's African-Americans and Mexican-Americans. They could not automatically assume that they would get better jobs working elsewhere in California. Discrimination restricted them to the bottom of the labor hierarchy and the lowest wages everywhere in the state. Once they had found an occupational niche in Riverside providing long-term dependable wage income (even if at seasonal employment), they would maximize their overall economic security by concentrating on building assets. Home ownership would be desirable for several reasons. Residential segregation restricted the rental housing market for minorities to one or two neighborhoods. They would therefore obtain maximum security of shelter by owning. Segregation sharply reduced the supply of high-quality rental housing, so they could improve the material quality of their homes mainly by owning and improving the dwelling in which they lived, though over-crowding made this difficult. Parents would maximize the livelihood security of their children by buying a home with the expectation of passing it on to their children, thereby guaranteeing them shelter.

In a city like Riverside with many small businesses, where hiring would be done by the business owner, building up personal ties with owners constituted asset building for Riverside's minorities. Orchard crew foremen and packing house managers, for instance, maintained a local core of employees for year-round work in the groves and for the long packing season. Seasonal migrant la-borers supplemented, but did not displace, core labor. Citrus agriculture's labor strategy required a small core of resident minority laborers to break strikes by unionized migratory pickers. Ethnic minority families similarly built up networks with local kin and close friends on whom they could call for support in emer-gencies. In a racially closed labor market like Riverside's, the ethnic neighbor-hoods would have a sizable core of long-term residents who occupied all the available small business and labor niches permitted by local segregation. By the early 1920s, for instance, Riverside's small African-American middle class owned small businesses that served the community itself. Without a significant increase in minority population, they had little opportunity to increase the num-ber of these businesses. Occupancy of these niches maximized the returns from long-term residency. Only households living in the community for a long time could accumulate assets requiring personal knowledge, such as a strong credit rating, community leadership, and working relationships with Anglo leaders. Home buying, often through a mortgage with a white-owned bank, required the confidence of white creditors built on a long-term relationship. An asset strat-egy therefore explains the high incidence of home ownership and long-term home tenure among Riverside's poor minority households.

Progressive policies for domestic electrical modernization distinguished be-tween wage security and asset security. Influenced by the rational housekeeping movement, progressives perceived domestic electrical modernization as a form of asset building bringing social modernization. From their point of view, the overwhelming majority of American households in the 1920s did not have the electrical technology that could significantly improve their health, comfort, and domestic moral life. Some electrical technology, such as the refrigerator, could increase cash flow by cutting down expenses. Enhancing family health and com-fort increased the capability of a family to earn an income outside the home. As David Lilienthal observed in the 1930s, higher assets, including housing qual-ity, increased the opportunity for social contact and living life on a higher moral plane. Progressives therefore approached social modernization from the point of view of building asset security, rather than wage security. This strategy obviously did not mean that they viewed wage security as unimportant, since their New

Deal sought to enhance wage income security through work relief programs, the National Industrial Recovery Act, National Labor Relations Act, and Fair Labor Standards Act. But New Deal programs built modernization, in the sense of raising American families to a high quality of living, on domestic electrical modernization. Owning the home one lived in represented the major asset for modernization. The New Deal approached electrical modernization through the policy of shifting households from renting to owning. This approach not only grew out of the traditional home ownership ideology but also drew on the observation that resident-owner homes were materially better than renters' homes, even when renters were at the same occupational and income level as owners.

The timing and diffusion of domestic electrical modernization in Riverside's neighborhoods show the distinction between asset and wage strategies. We expect households pursuing an asset strategy to obtain electrical modernization first in the 1920s, then households pursuing a wage strategy should obtain electrical modernization in the 1930s, as the New Deal moved them to an asset strategy. Riverside statistics on owner-renter proportionality in refrigerator use imply this sequence (see table 6.5). From 1926 to 1935, owner-resident households of professionals and the business class led the adoption of the refrigerator. Here we see that income level did not automatically bring adoption. Professionals and business families who rented homes presumably had sufficient income to buy refrigerators, but the great majority chose not to use them. Upper-class households who rented their homes largely followed a wage strategy. They may have been saving with the intention of eventually shifting to an asset strategy, which would include home ownership. They must have assumed that the refrigerator did not produce a sufficient stream of savings in a rental dwelling or that it would encumber moving. In 1936–1940, when the nation adopted mass refrigeration, both renters and owners adopted refrigerators, though it took renters five years to achieve the level of refrigerator ownership of home owners. The New Deal lowered the cost of refrigerators so much that they produced real savings, even for renters who had to move them around frequently. The Social Security Act provided an asset-based strategy for the nation's laboring classes. Other New Deal legislation also had this effect. Policy makers intended the National Housing Act and the diverse programs that sponsored mass adoption of domestic electric appliances to provide asset-based security. The refrigerator and other heavy appliances were part of this broad shift in the last half of the 1930s. Congressionally mandated renter eligibility for Title I loans to purchase appliances is more evidence of the legislators' desire to move renters to an asset strategy.[20]

Conclusion

In the booming 1920s, Riverside reflected the nation's social stratification, racial segregation, and unequal distribution of income and wealth. Power utilities and electrical manufacturers of the private electrical industry accepted the nation's fragmented society and segmented economy as the framework for marketing domestic electrical appliances, pitching their products to the households in the top quintile of the nation's income—white, upper-class, home owning professional and business families. Private enterprise did not try to develop a mass market for the new labor-saving technology that industrialists, politicians, and social commentators alike called the century's most important advance in home economy. Bourgeois elites used their political clout to bring cheap electricity to industry, rather than homes. As a consequence, in the 1920s, domestic electrical appliances were luxury gadgets, not everyday technology. Their potentially revolutionary effects in the home were unfulfilled, in telling contrast to the automobile, whose mass adoption in the 1920s dramatically changed the social and economic fabric of the nation. The control of housing by the local bourgeoisie reinforced the effects of the nation's unequal distribution of income and wealth. Lack of affordable homes to buy and lack of rental housing forced most households into inadequate houses. Segregation reduced the stock of quality dwellings even further for people of color. The combined effects of these national and local forces meant that housing quality for many Americans deteriorated in the 1920s.

Riverside's home electricity meter readings have given us the opportunity to study the role of electrical technology in this social system of the 1920s and to see its transformation in the following decades. The shift to an electricity-intensive style of life began in the late 1920s with the mass adoption of the radio, not a decade earlier after World War I. The radio created the mass domestic market for higher electrical consumption. Expensive to buy and expensive to use, the radio doubled home electricity consumption and could easily increase consumption more. Within five years, 1928–1932, the majority of Riverside's and the nation's homes made the jump to a new electrical style of domestic life created by the radio. Only the homes of manual laborers and racial and ethnic minorities did not benefit from the radio before 1933. Significantly, highly advertised electrical labor-saving technology of the 1920s did not convince households of the value of a high-energy new style of life.

Private industry made its first sustained effort to create a mass market for domestic electrical appliances in the depression. Deprived of industrial and commercial markets for their products, they turned to households as the remaining opportunity for sales. Despite the drop in appliance prices, private industry did not broaden the market for domestic appliances much beyond their primary market in the 1920s. The shift to a true mass market in domestic electrical appliances came between 1935 and 1940. The refrigerator led the way. Excepting minority households of the labor class, who remained trapped in local racism, American consumers broadly adopted the refrigerator as a labor-saving and home-economizing technology. As earlier with the adoption of the radio, once consumers became convinced that the device offered a significant benefit, they willingly leaped to a qualitatively higher consumption of electricity. The mass adoption of the refrigerator caused a shift of home lifestyle that involved more than simply frugality and cost savings. For the mass of Americans, it involved transforming home food management and meal preparation. It brought new attitudes toward home, reinforcing the historic shift to home owning and slowing residential mobility. It also required technological improvement in the wiring and electrical service of the dwelling, which the federal government promoted through the National Housing Act and other programs.

Labor-saving appliances took on new meaning in the depression. The progressive political tradition developed and sponsored a policy of domestic electrical modernization as a means to social modernization. Progressive politicians conceived of domestic technology as instruments to free individuals, rather than to conserve social status. With Franklin Roosevelt's election in 1932 and five years of New Deal legislation, the federal government reframed and restructured the national market, subsidized consumerism and home owning, and brought to the white middle and labor classes the quality of life progressives defined as electrically modern. Once the privilege only of the upper class, the federal government diffused the material benefits of modern technology to the mass of white households as a matter—in FDR's words—of right. After World War II, a change in the nation's racial philosophy permitted the nation's households of color to obtain the same benefits.

Appendix

Table 6.1.   Consumption Floors for Standards of Electrical Living, 1921–1950

Standard of Electrical Living	Electrified	[Radio Transition]	Standard Modern	Fully Modernized
Device configuration	Lights & iron	House-current radio	Electrical refrigerator	Electric range or water heater
Consumption floor in kwh/mo.	11.4	23.5	45.5	168.7

SOURCE: Tobey, "Statistical Supplement."
Appliance adoption cumulates in kwh/mo. from left to right.

*Table 6.2.   Radio Adoption by Neighborhood Class, Riverside, 1926–1950
(excluding Groves)*

Neighborhood Class	Percentage of Households Owning Radio				
	1926-1930	1931-1935	1936-1940	1941-1945	1946-1950
Upper	54.1	79.5	93.6	96.3	96.3
Middle	43.6	69.8	81.9	90.7	94.9
Labor*	37.4	47.9	66.6	79.7	93.8
Labor/nonwhite	27.3	31.3	50.7	71.7	94.7

SOURCE: Riverside Sample Data.
*Labor neighborhoods including nonwhite.
Probability: o.o.

Table 6.3. Radio Adoption by Occupation, Owners and Renters, Riverside, 1926–1945

Occupational Group	Percentage of Households Owning Radio			
	1926-1930	1931-1935	1936-1940	1941-1945
Professionals				
Owners	66.6	94.5	98.3	98.8
Renters	60.0	81.1	94.7	94.8
Citrus farmers, business proprietors, dealers				
Owners	58.9	82.8	95.3	98.4
Renters	55.2	84.7	84.5	94.2
Clerks, salesmen, office managers				
Owners	56.9	75.0	91.1	98.3
Renters	49.4	76.8	87.4	96.2
Skilled craftsmen, industrial foremen				
Owners	45.1	76.5	87.9	92.0
Renters	45.2	70.8	91.7	91.8
Semi-skilled workers, drivers				
Owners	47.4	76.4	89.4	90.0
Renters	46.1	65.5	91.6	93.2
Unskilled laborers				
Owners	22.7	32.9	58.5	82.2
Renters	47.3	47.7	68.6	80.2

SOURCE: Riverside Sample Data.

Probability: 0.0

Table 6.4.   Refrigerator Adoption by Neighborhood Class, Riverside, 1921–1950
             (excluding Groves)

Neighborhood Class	Percentage of Households Owning Refrigerator					
	1921-1925	1926-1930	1931-1935	1936-1940	1941-1945	1946-1950
Upper	1.2	10.9	37.8	77.3	88.6	92.1
Middle	0.0	3.9	18.1	52.4	75.3	87.3
Labor*	0.0	1.4	7.7	32.0	52.8	75.8
Labor/nonwhite	0.0	1.6	4.0	12.7	36.1	69.4

SOURCE: Riverside Sample Data.
* Labor neighborhoods including nonwhite.
Probability: 0.00.

Table 6.5.   Refrigerator Adoption by Occupation, Owners and Renters, Riverside,
             1926–1950

Occupational Group	Percentage of Households Owning Refrigerators				
	1926-1930	1931-1935	1936-1940	1941-1945	1946-1950
Professionals					
Owners	26.7	54.1	88.1	96.5	92.9
Renters	2.9	29.7	64.3	81.6	97.4
Citrus farmers, business proprietors, dealers					
Owners	17.3	44.9	80.9	91.4	91.9
Renters	6.3	29.1	63.1	83.7	90.1
Clerks, salesmen, office managers					
Owners	8.3	26.3	75.8	91.4	94.3
Renters	1.2	23.1	66.0	83.2	86.6
Skilled craftsmen, industrial foremen					
Owners	0.0	18.5	64.5	81.9	90.0
Renters	1.2	12.4	48.8	76.3	85.9
Semi-skilled workers, drivers					
Owners	0.00	17.7	53.2	70.0	88.9
Renters	3.2	16.1	63.2	75.7	83.5
Unskilled laborers					
Owners	1.9	6.3	18.3	58.9	85.6
Renters	5.6	6.9	31.4	50.6	76.0

SOURCE: Riverside Sample Data.
Probability: 0.00.

Table 6.6.   *Residential Survival Time by Neighborhoods, Riverside, 1921–1950*

	Median Survival Time in Years			
Neighborhood	Lights and Iron	Radio	Refrigerator	Range or Water Heater
Mile Square	0.64	0.72	0.91	3.22
Old East Side	0.97	0.83	1.70	4.0*
North East Side	0.64	0.72	1.43	2.42
South East Side	0.72	0.71	1.21	5.0*
Expansion	0.71	0.81	1.54	2.93
Country Club	0.69	2.00	1.93	3.30
Wood Streets	0.70	0.85	1.85	2.89
Casa Blanca	1.39	1.08	3.86	4.0*
Arlington	0.77	0.78	1.27	4.19
Groves	0.75	0.81	2.23	2.85
Tract	0.72	0.87	1.97	3.20

SOURCE: Riverside Sample Data.

* Survival times indicate too few cases to calculate. For example, there was only one case of a Casa Blanca resident with a range and water heater.

Probability: 0.01.

Table 6.7.   *Residential Survival Time by Consumption Floors, Riverside, 1921–1950*

Consumption Floor	Cumulative Proportion surviving 1 Year (%)	Cumulative Proportion Surviving 2 Years (%)	Median Survival Time (yr)
Lights and iron	30.5	15.9	0.72
Radio	35.7	16.2	0.78
Refrigerator	58.6	41.6	1.51
Range or water heater	75.2	60.1	3.14

SOURCE: Riverside Sample Data.

Probability: 0.00.

Table 6.8.   *Residential Survival Time by Occupational Groups, Riverside, 1921–1950*

| | Median Survival Time in Years | | | | | |
Consumption Floor	Professionals	Citrus growers, proprietors, dealers	Clerks, salesmen, assistant managers	Skilled craftsmen, industrial foremen	Semi-skilled workers	Unskilled workers, laborers, servants
Lights and iron	0.98	0.97	0.84	1.01	0.72	1.37
Radio	1.05	1.32	0.89	1.04	0.90	1.05
Refrigerator	2.62	3.02	2.11	3.27	1.37	2.63
Range or water water	5.80	6.34	5.53	4.71	1.54	4.68

SOURCE: Riverside Sample Data.
Probability: 0.00.

Table 6.9.   *Residential Tenure by Tenure Status, Occupation, and Neighborhood*

Tenure Status	Residential Tenure (mo.)
owners	59.1
renters	15.2
significance	.000
N	8,774

Occupation	Residential Tenure (mo.)
High white collar	61.8
Low white collar	38.0
Skilled	41.1
Semi-skilled	26.3
Unskilled	42.4
significance	.000
N	4,189

Table 6.9.   (continued)

Neighborhood	Residential Tenure (mo.)
Mile Square	23.5
Old East Side	37.8
New East Side	28.6
South East Side	28.0
Expansion	32.8
Country Club	54.2
Wood Streets	38.0
Casa Blanca	56.8
Arlington	27.2
Groves	36.9
Tract	35.4
significance	.000
N	8,702

SOURCE: Riverside Sample Data.

Figure 6.1.   Annual Monthly Mean, Household Electricity Consumption, 1921–1950

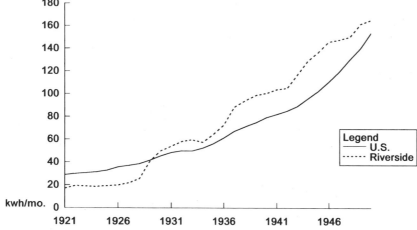

SOURCE: U.S. average monthly mean, household: series 108, residential service—
Annual use per customer (kwh), and 109, Percentage of dwelling units with electric
service—All dwellings. Bureau of the Census, *Historical Statistics of the United States*
(1976), 1:827.

Figure 6.2.   Riverside Consumption Levels, 1921–1950

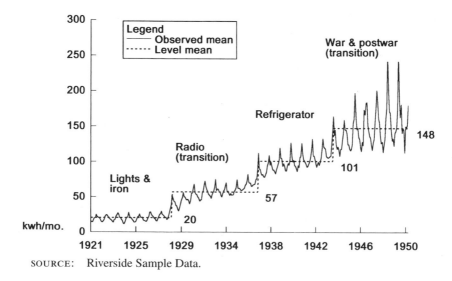

SOURCE: Riverside Sample Data.

Figure 6.3.   Electrical Consumption, Individual Dwellings, Riverside, 1921–1950

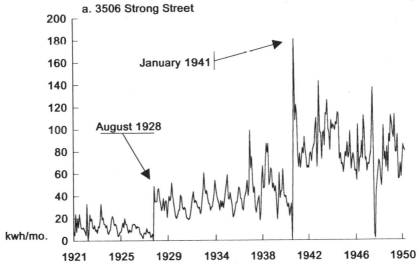

SOURCE: Riverside Sample Data.

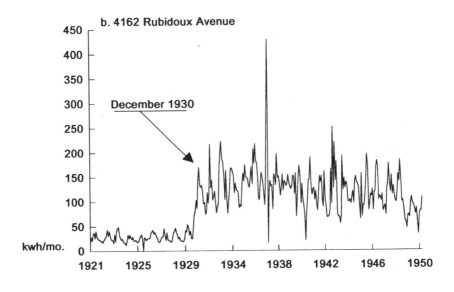

Figure 6.3.   (continued)

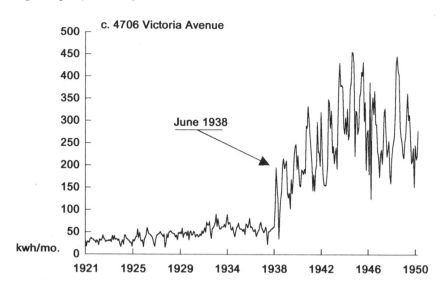

a. *3506 Strong Street*

Six households occupied this single-family dwelling. E. J. Swartout vacated the house in 1921, succeeded by J. P. Miller, who lived in the house until 1929. In city directories for 1923, 1925, and 1927, Miller identified himself as a fruit grower, as associated with Dean and Miller Auto Repair, and as a mechanic. It is likely that this property had a small citrus orchard, the care of which Miller contracted to a packing house. In 1929, P. W. Greenleaf made his home here through 1943. Minnie B. Greenleaf, probably his widow, next occupied the house. Miller and the Greenleafs owned their home. P. W. Greenleaf identified himself as a construction superintendent and an employee of a power company in eight city directories between 1929 and 1939. In 1943, Dale Von Riper, occupation unknown, rented the house. In 1948, its final resident, a secretary, Mrs. E. Ellen Showes, rented the dwelling.

b. *4162 Rubidoux Avenue*

Four households lived in this single-family residence. G. E. Degerholm lived in the house from 1921 to 1936 as owner. He identified himself variously as a draftsperson, civil engineer, surgeon, architect, and musician. The next two residents rented the dwelling. Lt. H. G. Montgomery, a member of the "U.S. military," lived in the house in 1936 and 1937, and W. A. Leonard lived in the house from 1937 to 1939. In 1939, the dwelling was sold to its last resident, W. S. Lay, who identified himself as an auditor and lived there during the 1940s.

c. *4706 Victoria Avenue*

Three households owned this single-family dwelling. Mrs. W. E. Clark lived in the house for fifteen years, from 1921 to 1936; H. N. Stearns lived eleven years in the house, from 1936 to 1947; and Joseph P. Wood, who identified himself as a driver and working in construction, lived in the house from 1947 to 1951.

Figure 6.4. *Neighborhood Average Residential Monthly Electrical Consumption,*
1921–1950

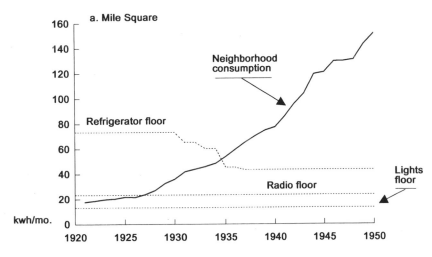

SOURCE: Riverside Sample Data.

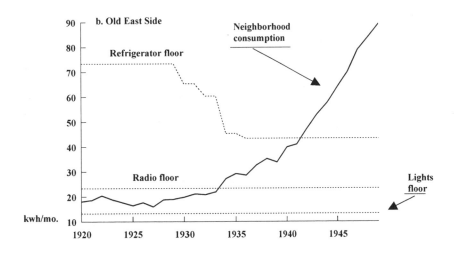

Figure 6.4.   *(continued)*

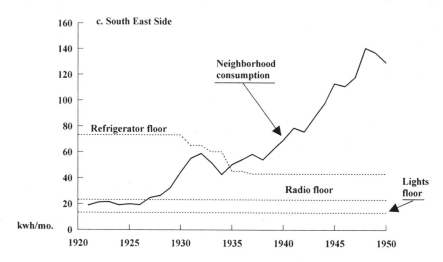

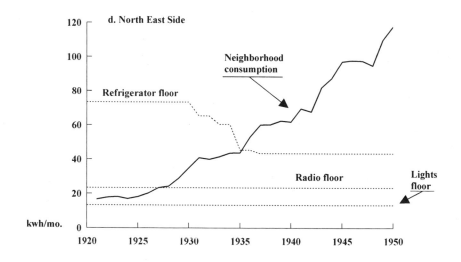

Figure 6.4. (continued)

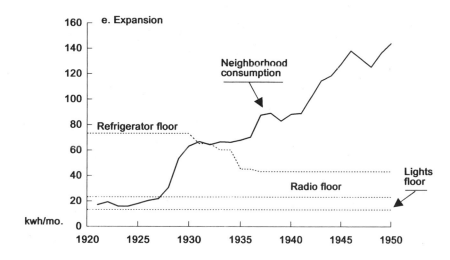

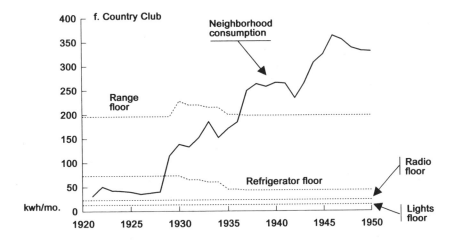

Figure 6.4.   (continued)

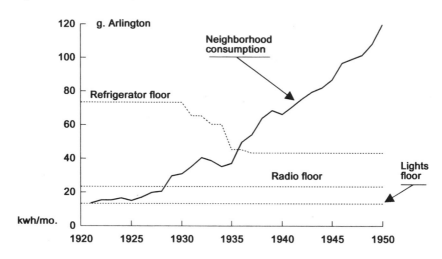

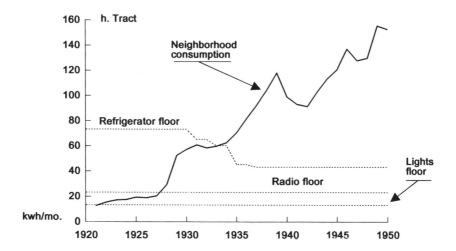

Figure 6.4.   *(continued)*

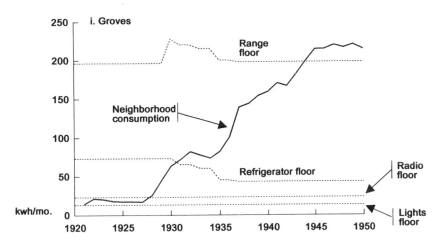

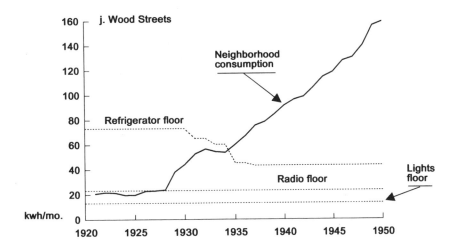

Figure 6.4. (continued)

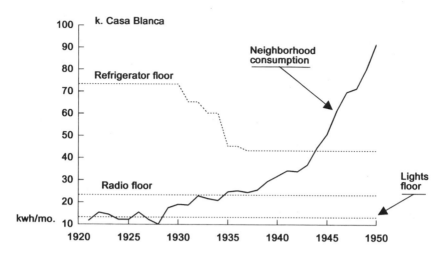

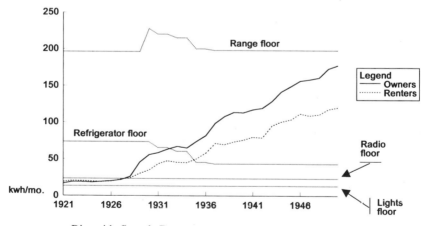

Figure 6.5. Average Monthly Electrical Consumption, Owners and Renters, 1921–1950

SOURCE: Riverside Sample Data.

Figure 6.6. *Cumulative Proportion Persisting,*
Country Club + Casa Blanca vs. Mile Square

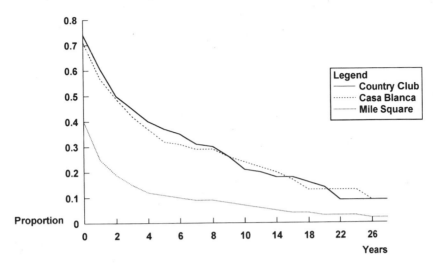

SOURCE: Riverside Sample Data.

Chapter 7
The Culmination of the New Deal in Electrical Modernization, 1945–1960

History's Armillary Sphere

President Harry Truman shared Franklin Roosevelt's vision of housing modernization as social justice. Electrical modernization would be the means to modernize housing in the Fair Deal programs of 1948. Truman added his presidential commitment to racial modernization, extending the New Deal's promise of social and material justice for the American people to the nation's racial minorities. For households of color around the nation, as for African-American and Mexican households in Riverside, improvement in the material comfort and health of their homes stood at the center of concentric spheres of historic context, like a medieval armillary sphere illustrating the earth-centered Ptolemaic cosmology. The *primum mobile* was the Second World War. The war accelerated the emigration of the African-American people out of the South that had begun before the First World War. The war created the great armament manufactories; African-American workers and their families moved to cities in the North and the West to take the new employment opportunities. Assigned by military service to new regions of the country, many African-American men brought their families to new homes after the war, and the African-American population in southern California dramatically increased. After growing slowly to 881 persons in 1940, Riverside's African-American community doubled to 1,600 persons in 1945, then grew more slowly to 1,805 persons in 1950, before again doubling to 3,938 persons in 1960. Similarly rapid increases in other cities made African-American voters a significant influence in the national political parties by 1944.

In America's voluntaristic society, the number of neighborhood organizations is the true gauge of community conscience. By this measure, the war years in Riverside brought profound change. The National Association for the Advancement of Colored People (NAACP) remained central, the African-American churches and their committees foundational, but expanding consciousness expressed itself in new or newly invigorated groups— the Women's Uplifting Club, the Negro Civic League, the Women's Political Study Group, the Lincoln Park Recreation Center Hospitality Group, the Los Angeles Urban League, the USO Traveler's Aid Society, the Cosmopolitan Club, and the annual war bond solicitation committees and air raid district committees. Each group signified repeated meetings, discourse, and politicking; each group conducted membership drives and fund raising and arranged programs, speakers, and special events. Each group socialized another individual's consciousness, forging another link in the chain of social causality from national events to the daily life of every person, and turning another wheel in the great armillary sphere of history by which the dramatic events of world war geared down to neighborhoods and households in Riverside's minority communities and to racial minority neighborhoods and households like Riverside's across the nation.[1]

The organized drive to end segregation that erupted during the Second World War provided the second armillary sphere of changing historical context. Pressed by the Congress of Industrial Organizations' Political Action Committee and national reform organizations, such as the NAACP, the leadership of organized labor began to desegregate their labor unions. The national political parties in the North and West courted African-American urban voters. Although African-American voters traditionally allied with the Republican party—an allegiance to Lincoln—significant numbers of them moved to the Democratic party. FDR's third reelection in 1944 demonstrated their political power. The shift enabled Truman to break the deadlock on racial progress held by Southern white Democratic voters. The breakthrough came in the 1948 presidential election. Liberals fought successfully to get a plank endorsing civil rights and opposing discrimination in the Democratic party platform. Dixie Democrats followed Gov. Strom Thurmond of South Carolina out of the Democratic party to form the States' Rights Democratic party. Four Southern states failed to vote for Truman; yet Truman squeaked out an electoral victory over Republican candidate Thomas Dewey.[2]

Housing crises comprised the third sphere. The nation built little new housing after 1931 and virtually no nondefense housing after 1941. Where defense industries and military bases swelled population, as in Riverside, severe housing shortages resulted. In the major industrial cities of the Midwest and California, racial restrictions compelled African-American immigrants to live in previously established "black belts." Wartime workers crowded into Chicago's South Side, Los Angeles's Central Avenue district, and Detroit's Paradise Alley. Similar ghettos burgeoned in Buffalo, Cincinnati, Cleveland, Dayton, Toledo, Portland, Philadelphia, Pittsburgh, and Oakland. Only Chicago and New

York City made strong political efforts during the war to increase the public housing for African-American defense workers. Federal policies exacerbated the
housing shortage for nonwhite persons. When the Office of Price Administration
froze rents in defense areas, as in Riverside, Robert Weaver pointed out, "the
Negro lost his most effective tool for entering new areas. Since rents were fixed,
he could not legally buy his way into white areas by paying higher prices." Federally subsidized public housing, intended to house defense workers, initially
discriminated against African-Americans. Detroit built 44,000 housing units for
war workers between 1941 and 1944, when over 60,000 African-Americans had
moved into the city to work in the defense plants; but the city opened only 3,070
units to them. Because of FHA reluctance to push for housing for African-
Americans, of all private priority housing permitted in defense areas during the
war, landlords allocated only 4.3 percent for African-Americans.[3]

War's end returned veterans to marriages and children, but did not bring nearly
enough new dwellings to shelter all the new households. The housing shortage
and its accompanying political crisis lasted through 1950 and provided the context in which minority Americans at last fulfilled the New Deal's promise of social justice through housing modernization. The National Housing Act of 1934
and veterans housing programs created a huge market for the home building industry and unleashed mass tract home building. Public housing programs
brought urban renewal and public housing to most of America's cities. The civil
rights movement sought to desegregate America's housing. In the late 1940s,
liberals finally defeated housing segregation in legislation, in the courts, and in
federal policy. For minority citizens, these wheeling contexts of change finally
brought electrical modernization, the standard of living, and the quality of life
to which Franklin Delano Roosevelt said a decade earlier all Americans had a
right.[4]

The Storm Breaks

The implosion of housing segregation in the United States after 1948 occurred
because local property owners lost their constitutional authority and much of
their direct, local governmental power to maintain the local social order against
federal civil rights. To extend the New Deal's promise of home modernization
and social modernization to racial minorities, racial custom—as Riverside
illustrates—had to change. Watching the reorganization of real estate and succession of federal housing programs after 1932, Riverside's Anglo elite understood that the New Deal inverted the political ontology of the nation's historic
freeholder society. The potential of the 1930s became the reality of the 1940s.
Administrative elites began to use the new power of the federal government in
regulating and insuring real estate, housing, and banking to modernize social
policy. Federal bureaucracies interposed themselves between local white elites
and discriminated minorities. Public hearing requirements gave minorities
voice and influence in community dialogues in which they had not previously

participated. For local Anglo elites, the urban world they had known seemed out of control. Change began almost immediately after Roosevelt's death. Harry Truman's appointees ended Federal Housing Administration support for real estate racial covenants. Then Truman changed the federal government's position on African-American civil rights. As a first specific step, Truman moved the federal government against racial housing covenants. Finally, in his Fair Deal, Truman sought to increase significantly the federal government's commitment to public housing. These presidential initiatives extended the New Deal promise in housing. Believing strongly in the constitutional equality of all citizens and appealing to African-American voters for electoral success, Truman made the first presidential commitment to racial justice and integration in the nation's history.[5]

The Federal Housing Administration's overt support for racial discrimination changed first. At its inception, the FHA linked housing modernization to racial segregation. To obtain FHA insurance for a dwelling or subdivision, a builder had to meet criteria to reduce the risk that the market value of the property would decline during the period of the mortgage. The FHA underwriters' manual repeatedly pointed to racial change in a neighborhood as one of the most serious threats to property values. "If a neighborhood is to retain stability, it is necessary that properties shall continue to be occupied by the same social and racial classes. A change in social or racial occupancy generally contributes to instability and a decline in values." The FHA required racial restrictions on deeds to supplement zoning protection of property. Since the nation already consigned minorities of color to its worst housing, the FHA's requirement for segregation of new residences effectively locked minorities out of decent housing. The federal program that sought to modernize the nation's dwellings thereby imposed a barrier preventing African-Americans and other racial minorities from participating in federal home modernization programs. To obtain dwelling modernization, minorities had first to modernize their civil rights.[6]

During the war, the NAACP tried to open housing in Northern industrial cities for African-American workers by breaking down racial covenants. The organization lobbied district FHA offices protesting discrimination and segregation. It prevailed on FHA directors to increase the assignment of priority housing to African-Americans. In 1944, the FHA also agreed to nondiscrimination in employment on FHA and Federal Public Housing projects, issuing administrative regulations to this effect. By the end of the war, African-Americans participated in nearly all public housing projects.[7]

Truman built on the progress made during the war in changing FHA practices. He appointed Raymond M. Foley to be its commissioner in July 1945, and subsequently its administrator. In fall 1946, guided by the president's clear desire to modernize racial practices, Foley instructed all FHA personnel to take an active interest in the housing problems of minorities. He distributed a packet of special agency publications, "Material for F.H.A. Offices on Minority Group Housing," to assist field personnel. He assigned racial advisers to attend all regional meetings conducted by the FHA for the building and real estate industry to speed construction of housing for veterans. In 1947, at the same time that the civil rights commission studied segregation around the nation, Foley ordered rewriting of the FHA's *Underwriting Manual* to remove FHA support for private racial covenants. The FHA continued to stress the desirability of homogeneous neighborhoods, but the agency now shifted its criterion to income, rather than racial, homogeneity. Implementation of nondiscrimination varied by locality, as it had during the war. In Los Angeles in 1946, for instance, local FHA officials stalled and weakened a Hollywood film union's application for financing for a biracial cooperative housing project, so that it eventually failed. Only in early 1948 did the FHA for the first time approve insurance for a biracial housing project (in Chicago).[8]

Truman deplored the renewal of white violence against African-Americans that broke out around the nation after the war. Lobbied by the NAACP, in 1946 he appointed the Committee on Civil Rights, chaired by Charles E. Wilson, chairman of General Electric, to review the nation's racial relations. The committee report, *To Secure These Rights,* in October 1947 called for the end of segregation and suggested forty federal actions to secure that goal. The report pointed to substandard housing as the prevalent condition among the nation's African-American urban minority and identified racially restrictive covenants as the reason African-American families could not move to better housing. "One of the most common practices is the policy of landlords and real estate agents to prevent Negroes from renting outside of designated areas. Again, it is 'good business' to develop exclusive 'restricted' suburban developments which are barred to all but white gentiles." The report cited Chicago, Cleveland, Washington, D.C., and Los Angeles for the large extent of their residential areas restricted to whites only. Investigators estimated that property owners of 80 percent of Chicago's residential property prohibited African-American residents. The committee invoked the Roosevelt heritage as one of the bases for federal action to end inadequate housing: "the right to housing." The committee also invoked the recent experience of war. American society should not deny returning African-American veterans the same housing open to white veterans, which they—along with white soldiers—had fought to protect. The committee specifically recommended that the federal government enter civil rights cases that sought to end the restrictive real estate covenant.[9]

Following the committee's recommendation, the Truman administration supported African-American plaintiffs in the housing discrimination suits, later known collectively as *Shelley v. Kraemer,* that the U.S. Supreme Court agreed to hear in June 1947. Thurgood Marshall and Charles Houston, lawyers for the NAACP, wrote the briefs against racially restrictive real estate covenants for presentation to the Court. Other integration advocates approached U.S. Attorney General Tom Clark to request that the federal government support the plaintiffs by filing an amicus brief. A week after release of the Civil Rights Committee report, Clark, whom Truman appointed after requesting that FDR's attorney general resign, agreed. The U.S. government for the first time entered a civil rights case involving only civil litigants. The federal attorneys argued that decent housing was a basic necessity of life and a fundamental right, equal opportunity to which the Fourteenth Amendment protected as a civil right. "Both Presidents Roosevelt and Truman have spoken of 'the right to a decent home' as part of 'a second Bill of Rights', and of the basic rights which every citizen in a truly democratic society must possess." Racially restrictive covenants denied African-Americans the opportunity to participate in social modernization through housing modernization. Indeed, by compelling African-Americans to live in overcrowded ghettos, the covenants imposed social disintegration, social pathology, and personal ill health on them. The legal brief addressed the modernization issue directly, in language that resonated with Franklin Roosevelt's vision of the meaning of the materially abundant life:

> [Racially restrictive covenants] are responsible for the creation of isolated areas in which overcrowded racial minorities are confined, and in which living conditions are steadily worsened. The avenues of escape are being narrowed and reduced. As to the people so trapped, there is no life in the accepted sense of the word; liberty is a mockery, and the right to pursue happiness a phrase without meaning, empty of hope and reality. This situation cannot be reconciled with the spirit of mutual tolerance and respect for the dignity and rights of the individual which give vitality to our democratic way of life.

Since the war, new housing developments had begun to provide modern housing for veterans and to solve the nation's housing shortage for white Americans. Racially restrictive covenants prohibited African-Americans and other minorities (the brief also cited Hispanic, Native American, Pacific Islanders, Arabic, and Jewish peoples) from having access to modern housing and thereby from participating in the new standard of living made possible by electrical modernization.[10]

In its brief in *Shelley v. Kraemer,* the NAACP mounted two large arguments against state enforcement of racially restrictive real estate covenants. The legal argument rested on the Fourteenth Amendment's guarantee to all citizens, regardless of color, of equal protection of the law. The amendment prohibited states from enforcing private contracts that denied equal treatment on the basis of race. The social argument claimed that housing discrimination prevented the social modernization of African-American households that white households took for granted. Robert Weaver's *The Negro Ghetto* stated the social thesis and provided empirical information for the social and economic brief submitted to the Court. The NAACP claimed first that restrictive covenants had kept the African-American population boxed in historic ghettos in major cities. The housing in these ghettos represented the antiquated housing stock abandoned by white households. Landlords cut these dwellings into smaller and smaller apartments, until many families were living in single rooms without private toilets or kitchens. In a word, restrictive covenants confined African-Americans to severely substandard and overcrowded housing. Population growth in the

African-American ghettos occurred at the same time that the federal government engaged in extensive home improvement programs and began public housing and defense housing for white households. Since the FHA supported restrictive covenants and the federal Public Housing Administration practiced discrimination, the federal government policy abetted widespread local policy in creating two categories of urban housing—homes being modernized under Federal programs for white households and substandard housing largely outside those programs for African-Americans (and Mexicans, as in Riverside).[11]

The war brought many changes to African-Americans. The major positive change, Weaver argued, was the first glimpse for many of the possibility of a new way of life. Leaving rural lives of poverty behind, migrating to thriving and energetic Northern industrial cities, they foresaw the possibility of decent housing, healthful neighborhoods, and possession of a wide range of consumer goods. Weaver did not use the exact phrase that Franklin Roosevelt used in his 1936 campaign for reelection, but he meant exactly what Roosevelt had meant. Roosevelt said the New Deal was all about "the abundant way of life." Restrictive covenants, supported by federal housing policy, denied the "American ideal of a high standard of living" that Roosevelt said the nation owed every American.[12]

In May 1948, Roosevelt's liberalized Supreme Court struck down state enforcement of private racially restrictive covenants. Without state enforcement, restrictions were useless. Private property, as lawyers are fond of pointing out, is a bundle of *enforceable* rights. After *Shelley v. Kraemer,* home owners and neighborhood associations could not obtain state enforcement of racial restriction on the sale of homes. The decision forced the FHA to complete rewriting of its administrative rules and put the federal bureaucracy behind social modernization of minority American homes. Responding to political pressure to implement *Shelley v. Kraemer,* the FHA adopted a new eligibility rule requiring applicants to establish that home owners filed no racial covenant on the subject property after the implementation date of the new eligibility rule.[13]

The Supreme Court's decision in *Shelley v. Kraemer* took practical effect immediately. President Truman's efforts to obtain a large national public housing program reinforced the Court's decision in bringing the issue of minority housing modernization to all levels of politics. No one could miss the connection between advancement of minority civil rights, housing issues, and social modernization. Liberals unsuccessfully attempted to insert antisegregation clauses into the 1948 and 1949 housing acts. Truman placed extension of civil rights and public assistance for housing at the center of his 1948 campaign for reelection. After his close victory over Thomas Dewey, the president proposed major civil rights and housing bills to Congress in early 1949 as part of his Fair Deal. When Truman signed the National Housing Act in July 1949, the national storm over racial integration of neighborhoods broke with full force. In this situation—a liberal presidential administration pressing for housing and social modernization from the top of the governmental hierarchy and minority organizations, such as the NAACP, pressing for modernization at the local level—

Riversiders debated whether to allow federal public housing projects in the city. Earlier, the city rezoned a large portion of the city for apartments, recognizing that minority citizens would rent them.[14]

Immediately upon passage of the National Housing Act in summer 1949, civic liberals in Riverside city called for public housing. Administrators of the County Housing Authority responded by starting the planning and review process. Since 1915, progressive civic groups had worried about the substandard dwellings occupied by immigrant Mexicans and African-Americans in Old East Side. In 1948, a group of social workers and volunteers conducted a housing survey of Old East Side, examining mainly the nonwhite blocks. The survey revealed dilapidation of overcrowded houses, lack of indoor plumbing, and failure of physical shelter. There was no question of approaching the electrical standard of living. In response, the executive director of the Riverside County Housing Authority applied for 765 new housing units for the city of Riverside under the 1949 National Housing Act.[15]

Federal public housing raised three issues related to control: (1) federal power intruded directly into the local community; (2) the federal housing bureaucracy challenged the power of the local private real estate and housing industry and public housing diminished the rental income of the local bourgeoisie; (3) federal housing threatened the local white community with unwelcome racial values. The issue of the intrusion of federal power appeared as different themes. Procedurally, the act required local housing authorities to hold public hearings on proposed public housing. Though meeting constitutional requirements for municipal control over real property, the public hearings ironically opened a forum for new local voices to be heard, besides those of the white civic-commercial elite. In 1922, demonstrating Anglo imperiousness during a desegregation controversy over a public swimming pool, Riverside park commissioners left a public meeting rather than listen to African-American petitioners. "'The members walked out, leaving us sitting here like a row of checkers,'" one petitioner described. Federal presence prohibited such arrogant abrogation of local minority rights at postwar public housing hearings. Federal housing officials spoke in support of minority housing rights. Local officials and local Anglo citizens listened to minority community speakers.[16]

Administratively, the federal housing programs broke old political arrangements by forcing creation of new governmental institutions and rearranging local elite coalitions. The City of Riverside did not have its own housing authority, for instance, and local administration of a federal housing program would be in the hands of the county government. The city's real estate industry did not have the same political clout with the County Board of Supervisors and its agencies, as it did in the city. Riverside County established its housing authority in 1942 to administer federally funded defense housing, which included several large developments to serve nearby military bases. Neither the City of Riverside nor the county took advantage of the short-lived 1937 Wagner Housing Act, which required establishment of local housing agencies to receive and manage the federal dollars for subsidized low-rent housing. When the county created its housing agency, the Riverside City Council legislated that its authority could extend inside the city, since lack of defense housing caused many of the city's housing problems also. California voters turned down a statewide initiative for state-funded public housing in November 1948—clearly indicating their opposition to public housing. The 1949 National Housing Act created a different scale and permanence of federal presence. If the federal government fully funded the Riverside County Housing Authority's application, over $10 million would be spent inside the city. Once again, rather than establish the city's own housing agency, the city council contracted with the County Housing Authority for administration of federally funded public housing. The city's realtors moved to have the city establish its own housing agency. They organized themselves as the Riverside Rental and Property Owners' Association, clearly identifying retention of private rental property as a major goal. During the course of the controversy, the local chapter of the Building Contractors' Association and the Real Estate Board joined the coalition seeking a city housing authority. Though the realtors political squeeze did not succeed, it pressed the bile of controversy through nearly every other local issue involving contracting, siting, building, and letting federal public housing and extended to related issues such as removing rent controls and regulating citrus growers' smudging.[17]

The second issue concerned the relative roles of the private housing market and the federal government in construction and control of the local dwelling stock. The real estate industry and some members of the local business and civic communities strongly believed that the private marketplace could and should determine housing stock and quality. They did not enjoy their experience with direct federal regulation of housing during the war. They pointed to the revival of housing construction in California in late 1948 as evidence that private capital could solve the housing problem, including providing adequate housing for lower income groups, except for the poorest families who could not afford mortgages. They saw the 1948 presidential contest between President Truman and Governor Dewey of New York as a referendum on "the issue of the New Deal." As southern California lurched conservatively into the epoch of the "red scare," they began to call government housing "socialism." Their major concerns leading to opposition to public housing had less to do with government ownership, however, than with what the government as owner might do with its property.[18]

The third issue concerned federal imposition of progressive racial values on local communities. The increasing legislative successes of the Truman administration's Fair Deal, President Truman's commitment to racial fairness, organized labor's effort to integrate the nation's unions and workplaces, and the U.S. Supreme Court's decision in *Shelley v. Kraemer* threatened the private property-based system of racial segregation in Riverside, in California, and elsewhere in the nation. Truman sought a civil rights provision in the 1949 refunding of the Federal Housing Administration. Though Congress struck out the provision, national progressive forces had declared their intentions. They wanted to use the administrative power of the national government to end residential racial segregation.

The centrality of the racial issue to the local housing issue is clear. Realty groups' opposition to housing integration remained unflagging. White social reformers occupied an ambiguous position. They favored social relief and housing reform in Old East Side, and they called for public housing, but they did not visibly lobby to locate integrated public housing in all-white neighborhoods. Other organizations supporting public housing included the Riverside Council of Church Women (with a special action committee, the Christian Social Relations Committee), the officers of the board of directors of the YWCA, the Latin-American Club, the Casa Blanca American Legion Post 838, the Eastside Neighborhood Council, the Riverside Ministerial Association, and the Central Labor Council of Riverside County of the American Federation of Labor.[19]

White Riversiders expressed racial fears when discussing tenant characteristics and site selection for public housing projects. Opponents of public housing disliked subsidization of lower-income tenants. Federal housing officials estimated that housing would cost about $10,000 per unit but would rent for no more than $25 a month. In addition, though the federal government would pay 10 percent of shelter rent in lieu of taxes to the city, public housing would not directly and fully pay for the municipal services it used, such as street improvements, schools, water, and fire protection. Public hearings in December 1949 brought the opposing factions together for a vociferous debate. Supporters argued that public housing improved the lives of tenants, thereby decreasing crime and indirect welfare costs; in terms of social accounting, the balance sheet of cost and benefit evened out. For them, the issue was clear. Americans of color had earned their right to a quality standard of living by fighting in the war. The federal government owed them enforcement of this right. Joseph Park, representing the Mexican community's Casa Blanca American Legion post, put it plainly: "'We carried a heavy burden during the war, and we can do it again. . . . There's been talk about the City taking care of housing by itself, but there's been talk before, and nothing has been done. This is our chance. We not going to sit by for 20 years. We going to do our utmost to get a share of it.'" John Sotelo, speaking for the Mexican and African-American East Side, erupted emotionally at a hearing: "'You people who are against the program, get hold of me. I'll take you to places there to be cleaned up. Just look at them and see if you don't think something should be done.'" Resentment seeped through civic dialogue about imputed subsidization. At a city council hearing, an opponent complained, "'These $10,000 homes are going to rent for $20 a month. Why rent a mansion for $20 a month and make the rest of us pay for it?' The opponents of the housing program applauded loudly." At a meeting of the city's Optimist Club, the regional director of federal housing defended public housing against the charge that "'Mexicans and Negroes up out of this slum class'" would destroy the better housing provided by the government.[20] (See pl. 9.)

The possibility that the federal government might site public housing proj-

Plate 9.   *The Promise of the New Deal for the Nation's Minority Families—
Electrically Modern Public Housing.* (Leonard Nadel, photographer. "L.A.—
Residences—Housing Projects—Aliso Village. The Louis Gillen family after
relocation into their new three-bedroom apartment [for $35/mo.] at Aliso Village."
Security Pacific National Bank Photograph Collection. Los Angeles Public Library.)

ects near white neighborhoods angered white Riverside opponents most of all.
So many persons lived crowded together in several blocks of Riverside's Old
East Side, federal agencies could not rehouse all of them in the same area after
they erected new buildings. The realtors' association coordinating the opposition campaign focused on the siting issue. It called for housing improvement
programs that kept slum residents in place while landlords improved their properties. At a meeting called by the association, a prominent realtor addressed the
audience with the explosive charge, "'You may have a housing project next to
where you live. How would you like that?'" The Riverside *Daily Press* later ed-
itorialized about the issue in less volatile, but nonetheless direct, language: "Public housing can change the character of a community."[21]

Local opposition protracted the housing approval process so that Riverside
did not get public housing until after the Korean War. Cities with blue-collar
voting strength, such as nearby San Bernardino, quickly received public housing contracts. Riverside realtors pushed a local initiative that would require voter
approval for siting public housing. Legal tacticians in the city maneuvered around

them, but the realtors then led a successful statewide initiative to achieve the same goal. Passage of the statewide initiative in 1950 pointedly measured white Californians' opposition to disruption of their community arrangements. Riverside realty interests led the statewide initiative (the president of the state building contractors' association was a Riversider who also led local opposition to public housing). The outbreak of the Korean War forced the Truman administration to shift its housing programs from public housing to defense housing. The public housing controversy briefly died down.[22]

The defeat of public housing left unresolved the issue of housing modernization for Riverside African-American and Mexican-American households. Riverside's private housing market boomed following the war. High prices for the new dwellings closed out for most of Old East Side's better-off residents the option of exercising their rights under *Shelley v. Kraemer* by buying new homes in white neighborhoods. In 1949, a few white property owners in neighborhoods bordering the Eastside began to move out, presumably in anticipation of integration and impending changes in the area. In these circumstances, the city's civic leaders decided to rezone a large neighborhood just north of the Eastside district. Rezoning from a uniform single-family home district to an apartment zone would greatly enlarge the stock of better rental dwellings to the Eastside's residents. In arguing for the rezoning, Henry Coil, a member of the commission, predicted, "The area seemed to be headed away from first-class residential development." The planning commission "should plan ahead of the tendency by recommending a wholesale rezoning instead of waiting for individual owners to request the zoning on their own." Only one of 162 property owners in the area protested the proposed rezoning.[23]

Within a few years of the rezoning in 1949, the racial and ethnic composition of the district began to shift. Although we lack racial identifications needed to track the migration of African-American residents by name, by February 1950 Longfellow Elementary School in the newly rezoned neighborhood enrolled 51 African-American children, 60 Mexican-American children, and 438 Anglo children. Presumably, the presence of these minority children in the school represented the movement of families into newly opened rental homes. We can observe the shift in Mexican-American residents by the appearance in the district of Spanish surnames. In 1947, of 213 households (listed in the city directory) in a small study area in North East Side, only two had Spanish surnames. In 1960, of 277 households, fourteen had Spanish surnames. In 1969, of 312 households, twenty-eight had Spanish surnames. In 1965, half of Longfellow's students were minorities, about evenly divided between African-American and Mexican-American children. The racial integration of North East Side did not take place overnight; it required a decade. Most settled white residents did not flee in panic. Residential integration would not be unopposed in Riverside or elsewhere in the nation. Local planning boards, the real estate industry, and white home owners had an arsenal of legal and nonlegal techniques to resist integration, including covertly antiracial zoning for design and health requirements, state constitutional mandates for local option voting, redlining, neighborhood pressure on sellers, white flight, and violence. Nonetheless, *Shelley v. Kraemer* shifted the burden of racial residential segregation in a manner that strengthened its foes. The decision deprived local white communities of their main positive tool for racial planning, forcing them into defensive strategies. In 1948, Riverside and many other communities began to walk the long gauntlet of racial animosity toward residential modernization.[24]

The Culmination of the New Deal

Harry Truman's Fair Deal brought civil rights to the nation's housing through the New Deal national housing agencies and policies. Truman also continued Roosevelt's public power policies. Though a hostile Eightieth Congress forced him to curtail his support for replicating the TVA in other river basins around the nation, Truman never backed off from his views that America needed public power to ensure cheap electricity and that modern housing required cheap electricity. In the name of New Deal, the national government under Truman began to modernize the local American social order. By making home buying as cheap as renting, the New Deal rapidly shifted the nation from renting to owning. Because of the New Deal's creation of a national market for electrical goods and because of innovative private marketing strategies, such as the "completed home plan," domestic electrical modernization accompanied the shift to home buying. Economists long ago observed the relationship between home ownership and adoption of electrical appliances. Carolyn Bell, a consumer economist, noted in 1967 that "consumer spending for appliances accelerated only after the major shift from renting to home ownership took place, for housekeeping arrangements reflect patterns of housing." We can now appreciate that housekeeping arrangements did not reflect patterns of housing by coincidence. Electric housekeeping reflected home ownership because New Deal and Fair Deal policy intended it to do so.[25]

The opening of housing opportunity for African-Americans and other minority groups after 1948 brought dramatic improvement in their living conditions. Between 1950 and 1960, the proportion of nonwhite families living in substandard housing declined by half. The urban home ownership rate for non-white households rose from 20 percent in 1940 to 33 percent in 1950 and 36 percent in 1960. The rise in the home owning rate does not by itself prove that nonwhite households improved their living conditions. Unlike the general situation of white families, where the rise of the home owning rate roughly signals an improvement in living conditions, the restrictions placed on nonwhite families before 1948 often meant that there was an inadequate rental market for them and that to have any housing at all they had to buy. That the median value of nonwhite-owned homes in 1950 ($3,000) was less than half that of white-owned homes ($7,700) supports—though not unambiguously—the thesis that lack of rental opportunities, not a desire for home owning, forced up nonwhite

Plate 10.   *The Promise of the New Deal for the Nation's Minority Families—*
Electrically Modern Private Homes. ([Amateur photographer.] "Picture of home
on Stanford near El Segundo and Avalon, called Carver Manor in 1945." Snapshot
donated in the "Shades of L.A." project, 1994/1995. Security Pacific National Bank
Photograph Collection. Los Angeles Public Library.)

home owning rates. As the Housing and Home Finance Agency noted in a review of the 1940s, regarding the housing problems of nonwhite households, "It
is especially difficult for nonwhites to acquire living quarters during periods of
general housing shortage because of prevailing restrictions upon their occupancy
as well as their relatively lower incomes." The removal of housing restrictions
after 1948 enlarged the opportunities for nonwhite families to live in better-
quality dwellings, whether as renters or as owners. The doubling of the percentage of home owning nonwhite households in standard-quality dwellings between 1950 and 1960 also indicates that the increase was not due simply to public
housing.[26] (See pl. 10.)

The New Deal's policies for electrical modernization of the home completed
their social revolution in the 1950s. After removal of the Second World War's
national restraints on construction and rent controls in 1946, the nation entered
a decade of unparalleled home building. In 1950, the agency insured 36 percent
and the VA insured another 15 percent, that is, over half of all new private housing financing. Federal building codes required that new homes be built at the
electrical standard. Rural electrification, urban rehabilitation, and urban renewal
brought many older dwellings up to the New Deal's electrical standard. By the
mid-1950s, an overwhelming majority of America's urban, suburban, rural, and
farm households used electrical technology and lived socially modernized lives.

At the same time, the percentage of all households possessing major electrical appliances (with the exception of the range) reached a ceiling and the growth rate in saturation leveled off. In just over twenty years, the nation had transformed the material fabric of its home life. In 1933, the electrical standard divided the nation's housing into two classes. One-fifth of the households benefited from the prosperity of the 1920s and lived in modern housing; four-fifths of the nation's households did not receive a proportionate share of the decade's wealth and lived in antiquated housing without electrical modernization. In 1955, over three-fourths of households lived in electrically modernized homes, while less than one-fourth remained in substandard dwellings. This inversion of the national statistics on distribution of wealth from 1933 to 1955 reveals the scope of the New Deal's ongoing revolution. Shifting ownership of the nation's housing stock to those who had previously been tenants constituted a vast redistribution of the nation's wealth.[27]

The nation at last made the celebrated social portrait of prosperous home life true for most Americans. Home ownership enabled accumulation of wealth. Although home "ownership" meant home buying for most households, the home mortgage nonetheless gave many of the benefits of fee simple ownership. It secured and enlarged the credit available to families. Credit provided financial flexibility for coping with the exigencies of capitalism's economic cycles. Home ownership eventually anchored the asset strategy life plan for three of four American families. Home ownership also brought higher-quality homes. Electricity enabled households to live in physically and socially detached dwellings with control over their own utilities. Refrigerators, electric washing machines, and small electric wares powered the productive activities of kitchen, cleaning, and home renovation. Recreation in the home, whether playing, reading, listening, or watching, also benefited from electrical devices. Social patterns whose mosaic is recognizable as a "style of life" distinctively reflected the capabilities of domestic electricity. Small machines enabled individualization and privacy in the home. Electrification of the home environment promoted bodily health through safer storage and preparation of fresh foods, environmental health from uniform warmth and air conditioning, and greater personal sanitation through private bathing and bodily hygiene. Greater wealth and health provided the means by which Americans could fulfill their individual talents and dreams. Electrical modernization gave Americans effective freedom.

In the 1950s, two decades of New Deal programs converged and fulfilled themselves. The REA and the TVA brought electricity to nearly every rural dwelling. The FHA and the VA, directly and through their stimulus to private lenders, extended home ownership, modernized existing homes, and placed new housing starts at the level of the electrical standard. The TVA demonstrated the possibility of a national mass market for electrical goods. Federal demonstration of the value of and subsidization of cheap consumer credit made possible purchase of electrical appliances for nearly all households. In 1940, the electric iron was the only electrical appliance owned by more than half of all American households; by 1950, half of all homes possessed the refrigerator, vacuum cleaner, and clothes washer; by 1960, most homes had the full range of electrical devices, now including, of course, the television.[28]

The Invisibility of the Revolution

Some revolutions are visible. The great national revolutions that wrenched colonial and autocratic states into modernity—the American Revolution, the French Revolution, the Bolshevik Revolution—are models of swift political change to which we apply the word *revolution.* Revolutions can also be invisible. Swift social and economic changes that leave political institutions nominally intact while they dramatically redistribute political power and wealth are also revolutionary. Such social and economic revolution is invisible, because preservation of political institutions pastes a patina of continuity over public life. News and public gossip endlessly stream through familiar channels and swirl around familiar rocks of institutional drama, without recognition that the material and social lives of the citizenry have fundamentally changed.[29]

The New Deal in domestic electrical modernization worked an invisible revolution. The New Deal shifted the majority of American families to an asset strategy for economic security through state-enframed home ownership of electrically modern dwellings. Geographic mobility declined. Unrestrained domination of local politics by a locally resident real estate elite ended. Material accumulation based in the owner-occupied home created unprecedented material affluence. The dwellings modernized their occupants, as households rebuilt their social and labor relations around new technologies. Minority groups previously locked out of affluence gained the keys to their future. The New Deal created the 1950s.

The role of the New Deal rapidly faded in popular consciousness in the 1950s. How could consumers notice less the visible hand of the state than the invisible hand of the marketplace? Although New Deal relief programs ended in the year before U.S. entry into the war, federal price and production controls, restraint on consumer spending, and execution of the war effort kept the national government in front of all eyes. The war certainly did not push the hand of the state behind the scenes. Four other events played the important roles in normalizing the New Deal. Two of them developed before the war: the court-packing controversy of 1937 and acceptance of the lessons of the TVA and the REA by private enterprise between 1935 and 1939. Two events played themselves out following the war: the moderation of labor-capital conflict and the democratization of material abundance.

The political controversy over Roosevelt's court-packing scheme of 1937 drew attention away from the New Deal's revolution in local property. Riverside illustrates how the controversy suspended the bourgeoisie's pragmatic acceptance of the New Deal, compelling them to recast their opinions about the New Deal in terms of moralistic and legalistic constitutional principles. Critics argued that if Roosevelt succeeded in packing the Supreme Court, a Rooseveltian majority would not block expansion of presidential power. Legislative intrusion into property relations could proceed unchecked. By stating opposition to the court-packing plan in terms of constitutional absolutes, critics obscured from themselves the New Deal's practical intrusion into local property capitalism accomplished through indirect restructuring and underwriting of the nation's real estate and home industries. Blinded by the exploding political fireworks of the court-packing controversy, Roosevelt's local critics could not see the gnomes of the New Deal quietly rebuilding the nation's political economy under their feet. Riverside's white civic leaders called public meetings, remonstrated in civic clubs, argued in the columns of the newspapers. The Riverside *Daily Press* interviewed civic leaders to obtain their opinion. They feared that if the Court lost independence, there would be no check to executive power. Eugene Best, Riverside city attorney, hinted at a subversive president: "'The proposal is plainly an effort to control the courts, and dictate their decision by one admittedly not friendly to the court or our Constitution.'" Local opponents invoked the purest Lockean philosophy of property as the source and basis for government. Francis Cuttle, a regionally prominent water administrator, saw capitalism attacked: "'Capitalists are still legal owners of their property, but apparently they have no control over their income.'" The local newspapers sponsored a reader referendum approving or disapproving Roosevelt's scheme as part of a national ballot on the plan organized by the National Editorial Association. Riverside's newspaper readers disapproved Roosevelt's plan by 993 votes against 55 in favor. In similar polls, Los Angeles voters favored the court scheme by 2 to 1. The defeat of Roosevelt's court-packing bill ended the controversy and—apparently— saved the Supreme Court as the last line of defense against executive aggrandizement and legislative erosion of property rights. This misimpression obscured the manner in which New Deal programs, such as the National Housing Act, diminished the rights of private property ownership in favor of governmental regulation even though they were not at issue in the controversy.[30]

The second factor normalizing the New Deal was the muting of antagonism between the powerful electrical utility and manufacturing industries and the federal government on key issues of governmental activity. By the late 1930s, private enterprise had accepted the public power thesis behind the TVA and the REA. The New Deal created a truly mass consumer market. Behind the loud outrage over the earlier "court packing," private corporations quietly accepted the new economic framework and planned to prosper in it.[31]

Subsiding industrial conflict between labor and management, as a third factor, normalized the New Deal. For laborers, the Wagner Act's legalization of collective bargaining for industrial unions partially achieved the New Deal goal of distributive justice. While laborers did not gain control of the workplace, collective bargaining enabled industrial labor to obtain a greater share of the wealth generated by private industry in the postwar boom. The Taft-Hartley Act of 1947 also blunted labor militancy. The federal government could enter into the labor-capital bargaining process to compel strikers to return to work, thereby defusing protracted conflict and keeping key industries, such as coal and steel, up and running. The subsidence in the 1950s of the ferocious class antagonisms between labor and capital that had alarmed the nation from the 1870s to the 1930s naturally brought a concomitant diminution of the New Deal's direct presence in the everyday lives of unionized laborers.[32]

The extraordinary material abundance brought within reach of nearly every American household after 1947, as a fourth factor, normalized the New Deal. Material abundance lessened differences between lifestyles of wage earners, salaried workers, and the wealthy. New Deal policies in social welfare, labor, and housing gave most wage-earning households enough assets for them to identify with the middle class, with whom their economic similarities became more obvious than their differences. Obtaining this abundance in the marketplace, consumers perceived their material affluence as resulting from the free enterprise system, rather than state-enframed capitalism. The extension of home ownership put American families' wealth on the same plane, a fact each perceived in daily life. Mass deprivation drove New Deal politics. When deprivation disappeared amid material affluence, the intensity of anyman's political identity lessened.[33]

The postwar state no less actively guided the national economy toward social ends than did the New Deal state of the 1930s. Active guidance only apparently disappeared, because the position of the state relative to the consumer had changed. The nature of the New Deal achievement disguised the postwar role of the state in the manufacture of commodities and in making material abundance possible. Guaranteeing the solvency of capital institutions put the national government behind the facade of the private banking and financial institutions with which the consumer and home owner dealt directly. By requiring dwellings to meet an electrically modern standard, the New Deal literally stood inside the dwellings Americans lived in, behind drywall with its private manufacturer's name printed on it, out of sight and out of mind. The consumer consumes pleasures and utilities. As long as goods pour from the cornucopia, the mixed economy of supply and demand need not concern her. Similarly, the government's new Keynesian role of underwriting prosperity by managing aggregate demand hid the government from the consuming household's direct view.[34]

When Democrats lost the presidency in the 1952 elections, they lost the enormous capability of the president, as a single symbolic voice, to represent the New Deal as a unified political vision. In the era of television and radio, mass broadcast media provided the means to determine the general impression voters had of national political issues. Democrats could not effectively contest Republican claims about the power of American capitalism. No one told consumers that the corporations producing the goods of mass abundance did not ultimately cause that abundance. Consumers mistook the mechanism of prosperity—the corporations—for its cause. Corporate advertising continued the 1920s' tradition of disinformation and ideological promotion of the private electrical utilities, giving the private sector credit for electrical modernization and social modernization in the home. Living in the house that the New Deal built, their consciousness in thrall to fashion, households saw only the furnishing and appliances that filled up their homes, but not the design and designers of it. They had historical amnesia.[35]

The New Deal strategy of hooking social modernization and electrical modernization to home ownership similarly disguised the role of the national government. The home buyer experiences home ownership as individual ownership obtained through a local lender, rather than as publicly enabled ownership. The role of home ownership is crucial here. The vast shift of the American households from renting to home owning generated prosperity after World War II. Home ownership even boosted the automobile industry, whose growth in turn contributed to the nation's prosperity. The New Deal's sponsorship of suburban home owning reinforced and diffused a dependence on the automobile that guaranteed the auto industry's growth.[36]

The New Deal did not end in the late 1930s. It transmuted from process to structure. It enframed the prosperity of the postwar era, out of sight like studding, like Romex, like plumbing, behind drywall. Before 1942, the New Deal constituted a group of programs, actively implemented in the midst of political controversy to achieve politically sponsored goals. After 1945, the New Deal constituted a framework of institutions within which private enterprises pursued profit in a way that achieved social goals. People did not see that the New Deal remained around them as the infrastructure of prosperity because the social phenomenology of mass perception had changed. Political consensus restructured what individuals and groups perceived in their political and social worlds. Consensus painted over social division and class difference. Before 1942, politics built the New Deal much as architects build a home. Consciousness of intent animates every step of creating the home, from envisioning the design to constructing the dwelling and moving in. In the early stages of construction, as carpenters define rooms and hallways with studding frame, the floor plan is evident to its future occupants when they walk around. The carpenter's chalk lines on the concrete slab, two-by-four wall plates gun-nailed to the concrete, armored electric wires tunneling through bare studding, the unattached plumbing pipes, and the grease pencil instructions and dimensions on window and door frame reveal the architect's mind. As carpenters finish the interior, fill wall frames with insulation and cover studs with drywall, hang doors and windows, sct floor boards and lay carpets, the floor plan disappears from view. Having moved in, residents experience spaces and functions. The social patterns of living inside the dwelling prevent them from perceiving the floor plan. The completion of the dwelling and moving in changes the phenomenology of the family living in it. After 1945, the New Deal was like a largely completed house. The floor plan guides the residents' social pattern, but they do not experience the floor plan by living in the home; they experience the home. Asked why they move about their home as they do, why they eat and sleep in the rooms they do, most households would answer in terms of their immediate intentions, not in terms of the floor plan. Building the home could no longer be their goal. Their minds would now be conscious of other goals and values. With what material objects to fill up their new home would certainly be central. The dwelling thereby silently transforms itself from process to structure, from conscious goal seeking to unconscious guidance. This transformation does not mean that the architectural design of the house ceased to exist. Similarly, the transformation of the New Deal from process to structure did not mean that it ceased to exist. Rather, the nation bracketed the New Deal outside the foreground of its experience.

After 1948, everyday material technology underwent a transformation paralleling the postwar normalization of the New Deal. As the New Deal ceased to be a political project, the world of objects it had previously sustained as technologies also normalized. Electric appliances became transparent and unproblematic. They disappeared into the anonymity of the domestic background, along with the ubiquitous telephone and radio. Consumers need think about them only in terms of immediate usefulness. The many considerations about electrical technologies that animated public debate in the 1920s and 1930s were no longer relevant. Consumers did not need to know that using a refrigerator would decrease the probability of food poisoning by retarding spoilage, or would improve the health of the family by increasing their consumption of fresh fruits, vegetables, and meats. Homemakers did not need to know that serving meals with a variety of nonseasonal foods made possible by refrigeration would enhance family togetherness as family members looked forward to meals. The consumer did not need to know that owning a refrigerator would pay for itself by generating a flow of savings, because she took fewer trips to the market. She did not need to know the physics and engineering that made a "refrigerator" work; she did not need to know how the components fit into the refrigerator's box; she did not need to know how to fix one if it broke. To buy one, she did not need special shopping expertise or vocabulary. She did not need to know the nearly endless succession of persons, from assembly line laborers to sales persons, whose hands touched the refrigerator. She did not have to know anything about any of the other electrical appliances she used, whether television, vacuum cleaner, air conditioner, or water heater. She did not have to engage in political activity to shop. She did not have to pressure legislatures to set commodity safety standards. She did not have to remonstrate with businessmen for the lack of stores carrying electrical appliances, or lobby utilities for reduction of electric rates, or convert other voters to the view that they had a right to an electrically modernized domestic life, a right other property owners could not deny by reason of skin color or religion or low income. With normalization of the New Deal, electrical modernization of the home became a personal environment in which electrical appliances were simply commodities.[37]

Social thinkers accept the transparency of household appliances as a natural consequence of wealth and abundance, as if ease of acquisition and familiarity made material objects invisible. The naturalness of "commodities" is part of the reason that the culture of the 1950s seems, sui generis, unconnected to the history of the New Deal. The history of the political creation of technology ought to caution us not to think that commodification of technology is a "natural" process. If politics made appliances into technology, we might suspect that politics makes technology into commodities. As the New Deal ceased to be a primary political project in the nation, the process by which household appliances were technologized reversed itself. As the mass of households achieved the New Deal standard of living, the technological status of appliances faded and the appliances became commodified. Normalization occurred, not because of the commonness of electrical technology or the affluence of households buying them, but because most households no longer acquired and used appliances within political projects.[38]

When appliances lapsed into the status of commodities, American culture came full circle in development of the domestic values of electricity. In the 1920s, private enterprise marketed electrical household appliances to a small percentage of the nation's households. In that social context, appliances were not technologies and their employment did not challenge the bourgeois values held by that social class. The depression brought into political power a statist-tending progressive political party that sought to democratize the material benefits of the electrical age. The New Deal redefined 1920s luxury commodities into the necessities of the many, from the material symbols of the upper class's conservative retention of an unequal social structure to the material instruments of mass freedom and material justice. As a political issue, the New Deal pointed to those luxuries as the material condition of freedom to which the mass of American households had a right. New Deal policies embedded electrical devices in a primary project shared by most Americans. The New Deal made electrical home appliances into technology. The fading of the New Deal as a project, ironically involving its transubstantiation into structure, stripped electrical household appliances of their technological status. Commodification of household technology worked reciprocally to normalize the New Deal. Situated in homes as commodities, appliances obtained meaning only through personal pleasure. Personalizing of objects thereby separated the private environment of the household from the anonymous public environment. Separation of the private and public environments distanced families from mass institutions of the public environment, thereby reinforcing the withdrawal of New Deal politics. Privatization of American life in suburbia in the 1950s appeared as the New Deal's mass politics declined.[39]

Notes

Introduction

1. "He dreamed" quoted from Sinclair Lewis, *Dodsworth* (New York: Modern Library, [1929] 1947), 21. "Decided that" quoted from p. 255 and "to us, diversity" quoted from p. 256 of Richard Nixon, *Six Crises* (New York: Simon & Schuster, [1962] 1990), 235–291; see also Elaine Tyler May, *Homeward Bound: American Families in the Cold War Era* (New York: Basic Books, 1988), 16–20.

2. "All those women" quoted from Ruth Schwartz Cowan, *More Work for Mother: The Ironies of Household Technology from the Open Hearth to the Microwave* (New York: Basic Books, 1983), 148; see also pp. 145–150. "For the most part" quoted from Harold L. Platt, *The Electric City: Energy and the Growth of the Chicago Area, 1880–1930* (Chicago: University of Chicago Press, 1991), 243. See also David E. Nye, *Electrifying America: Social Meanings of a New Technology, 1880–1940* (Cambridge: MIT Press, 1990), xiv, 16–18, 27; Thomas P. Hughes, *Networks of Power: Electrification in Western Society, 1880–1930* (Baltimore: Johns Hopkins University Press, 1983); Mark H. Rose, *Cities of Light and Heat: Domesticating Gas and Electricity in Urban America* (University Park: Pennsylvania State University Press, 1995).

3. See note 2. In the latest addition to this literature, Rose argues that private capital constructed local consumer environments of technology to expand their domestic market; the clear implication is that industry raised a veil between the private home and organized political debate (*Cities of Light and Heat,* 91–109).

4. On the paradox of mass consumption, see Daniel Horowitz, *The Morality of Spending: Attitudes toward the Consumer Society in America, 1875–1940* (Baltimore: Johns Hopkins University Press, 1985); Thomas Richards, *The Commodity Culture of Victorian England: Advertising and Spectacle 1851–1914* (Stanford: Stanford University Press, 1990); David M. Tucker, *The Decline of Thrift in America: Our Cultural Shift from Saving*

to Spending (New York: Praeger, 1991); and Rosalind H. Williams, *Dream Worlds: Mass Consumption in Late Nineteenth-Century France* (Berkeley, Los Angeles, and Oxford: University of California Press, 1982). Lizabeth Cohen, *Making a New Deal: Industrial Workers in Chicago, 1919–1939* (New York: Cambridge University Press, 1991), explains how ethnic values mediated mass consumption, pp. 99–158. Andrew R. Heinze, *Adapting to Abundance: Jewish Immigrants, Mass Consumption, and the Search for American Identity* (New York: Columbia University Press, 1990), describes a group project providing meaning through recontextualization of consumer goods. On social positioning, see Pierre Bourdieu, *Distinction: A Social Critique of the Judgment of Taste* (Cambridge: Harvard University Press, [1979] 1984); see also the discussion of Bourdieu in Daniel Miller, *Material Culture and Mass Consumption* (Oxford: Basil Blackwell, 1987).

5. "Consumerism" refers to commodity consumption as characterized by the paradox of commodity consumption and is distinguished from material consumption generally; see Richards, *The Commodity Culture,* 268 n. 26. Commodity consumption was socially constructed at the end of the nineteenth century; see Susan Strasser, *Satisfaction Guaranteed: The Making of the American Mass Market* (New York: Pantheon Books, 1989), 17–21, 26–28, 89–91, 286–290. See also her discussion of social and political movements by consumers, ibid., 52–85, and the notes, pp. 321–325. On mass marketing, see Richard S. Tedlow, *'New and Improved': The Story of Mass Marketing in America* (New York: Basic Books, 1990), which periodizes the history of marketing and then narrates struggles involving major corporations, such as Coca-Cola. Historians of technology view technology as a social construction, but they have not generally treated electoral political parties and consumers as significant direct participants in the process, except at the local level, the consumer's role being channeled through the marketplace. See Wiebe E. Bijker, Thomas P. Hughes, and Trevor J. Pinch, eds., *The Social Construction of Technological Systems: New Directions in the Sociology and History of Technology* (Cambridge: MIT Press, 1987), especially Trevor J. Pinch and Wiebe E. Bijker, "The Social Construction of Facts and Artifacts: Or How the Sociology of Science and the Sociology of Technology Might Benefit Each Other," pp. 18–50; see also C. E. Bose, Philip L. Bereano, and Mary Malloy, "Household Technology and the Social Construction of Housework," *Technology and Culture* 25 (1984): 53–82. Outstanding examples of the social construction of technology are Hughes, *Networks of Power;* Thomas P. Hughes, *American Genesis: A Century of Invention and Technological Enthusiasm, 1870–1970* (New York: Penguin Books, 1990); Nye, *Electrifying America;* Claude S. Fischer, *America Calling: A Social History of the Telephone to 1940* (Berkeley, Los Angeles, and Oxford: University of California Press, 1992); and Rose, *Cities of Light and Heat.* At the local level, the social construction of electrical systems involved politics when local commercial and civic elites utilized franchising powers to guide utilities toward their own class economic benefit. See Hughes, *Networks of Power,* chaps. 7–9 passim; Nye, *Electrifying America,* 138–184; Platt, *The Electric City,* passim; Rose, *Cities of Light and Heat,* esp. chaps. 1 and 2 on the city-growth game. These historians see mature utilities as evolving beyond effective local political control.

6. Platt, *The Electric City,* 235–236; Cowan, *More Work for Mother,* 192; Loren Baritz, *The Good Life: The Meaning of Success for the American Middle Class* (New York: Alfred A. Knopf, 1989), 71–85; Rose, *Cities of Light and Heat,* does not mention the New Deal and describes postwar modernization in terms of prewar electrification, pp. 171–188.

7. Cowan, *More Work for Mother,* 172–180; Nye, *Electrifying America,* 247–259, 279–283; Martha L. Olney, *Buy Now, Pay Later: Advertising, Credit, and Consumer*

Durables in the 1920s (Chapel Hill: University of North Carolina Press, 1991), 9–40; Joann Vanek, "Keeping Busy: Time Spent in Housework, United States, 1920–1970," *Scientific American* 231 (November 1974), 116–120.

8. "Few neighborhoods" quoted from Rose, *Cities of Light and Heat,* 9. General histories of household appliance technology are provided by Earl Lifshey, *The Housewares Story: A History of the American Housewares Industry* (Chicago: National Housewares Manufacturers Association, 1973); Sigfried Giedion, *Mechanization Takes Command* (New York: Oxford University Press, 1948); Louise J. Peet and Lenore Sater Thye, *Household Equipment,* 4th ed. (New York: John Wiley, 1955); Calvin C. Burwell and Blair G. Swezey, "The Home: Evolving Technologies for Satisfying Human Wants," pp. 249–270 in Sam H. Schurr, Calvin C. Burwell, Warren D. Devine, Jr., and Sidney Sonenblum, eds., *Electricity in the American Economy: Agents of Technological Progress,* published under the auspices of the Electric Power Research Institute (Westport, Conn.: Greenwood Press, 1990); Lewis Mumford, *Technics and Civilization* (New York: Harcourt, Brace & World, [1934] 1963). Historians' current interpretation of the history of the domestic refrigerator is dominated by Cowan, *More Work for Mother,* 128–145, and bibliography, pp. 228–229. Basic references include Oscar Edward Anderson, Jr., *Refrigeration in America: A History of a New Technology and Its Impact* (Princeton: Princeton University Press, 1953), esp. pp. 195–199, 207–223; Donald MacKenzie and Judith Wajcman, eds., *The Social Shaping of Technology: How the Refrigerator Got Its Hum* (Stratford: Open University Press, 1985); Platt, *The Electric City,* 220–223, 277–278; and Nye, *Electrifying America,* 275–276, 293, 356. Two older industry articles provide good background; see Dr. D. K. Tressler, "Home Freezers—Past, Present, and Future," *Electrical Merchandising* 72 (October 1944): 58 f.; and Tom F. Blackburn, "Time for Advancement," ibid., 65 (April 1941): 6 f., which reviews each major refrigerator manufacturer. For a microeconomic theory of refrigerator demand, showing that price per unit of service declined in the 1930s, see M. L. Burstein, "The Demand for Household Refrigeration in the United States," pp. 99–145 in Arnold C. Harberger, ed., *The Demand for Durable Goods* (Chicago: University of Chicago Press, 1960). Tanis Day confirms Burstein's thesis for Ontario, Canada, for the range, refrigerator, washer, and vacuum cleaner; see Day, "Capital-Labor Substitution in the Home," *Technology and Culture* 33 (April 1922): 320–321. On the history of stoves, ranges, and ovens, see Josephine Peirce, *Fire on the Hearth: The Evolution and Romance of the Heating Stove* (Springfield, Mass.: Pond-Ekberg, 1951); Lawrence Wright, *Home Fires Burning: The History of Domestic Heating and Cooking* (London: Routledge & Kegan Paul, 1964); and Jane Busch, "Cooking Competition: Technology on the Domestic Market in the 1930s," *Technology and Culture* 24 (April 1983): 222–245. On the history of the vacuum cleaner, see Frank G. Hoover, *Fabulous Dustpan: The Story of the Hoover Company* (Cleveland: World, 1955). On the history of the radio, see chapter 1, note 30. On the history of the clothes washing machine, see "Washers are Getting Better and Better," *Electrical Merchandising* 64 (November 1940): 6–15, 16–17.

9. The thesis that electrical technologies conservatively reinforced social values is argued by Giedion, *Mechanization Takes Command;* Gwendolyn Wright, *Building the Dream: A Social History of Housing in America* (New York: Pantheon Books, 1981); Cowan, *More Work for Mother;* Bose, Bereano, and Malloy, "Household Technology," 53–82; Fischer, *America Calling,* 260; Charles A. Thrall, "The Conservative Use of Modern Household Technology," *Technology and Culture* 23 (1982): 175–194; Jo Ann Vanek, "Household Technology and Social Status: Rising Living Standards, Status and Resi-

dence Differences in Housework," *Technology and Culture* 19 (1978): 361–375; and Vanek, "Keeping Busy." The notion that the electrification of American housing was culturally conservative is also widely held; see Giedion, *Mechanization Takes Command;* Wright, *Building the Dream;* and Kenneth T. Jackson, *Crabgrass Frontier: The Suburbanization of the United States* (New York: Oxford University Press, 1985). Industry biased its advertising toward the middle class and ignored the working class; see Elizabeth Sprenger and Pauline Webb, "Persuading the Housewife to Use Electricity? An Interpretation of Material in the Electricity Council Archives," *British Journal for the History of Science* 26 (March 1993): 63–64.

Chapter 1. Limits of Private Electrical Modernization, 1919–1929

1. Hughes, *Networks of Power,* 285–265, 369; "Distribution of Central Station Energy, 1920–1930," *Electrical World* 97 (January 3, 1931): 28; "Revenue of the Electric Light and Power Industry," ibid., 97 (January 3, 1931): 28. Nye believes utility resistance to the home market largely disappeared in the 1920s; see Nye, *Electrifying America,* 261; see also Platt, *The Electric City,* 235–245, 253–261; and Rose, *Cities of Light and Heat,* passim.

2. The statistic was provided by the president of the National Electric Light Association in an address in 1930 and cited in the editorial, "A Word of Warning," *Electrical World* 96 (September 13, 1930): 471.

3. See table AII.7.5, "Percentage Distribution of Energy and Electricity to Manufacturing and Nonresidential Use," in Sidney Sonenblum, Appendix II, "Basic Statistical Data: Long-Term Quantitative Trends," p. 426 in Sam H. Schurr et al., *Electricity,* Milton F. Searl, "The Growth of Electricity Consumption in Historical Perspective," pp. 342–343, in Schurr, *Electricity,* esp. pp. 343–346, figs. AI.2 and AI.3. For electrification of the factory, see Nye, *Electrifying America,* 184–237. For an economic examination of electrification of industrial power processes, see Schurr, *Electricity;* see especially the overviews by Warren D. Devine, Jr., "Electrified Mechanical Drive: The Historical Power Distribution Revolution," ibid., pp. 21–42, and Sidney Sonenblum, "Electrification and Productivity Growth in Manufacturing," ibid., pp. 277–423, which provides a four-stage history for the application and development of electricity in manufacturing production. Sonenblum's footnotes contain extensive citations to the historical literature. See also Sidney Sonenblum and Sam H. Schurr, "Electricity Use and Energy Conservation," ibid., pp. 325–339, where the rapidity of application of electricity to manufacturing in the 1920s is explained, from the manufacturing user's point of view, in terms of the increase of productivity and savings due to total energy conservation. The cost-revenue analysis of the residential customer is discussed in "The Residence Consumer—What He Costs and What He Is Worth," *Electrical World* 81 (June 2, 1923): 1269–1272. On connecting isolated stores to central stations in Chicago, see Platt, *The Electric City,* 101–103, 107–108.

4. "Outstanding Facts," *Electrical World* 103 (January 6, 1934): 16. In 1922, 80.3 percent of total customers were residential: "Business Facts for Electrical Men," ibid., 81 (January 13, 1923): 137. For other representative opinion of industrial versus residential electrical sales, see E. S. Hamblen, "Economic Value of Load Diversity," ibid., 78 (July 16, 1921): 110; "The Residence Consumer—What He Costs and What He Is Worth"; "Keeping Dollars at Work," ibid., 85 (March 28, 1925): 658–660; "An Industry Balance Sheet," ibid., 87 (May 8, 1926): 971–982. The ten-year projection was pro-

vided by Robert M. Davis, "Looking Ahead Ten Years," ibid., 83 (January 5, 1924): 17–24. Before World War I, the telephone industry similarly targeted the industry and business markets, leaving development of the residential market until the 1920s and 1930s; see Fischer, *America Calling*, 42–50.

5. "It would appear" quoted from Charles J. Russell (vice president, Philadelphia Electric Company), "Philadelphia Residence Studies," *Electrical World* 87 (May 8, 1926): 1004. "Actual demand" quoted from C. F. Lacombe (consulting engineer, New York), "The Competitive Market for Domestic Electric Service," ibid., 89 (May 28, 1927): 1140.

6. *Electrical World* estimated in 1929 that only 20 percent of private utility electric customers were capable of buying "complete electrical service"; see "This Domestic Business," ibid., 93 (May 25, 1929): 1033; "prospects" quoted from ibid., p. 1037. Market survey in Lacombe, "The Competitive Market," 1139–1147. On market segmentation, see ibid., 1140, and "Relation of Appliance Sales to Family Income," ibid., 86 (September 12, 1925): 523–524. On the basis of aggregate data, Platt believes that Chicago Edison successfully marketed to the suburban middle class, in addition to the "luxury" class, in the 1920s but does not know the share of total households comprised by these groups in order to test the utility's claims; see Platt, *The Electric City*, 240–252, esp. table 30, p. 251. On utility marketing, see Nye, *Electrifying America*, 262–287, and table 6.1, p. 268; and Rose, *Cities of Light and Heat*, 65–109, 112–146 on marketing to and educating upper-class consumers. Sicilia argues that Boston Edison targeted the home luxury market before World War I and afterward included the middle-class consumer but implies that the upscale bias continued in the 1920s; see David B. Sicilia, "Selling Power: Marketing and Monopoly at Boston Edison, 1886–1929" (Ph.D. dissertation, Brandeis University, 1991), 330, 373, 467–469, 486–489. Before the 1920s, phone companies similarly ignored lower-income households; see Fischer, *America Calling*, 108–109.

7. Fischer, *America Calling*, 75–80, 260; Lacombe, "The Competitive Market," 1139–1147. I found only one organized effort by the utility industry in the 1920s to understand housekeeping. In 1925, the National Electric Light Association cooperated with the General Federation of Women's Clubs to survey households for the home equipment they contained. See Mrs. John D. Sherman, president of the General Federation of Women's Clubs, "Home Making an Occupation," *Electrical World* 87 (May 22, 1926): 1124–1125. Sicilia's discussion of Boston Edison's innovative marketing strategies in the 1920s shows how far most companies, who did not follow Edison, had to go; see Sicilia, "Selling Power," 465–560.

8. "Almost a total" quoted from "The Residence Consumer—What He Costs and What He Is Worth," *Electrical World* 81 (June 2, 1923): 1269; Alex Dow, "Evolution of Rate Making," ibid., 84 (September 20, 1924): 629–631; Platt, *The Electric City*, 82–89, 98–99, 127–137, on the history of rate making and Samuel Insull's role. Platt's discussion of the role of gas utility rate setting, *The Electric City*, 127–130, helps explain the political dynamics in electrical rate setting. See also Forrest McDonald, *Insull* (Chicago: University of Chicago Press, 1962). Chandler emphasizes the role of accounting in enabling producers to enter mass production, but more research is needed to evaluate the importance of inadequate accounting relative to other constraints; see Alfred D. Chandler, Jr., *The Visible Hand: The Managerial Revolution in American Business* (Cambridge: Belknap Press, 1977), 445–450.

9. "As a matter of fact" quoted from "Domestic Load and the Lesson of the Factory," *Electrical World* 87 (May 1, 1926): 904; George H. Davis (Idaho Power Company, Boise), "Does Residence Business Pay?" ibid., 80 (December 1922): 1398–1399; John L. Haley,

"Revised Rate Structures," ibid., 92 (October 20, 1928): 791; Fischer, *America Calling,* 38–42.

10. "Hartford's Combination Residence Rate," *Electrical World* 91 (April 21, 1928): 917–921; Samuel Ferguson (president, Hartford Electric Light Company), "Inducement Rates, Key to Progress," ibid., 93 (March 2, 1929): 435–437; "Customer Psychology," ibid., 93 (April 20, 1929): 787–789; "Promotional Rates Improve Usage Classification," ibid., 94 (July 27, 1929): 1919–1920; "Three-Cent Energy Rate for Hartford Homes," ibid., 96 (November 8, 1930): 850.

11. C. L. Campbell, "Residential Rates That Encourage Use," *Electrical World* 86 (December 19, 1925): 1249–1250; "Low Rates Attract Domestic Power Load," ibid., 90 (September 24, 1927), 619; John L. Haley, "Revised Rate Structures," ibid., 92 (October 20, 1928): 791–793; C. F. Lacombe and W. S. Leffler, "Defects of Straight-Line Rate," ibid., 93 (February 2, 1929): 243–246; Barclay J. Sickler, "Lower Rates—More Business," ibid., 95 (May 3, 1930): 888–889; "New York City Offered Lower Rates," ibid., 96 (August 9, 1930): 257–258; "Promotional Rates Quicken Commercial Pulse," ibid., 98 (August 1, 1931): 207; "Rates Go Down, Consumption Goes Up," ibid., 98 (November 21, 1931): 908; "Sixteen Months to Recover with Inducement Rates," ibid., 98 (December 19, 1931): 1084–1086; F. A. Newton, "This Business of Rates," ibid., 101 (June 10, 1933): 769–773.

12. See the negotiations of New York Edison with New York State in 1930 in "Sloan for 5-Cent Rate Plus 60 Cents—Boston and Philadelphia Rates Cut," *Electrical World* 96 (August 9, 1930): 240–241.

13. "Interest has" quoted from "Selling Centers on Homes," *Electrical World* 105 (January 5, 1935): 60. "While private" quoted from Richard F. Hirsh, *Technology and Transformation in the American Electric Utility* (Cambridge: Cambridge University Press, 1989), 35; see also pp. 33–35. Table AII.7.5, "Percentage Distribution of Energy and Electricity to Manufacturing and Nonresidential Use," in Sonenblum, "Basic Statistical Data," 426.

14. On General Electric's advertising campaign, see Nye, *Electrifying America,* 268–271. Electrical manufacturing establishments from Table I, "Thirteen Years' Growth in Electrical Manufacturing," in "Value of Electrical Goods Doubled in Eight Years," *Electrical World* 94 (October 26, 1929): 837; the data refer to all electrical manufacturers, including makers of appliances. On General Electric, see David Loth, *Swope of G.E.: The Story of Gerard Swope and General Electric in American Business* (New York: Simon and Schuster, 1958), 113–116, 132–133, 144–148, 164–166, 180.

15. On the relationship between electrical manufacturers and operating utilities, see Sidney Alexander Mitchell, *S. Z. Mitchell and the Electrical Industry* (New York: Farrar, Straus & Cudahy, 1960), 62–151. Mitchell's biography defends the holding company movement from the industry point of view. Gifford Pinchot portrayed General Electric as one of the five electric trusts; see "Pinchot Tells of Trust with Five Heads," *Electrical World* 90 (December 3, 1927): 1164. See also Ralph G. M. Sultan, *Pricing in the Electrical Oligopoly,* vol. 1, *Competition or Collusion* (Cambridge: Harvard University Press, 1974), 1–36. On electrical manufacturers' ownership of utilities, see also Hughes, *Networks of Power,* 126–129; on holding companies, ibid., 392–402. Hughes interprets holding companies as the natural outcome of operating utility growth and considers his research a correction of misunderstanding of holding companies in the 1920s due to government investigations and criticisms by public power advocates.

16. Table III, "Value of Electrical Manufactures by Classes," in "Value of Electrical

Goods Doubled in Eight Years," *Electrical World* 94 (October 26, 1929): 838. On G.E. product diversity, see Loth, *Swope,* 114, and Jules Backman, *The Economics of the Electrical Machinery Industry* (New York: New York University Press, 1962), 4. Thomas Hughes argues that military research was a major source of industrial invention by World War I; see Hughes, *American Genesis,* 96–137. On G.E. investment figures, dollar amounts refer to 1953; the report does not state the dollar amount for earlier administrative guidelines on capital requests; see W. C. Wichman (vice president-general manager, Industrial Power Components Division), "The Product Division General Manager's Responsibilities and Role in Planning and Control," in *Controllers Institute of America: A Case Study of Management Planning and Control at General Electric Company* (New York: Controllership Foundation, 1955), 23–28. On divisional competition, I rely on General Electric's practices; see Robert W. Lewis, "Measuring, Reporting and Appraising Results of Operations with Reference to Goals, Plans and Budgets," in *Controllers, Case Study,* 29–41. On General Electric research, see George Wise, *Willis R. Whitney, General Electric, and the Origins of U.S. Industrial Research* (New York: Columbia University Press, 1985), 170–171; John Winthrop Hammond, *Men and Volts: The Story of General Electric* (Philadelphia: J. B. Lippincott, 1941), 325 f.; and Ronald R. Kline, *Steinmetz: Engineer and Socialist* (Baltimore: Johns Hopkins University Press, 1992).

17. Ralph Sultan demonstrated the "stickiness" of prices in electrical equipment destined for industrial purchasers after the three major corporations—G.E., Westinghouse, and Allis-Chambers—worked out their market shares; see Sultan, *Pricing,* 1–36, 37–83, 170–193. Sultan concludes, despite oral testimony of informal price fixing among electrical manufacturers and several prosecuted cases of collusion to fix prices, that the market for apparatus was not conspiratorially "administered" and that a combination of market forces and technological evolution of products accounts for what appears as price fixing; see ibid., 301–320. On incandescent lamp patent pooling for the purpose of controlling the market, see ibid., 26–28. For Swope's views, see Loth, *Swope,* 179–180; Hammond, *Men and Volts,* 389–393. Riverside appliance prices are from an impressionistic sample of the Riverside *Daily Press,* 1928–1940 (n = 118), conducted for the purposes of illustration.

18. Percentage changes in price calculated from average national retail prices in "10 Years Sales and Retail Value of Electrical Merchandise [1926–1935]," *Electrical Merchandising* 55 (January 1936): 2–5; "10 Years Sales and Retail Value of Electrical Merchandise [1930–1939]," ibid., 63 (January 1945): 8–9. Unit price determined as aggregate retail value divided by number of retail units sold.

19. "Some representatives" quoted from "Ideal Refrigerator Motor Specified," *Electrical World* 85 (May 16, 1925): 1051. On the history of refrigerators, see Cowan, *More Work for Mother,* 127–150, and Anderson, *Refrigeration in America.* Anderson's story of the advance of technology can be read backward as the persistence of technological failings; ibid., 195–200. My discussion of problems with mass market mechanical refrigeration draws from the following sources: "Electrical Refrigerating Outfits Moving Well," *Electrical World* 81 (April 1923): 1006; "Electric Refrigeration in Chicago," ibid., 84 (December 20, 1924): 1316; "Better Motors Wanted for Refrigerators," ibid., 85 (February 28, 1925): 484; "To Find the Ideal Refrigerator Motor," ibid., 85 (March 7, 1925): 496; "Ideal Refrigerator Motor Specified," ibid., 85 (May 16, 1925): 1051; "Domestic Electric Refrigeration Featured," ibid., 85 (June 20, 1925): 1352; "Status of Electric Refrigeration," ibid., 88 (October 30, 1926): 895–903; "Better and Lower-Priced Refrigerators Wait on Sales Volume," ibid., 89 (January 22, 1927): 187; "The Nation's Ice Bill," ibid., 90

(August 6, 1927): 249; "Refrigerators, Yes, But Who Owns Them," ibid., 106 (July 20, 1935): 21; "Time for Replacement," *Electrical Merchandising*, 65 (April 1941): 6–24.

20. "Cleared for Marketing Action," *Electrical World* 105 (May 25, 1935): 37–41; "Electrification" quoted from ibid., 37. Also see Loth, *Swope*, 179–181.

21. "Joke" quotation by John F. Gilchrist, vice president of Commonwealth Edison, Chicago, reported in "Appliance Distribution Methods a 'Joke,'" ibid., 82 (October 13, 1923): 777.

22. *Electrical World* surveyed one city of each population category. These reports are devoted to each city as follows: "Who Sells Electrical Appliances—A City of 500,000," *Electrical World* 82 (December 8, 1923): 1170; "II. A City of 200,000," ibid., 82 (December 22, 1923): 1271; "III. A City of 800,000," ibid., 83 (January 12, 1924): 92; "IV. A City of 250,000," ibid., 83 (February 2, 1924): 234; "V. A City of 800,000," ibid., 83 (March 1, 1924): 429; "VI. A City of 800,000 [city whose utility does not retail]," ibid., 83 (March 22, 1924): 573.

23. "Central-Station Appliance Sales," *Electrical World* 87 (January 2, 1926): 57. "If other dealers" quoted from [editorial], ibid., 87 (January 2, 1926): 1. Marshall E. Sampsell, vice president, National Electric Light Association, "Anti-Utility Legislation vs. Industry Co-operation," ibid., 98 (November 14, 1931): 870–871; Earl Whitehorne, "Oklahoma-Kansas Experience," ibid., 105 (February 16, 1935): 36–39.

24. Marshall E. Sampsell (vice president, National Electric Light Association), "Anti-Utility Merchandising Legislation vs. Industry Co-operation," *Electrical World* 98 (November 14, 1931): 870–871; "Department Store Sales Shown in Committee Report," ibid., 100 (December 23, 1932): 737.

25. Olney, *Buy Now, Pay Later*, table 2.1A, p. 10; table 2.6A, "Average Shares of Expenditure for Major Durable Goods, Current Price Estimates, 1869–1986," p. 34; table 4.2, "Outstanding Consumer Debt by Product Group, 1919–1939," pp. 93–94.

26. Automobile retail sales statistics from Gregory Chow, *Demand for Automobiles in the United States* (Amsterdam: North-Holland, 1957).

27. Technological developments enabling clear transmission and receipt of voice (as distinguished from nonvoice codes) made possible the radio boom of the 1920s; see Hugh G. J. Aitken, *The Continuous Wave: Technology and American Radio, 1900–1932* (Princeton: Princeton University Press, 1985). On the early history of broadcasting, see Susan J. Douglas, *Inventing American Broadcasting, 1899–1922* (Baltimore: Johns Hopkins University Press, 1987); and Erik Barnouw, *A Tower in Babel: A History of Broadcasting in the United States,* vol. 1, to 1933 (New York: Oxford University Press, 1966). For Montgomery Ward's first radio, see Barnouw, *A Tower of Babel*, 1:186; on the creation of the National Broadcasting Company, ibid., 201; for the history of the Radio Act of 1927, ibid., 195–200, 215–217, 300–315. The importance of the plug-in radio for mass marketing is stressed by the trade journals; see "Make Radio Another Standard Household Electric Service," *Electrical World* 86 (September 12, 1925): 501, and "A New Trend in Radio," ibid., 86 (October 10, 1925): 734. The number of radio sets in use through 1925 is provided by "Estimated Total Radio Sets, 1922–1945," *Television Factbook*, no. 37 (Washington, D.C.: Television Digest, 1967), 52a. "The more impressive thought" quoted from "In Two Years Radio Runs Neck and Neck," *Electrical World* 85 (March 21, 1925): 600. Radio stock after 1925 determined by depreciating the annual sales of radios over a twelve-year life span. Residential saturation determined by dividing the stock of radios by the number of households in the United States and the number of electrified households. Source for radio sales is annual ten-year merchandising review in *Electrical Merchandising*, 1936 and later.

28. "It is impossible" quoted from "Points Way to Greater Domestic Loads," *Electrical World* 88 (November 27, 1926): 1126. For the peril of appliances, see Ernest B. Slade, "Remove this Obstacle to Appliance Use [on nonstandardized plugs]," ibid., 82 (September 1923): 458–459; E. S. Lincoln, "An Engineer's Analysis of Why Some Appliances Are Not in Use," ibid., 82 (October 20, 1923): 807–809; L. R. Parker, "Development of Domestic Refrigerator," ibid., 81 (June 6, 1923): 1219–1222; "Interchangeable Appliance Plug Advances Interests of Entire Industry," ibid., 84 (October 18, 1924): 869; "Keeping Appliances at Work," ibid., 84 (November 8, 1924): 1008–1009; H. E. Young, "Servicing Domestic Electric Refrigerators," ibid., 84 (November 29, 1924): 1149–1152; "Electric Refrigerator Service Costs," ibid., 86 (July 4, 1925): 24; L. W. W. Morrow, "Action Urged on Standardization," ibid., 89 (May 21, 1927): 1057–1060; "An Industry Move to Stimulate Better Appliances," ibid., 93 (April 27, 1929): 835–836; "To Keep Appliances Working," ibid., 95 (January 18, 1930): 153. On retailer cooperation to remove unsafe appliances, see "Retailers Aiding Drive for Quality Appliances," ibid., 92 (October 20, 1928): 773. On local ordinances against unsafe appliances, see Earl Whitehorne, "This Matter of Quality in Appliances," ibid., 101 (April 15, 1933): 488–489. On plug standardization, see Fred E. H. Schroeder, "More 'Small Things Forgotten': Domestic Electrical Plugs and Receptacles," *Technology and Culture* 27 (July 1986): 535–543. On difficulty of using appliances, see also C. E. Bose, Philip L. Bereano, and Mary Malloy, "Household Technology and the Social Construction of Housework," ibid., 25 (1984): 66.

29. Martha E. Dresslar, "Relative Cost of Gas and Electricity," *Journal of Home Economics* 15 (February 1923): 71–80; Ruth A. Potter and Martha E. Dresslar, "Further Data on the Cost of Gas and Electricity for Cooking," *Journal of Home Economics* 23 (January 1931): 67–70; Busch, "Cooking Competition," 222. On the competition of ice and mechanical refrigeration, see Anderson, *Refrigeration,* 215–221.

30. Margaret G. Reid, *Economics of Household Production* (New York: John Wiley, 1934), 97, 104–106; "Curling Irons and Bobbed Hair," *Electrical World* 93 (March 23, 1929): 575. Riverside Business Licenses, Riverside Police Department, ledgers for 1922 and 1926, Riverside Municipal Archives, University of California, Riverside, Rivera Library Special Collections. Hardening of local attitudes toward strangers at the door is seen in the mid-1930s: "Charities Irked by Hoboes Here," Riverside *Daily Press,* November 24, 1937, 7; "Bums Coming to City Will Labor," ibid., October 27, 1936, 4; Riverside County considered joining Los Angeles city's blockage in October 1936: "County's Supervisors Invited to Meeting on Barring Unemployed Transients from Southland," ibid., October 30, 1936, 4; "Riverside Housewives Asked Not to Give Any Help to Transients," ibid., March 6, 1934; "Kiwanians Back 'Bums Blockade,'" ibid., November 19, 1936, 4; "Residents Asked Not to Feed Transients," ibid., December 7, 1939, 4.

31. "Profound" quoted from Cowan, *More Work for Mother,* 174, and see also pp. 107–108. Cowan's argument was preceded by Heidi Irngard Hartmann's "Capitalism and Women's Work in the Home, 1900–1930," Ph.D. dissertation, Yale University, 1974. Hartmann's thesis also influenced Julie Matthaei; see Julie A. Matthaei, *An Economic History of Women in America: Women's Work, the Sexual Division of Labor, and the Development of Capitalism* (New York: Schocken Books, 1982), 352 n. 1, 356 n. 3, 361 n. 5. See also Nye, *Electrifying America,* 272.

32. See introduction, table I.1.

33. Isabel Ely Lord, *Getting Your Money's Worth: A Book on Expenditure* (New York: Harcourt, Brace, 1922), 48–49, 51, 80, 82. On the 1928 survey, see Ruth Lindquist, *The Family in the Present Social Order: A Study of Needs of American Families* (Chapel Hill:

University of North Carolina Press, 1931), 31–32, 150. Phyllis Palmer, *Domesticity and Dirt: Housewives and Domestic Servants in the United States, 1920–1945* (Philadelphia: Temple University Press, 1989), 9–10.

34. Wet-wash statistics from "The Real Appliance Sales Problem," *Electrical World* 88 (August 7, 1926): 258; and "Laundry-Tested," *Business Week* (August 18, 1934): 24. Gross receipts from table 3, "Rise in Annual Laundering Sales Volume," in Fred DeArmond, *The Laundry Industry* (New York: Harper & Brothers, 1950), 21. On black laundresses, see Geo. H. Watson, "Competition with Muscle," *Electrical Merchandising* 53 (March 1935): 9; and Palmer, *Domesticity,* 9–10; see also ibid., 9, for Palmer's analyses of the Bureau of Labor household survey. On the 1934 laundry campaign, see "Laundries Hit Back," *Business Week* (March 24, 1934): 12–13. Other statistics from *Household Management and Kitchens, Reports of the Committees on Household Management,* Effie I. Raitt, Chairman, and *Kitchens and Other Work Centers,* Abby L. Marlatt, Chairman, vol. 9, *President's Conference on Home-building and Home Ownership, 1931,* publications edited by John M. Gries and James Ford, General Editors (Washington, D.C.: President's Conference on Home Building and Home Ownership, printed by National Capital Press, 1932), 64; from data compiled by the Bureau of Home Economics, U.S. Department of Agriculture. Also see, table 16, "Percentage of Families Sending Laundry Out," in Reid, *Economics,* 97.

35. Ronald Tobey, Charles Wetherell, and Jay Brigham, "Moving Out and Settling In: Residential Mobility, Home Owning, and the Public Enframing of Citizenship, 1921–1950," *American Historical Review* 95 (December 1990): 1395–1422. Mildred Weigley Wood, Ruth Lindquist, and Lucy A. Studley, *Managing the Home* (Boston: Houghton Mifflin, 1932), 161.

36. Housing data from "New Housing Units Started, by Ownership, Type of Structure, Location, and Construction Cost: 1889–1970," in Series N 162, "Urban Areas, New Housing Units Started [1,000s]," Bureau of the Census, *Historical Statistics of the United States, Colonial Times to 1970,* 2 vols., Bicentennial edition (Washington, D.C., 1975), 2: 639–640. Pearson correlations between appliance growth rates and households growth rate, 1921–1941: vacuum cleaner $r = .32$; range $r = .43$; refrigerator $r = .45$; heating pad $r = .52$; washing machine $r = .06$; flatiron $r = .14$.

37. Normalized rate is defined as absolute annual sales of the appliance per hundred households living in dwellings capable of servicing the appliance.

38. "Some six or seven" quoted from "Why Appliances Do Not Sell More Rapidly, An Answer in Present Housewiring Incompleteness," *Electrical Merchandising* 35 (March 1926): 6133. "Electrical articles" quoted from "Why Appliances Do Not Sell More Rapidly [editorial]," ibid. See the confusion in Nye, *Electrifying America,* 262, 265.

39. "Residential wiring" quoted from E. S. Fitz, "Residential Load Possibilities," *Electrical World* 102 (September 23, 1933): 400.

40. Not distinguishing between electrification and electrical modernization are Cowan, *More Work for Mother,* 151–191; Alice Kessler-Harris, *Women Have Always Worked: A Historical Overview* (Old Westbury, N.Y.: Feminist Press, 1981), 40, 52; Nye, *Electrifying America,* 238–286; Platt, *The Electric City,* 235–267; Michael Doucet and John Weaver, *Housing the North American City* (Montreal: McGill-Queen's University Press, 1991), 423–445; and Witold Rybczynski, *Home: A Short History of an Idea,* repr. (New York: Penguin Books, 1987), 150–154. Hints about physical quality of housing are not followed up in Cowan, *More Work for Mother,* 155, 162, 173, 182–183; Nye, *Electrifying America,* 17, 266, 275; or Platt, *The Electric City,* 241.

41. Bakersfield, California, Ordinance no. 154, New Series, An Ordinance Creating a Department to Be Known as the 'Department of Electricity,' Providing for the Greater Safety to Life and Property by Regulating the Installation, Repair, Operation, and Maintenance of all Electrical Conductors [etc.], January 2, 1923, articles 2b, 11; Pasadena, California, Ordinance no. 1969, An Ordinance of the City of Pasadena Fixing the Duties and Powers of the City Electrician; Regulating the Installation, Alteration and Repair of Inside and Outside Electrical Construction, and Providing for the Inspection of Same, March 28, 1922, articles 9, 15. The National Board of Fire Underwriters' model building code stipulated that building codes require electrical installations to meet the National Electrical Code; see [National Board of Fire Underwriters] *Building Code Recommended by the National Board of Fire Underwriters,* 4th ed. (New York: [National Board of Fire Underwriters], 1922), sec. 261.

42. History of the National Electrical Code from Terrell Croft, *Wiring for Light and Power: A Detailed and Fully Illustrated Commentary on the National Electrical Code,* 4th ed. (New York: McGraw-Hill, 1924), preface to the 1923 National Electrical Code, x; see also Charles S. Morgan, *Public Advocate for Fire Safety: The Story of the National Fire Protection Association* (New York: Newcomen Society in North America, 1977); branch circuiting comparison of 1920 and 1923 codes refers to circuits of no. 14 conducting wire, Croft, *Wiring for Light and Power,* 201–202. The code stipulated no. 18 wire for lamps, no. 14 wire for small motor appliances, and no. 12 wire for large-base lamps ("mogul" base lamps) on two-wire circuits; ibid., 200–202. Chicago's 1923 code revisions referenced, ibid., 375–376. On separate appliance circuits, also see H. C. Cushing, Jr., *Standard Wiring for Electric Light and Power, as Adopted by the Fire Underwriters of the United States,* 31st ed. (New York: H. C. Cushing, Jr., 1925), 239, 246. Popularization of the National Electrical Code was provided by Blanche Halbert, ed., *The Better Homes Manual,* published in cooperation with Better Homes in America (Chicago: University of Chicago Press, 1931), 287–309.

43. For heavy heating appliances, see Halbert, *Better Homes Manual,* 395–397. See also Cushing, *Standard Wiring,* 136, 161–168.

44. "It is very difficult" quoted from Terrell Croft, *Wiring of Finished Buildings, a practical treatise . . .* (New York: McGraw-Hill, 1915), 102; see also pp. 61–63, 101–143, and the discussion, "Neatness and How Obtained," 157–159. See also Arthur L. Cook, *Electric Wiring for Lighting and Power Installations* (New York: John Wiley, [1917] 1933), 177–223.

45. My conclusion that inadequate wiring divided the nation's housing stock into classes of technological capability is supported by the following references: W. J. Canada (Electrical Field Secretary, National Fire Protection Association), "Wiring Code National Standardization," *Electrical World* 85 (June 27, 1925): 1424–1425, which argued for replacement of local building codes on wiring by a national standard. The "Red Seal" plan originated in 1924 in an effort to induce the home building industry, utilities, and electrical manufacturers to raise wiring standards. How the industry intended the plan to work is discussed in "California Electrical Men Organize Behind the Red Seal Plan" [subtitle: "Adequate Wiring the Basic Need in All Market Development Work"], *Electrical Merchandising* 34 (October 1925): 5619–5620. M. Luckiesh, "40,000,000 Outlets in Prospect," *Electrical World* 86 (October 24, 1925), 851–852. M. Luckiesh (Director of the Lighting Research Laboratory, Nela Park [National Electric Light Association research facility], "Good Business in Fixtures," ibid., 86 (November 14, 1925): 995–996, which cites a national NELA survey that found 23 percent of all lightbulbs

unshaded and 31 percent of all fixtures "obsolete." "Why Appliances Do Not Sell More Rapidly: An Answer in Present Housewiring Incompleteness," *Electrical Merchandising* 35 (March 1926): 6133. "Convenience Outlets and Residential Electrification," *Electrical World* 89 (April 30, 1927): 898. Earl A. Graham, "Home Lighting—an Unsaturated Market," ibid., 98 (September 12, 1931): 464–466, which estimated that 70 percent of electrified dwellings did not have lights at "the level considered at present to be minimum good practice" (p. 464). "What Is Adequate House Wiring?" ibid., 100 (October 29, 1932): 603–605, stated, matter-of-factly, that "inadequate wiring for residences has long been a stumbling block to complete home electrification." E. S. Ritz, "Residential Load Possibilities," ibid., 102 (September 23, 1933): 400. "Facing the Facts on the American Home [editorial]," ibid., 104 (July 28, 1934): 102, interprets the Real Property Inventory of 1934 as showing that the American urban housing stock on average was substandard. Laurence Wray, "How to Make Money in Lighting," *Electrical Merchandising* 62 (November 1939): 1–5, reports a *Women's Home Companion* survey of wiring and lighting upgrade needed in 1,000 homes, as part of a national "Better Lighting" campaign. Irving W. Clark (Manager, Home Building Division, Westinghouse Electric Appliance Division), "Electrifying Postwar Housing," *Electrical Merchandising* 69 (June 1943): 20, 59, argued that utilities should join manufacturers in obtaining new wiring standards for the expected postwar building boom. Michael Doucet and John Weaver do not distinguish between electrification and electrical modernization. I have been unable to relate their impressive data to the categorization of housing grades in this chapter. They utilize the number of rooms per resident and assessed valuation as measures of the quality of housing, supplemented by national censuses on sanitation facilities in homes. See Doucet and Weaver, *Housing the North American City,* 423–445. Doucet and Weaver mention the deterioration of housing after the onset of the depression in 1930 and attempt to measure it. They find that the passage of better owned houses into rentals increased the availability of better rental units (but see pp. 428, 457–462).

Chapter 2. The Reform Tradition

1. Norris quoted by Richard Lowitt, *George W. Norris: The Persistence of a Progressive, 1913–1933* (Urbana: University of Illinois Press, 1971), 359. See also Jay Lawrence Brigham, "Public Power and Progressivism in the 1920s" (Ph.D. dissertation, University of California, Riverside, 1992).

2. "After two years" quoted from Robert M. La Follette, *La Follette's Autobiography: A Personal Narrative of Political Experience,* with a foreword by Allan Nevins (Madison: University of Wisconsin Press, 1960), 153–154. See also *California Progressive Campaign Book for 1914: Three Years of Progressive Administration in California under Hiram W. Johnson* (San Francisco: [s.n.], 1914), 141, 158–160. Morton Keller perceives an important difference between the railroads and public utilities as subjects of regulation; see Keller, *Regulating a New Economy: Public Policy and Economic Change in America, 1900–1933* (Cambridge: Harvard University Press, 1990), 59, 63.

3. *California Progressive Campaign Book,* 50; Charles Evans Hughes, "Speech at the Dinner of the Republican Club of the City of New York, October 18, 1907," in Charles Evans Hughes, *Addresses of Charles Evans Hughes 1906–1916,* 2d ed. (New York: G. P. Putnam's Sons, 1916), 71–72; La Follette, *Autobiography,* 171.

4. Charles Evans Hughes, "Speech Before the Republican Club of the City of New York, January 31, 1908," in Hughes, *Addresses,* 91; Robert F. Wesser, *Charles Evans*

Hughes: Politics and Reform in New York, 1905–1910 (Ithaca: Cornell University Press, 1967), chap. 4.

5. U.S. Bureau of the Census, *Historical Statistics of the United States, Colonial Times to 1970, Bicentennial Edition, Part 1* (Washington, D.C., 1975), 2: 827, Series S 108–119, "Growth of Residential Service, and Average Prices for Electric Energy: 1902 to 1970," Series 112, "Residential Service, Average Price (cents per kw.-hr.) monthly use 0–25 kw.-hr."

6. The distinction between normal or average load and peak load enabled the industry to argue in the late 1920s that it did not have excess capacity and was not overcapitalized; see Edwin G. Nourse and associates, *America's Capacity to Produce: Study of Consumption in the 1920s* (Washington, D.C.: Brookings Institution, 1934), 313–339.

7. See Twentieth Century Fund, *Electric Power and Government Policy: A Survey of the Relations Between the Government and the Electric Power Industry* (New York: Twentieth Century Fund, 1948), 39–44, for an overview of pricing; pp. 19–23, 223–230, for analysis of the historical decline in rates and costs in the 1920s and 1930s; pp. 28–29, on marginal generating costs. From the industry side, this analysis is presented by Edwin Vennard (a managing director of the Edison Electric Institute), *Government in the Power Business* (New York: McGraw-Hill, 1968), 205. Analysis of the historic decline in rates from the reformers' perspective is made by James C. Bonbright (a Roosevelt adviser and an original member of the New York State Power Authority), *Public Utilities and the National Power Policies* (New York: Columbia University Press, 1940), 18–19.

8. H. S. Rauschenbush and Harry W. Laidler, *Power Control* (New York: New Republic, 1928), 104–105.

9. For the debt-capitalization ratio, see table 1-14, "Ratio of Debt to Capitalization of Electric Operating Companies, All Manufacturing and Domestic Corporations, 1917–1938," in Twentieth Century Fund, *Electric Power,* 38. The accusation that high rates were needed to pay fraudulent debts was reviewed in Bonbright, *Public Utilities,* 10, 24–26. Twentieth Century Fund, *Electric Power,* 20–21, discusses the legal problem, and pp. 252–253, 260–262, and 271–274 review the problem of inflated securities and rates. "Premium" quotation by Norris is from Lowitt, *Norris: The Persistence,* 264. Twentieth Century Fund, *Electric Power,* 187–194.

10. "Intimately bound" quoted from Franklin D. Roosevelt, *The Public Papers and Addresses of Franklin D. Roosevelt,* ed. Samuel I. Rosenman (New York: Random House, 1938), 1: 106. An influential discussion of the effect of holding companies on state regulation was provided by Rauschenbush and Laidler, *Power Control,* 116–157. On the regionalization of American operating utilities, see Hughes, *Networks of Power,* 363–460.

11. Table 1.1, "Municipal Electric Systems in the United States, 1882–1981," p. 9 in David Schap, *Municipal Ownership in the Electric Utility Industry: A Centennial View,* Praeger Special Studies, Praeger Scientific (Westport, Conn.: Greenwood Press, 1986).

12. For Norris's career, see Lowitt, *Norris: The Persistence,* 264–267. See also Hughes, *American Genesis,* 362–364.

13. "Every stream" quoted from George W. Norris, *Fighting Liberal: The Autobiography of George W. Norris* (New York: Macmillan, 1945), 161.

14. All quotations from David E. Lilienthal, *TVA: Democracy on the March,* rev. ed. (New York: Harper & Brothers, [1944] 1953), 218–225, passim. Lilienthal's characterization of the TVA as a form of democratic, grassroots planning has been repeatedly challenged, beginning with Donald Davidson, *The Tennessee,* 2 vols. (New York: Rinehart, 1946–1948). For a review of Lilienthal's versus Davidson's vision of the Tennessee River

valley, see William C. Havard, Jr., "Images of TVA: The Clash over Values," in Erwin C. Hargrove and Paul K. Conkin, ed., *TVA: Fifty Years of Grass-Roots Bureaucracy* (Urbana: University of Illinois Press, 1983), 297–315; see also Victor C. Hobday, *Sparks at the Grassroots: Municipal Distribution of TVA Electricity in Tennessee* (Knoxville: University of Tennessee Press, 1969), 32–73. A more generous interpretation of the TVA is provided by Philip Selznick, *TVA and the Grass Roots: A Study in the Sociology of Formal Organization* (New York: Harper & Row, [1949] 1966).

15. All quotations from Lilienthal, *TVA,* 218–225, passim.

16. For Lilienthal's conceptualization of TVA planning, see Lilienthal, *TVA,* 218–225.

17. Schap, *Municipal Ownership,* 66.

18. On Ford's vision, see Preston J. Hubbard, *Origins of the TVA: The Muscle Shoals Controversy, 1920–1932* (Nashville: Vanderbilt University Press, 1961), 39, 55, 86–87, 92, 129, 140–141: and Reynold M. Wik, *Henry Ford and Grass-roots America* (Ann Arbor: University of Michigan Press, 1972), 112, 120, 230. See also Walter L. Creese, *TVA's Public Planning: The Vision, the Reality* (Knoxville: University of Tennessee Press, 1990), 28–29; Nye, *Electrifying America,* 298–299.

19. On Boston Edison's participation in the educational campaign, see Sicilia, "Selling Power," 527–539.

20. On social conservatism and class advertising in magazines, see Roland Marchand, *Advertising the American Dream: Making Way for Modernity, 1920–1940* (Berkeley, Los Angeles, and London: University of California Press, 1985), xvii, 63–66, 127–132, 194–200, 248–254. On electrical advertising, see Cowan, *More Housework,* 137–138, 187–188; Pamela W. Laurito, "The Message Was Electric," *IEEE Spectrum* 21 (September 1984): 84–95; and Nye, *Electrifying America,* 267–277. Nye argues that electrical appliances socially meant both "tools of psychological maintenance and symbols of transformation" (ibid., 281). While his text makes clear the evidence for interpreting the advertising message as psychological maintenance, his evidence is less convincing that appliances promised transformation for middle-class households. Rather than "transformation," the ads promise more efficient and capable achievement of traditional values. On New Deal pictorial symbolism, see Creese, *TVA's Public Planning;* see also Richard Lowitt and Maurine Beasley, eds., *One Third of a Nation: Lorena Hickok Reports on the Great Depression* (Urbana: University of Illinois Press, 1981). On the political activities of the electrical associations and the disinformation campaign involved in private advertising of electrical products, see Rauschenbush and Laidler, *Power Control,* passim. On Norris's struggle over Ford's vision, see Lowitt, *Norris: The Persistence,* 208, 214–215, 245, 264, 359–360.

21. On Cooke's career, see Kenneth Trombley, *The Life and Times of a Happy Liberal, Morris Llewellyn Cooke* (New York: Harper & Brothers, 1954). D. Clayton Brown, *Electricity for Rural America: The Fight for the REA* (Westport, Conn.: Greenwood Press, 1980), 22–57.

22. "The change from muscle" quotation is from Gifford Pinchot, Introduction, in *Giant Power: Large-Scale Electrical Development as a Social Factor,* ed. Morris Llewellyn Cooke, *Annals of the American Academy of Political and Social Science,* 118, (1925): viii; Pinchot's contribution hereafter cited as Pinchot, "Introduction," and the whole volume as Cooke, *Giant Power.* "Decline in country life" quotation and "decentralization" quoted from Pinchot, "Introduction," xi. Pinchot wrote that public ownership of utilities was not needed; social modernization could be achieved through state planning and regulation of privately owned utilities. Alfred Bettman thought contrarily

that public ownership might be necessary to achieve social goals, though this ownership ought to be accomplished at the state level rather than the federal level (which should limit itself to regulation). See Pinchot, "Introduction," vii–xii, and Alfred Bettman, "Is Giant Power a State or Federal Utility? Should Its Control be Through Public Ownership or Regulation?" ibid., 168–175. Thomas Hughes interprets *Giant Power* from a point of view in opposition to public power; see Hughes, *Networks of Power,* 297–313; and Hughes, "The Industrial Revolution That Never Came," *American Heritage of Invention and Technology* (Winter 1988): 58–64. Cooke's and Pinchot's positions in corporate liberalism are analyzed in terms of the Super Power and Giant Power projects of the 1920s in Leonard DeGraaf, "Corporate Liberalism and Electric Power System Planning in the 1920s," *Business History Review* 64 (Spring 1990): 1–31. On the community vision of the Regional Planning Association and its progenitors, see James W. Carey and John J. Quirk, "The Mythos of the Electronic Revolution," *American Scholar* 39 (Spring 1970): 219–241 and 40 (Summer 1970): 395–424, and Hughes, "The Industrial Revolution," 63–64.

23. "Life born" quoted from Martha Bensley Breùere, "What Is Giant Power For?" in Cooke, *Giant Power,* 123; "There must be" quoted from Mary Pattison, "The Abolition of Household Slavery," in Cooke, *Giant Power,* 126.

24. Helen Campbell, *Household Economics: A Course of Lectures in the School of Economics of the University of Wisconsin,* rev. (New York: G. P. Putnam's Sons, 1896); Isabel Gordon Curtis, *The Making of a Housewife* (New York: Frederick A. Stokes, 1906); Lucy H. Salmon, *Progress in the Household* (Boston: Houghton Mifflin, 1906); Bertha J. Richardson, *The Woman Who Spends: A Study of Her Economic Function,* rev. (Boston: Whitcomb & Barrows, 1910); Georgie Boynton Child, *The Efficient Kitchen: Definite Directions for the Planning, Arranging and Equipping of the Modern Labor-saving Kitchen—A Practical Book for the Home-Maker* (New York: McBride, Nast, 1914); Mary (Mrs. Frank A.) Pattison, *Principles of Domestic Engineering, Or the What, Why and How of a Home; An Attempt to Evolve a Solution to the Domestic "Labor and Capital" Problem—To Standardize and Professionalize Housework—To Re-Organize the Home Upon 'Scientific Management' Principles—And To Point Out the Importance of the Public and Personal Element Therein, As Well As the Practical* (New York: [Women's Club of New Jersey], 1915); Christine Frederick, *Household Engineering: Scientific Management in the Home; A Correspondence Course on the Application of the Principle of Efficiency Engineering and Scientific Management to the Every Day Tasks of Housekeeping* (Chicago: American School of Home Economics, 1919); see also the 1925 edition of Christine Frederick's work, titled *Efficient Housekeeping or Household Engineering: Scientific Management in the Home. A Correspondence Course on the Application of the Principles of Efficiency Engineering and Scientific Management to the Every Day Tasks of Housekeeping* (Chicago: American School of Home Economics, 1925); Lillian Gilbreth, *The Homemaker and Her Job* (New York: D. Appleton-Century [1927] 1935). On concerns about the shift from the farm to the urban home kitchen, see Child, *The Efficient Kitchen,* 13, and Frederick, *Household Engineering,* 19. "We can foresee" quoted from Mary Pattison, *Principles of Domestic Engineering,* 121. Ernest Flagg, *Small Houses: Their Economic Design and Construction; Essays on the Fundamental Principles of Design and Descriptive Articles on Construction* (New York: Charles Scribner's Sons, 1922), ix–x. Robert T. Jones, *Small Homes of Architectural Distinction: A Book of Suggested Plans by the Architects' Small House Service Bureau, Inc.* (New York: Harper & Brothers, 1929), 2, 5–6, 8, 22, 62, 118. Child, *The Efficient Kitchen,* 20.

25. Marion Talbot and Sophonisba Preston Breckinridge, *The Modern Household* (Boston: Whitcomb & Barrows, 1912), 47–55; Martha Bensley Bruère and Robert W. Bruère, *Increasing Home Efficiency* (New York: Macmillan, [1911] 1916), 11–12. Gilbreth provides one of the more extensive discussions of time and motion studies in the home; See Gilbreth, *The Homemaker,* 55–56, 86–142.

26. "This principle" quoted from Frederick, *Household Engineering,* 22.

27. "The health" quoted from Frederick, *Household Engineering,* 267; see also pp. 286–296. Ellen Richards feared families would purchase housing so expensive they would skimp on clothes and food, for which careful budgeting was the only answer; see Ellen H. Richards, *The Cost of Shelter* (New York: John Wiley & Sons, 1905), 15–17. "It is clearly" quoted from C. W. Haskins, *How to Keep Household Accounts: A Manual of Family Finance* (New York: Harper & Brothers, 1903), 9. See also Richardson, *The Woman Who Spends,* 16–17.

28. "Unbusinesslike" quoted from Frederick, *Household Engineering,* 269. See also Gilman, *The Home,* 70.

29. "Whether it is" quoted from Child, *The Efficient Kitchen,* 201–202. Lord, *Getting Your Money's Worth,* 1–2, 125–127, 131–320. On asset accumulation, see Lord, *Getting Your Money's Worth,* 7, 19–24, 77–79.

30. "If marriage" quoted from Lord, *Getting Your Money's Worth,* 14. "The greatest" quoted from ibid., 12. See Bertha Richardson's introductory remarks in Richardson, *The Woman Who Spends,* 49–50. See also Pattison, *Principles,* preface and 49, 181, 191. Gilbreth, *The Homemaker,* 27–48. "Humiliating" and "demoralizing" from Lord, *Getting Your Money's Worth,* 12, 117.

31. "The whole family" quoted from Frederick, *Household Engineering,* 268.

32. "Is one" quoted from Norris, *Fighting Liberal,* 161. Frank Freidel, *Franklin D. Roosevelt: The Triumph* (Boston: Little, Brown, 1956), 43. "The most weighty" and "Hydroelectric power" quotations from Arthur M. Schlesinger, Jr., *The Age of Roosevelt: The Crisis of the Old Order, 1919–1933* (Boston: Houghton Mifflin, 1957), 124. "One of the most important" quoted from "Important Notice to Members of the Academy," *Annals of the American Academy of Political and Social Science* 156 (July 1931), inside back cover; I appreciate Gabriele Carey for bringing this item to my attention. See also Brigham, "Public Power."

33. Martin J. Sklar, *The Corporate Reconstruction of American Capitalism, 1890–1916: The Market, the Law, and Politics* (New York: Cambridge University Press, [1988] 1989), 35–40. See also Ellis W. Hawley, *The New Deal and the Problem of Monopoly* (Princeton: Princeton University Press, 1966).

34. For the ideological positions regarding public power, see Philip J. Funigiello, *Toward a National Power Policy: The New Deal and the Electric Utility Industry, 1933–1941* (Pittsburgh: University of Pittsburgh Press, 1973), xi–xvi, 3–31; Brigham, "Public Power," 1–60, 112–158; Kline, *Steinmetz,* 200–264.

35. John G. Clark, *Energy and the Federal Government: Fossil Fuel Policies, 1900–1946* (Urbana: University of Illinois Press, 1987), 169; Clark's remarks pertain to fossil fuel industrialists but are applicable to the electrical industry.

36. On Roosevelt's economic views, see Daniel G. Fusfield, *The Economic Thought of Franklin D. Roosevelt and the Origins of the New Deal* (New York: Columbia University Press, 1956). Biles emphasizes Roosevelt's commitment to economy in government as helping to unify the various New Deal programs; Roger Biles, *A New Deal for the American People* (DeKalb: Northern Illinois University Press, 1991), 55.

37. "Intensive study" quoted from Freidel, *Franklin D. Roosevelt,* 101; see also pp. 264–265. "Brain trust" quoted from Kenneth S. Davis, quoting Roosevelt, in *FDR: The New York Years, 1928–1933* (New York: Random House, 1985), 289; on Roosevelt's sense of personal destiny, see pp. 13–16.

38. Roosevelt, *Public Papers,* 1: 159–166; Freidel, *Franklin D. Roosevelt,* 45.

39. Roosevelt discussed his position on rate-setting in the message to the legislature, March 12, 1929, in Roosevelt, *Public Papers,* 1: 171–178.

40. See Freidel, *Franklin D. Roosevelt,* and Schlesinger, *The Age of Roosevelt,* on Roosevelt's political strategy.

41. Roosevelt, *Public Papers,* 1: 15.

42. Campaign speech at Syracuse, New York, October 23, 1928, pp. 44–45. Annual Message to the New State Legislature, January 1, 1930, 92.

43. Campaign address, Syracuse, New York, October 22, 1930, p. 20.

44. Ibid., 20–21.

45. "First consideration" quoted from memorandum to the legislature accompanying transmittal of the Report of the St. Lawrence Power Development Commission, January 19, 1931, p. 187; "primary purpose" quoted from memorandum to the legislature concerning the bill to develop St. Lawrence hydroelectric power, March 4, 1931, p. 194.

Chapter 3. Homes or Industry?

1. "Ten thousand towns" is from Sinclair Lewis, *Main Street,* chap. 1. On the "city growth game," see Eric H. Monkkonen, *America Becomes Urban: The Development of U.S. Cities and Towns, 1780–1980,* (Berkeley, Los Angeles, and London: University of California Press, 1990), 138–144.

2. "One of the eras" quoted from Robert S. Lynd and Helen Merrell Lynd, *Middletown: A Study in American Culture* (San Diego: Harcourt Brace Jovanovich, [1929] 1957), 5; "a small" and "homogeneous" quoted from ibid., p. 8; "the mere fact" quoted from ibid., pp. 23–24. For use of the Middletown portrait, see Nye, *Electrifying America,* chap. 1, "Middletown Lights Up"; Cowan, *More Work for Mother,* 82–83, 96–97, 107, 123, 173–174, 182, 189; Platt, *The Electric City,* 221, 222, 226, 244, 252; Baritz, *The Good Life,* 125–128. Historians of domestic electricity do not treat race as a factor in differential modernization. Doucet and Weaver do not take up the racial variable, since Hamilton, Ontario, did not have a significant nonwhite population; see their *Housing the North American City,* 446–466. On the typicality of Riverside, see Tobey, Wetherell, and Brigham, "Moving Out and Settling In," 1421–1422.

3. Riverside shared southern California's growth, increasing to 29,696 persons in 1930 and 46,764 in 1950. Throughout this chapter, general details of local history are from Thomas Patterson, *A Colony for California: Riverside's First Hundred Years* (Riverside: Press-Enterprise, 1971). Historical population statistics for white and nonwhite peoples in Riverside are estimates based on U.S. Census sources from 1900 to 1960, including use of the 1910 manuscript census; see Tobey, "Statistical Supplement."

4. By "upper class," I mean bourgeoisie. The bourgeoisie is distinguished from other social classes by having a significant portion of its income from real property investment or shares in capital ventures. "Middle class" refers to white-collar, salaried employment and skilled labor employment in which the laborer works by contract. "Labor class" refers to manual labor, wage-earning occupations. Carpenters who take construction contracts would be middle class: carpenters who work for contractors for wages would be classed

as laborers. See table 3.1. For historical accuracy, I follow without approving the local Anglo convention of classifying Mexican and Hispanic persons as "nonwhite." On Riverside's Anglo elite, see Kevin Starr, *Inventing the Dream: California Through the Progressive Era* (New York: Oxford University Press, [1985] 1986), 89–98, 144–147, and Kevin Starr, *Material Dreams: Southern California Through the 1920s* (New York: Oxford University Press, 1990), 136–139, 186–187, 205–209. With regard to the capability of a capitalist class to make social relations, see David Montejano, *Anglos and Mexicans in the Making of Texas, 1836–1986* (Austin: University of Texas Press, 1987). Citrus employment statistics are from 1938 but are roughly applicable to the 1920s; "Citrus Packing Plants Employ 1200 Workers," Riverside *Daily Press,* May 5, 1938, p. 7. California's first "captive" agricultural labor force was Chinese; see Cletus E. Daniel, *Bitter Harvest: A History of California Farmworkers, 1870–1941* (Berkeley, Los Angeles, and London: University of California Press, [1981] 1982), 27. On the importance of the open shop to the regional industrialization strategy, see Robert Phelps, "Dangerous Class on the Plains of the Id: Ideology and Home Ownership in Southern California, 1880–1920" (Ph.D. dissertation, University of California, Riverside, 1996).

5. Some of my neighborhood names do not correspond to local place-names. "Expansion," "Government Tract," "Groves," and the geographic differentiation of three East Side neighborhoods designate historically and socially distinguishable districts but are not contemporary place-names. Today, the three East Side neighborhoods are known simply as "Eastside." I defined the geographic boundaries of Riverside's historic neighborhoods in terms of street boundaries for distinctive racial, class, and historical characteristics. The boundaries are static but encompass socially dynamic areas for three decades, 1921–1950. The boundaries should therefore be thought of as containing the central tendencies in social and geographic definition of neighborhoods, rather than mutually exclusive neighborhood characteristics. Over time, social characteristics changed near the boundaries, perhaps sufficiently by 1950 that households along particular street boundaries no longer reflected the central tendency of the neighborhood. I defined the street boundaries for Old East Side in terms of the 1948 housing survey of the area; see "Nearly all residents" quotation and other information regarding the survey from "Church Women Make Survey of Housing Conditions on East Side," Riverside *Daily Press,* September 22, 1948, p. 4. In 1921, the African-American and Mexican-American populations in the neighborhood were smaller and more confined than in 1948, so that at the outset of the period there were more Anglo households than minority households along the neighborhood's boundary streets. Table 3.1 demonstrates that the boundaries capture distinguishing characteristics for the entire period.

6. To supplement Riverside Sample Data (see n. 7), I drew on the class analysis of households in Mile Square in 1889 and 1923 by Robert Phelps, "The Riverside and Arlington Railroad Company: Social Control in the Citrus Community" (unpublished graduate research paper, Department of History, University of California, Riverside, 1989), 61–64, 74–76. "Four Hundred and Three New Houses Have Been Erected Here in Last Twelve Months," *Riverside Enterprise,* December 31, 1924, p. 9.

7. Data on social characteristics, residential characteristics, housing quality, electrical status, and neighborhood zones of Riverside households are drawn from three data sets. The first consists of 1,573 electrified houses drawn from the utility billing records of the City of Riverside, California, between 1921 and 1950; the second, for information pertaining to the 9,080 individuals and business enterprises, was obtained from city directories listing who occupied those houses and consumed electricity; and the third,

of 276,399 monthly observations of electrical consumption. As the source for the data and analysis of Riverside, the data are referenced as "Riverside Sample Data." Research on the Riverside Sample Data was conducted by chapter 6 co-author, Charles Wetherell. Unless otherwise referenced, all quantitative data about Riverside is from this source. See Tobey, "Statistical Supplement." See also chapter 6, note 3.

8. On Riverside's minorities, see Joyce Carter Vickery, *Defending Eden: New Mexican Pioneers in Southern California, 1830–1890* (Riverside: Department of History, University of California, Riverside, and the Riverside Museum Press, 1977); Mark Howland Rawitsch, *No Other Place: Japanese American Pioneers in a Southern California Neighborhood* (Riverside: Department of History, University of California, Riverside, 1983); and Great Basin Foundation, ed., *Wong Ho Leun: An American Chinatown* (San Diego: The Foundation, 1987). Riverside's Chinatown followed a model similar to San Jose's Chinatown; see Timothy J. Lukes and Gary Y. Okihiro, *Japanese Legacy: Farming and Community in California's Santa Clara Valley,* Local History Studies 31, California History Center (Cupertino: California History Center, 1985), 19–25. See also Roger Daniels, *The Politics of Prejudice: The Anti-Japanese Movement in California and the Struggle for Japanese Exclusion* (New York: Atheneum, [1969] 1970). On employment segregation, see Tobey, "Statistical Supplement." On the racial context of Riverside zoning, see "Race Relations Survey Is Plan," Riverside *Daily Press,* August 15, 1924, p. 2; "Mexican Housing Being Studied," *Riverside Enterprise,* July 11, 1924, p. 2; "Will Oppose Any Entrance of Orientals: Northsiders Plan to Take Action to Meet Situation," ibid., July 29, 1924, p. 5; "[Berkeley, California] Adopt[s] Covenant on Race Problem," Riverside *Daily Press,* August 13, 1924, p. 6; "Mexican Problem Theme of Meeting," *Riverside Enterprise,* November 16, 1924, p. 1. "Council Overrules Planning Body on Duplex Rezoning," Riverside *Daily Press,* June 18, 1940, p. 4. "Big Subdivision Project on Rubidoux Slope Approved," ibid., February 7, 1941, 9. "Subdivision Rezoning Given Tentative Approval," ibid., March 5, 1943, 5. "City's Housing Problems Aired," ibid., February 12, 1947, p. 1. "Planners O.K. Housing Zone," ibid., April 8, 1949, p. 9. "44-Home Project Now Underway on Eastside," ibid., April 6, 1950, p. 12. Morton Keller opposes but does not disprove the thesis that zoning resulted from elites attempting to maintain social control of an ever-changing population and does not mention control of race relations; see Keller, *Regulating a New Economy,* 181–191. My claim that zoning deliberately suppressed minority population growth is partly based on comparison of Riverside's and regional minority population trends; see Tobey, "Statistical Supplement." On Mexican immigration, see Carey McWilliams, *North from Mexico: The Spanish-speaking People of the United States,* new ed., updated by Matt S. Meier (New York: Praeger, [1948] 1990). On zoning for race separation, see Christopher Silver, *Twentieth-Century Richmond: Planning, Politics, and Race* (Knoxville: University of Tennessee Press, 1984), 11, 31–34, 97–129; and Barbara J. Flint, "Zoning and Residential Segregation: A Social and Physical History, 1910–1940" (Ph.D. dissertation, University of Chicago, 1977), 12–16, on California's leadership in racial zoning, and pp. 35–39, 103–107, 226–28, 238–241, 300–358 on planned zoning and racial residential segregation in twentieth-century Atlanta, St. Louis, and Chicago.

9. Hunter Douglas Corporation built a $290,000 plant on Kansas Avenue in 1947–1948; see "Building Permits in Riverside Up in 1947," Riverside *Daily Press,* January 1, 1948, p. 4.

10. One Hispanic family lived in the North East Side before 1941, that of Miguel Estudillo, city attorney and descendant of Mexican land grant holders. See "Miguel

Estudillo Tells of Political Battle in County," Riverside *Daily Press,* September 25, 1943, 2:A-7, and "Miguel Estudillo, Son of State Pioneers, Dies," ibid., April 29, 1950, p. 9.

11. "Alternate Lots Free to All Who Build," *Riverside Enterprise,* April 1, 1923, p. 13. Patterson, *A Colony for California,* 376.

12. For the profiles of Diaz and Machado, see Arthur Gordon, "Potential Value of Latins to Their Community Told," Riverside *Daily Press,* May 11, 1940, p. 2.

13. "Names Are Wanted for Subdivision," *Riverside Enterprise,* April 6, 1922, p. 2. "Four Hundred and Three New Houses Have Been Erected Here in Last Twelve Months," ibid., December 31, 1924, p. 1. "Magnolia Area Continues Home Building Center," Riverside *Daily Press,* July 9, 1938, p. 16; twenty of eighty-two permits from January 1 to July 1 were in the area. "60-Home Project to Be Built at Once," Riverside *Daily Press,* July 15, 1947, p. 4; "60-Home Building Project Invites Public Inspection," ibid., November 15, 1947, p. 7. On tract development in the Government Tract area, see "Mayor Guessed Wrong—City Building Boom Still Booming," ibid., April 13, 1950, p. 10. Kenneth T. Jackson, "Race, Ethnicity, and Real Estate Appraisal," pp. 210–232 in Leonard Dinnerstein and Kenneth T. Jackson, eds., *American Vistas, Vol. 2: 1877 to the Present* (New York: Oxford University Press, 1995); see also Federal Housing Administration, *Underwriting Manual: Underwriting and Valuation Procedure under Title II of the National Housing Act,* rev. ed. (Washington, D.C.: Federal Housing Administration, February 1938), pars. 909, 936, 1379(6). Greg Hise, "Home Building and Industrial Decentralization in Los Angeles: The Roots of the Postwar Urban Region," *Journal of Urban History* 19 (February 1993): 95–125, and Marc A. Weiss, *The Rise of the Community Builders: The American Real Estate Industry and Urban Land Planning* (New York: Columbia University Press, 1987), 145–162.

14. Average Number of Light Bulbs in Residences, 1923–1924, from Table I, "Summary of Various Major Items in Residential Lighting Survey," in "Possibilities of Residence Lighting," *Electrical World* 85 (June 20, 1925): 1319. In the early 1920s, home owners used only low-wattage bulbs. In a survey of 7,000 homes in 1922, the National Electric Lighting Association found that 75 percent of all bulbs rated at fifty watts or less; see fig. 3, "Lamp Wattage Distribution in Residences," in M. Luckiesh, "More Wattage in the Home Lights," *Electrical World* 86 (November 28, 1925): 1106. In table 3.6, below, a small number of residences with more than 100 lightbulbs were eliminated because they provided an insufficient basis for statistical analysis. On the connection between income, assessed value of residential property, and the number of rooms, see Doucet and Weaver, *Housing the North American City,* 428:table 10.2, 430:table 10.3.

15. Phelps, "The Riverside and Arlington Railroad Company," 44; Patterson, *A Colony for California,* 185. "Accepted the Agnew Agency" quoted from "Riverside Snap Shots" personals column by "Jay Hawker" [H. H. Williamson], *California Eagle,* December 30, 1922, p. 6. "Has bought" quoted from ibid., November 11, 1922, p. 13.

16. "Strict Economy of Electric Power Urged," *Riverside Enterprise,* March 17, 1924, p. 1. "Utilities Board to Force Reduction in Local Use of Electricity Immediately," ibid., June 20, 1924, p. 4. "Power Curtailed 25 Per Cent in Southern California," *Electrical World* 84 (July 19, 1924): 135. H. G. Butler, "California Power Shortage of 1924," ibid., 85 (January 24, 1925): 193–197.

17. Cf. Platt, *The Electric City,* 235–267.

18. "Gas Company Believed to Have No Franchise," Riverside *Daily Press,* January 26, 1939, p. 5; Riverside *Morning Mission,* September 3, 1909, p. 2; "Gas Company to Build Own Office Here," Riverside *Daily Press,* January 7, 1930, p. 5. Statistics on

Riverside meters are provided in "Riverside Public Utilities," *Riverside Press and Enterprise* Progress Edition supplement, February 11, 1949, p. 7. On continuing use of oil lamps, see "Change in Rates Here for House Lighting Is Unlikely," *Riverside Enterprise,* April 14, 1925, p. 2.

19. For the appearance of technologies, see: [advertisements for] "Samuel Hill [oil]," Riverside *Press,* July 6, 1878, p. 3; "Ruffen and Biays [oil stoves]," ibid., August 24, 1878, p. 4; "Standard Oil Co.," ibid., November 30, 1979, p. 3; "Hutchings & Co , Oil," ibid., December 21, 1878, p. 3; "Weister & Co. [oil stoves]," ibid., December 28, 1878, p. 3; "Trowbridge and Wakeman [gasoline stoves]," ibid., November 12, 1889, p. 1; "The Riverside Transfer [coal]," ibid., 1; "Wood & Cunningham [stoves]," ibid., November 18, 1889, p. 4; "C. C. Birdsall [gasoline and coal oil]," Riverside *Morning Enterprise,* August 3, 1900, p. 3; "Findlay & Knight [wood and coal heaters, coal oil heaters]," ibid., December 18, 1900, p. 8; "Riverside Milling & Fuel Company [coal]," ibid., September 1, 1910, p. 5; "Southern California Gas Company [ad for service]," ibid., September 4, 1912, p. 3; "Southern California Gas Company [ovens]," ibid., July 23, 1915, p. 6; "Florence Oil Range," ibid., May 6, 1925, p. 3; "Gas Ranges and Heaters," ibid., January 15, 1928, p. 5; "Sears, Roebuck, and Co. ['Dispatch' Gas Ranges]," ibid., February 24, 1929, p. 6. As the housing boom of the 1920s finally got under way, businesses affiliated with gas service took out full-page ads in the *Riverside Enterprise* to promote heaters and ranges: "Why Have New Houses No Chimneys?" ibid., November 16, 1922, p. 3, and "Gas Equipment Exhibit," ibid., April 7, 1924, p. 4. Typical stories about improving gas service are "Gas Improvements Are Planned Here," ibid., March 3, 1921, p. 8; "Gas Service Is Improved Here," ibid., November 10, 1921, p. 3; "Gas Assured for Elsinore," ibid., February 22, 1923, p. 7; "Corona Good Field for Gas Company," ibid., February 29, 1923, p. 2; "Big Sum Will Be Expended," ibid., February 5, 1924, p. 9; "Huge Gas Line Is Being Constructed," ibid., December 25, 1926, p. 4. "Electricity can be safely" quoted in "All Riverside Property Owners Are Stockholders in Their Municipal Electric Light Plant [advertisement]," Riverside *Daily Press,* March 20, 1935, p. 8. On the state of gas cooking technology and the competition between gas and electric cooking, see Jane Busch, "Cooking Competition," 222–245. On the advancement of residential technologies and quality of home life, see Cowan, *More Work for Mother,* passim.

20. See Norris Hundley, Jr., *Dividing the Waters: A Century of Controversy Between the United States and Mexico* (Berkeley, Los Angeles, and London: University of California Press, 1966); Norris Hundley, Jr., *Water and the West: The Colorado River Compact and the Politics of Water in the American West* (Berkeley, Los Angeles, and London: University of California Press, 1975); Norris Hundley, Jr., *The Great Thirst: Californians and Water, 1770s–1990s* (Berkeley, Los Angeles, and Oxford: University of California Press, 1992), 203–220; and Donald J. Pisani, *From the Family Farm to Agribusiness: The Irrigation Crusade in California and the West, 1850–1931* (Berkeley, Los Angeles, and London: University of California Press, 1984); and Donald Worster, *Rivers of Empire: Water, Aridity, and the Growth of the American West* (New York: Pantheon Books, 1985). On Los Angeles's struggle for the Colorado River, see Brigham, "Public Power," 273–304. On Southern California Edison, see William A. Myers, *Iron Men and Copper Wires: A Centennial History of the Southern California Edison Company* (Glendale, Calif.: Trans-Anglo Books, 1983), and William Allan Myers, "Electricity in Orange County, California, 1890–1914: A Case Study in the Socio-Economic Impact of Technology" (M.A. thesis, California State University, Fullerton, 1991).

21. Carey McWilliams, *Southern California: An Island Upon the Land* (Salt Lake

City: Peregrine Smith Books, [1946] 1973), 273–283; Starr, *Material Dreams,* 90–95; Robert M. Fogelson, *The Fragmented Metropolis: Los Angeles, 1850–1930* (Cambridge: Harvard University Press, 1967), 108–134; Roger W. Lotchin, *Fortress California, 1910–1961* (New York: Oxford University Press, 1992), 5–17, 64–130. On the Southern industrialization strategy, see James C. Cobb, *Industrialization and Southern Society, 1877–1984* (Lexington: University of Kentucky Press, 1984), 27–50, 88; and James C. Cobb, *The Selling of the South: The Southern Crusade for Industrial Development, 1936–1980* (Baton Rouge: Louisiana State University Press, 1982), 92–98.

22. See Daniel, *Bitter Harvest,* passim. See also Mike Davis, *City of Quartz: Excavating the Future in Los Angeles* (New York: Vintage Books, [1990] 1992), 101–106.

23. In the city's mayoralty election in November 1927, six candidates debated issues of agriculture and industry in the city. Industrialization was strongly supported, even by the candidate who ran on an agricultural platform. See "Half Dozen Candidates to Run for Office of Mayor," *Riverside Enterprise,* October 27, 1927, p. 7; "Candidate for Mayor Sees Benefit of Farm Activity," ibid., November 4, 1927, p. 7; "Community Prosperity Is Dependent on the Payroll," ibid., November 5, 1927, p. 7. "The middle class" quoted from Baritz, *The Good Life,* 71, and see also pp. 71–85, 125–129, 171.

24. "Mayor Porter at Sacramento Power Meeting," *Riverside Enterprise,* January 29, 1921, p. 1. Dr. Porter elaborated his political philosophy in favor of municipal ownership of utilities in a debate with A. B. West, vice president of the Southern Sierras Power Company, who attacked municipal ownership as socialism by another name, at a meeting of the Present Day Club in Riverside, March 28, 1921. Porter's view was supported by E. A. Scattergood, chief engineer of the Los Angeles Bureau of Power and Light. "Will Riverside Build Power Plant?" ibid., March 29, 1921, p. 3. See also Van Valen, "Power Politics," 210–212, 232–233.

25. "Half Dozen Candidates to Run for Office of Mayor," *Riverside Enterprise,* October 27, 1927, p. 7; Patterson, *Colony for California,* 283. See also C. Howard Hopkins, *The Rise of the Social Gospel in American Protestantism, 1865–1915* (New Haven: Yale University Press, [1940] 1976), and Ira V. Brown, *Lyman Abbott, Christian Evolutionist: A Study in Religious Liberalism* (Westport, Conn.: Greenwood Press, [1953] 1970).

26. "Representatives Southern California Cities Urge Early Investigation Marshall Plan," *Riverside Enterprise,* February 23, 1921, p. 3; Hundley, *Water and the West,* 116–117.

27. "Principal private developer" quoted from William L. Kahrl, *Water and Power: The Conflict over Los Angeles' Water Supply in the Owens Valley* (Berkeley, Los Angeles, and London: University of California Press, 1982), 236. Riverside newspapers followed the L. A.–Southern Sierras fight daily. See "Los Angeles Begins Southern Sierras Suit," *Riverside Enterprise,* June 3, 1921, p. 1; "L.A. Seeks to Grab Power Is Asserted," ibid., June 4, 1921, p. 2; "Los Angeles Attempting to Secure Power Monopoly, A. B. West Asserts to C. of C.," ibid., June 24, 1921, p. 3; "Mayor Snyder's Statement of City Power," ibid., July 4, 1921, p. 3; "Where Filings Are," ibid., July 5, 1921, p. 4. Also see "Mass Meeting Denounces L.A. Grab Attempt," ibid., March 23, 1923, p. 1; "Power Bill Is Under Protest in Resolution," ibid., February 20, 1923, p. 1; See also Van Valen, "Power Politics," 206; Hundley, *Water and the West,* 117.

28. "Mayor Snyder's Statement of City Power," *Riverside Enterprise,* July 4, 1921, p. 3; "Where Filings Are," ibid., July 5, 1921, p. 4.

29. Brigham, "Public Power," 293 f. "Los Angeles Is Empowered to Buy Big Edison Plan," *Riverside Enterprise,* April 2, 1921, p. 1. R. H. Ballard (president, Southern California Edison Company), "Every Sixth Home—A Stockholder," *Electrical World* 92

(August 18, 1928): 319. "Hydro Power Plan Proposed," *Riverside Enterprise*, June 3, 1921, p. 1.

30. "The smaller cities" quoted from "Municipalities are Busy on Plan to Form Power Merger," *Riverside Enterprise*, June 29, 1921, p. 2. "Representatives Southern California Cities Urge Early Investigation Marshall Plan," ibid., February 23, 1921, p. 3. "Will Riverside Build Power Plant?" ibid., March 29, 1921, p. 3. A. B. West was also president of the Pacific Coast Electrical Association in 1922; see his address in "Power Industry Stands on What It Has Done," ibid., June 1, 1922, p. 6. "Dr. Porter Made Secretary of Committee," ibid., July 26, 1921, p. 4; "Bitter Attack on Riverside Made by Committee Starting Campaign for State Control," ibid., August 29, 1921, p. 3. On Haynes and Spreckels, see Tom Sitton, *John Randolph Haynes, California Progressive* (Stanford: Stanford University Press, 1992), 164–165.

31. "The mechanical revolution" quoted from "Porter Wants Cheap Power," *Riverside Enterprise*, September 30, 1921, p. 1. "Our prosperity" quoted from "Forensic Tilt Brings Issues Out Squarely," ibid., June 24, 1922, p. 1. "The water" quoted from "Dr. Porter Made Secretary of Committee," ibid., July 26, 1921, p. 4.

32. "Constitutional Amendment Will Be Fought Hard," ibid., August 5, 1921, p. 1.

33. "California State Ownership Campaign to Begin Anew," *Electrical World* 80 (December 9, 1922): 1287. "The Pacific Coast Rejects Public Ownership," ibid., 84 (November 15, 1924): 1035. "Public Ownership Up Again," ibid., 88 (October 16, 1926): 818; "California and Oregon Stand Firm," ibid., 88 (November 6, 1926): 977.

34. "Bitter Attack on Riverside Made by Committee Starting Campaign for State Control," *Riverside Enterprise*, August 29, 1921, p. 3; "Congressman Phil D. Swing in League Address Pleads for Solid Support of Fall Plan," ibid., December 11, 1921, p. 3; "Development of Colorado Approved," ibid., May 17, 1922, p. 2; "Power Act Is Condemned by Mass Meeting," ibid., May 16, 1922, p. 1; "Forensic Tilt Brings Issues Out Squarely," ibid., June 24, 1922, p. 1; "Water, Power Act Opposed By Realtors," ibid., October 26, 1924, p. 1; "Water and Power Act to Be Fought by Mutual Concerns," ibid., July 27, 1926, p. 3.

35. "Industries Being Sought," *Riverside Enterprise*, February 1, 1922, p. 3; "How to Bring Industries to City Discussed," ibid., April 25, 1923, p. 1; "The lifeblood" quoted from "Industries for Riverside Are C. of C. Theme," ibid., June 28, 1923, p. 1; "To Develop All of California Industries," ibid., July 29, 1923, p. 8. Arnold's address reprinted in "Los Angeles Chamber Brings Industrial Opportunities to All of Southern California," ibid., June 28, 1923, p. 7. See also Brigham, "Public Power," 279, 289 f.

36. All quotations from Arnold's address in "Los Angeles Chamber Brings Industrial Opportunities to All of Southern California," *Riverside Enterprise*, June 28, 1923, p. 7.

37. All quotations and "Is it not then" from Arnold's address in ibid. "White spot" refers to the realty practice of marking with a white spot on a map where real estate sales were booming. On the BAWI (Balance Agriculture with Industry) campaign and TVA liberals' development strategy, see Cobb, *Industrialization,* 38–40, and Cobb, *Selling of the South,* 5–34.

38. "Los Angeles Chamber Brings Industrial Opportunities to All of Southern California," *Riverside Enterprise*, June 28, 1923, p. 7; "Mayor Snyder's Statement of City Power," ibid., July 4, 1921, p. 3. "How to Bring Industries to City Discussed, Chamber of Commerce Has Interesting Discussion at Court House," ibid., April 25, 1923, p. 1; "Many Matters of Interest at Chamber Commerce," ibid., July 12, 1923, p. 3. "Industrial Survey of County Being Prepared; Interesting Data Is Already Available," ibid., July 26, 1923, p. 1; "Preliminary C. of C. Survey Is Completed," ibid., July 28, 1923, p. 7.

39. "Industrial Center for Riverside Is Favored," *Riverside Enterprise,* September 2, 1923, p. 1; "How to Bring Industries to City Discussed, Chamber of Commerce Has Interesting Discussion at Court House," ibid., April 25, 1923, p. 1; "Endorsement for Project," ibid., October 21, 1924, p. 2; "With streets" quoted from "Endorsement Is Voted on New Project," ibid., October 30, 1924, p. 6; "Change in Rates Here for House Lighting Is Unlikely, but Charges for Electric Power for Industrial Purposes Will be Investigated by Utilities Board," ibid., April 14, 1925, p. 2; "Power Rates Lowered by City Board, New Industrial Schedule Goes into Effect Here," ibid., May 12, 1925, p. 3.

40. "Industrial Report on Riverside Presented," *Riverside Enterprise,* March 19, 1927, p. 2; "L.A. Chamber Head Is Here," ibid., September 8, 1927, p. 7. "Development Is Objective," ibid., October 7, 1927, p. 2. "Chambers of Commerce Agree to Los Angeles Metropolitan Area," ibid., December 6, 1927, p. 1. "Big brother" quoted from "Relations with Los Angeles [editorial]," ibid., January 15, 1928, p. 12; "Insane Fear of Los Angeles [editorial]," ibid., February 26, 1928, p. 14; "Los Angeles Chamber of Commerce [editorial]," ibid., May 24, 1929, p. 10.

41. "Steps Taken to Draw Bill for Creation of District," *Riverside Enterprise,* October 16, 1924, p. 1; "Will Submit Bill for Approval," ibid., January 9, 1925, p. 1; "Water Supply of South Is Report Topic," ibid., July 23, 1926, p. 1.

42. "Colorado River Development of Tremendous Importance to Southwest Asserts Speaker," *Riverside Enterprise,* June 17, 1923, p. 2; "Mayor Evans Back from Journey to Washington to Aid Boulder Canyon Project," ibid., February 25, 1924, p. 2; "Will Submit River Bill for Approval," ibid., January 9, 1925, p. 1; "L.A. Aqueduct Is Discussed," ibid., February 18, 1925, p. 2; "Chamber Commerce Against Proposed Legislative Bills, Metropolitan Water District Meets with Particular Disfavor from Board of Directors," ibid., March 19, 1925, p. 4.

43. "If Riverside" quoted from "L.A. Aqueduct Is Discussed," *Riverside Enterprise,* February 18, 1925, p. 2. "Development" quoted from "Development of Community Termed Issue," ibid., March 10, 1931, p. 11. "L.A. Aqueduct Work to Start this Week," ibid., March 29, 1926, p. 1.

44. "The tremendous" quoted from "Metropolitan Water Scheme Is Commended," *Riverside Enterprise,* January 16, 1929, p. 1. "Riverside is" quoted from "Needs of City Are Outlined by Executive," ibid., January 1, 1931, p. 5. "Economic ruin" quoted from "Development of Community Termed Issue," ibid., March 10, 1931, p. 11. For an obituary of William B. Mathews, see *Electrical World* 98 (December 26, 1931): 1148.

45. "If the city" quoted from "Necessity of Water from New Source Outlined in Statement," *Riverside Enterprise,* March 22, 1931, p. 5.

46. "Necessity of Water from New Source Outlined in Statement," *Riverside Enterprise,* March 22, 1931, p. 5. "The best" quoted from "Opponents of District Plan Hold Meeting," ibid., March 11, 1931, p. 11. "The Santa Ana" quoted from "Eminent Engineer Makes Clear Urgent Need of Water if this City Shall Continue to Grow," ibid., March 17, 1931, p. 11. "Mayor Long Replies to Water Questions," ibid., March 11, 1931, p. 11.

47. "Directors of Project Take Quick Action," *Riverside Enterprise,* March 14, 1931, p. 11. The local debate over joining the MWD occupied the city for over six years, and after 1929, on a daily basis. For major turning points, see "Chamber Commerce Against Proposed Legislative Bills, Metropolitan Water District Meets with Particular Disfavor from Board of Directors," ibid., March 19, 1925, p. 4; "To Seek Water from Colorado, Cities Will Join in Organizing of Metropolitan District," ibid., August 7, 1927, p. 1; "Metropolitan Water Scheme Turned Down, Membership in District Decided Against by City

Council," ibid., August 15, 1928, p. 7; "C. of C. Votes Against Metropolitan Water District, Entry Found Inadvisable at this Time," ibid., October 16, 1930, p. 1; "Group Studies Issue of City Joining Move," ibid., December 13, 1930, p. 13; "Directors of District Vote after Report, Engineers Explain Reasons Why Parker Line Chosen, Formal Approval Is Then Given," ibid., December 23, 1930, p. 1; "Initial Step Taken Toward Joining Body," ibid., January 14, 1931, p. 1; "Construction of Project in County Voted," ibid., January 17, 1931, p. 11; "April 20 Last Date for Vote on Admission," ibid., January 31, 1931, p. 11; "Metropolitan District Vote Set March 21," ibid., February 11, 1931, p. 9; "Information on Issue Will be Broadcast, Group of 20 Prominent Citizens to Back Proposal City Enter Metropolitan Area," ibid., February 22, 1931, p. 9; "Water Issue's Opponents Act, 'Protective Association' to Oppose City's Joining District Calls Parley," ibid., March 4, 1931, p. 11; "Alterations to Water Act Opposed Here," ibid., March 5, 1931, p. 3; "Development of Community Termed Issue," ibid., March 10, 1931, p. 11, reporting a heavily attended public meeting; "Directors of Project Take Quick Action, Move to Prevent Any Possible Cause for Criticism of Metropolitan Plan," ibid., March 14, 1931, p. 11; "Present Day Members Hear All Phases," ibid., March 24, 1931, p. 4, reporting on another heavily attended public debate.

Supporting entry into the district were the current mayor, Joseph S. Long, Oscar Ford, former mayor, Horace Porter, former mayor and advocate of publicly owned water and power, Joseph Jarvis, former president of the Riverside Water Company, Frank Tetley, land developer and member of the State Highway Commission, Frank A. Miller, and Howard H. Hays, a land developer who would later purchase the Riverside *Daily Press,* one of the city's two major daily newspapers. S. C. Evans, long a proponent of entry, withheld a public position on the issue in 1931 but finally sided with the opponents of entry without taking an active role in the debate. The other Evans family businessmen— W. C. Evans and P. T. Evans—openly opposed entry to the district. Other prominent citizens lining up against entry included A. M. Lewis, J. R. Gabbert (*Riverside Enterprise* owner), L. D. Batcheldor, director of the University of California's Citrus Experiment Station at Riverside, A. B. West of Southern Sierras Power, and Henry Coil, attorney for Southern Sierras Power, and E. B. Criddle, Southern Sierras vice president, the Chase family, long associated with Riverside citrus, Miguel Estudillo, city attorney, and Henry Coil, head of the planning commission and advocate of master planned zoning.

48. "Big Majority Is Tabulated Against Plan," *Riverside Enterprise,* April 1, 1931, p. 1; "District Plan Meets Defeat in Close Vote," ibid., August 12, 1931, p. 3; "$220,000,000 for Aqueduct Gets Big Poll," ibid., September 30, 1931, p. 1; Camille Guerin-Gonzales, *Mexican Workers and American Dreams: Immigration, Repatriation, and California Farm Labor, 1900–1939* (New Brunswick: Rutgers University Press, 1994).

Chapter 4. The New Deal in Electrical Modernization

1. In discussing the New Deal, I do not reference individual titles in the enormous literature on the 1930s, unless the title is specifically significant to the text; instead, I cite *A New Deal,* Roger Biles's recent summary of scholarship. For a bibliography, see David E. Kyvig and Mary-Ann Blasio, compilers, *New Day/New Deal: A Bibliography of the Great American Depression, 1929–1941,* Bibliographies and Indexes in American History, no. 9 (New York: Greenwood Press, 1988). Useful anthologies of reinterpretations

of the New Deal are provided by Wilbur J. Cohen, ed., *The Roosevelt New Deal: A Program Assessment Fifty Years After* ([Austin]: Lyndon B. Johnson School of Public Affairs, the University of Texas, 1986); Robert Eden, ed., *The New Deal and Its Legacy: Critique and Reappraisal,* Contributions in American History, no. 132 (New York: Greenwood Press, 1989); and Steve Fraser and Gary Gerstle, eds., *The Rise and Fall of the New Deal Order, 1930–1980* (Princeton: Princeton University Press, 1989). For older reinterpretations of the New Deal, see Melvyn Dubofsky, ed., *The New Deal: Conflicting Interpretations and Shifting Perspectives* (New York: Garland, 1992).

2. Biles, *A New Deal,* 41; Paul K. Conkin, "Intellectual and Political Roots of TVA," in Hargrove and Conkin, *TVA,* 24–26; Creese, *TVA's Public Planning,* 32–52. Graham sees the New Deal as lacking a power policy because it could not arrive at a formal statement, a rather different perspective on the fundamental unity of New Deal goals from what I present; see Otis L. Graham, Jr., *Toward a Planned Society: From Roosevelt to Nixon* (New York: Oxford University Press, 1976), 60.

3. "The supply" quoted from "Northwestern Power," *Business Week* (August 11, 1934): 11. Nye dismisses Roosevelt's vision: "As was so often the case, Franklin D. Roosevelt caught the popular mood in a speech." See Nye, *Electrifying America,* 304.

4. "What I saw" quoted from "Extemporaneous Remarks at Tupelo, Mississippi," November 18, 1934, in Roosevelt, *Public Papers,* 3: 460–462.

5. "Power is" quoted from "The One Hundred Sixtieth Press Conference (Excerpts)," Warm Springs, Georgia, November 23, 1934, in Roosevelt, *Public Papers,* 3: 466.

6. "Social revolution," "sound and courageous public policy," and "it seems to me" quotations from "'Are You and I Paying Enough Attention to Human Engineering?'" Address to the Third World Power Conference, Washington, D.C., September 11, 1936, in Roosevelt, *Public Papers,* 5: 352–353.

7. For bibliographies on the history of the nation's housing, see Jackson, *Crabgrass Frontier,* and Wright, *Building the Dream.* The following citations pertain to points and personalities in the text: Michael J. Doucet and John C. Weaver, "Material Culture and the North American House: The Age of the Common Man, 1870–1920," *Journal of American History* 72 (1985): 560–587; Doucet and Weaver, *Housing the North American City;* Gertrude Sipperly Fish, ed., *The Story of Housing* (New York: Macmillan, 1979); Nathaniel S. Keith, *Politics and the Housing Crisis since 1930* (New York: Universe Books, 1973); Constance Perin, *Everything in Its Place: Social Order and Land Use in America* (Princeton: Princeton University Press, 1977); Irving Welfeld, *Where We Live: A Social History of American Housing* (New York: Simon & Schuster, 1988); and Wright, *Building the Dream.* Major contemporary contributions that argued for a greater federal presence in the nation's housing problems and provided a large amount of useful information on contemporary housing conditions were Louis Pink, *The New Day in Housing* (New York: John Day, 1928); Edith Elmer Wood, *Recent Trends in Housing* (New York: Macmillan, 1931); and Catherine Bauer, *Modern Housing* (New York: Arno, [1934] 1974). On the history of housing reform before the New Deal, see Eugenie Ladner Birch, "Edith Elmer Wood and the Genesis of Liberal Housing Thought" (Ph.D. dissertation, Columbia University, 1976); Pearl Janet Davies, *Real Estate in American History* (Washington, D.C.: Public Affairs Press, 1958), 128–149; Lawrence Friedman, *Government and Slum Housing: A Century of Frustration* (New York: Arno Press, [1968] 1978), 25–72, 73–131; Roy Lubove, *The Progressives and the Slums: Tenement House Reform in New York City, 1890–1917* (Pittsburgh: University of Pittsburgh Press, 1973); John F. Sutherland, "A City of Homes: Philadelphia Slums and Reform-

ers, 1880–1920," (Ph.D. dissertation, Temple University, 1973). On New Deal housing programs, see Miles L. Colean, *A Backward Glance—An Oral History: The Growth of Government Housing Policy in the United States, 1934–1975* (Washington, D.C.: The Fund, 1975); Gertrude S. Fish, "Housing Policy During the Great Depression," in Fish, *The Story of Housing,* 177–241; Jesse H. Jones, with Edward Angly, *Fifty Billion Dollars: My Thirteen Years with the RFC* (New York: Macmillan, 1951); C. Lowell Harriss, *History and Policies of the Home Owners' Loan Corporation* (New York: National Bureau of Economic Research, 1951); and Marriner S. Eccles, *Beckoning Frontiers: Public and Personal Recollections,* ed. Stanley Hyman (New York: Alfred A. Knopf, 1951). For assessments of the nation's housing by federal housing officials, see Glenn H. Beyer, *Housing: A Factual Analysis* (New York: Macmillan, 1958); Miles Colean, *American Housing* (New York: Twentieth Century Fund, 1944); and Nathan Straus, *Two Thirds of a Nation: A Housing Program* (New York: Knopf, 1952). On the history of public housing, see Henry J. Aaron, *Federal Housing Subsidies: History, Problems, and Alternatives* (Washington, D.C.: Brookings Institution, 1973); Harry C. Bredemeier, *"The Federal Public Housing Movement"* (Ph.D. dissertation, Columbia University, reprint New York: Arno Press, [1955] 1980); J. Joseph Huthmacher, *Senator Robert F. Wagner and the Rise of Urban Liberalism* (New York: Atheneum, [1968] 1971), 205–216, 224–230; Timothy McDonnell, *The Wagner Housing Act* (Chicago: Loyola University Press, 1957); Robert Moore Fisher, *Twenty Years of Public Housing* (New York: Harper & Brothers, 1959); Eugenie Ladner Birch, "Woman-made America: The Case of Early Public Housing Policy," *Journal of the American Institute of Planners* 44 (April 1978): 130–144. On New Deal new towns programs, see Paul Conkin, *Tomorrow a New World: New Deal Community Programs* (Ithaca: Cornell University Press, 1959); Joseph L. Arnold, *The New Deal in the Suburbs: A History of the Greenbelt Town Program, 1935–1954* (Columbus: Ohio State University Press, 1971); George A. Warner, *Greenbelt: The Cooperative Community: An Experience in Democratic Living* (New York: Exposition Press, 1954). On housing in cities, see Mark I. Gelfand, *A Nation of Cities: The Federal Government and Urban America, 1933–1965* (New York: Oxford University Press, 1975); and Jackson, *Crabgrass Frontier.*

8. Steven E. Andrachek, "Housing in the United States: 1890–1929," in Fish, *The Story of Housing,* 123–176; Wright, *Building the Dream,* chap. 10, "Welfare Capitalism and the Company Town"; Beyer, *Housing,* 39; Weiss, *The Rise of the Community Builders.*

9. John Gries and James Ford, eds., *The President's Conference on Home Building and Home Ownership,* vol. 2, *Home Finance and Taxation* (Washington, D.C.: President's Conference on Home Building and Home Ownership, 1932), 16, 19–20.

10. Ibid., 103, 104, 153, 158, 160; see also the report, "Appendix III, Increasing Tax Delinquency," pp. 184–187.

11. "'In 1933'" quoted from Cecelia M. Gerloff, ed., *The Federal Home Loan Bank System* (1971), by Fish, "Housing Policy During the Great Depression," 186. Carey Winston, untitled section in ibid., 189. Bureau of the Census, *Historical Statistics of the United States,* Bicentennial Edition, 2 vols. (Washington, D.C.: U.S. Government Printing Office, 1976), Series N 243, 2: 646; hereafter cited as Census, *Historical Statistics* (1976). Studies for the President's Conference on Home Building and Home Ownership, 1931, established that most families with less than $1,250 annual income were unable to afford home ownership. The report of the Committee on the Relationship of Income and the Home cautiously generalized this income threshold to the nation's urban areas; see

Gries and Ford, *The President's Conference,* 4: 52. Since 65 percent of American families and not married individuals in 1929 had less than $2,000, I have generalized that in 1930, some two-thirds of the nation's urban households could not afford home ownership; see Census, *Historical Statistics,* Series G 270–271, vol. 1. Participants in the President's Conference testified: "The results of careful research cited in the reports of other committees have established the fact that practically no new dwellings, and certainly no desirable types of houses, have been constructed in recent years at costs within the means of two-thirds of our population"; see Gries and Ford, *The President's Conference,* 3: 67. Also see Wood, *Recent Trends in American Housing.*

12. "Objectives" quoted from Franklin D. Roosevelt, "Message to the Congress Reviewing the Broad Objectives and Accomplishments of the Administration," June 8, 1934, in Roosevelt, *Public Papers,* 3: 288. Roger Biles places FDR's belief in the importance of home ownership at the center of his social vision of the home; Biles, *A New Deal,* 214. See also Tobey, Wetherell, and Brigham, "Moving Out and Settling In," 1395–1422.

13. Speech reprinted with explanatory foreword by Richard Hofstadter in Richard Hofstadter, ed., *Great Issues in American History: A Documentary Record* (New York: Vintage, 1958), 2: 343–351. Charles Kesler defends the notion that the Commonwealth Speech represented Roosevelt's own views and also analyzes the speech in Charles R. Kesler, "The Public Philosophy of the New Freedom and the New Deal," in Eden, *The New Deal and Its Legacy,* 154–166.

14. Foreword by Herbert Hoover, in John M. Gries and James S. Taylor, "How to Own Your Home: A Handbook for Prospective Home Owners," Department of Commerce (Washington, D.C.: Government Printing Office, 1923), v. The Department of Commerce, Building and Housing reprinted the pamphlet in 1931 as Publication no. BH17.

15. Eva Whiting White, "Housing and Citizenship, Recreation and Education," Report of the Group on Housing and Citizenship, Housing and Community—Home Repair and Remodeling, in Gries and Ford, *The President's Conference,* 86.

16. "Message to the Congress Reviewing the Broad Objectives and Accomplishments of the Administration," June 8, 1934, in Roosevelt, *Public Papers,* 3: 292.

17. "When land" and "the ultimate objective," from Roosevelt, *Public Papers,* 3: 288–289. "Many Tenants" quoted from "A Message to the Congress on Farm Tenancy," February 16, 1937, ibid., 6: 81. FDR repeated the ideological theme of security and stability in the home at important occasions, e.g., the "Annual Message to Congress," January 4, 1935, ibid., 4: 17; "The Resettlement Administration Is Established, Executive Order No. 7027," May 1, 1935, ibid., 5: 143; the footnote, beginning on page 144, written in 1937 or 1938 better conveys the vision behind the Resettlement Act.

18. "I need not remind" quoted from "Campaign Address at Kansas City, Missouri, 'America Will Have to Be Led in the Days to Come by the Youth of Today,'" October 13, 1936, in Roosevelt, *Public Papers,* 5: 470. "Should live" and "a settled place" quoted from "Address at the White House Conference on Children in a Democracy," April 23, 1939, ibid., 9: 244.

19. "Fireside Chat on Present Economic Conditions and Measures Being Taken to Improve Them," April 14, 1938, in Roosevelt, *Public Papers,* 7: 240, 242–243.

20. "Radio Address on Behalf of the Mobilization for Human Needs, White House, Washington, D.C.," in Roosevelt, *Public Papers,* 9: 535.

21. For a contemporary assessment of New Deal housing programs, see Albert Mayer, "The Nation Weighs a Vast Housing Program," *New York Times Magazine,* March 14,

1937; reprinted in Carl N. Degler, ed., *The New Deal* (Chicago: Quadrangle Books, 1970), 128–135. See also Jackson, *Crabgrass Frontier,* 190–218; Biles, *A New Deal,* 55–56, 206–224, 212–216; and Weiss, T*he Rise of the Community Builder,* 141–158.

22. Gertrude S. Fish discusses these eight programs in "Housing Policy During the Great Depression," 177–241. Lizabeth Cohen argues that the HOLC had an important impact on laboring-class neighborhoods, even though most residents did not own their homes and did not participate directly in the HOLC; see Cohen, *Making a New Deal,* 274–277.

23. Joseph D. Coppock, *Government Agencies of Consumer Installment Credit,* Financial Research Program, Studies in Consumer Installment Financing, no. 5 (New York: National Bureau of Economic Research, 1940), 1.

24. Biles, *A New Deal,* 186.

25. "Decision" and "Some one" quotations from Eccles, *Beckoning Frontiers,* 145.

26. Ibid., 147.

27. Coppock, *Government Agencies,* 21–33.

28. Ibid., 28; see also pp. 27–29.

29. Ibid., Table A-1. "Number, Amount and Average Amount of Notes Insured with FHA, 1934–37, by Month Insured," 157. The number of occupied residences is from Series N238 and N242, "Occupied Housing Units and Tenure of Homes: 1890–1970," Census, *Historical Statistics of the United States* (1975), 2: 646. The statistic of 84.8 percent is calculated from Table A-2, "Percentage Distribution of Number and Amount of Notes Insured with FHA. . . ," Coppock, *Government Agencies,* 158.

30. "The big thing" quotation by McDonald, in Coppock, *Government Agencies,* 22. Bank loan statistics calculated from Table D-4, "Components of Short-Term Consumer Debt," in Raymond W. Goldsmith, *A Study of Savings in the United States,* Vol. 1: *Introduction; Tables of Annual Estimates of Saving, 1897–1949* (Princeton: Princeton University Press, 1955), 703.

31. Coppock, *Government Agencies,* Table 6, "Percentage Distribution of Number and Amount of Notes Insured with FHA, 1934–37, with Average Note, by Type of Property and Type of Improvement," 41. Ibid., Table 28, "Percentage Distribution of Number of Appliances Financed by EHFA, Fiscal Years 1935–38, by Type of Appliance," 116. REA statistic from footnote 27, ibid. Title I statistics from Tom F. Blackburn, "Finance Houses Battle Banks for Installment Paper," *Electrical Merchandising* 57 (June 1937): 15.

32. "Has consistently" quoted from Federal Housing Administration, *Principles of Planning Small Houses,* Technical Bulletin no. 4, May 1, 1936 (Washington, D.C.: Federal Housing Administration), 2. Perin, *Everything in Its Place,* 13–14, Jackson, *Crabgrass Frontier,* 190–218.

33. "Electric wiring" quoted from Federal Housing Administration, *Principles of Planning Small Houses,* 4. "The use of" quoted from ibid., 20; see also p. 21. "The feeders," "Power circuits," and "There are" quoted from Federal Housing Administration, *Underwriting Manual: Underwriting and Valuation Procedure under Title II of the National Housing Act,* rev. 1938 (Washington, D.C.: U.S. Federal Housing Administration, 1938), par. 849, and see also par. 418, 421, 532, 619, 1334, 1624, 1719, 1726, 1873. The National Electrical Code is specifically referenced in ibid., par. 1873. In the mid-1930s, some states adopted state building and electrical codes, thereby compelling municipalities to come up to the new standards. Oregon adopted the National Electrical Code as part of its state code in 1935 and required that dwellings have wall base receptacles for

appliances; see Bureau of Labor, State of Oregon, *Rules Covering Installation of Wires and Electrical Equipment* (1940). The California State Chamber of Commerce proposed a building code for California in 1937 to establish seismic standards and proposed establishing the National Electrical Code; see California State Chamber of Commerce, *Building Code for California* (San Francisco: California State Chamber of Commerce, 1939), sec. 3301.

34. "Today, FHA" quoted from George Nelson and Henry Wright, *Tomorrow's House How to Plan Your Post-War Home Now* (New York: Simon & Schuster, 1945), 199. "New standards" and "Will protect" quoted from "Better Building Required by FHA," Riverside *Daily Press,* December 18, 1937, p. 5. Riverside's attention to increasing FHA standards is seen in the following articles: "Better Building Required by FHA," ibid.; "Lumber Rules of FHA Announced," ibid., December 21, 1937, p. 3; "FHA Inspections Protect Owners," ibid., May 7, 1938, sec. 2, p. 1; "'Jerry Building' Being Eliminated," ibid., December 3, 1938, p. 5; "New Bill Expected to Boost Building," ibid., June 10, 1939, p. 4.

35. "I asked" and "'I think'" quotations from Perin, *Everything in Its Place,* 14, 61. In Houston, land use is restricted by deed covenants, which can run a half-dozen pages. These agreements were drawn up by attorneys, hence the interviewee's reference.

36. Beyer, *Housing,* 203.

37. Weiss, *The Rise of the Community Builders,* passim.

38. "The broader the base" quoted from an address to the Third World power conference, 1936, in Roosevelt, *Public Papers,* 5: 354. "Household use" quoted from "Selling Centers on Homes," *Electrical World* 105 (January 5, 1935): 60.

39. National Emergency Council, *Report on Economic Conditions of the South* (New York: Da Capo Press, [1938] 1972), 13–14, 23–24, 39, 63–64; John V. Krutilla, "Economic Development: An Appraisal," in Roscoe C. Martin, ed., *TVA: The First Twenty Years, A Staff Report* ([n.p.]: University of Alabama Press and the University of Tennessee Press, 1956), 219–233. Bruce J. Schulman, *From Cotton Belt to Sunbelt* (New York: Oxford University Press, 1991), 1–52.

40. Nye, *Electrifying America,* 287–338, and notes, pp. 427–433, on rural electrification; O. S. Wessel, "The Power Program," in Martin, *TVA,* 113, 119–120; Brown, *Electricity for Rural America;* Morris Llewellyn Cooke, "The Early Days of the Rural Electrification Idea: 1914–1936," *American Political Science Review* 42 (June 1948): 431–447. On Cooke, see Jean Christie, *Morris Llewellyn Cooke, Progressive Engineer* (New York: Garland, 1983); Trombley, *Life and Times of a Happy Liberal.*

41. Tom F. Blackburn, "Finance Houses Battle Banks for Installment Paper," *Electrical Merchandising* 57 (June 1937): 15. Anderson does not mention the federal contribution to adoption of the refrigerator; see Anderson, Jr., *Refrigeration in America,* 213–215.

42. "By 1938" quoted from "Electric Home and Farm Authority," in James S. Olson, *Historical Dictionary of the New Deal: From Inauguration to Preparation for War* (Westport, Conn.: Greenwood Press, 1985), 143; reference to James S. Olson, "The Reconstruction Finance Corporation, 1932–1940" (Ph.D. dissertation, State University of New York at Stony Brook, 1972). Hobday, *Sparks at the Grassroots,* 102.

43. James Olson, "Farm Security Administration," in Olson, *Historical Dictionary,* 165–167, references Sidney Baldwin, *Politics and Poverty: The Rise and Decline of the Farm Security Administration* (1968).

44. "The holding company" quoted from Ralph F. De Bedts, *The New Deal's SEC:*

The Formative Years (New York: Columbia University Press, 1964), 114; see also pp. 112–143. Hawley, *The New Deal and the Problem of Monopoly,* 325–343, sees the Public Utility Holding Company Act and TVA as closely coupled strategies in Roosevelt's attack on the power trust.

45. "What the Utility Decisions Mean," *Business Week* (February 29, 1936): 18.

46. William Leuchtenburg, "Roosevelt, Norris, and the 'Seven Little TVAs,'" *Journal of Politics* 14 (August 1952): 418–441. To establish chronology for the "Seven Little TVAs," I used the following articles: "President Asks TVA Duplication in Seven Areas," Riverside *Daily Press,* June 3, 1937, p. 1; "Pile Up Seven TVA's—and You'll Have the Widespread AVA," ibid., March 7, 1941, p. 6; "Plan to Harness Missouri River Embraces One-sixth of United States," ibid., July 20, 1946, p. 2; "President Wants Lessons of TVA Applied to Western River Basins," ibid., January 6, 1949, p. 1; "Administration Plans 'TVA' for Northwest," ibid., January 21, 1949, p. 3. See also Crawford D. Goodwin, "The Valley Authority Idea—The Fading of a National Vision," pp. 263–296 in Hargrove and Conkin, *TVA;* Marguerite Owen, *The Tennessee Valley Authority* (New York: Praeger, 1973), 234–255; Richard Rudolph and Scott Ridley, *Power Struggle: The Hundred-Year War over Electricity* (New York: Harper & Row, 1986), 57–86.

47. Coppock, *Government Agencies,* 1.

48. Laurence Wray, "After FHA . . . What?" *Electrical Merchandising* 55 (June 1936): 1; Tom F. Blackburn, "Finance Houses Battle Banks for Installment Paper," ibid., 57 (June 1937): 15.

49. Rolf Nugent, *Consumer Credit* (New York: Russell Sage Foundation, 1939), 109; Duncan McC. Holthausen, Michael L. Merriam, and Rolf Nugent, *The Volume of Consumer Instalment Credit, 1929–38,* Studies in Consumer Instalment Financing, no. 7 (New York: National Bureau of Economic Research, 1940), 14.

50. "Their importance" quoted from Coppock, *Government Agencies,* ix. "Most notable" quoted from Nugent, *Consumer Credit,* 108. "Most striking" quoted from Thomas Juster, *Household Capital Formation and Financing, 1897–1962,* National Bureau of Economic Research, General Series, no. 83 (New York: Distributed by Columbia University Press, 1966), 54, 55. Data on amount and distribution of agencies making consumer loans in Tables B-4 and B-5, in Holthausen, Merriam, and Nugent, *Volume of Consumer Instalment Credit,* 77.

51. Blanche Bernstein, *The Pattern of Consumer Debt, 1935–36: A Statistical Analysis,* Studies in Consumer Instalment Financing, no. 6 (New York: National Bureau of Economic Research, 1940), 19. The WPA 1935–1936 survey was of nonfarm families not on relief. "'One-Third of a Nation . . . '," *Business Week* (September 10, 1938): 18–22, provided a detailed analysis. For comparative statistics on income, expenditures, and savings, see Table H-10, "Expenditures and Savings of Urban Families Averaging 3.5 Persons and Having Incomes Near the Average Income, Specified Dates: 1888–1947," in Raymond W. Goldsmith, Dorothy S. Brady, and Horst Mendershausen, *A Study of Saving in the United States,* vol. 3 (Princeton: Princeton University Press, 1956), 154. On the refrigerator, see Introduction, ibid., table 1.

52. Earl Whitehorne, "Selling Complete Home Electrification," *Electrical World* 95 (June 21, 1930): 1297. "The fact" quoted from "The plan for complete new-residence equipment sales [editorial]," ibid., 99 (April 16, 1932): 685. Historical sketch of the complete appliance home plan drawn from the following publications: "One Sale Electrifies the Home," ibid., 95 (March 15, 1930): 544; L. W. W. Morrow, "Selling the Homes," ibid., 95 (June 7, 1930): 1155–1157; Earl Whitehorne, "Selling Complete Home Elec-

trification"; E. R. Acker, "Full-Use Electric Home," ibid., 95 (June 7, 1930): 1158–1161; "The plan for complete new-residence equipment sales [editorial]"; "Sell the Home, Not the Appliance," ibid., 99 (April 16, 1932): 685, 688–691; George Potter, "A Plan for Complete Home Electrification," ibid., 100 (August 6, 1932): 182–185.

53. This brief history is drawn from "Long Terms for the Buyer . . . Cash for the Seller," *Electrical Merchandising* 72 (September 1944): 18–19; "Home Equipment as It Looks to the F.H.A.," ibid., 73 (February 1945): 25 f.; "A Fresh Start," ibid., 73 (March 1945): 1; "The Packaged Mortgage," ibid., 74 (July 1944): 38–39. A table listing appliances by state as eligible for FHA mortgage coverage is provided in the article, M. E. Skinner, "Electrical Living in the Homes of Tomorrow," ibid., 71 (May 1944): 54.

54. "Complete Home Plan," ibid., 73 (June 1945): 25 f. "The Packaged Mortgage," ibid., 74 (July 1945): 39.

55. [Table] "Type of Home Appliances included in value at time of purchase, 1-family homes, Sec. 203," [FHA] *Series Data Handbook, A Supplement to F.H.A. Trends,* Covering Section 203b Home Mortgage Characteristics (Department of Housing and Urban Development, Housing—F.H.A., Management Information Systems Division, Single Family Insured Branch), 18.

56. "TVA believes" quoted from "TVA Sales Plan," *Business Week* (December 23, 1933): 12. Utilizing the Lilienthal Papers, Gregory Field demonstrates that the philosophy of using the state's power to expand the mass market was present during the "first New Deal" and relates the history of the Electric Farm and Home Authority; see Gregory B. Field, "'Electricity for All': The Electric Home and Farm Authority and the Politics of Mass Consumption, 1932–1935," *Business History Review* 64 (Spring 1990): 32–60. TVA's policy of low rates and encouragement of electrical consumption is also reviewed in chap. 3, "Power Rates: An Overheated Issue," in Hobday, *Sparks,* 74–109, and Thomas K. McCraw, *TVA and the Power Fight, 1933–1939* (Philadelphia: Lippincott, 1971), 61–62. Hobday reviews the issue of whether low rates in fact succeeded in encouraging increased use of electricity; *Sparks,* 77–81, 102–104. Hughes does not believe that TVA lowered rates on ideological grounds, but for reasons of load-factor; see Hughes, *American Genesis,* 372–374. The bibliography on TVA in Kyvig and Blasio, *New Day/New Deal,* should be supplemented with the primary sources cited in North Callahan, *TVA: Bridge Over Troubled Waters* (South Brunswick: A. S. Barnes, 1980), 371–412. In interpreting TVA as part of a New Deal policy of social modernization, I do not imply that TVA (or the New Deal) also sponsored a policy of racial modernization. TVA maintained a hiring quota system to guarantee that its workforce reflected the proportion of African-Americans in the local population, and it did not oppose segregation. Lilienthal's and Harcourt Brown's philosophy that TVA should reflect "grass-roots democracy" placed the agency under regressive local racial policies. See Nancy L. Grant, *TVA and Black Americans: Planning for the Status Quo* (Philadelphia: Temple University Press, 1990), 19–44, 73–99.

57. "Existing systems" quoted from "Power Squeeze on All Sides," *Business Week* (June 7, 1933): 14–15. "Muscle Shoals Message," ibid. (April 9, 1933): 14–15. "Electrification is not" is a paraphrase of the Chamber of Commerce report in "The Rate Question," ibid. (August 11, 1934): 11.

58. "Are they" quoted from "TVA Sales Plan," *Business Week* (December 23, 1933): 12; the quotation referred to the fact that in the first several years, TVA generated more electricity than they had signed contracts for, leading to the necessity to increase loads on lines if they were to sell it all and disprove private industry's thesis that there was sufficient electric power for the region without TVA's adding more.

59. Quotations from David E. Lilienthal, "T.V.A. Seen Only as Spur to Electrification of America," *Business Week* 102 (November 25, 1933): 687–690; reprint of a speech by Lilienthal before the Lawyers' Club, Atlanta, Georgia. The TVA thesis on low rates and modernization is presented more systematically by the TVA board chairman, Gordon Clapp, who succeeded Lilienthal; see Gordon R. Clapp, *The TVA: An Approach to the Development of a Region* (Chicago: University of Chicago Press, 1955), 93–113.

60. Laurence Wray, "One Year Later," *Electrical Merchandising* 53 (February 1935): 6–9.

61. "This little town" quoted from "Tupelo—TVA's Guinea Pig," *Electrical Merchandising* 58 (November 1937): 33 f. "Here we'd like" quoted from ibid. *Business Week* had already pronounced the "anxiously awaited test" at Tupelo a success; "Tupelo Results," *Business Week* (June 9, 1934): 21. On the significance of Tupelo, see McCraw, *TVA*, 64, 70.

62. "The goal" and "old prejudice" quotations from "Selling Centers on Homes," *Electrical World* 105 (January 5, 1935): 60. "TVA-Buy Now," *Business Week* (February 10, 1934): 10.

63. "This industry" quoted from "TVA Appliances," *Business Week* (March 17, 1934): 10. "What GE" quoted from "Model T Appliances," ibid. (June 16, 1934): 11.

64. "The prices of energy" and "The plan is not brand new" quotations from T. K. Quinn, "What Can the Consumer Afford?" *Electrical World* 103 (June 9, 1934): 846. See also "Range Taps New Market," ibid. (September 8, 1934): 12. Nye argues that the appliance manufacturers, General Electric and Westinghouse, cooperated with the federal government from the start in planning electrical modernization through TVA and REA, because their interests fundamentally diverged from those of the utilities, who opposed public power; see Nye, *Electrifying America,* 318, 329–333. See also Field, "'Electricity for All,'" 44–45, 48–52. For a retrospective assessment not supporting the idea that cheap electricity was necessary for economic development, see Bruce C. Netschert, "Electric Power and Economic Development," pp. 1–23, and Gilbert Banner, "Toward More Realistic Assumptions in Regional Economic Development," pp. 121–143, in John R. Moore, ed., *The Economic Impact of TVA* (Knoxville: University of Tennessee Press, 1967).

65. "Company could not lose" quoted from McCraw, *TVA,* 76. On the "Objective Rate Plan," see ibid., 74–77. The Objective Rate Plan represented a split schedule or block schedule plan and resembled, although McCraw does not point this out, private utility rate experiments conducted in the late 1920s and early 1930s; see my discussion in chapter 1. "Earnings Make It 'Recovery,'" *Business Week* (May 4, 1935): 8–9. The generalizations regarding the timing of the industry's appreciation of REA markets are based on the following titles from the trade magazine, *Electrical Merchandising.* Tom Blackburn, "Selling Between the Highlines," 61 (March 1939): 24–26; Donald S. Stophlet and Tom Blackburn, "Selling Appliances on New Rural Lines—2 Reports," 61 (May 1939): 8 f.; "What to Expect from the Farm Appliance Market," 63 (April 1940): 35 f.; Thelma Beall, "The Royal Road to Farm Appliance Sales," 64 (September 1940): 12 f.; "The Farm Market," 65 (May 1941): 17 f., including Tom F. Blackburn, "Selling 'Work' Appliances to the Farmer," p. 18 f., "Work Appliances Do a Job," p. 20 f., "Jobs Electricity Makes Easier on the Farm," p. 27 f.; Tom Blackburn, "Rural Electrification Has Jelled," 68 (December 1942): 10–11; "The Farm Market as a Woman Sees It," 71 (March 1944): 22 f.; "Can the Cooperative Succeed in Selling Electrical Appliances," 74 (September 1945): 65 f.; Clotilde Grunsky, "Urban and Rural Buying Intentions Compared," 74 (December 1945): 50 f.

66. "The greatest" quoted from "The $25 a Week Family . . . A Market for Small Appliances," *Electrical Merchandising* 62 (December 1939): 10–12. A similar "discovery" of a previously neglected market that had been brought forward and economically enfranchised by the federal government occurred in the late 1940s and 1950s, when the electrical industry discovered the Northern urban African-American market; see Frank A. Muth, "Are You Overlooking the Growing Negro Market," ibid., 83 (May 1951): 60–61, 104, 162. "Load building," quoted from Wendell Willkie, "Spending for Load Building," *Electrical World* 104 (December 8, 1934): 21. J. Ronnie Davis, *The New Economics and the Old Economists* (Ames: Iowa State University Press, 1971), 24, 151–153.

67. Wendell Willkie, "Spending for Load Building," *Electrical World* 104 (December 8, 1934): 21.

68. "Automobiles, radios" quoted from Gerald E. Stedman, "Time Payment Paper," *Electrical Merchandising* 53 (April 1935): 24. For an oblique discussion of this thesis, see Field, "'Electricity for All,'" 58–60.

Chapter 5. The New Deal Saves the Home

1. Morris Janowitz summarizes sociological and political science literatures on the transformation of local power structures in *The Last Half-Century: Societal Change and Politics in America* (Chicago: University of Chicago Press, 1978), 242–244. Janowitz observes that federal sponsorship of home ownership severely undermined the ability of local capitalism to create and maintain social inequalities through control of housing; ibid., p. 145. Politicization of local ethnic and lower-income groups by Roosevelt's Democratic party and social organization of neighborhoods through community hearing requirements in public housing administration gave local groups significant power over neighborhood destiny separated from the requirement of property ownership; ibid., pp. 270–272, 300–305, 317, 456–457. On the federal challenge to local elites in the Midwest, see Catherine McNicol Stock, *Main Street in Crisis: The Great Depression and the Old Middle Class on the Northern Plains* (Chapel Hill: University of North Carolina Press, 1992), 86–127. For the rise of a Southern liberal New Deal administrative elite to challenge Southern traditional county elites, see Schulman, *From Cotton Belt to Sunbelt,* viii, 40–47. Schulman describes the first New Deal's effort to compromise with local property elites, ibid., pp. 15–20, the inadvertent politicization of Southern African-Americans, ibid., 44–47, FDR's effort to organize his new Southern liberals, ibid., pp. 48–53. See also Peter J. Coleman, "The World of Interventionism, 1880–1940," in Eden, *The New Deal and Its Legacy,* 50–75; John A. Wettergreen, "The Regulatory Policy of the New Deal," in Eden, *The New Deal and Its Legacy,* 199–213, esp. p. 200; Charles R. Kesler, "The Public Philosophy of the New Freedom and the New Deal," ibid., p. 163; and Morton J. Frisch, "An Appraisal of Roosevelt's Legacy: How the Moderate Welfare State Transcended the Tension Between Progressivism and Socialism," ibid., pp. 194–195. On New Deal policy of re-creating the middle class in terms of enlarging and invigorating home buying, see John A. Wettergreen, "The Regulatory Policy of the New Deal," ibid., pp. 208–209, and Robert Eden, "Introduction: A Legacy of Questions," ibid., pp. 2–3. For a brief review of the historiography of the issue of whether the New Deal saved capitalism, see James E. Anderson, "The New Deal, Capitalism, and the Regulatory State," in Cohen, *The Roosevelt New Deal,* 105–119.

2. "Rolph Places Signature on Leniency Bill," *Riverside Enterprise,* April 18, 1933, p. 1. "Unpaid Taxes at New High Record," ibid., July 4, 1933, p. 4; "Tax Rates for Cities

and Special Districts Announced by Auditor," ibid., August 30, 1933, p. 9; "Delinquent Tax Plan Explained," Riverside *Daily Press,* March 28, 1934, p. 6; "Tax Delinquency Shows Drop Here," ibid., May 21, 1935, p. 3. See also David T. Beito, *Taxpayers in Revolt: Tax Resistance during the Great Depression* (Chapel Hill: University of North Carolina Press, 1989), 1–80, Keller, *Regulating a New Economy,* places the rise in tax delinquencies in the context of the shift from local to national regulation of property.

3. "Moratoria on Mortgages in State Signed," *Riverside Enterprise,* May 10, 1933, p. 1; "Mortgage Moratorium Act Signed," Riverside *Daily Press,* February 1, 1935, p. 1.

4. Riverside voted almost 2 to 1 for Hoover against Roosevelt in 1932; see "Complete Unofficial Election Returns," *Riverside Enterprise,* November 9, 1932, p. 10. "Nation Ready to Follow New Leader," editorial, ibid., March 1, 1933, p. 14.

5. "Roosevelt Asks" quoted from *Riverside Enterprise,* April 14, 1933, p. 1. The act authorizing the president to set up the HOLC was signed by the president on June 13, 1933. "His purpose" and "Ultimately" quoted from "News & Views, by R.C.H.," ibid., April 14, 1933, p. 1.

6. "Plans to Put U.S. in Realty Loan Writing," ibid., April 14, 1933, p. 1.

7. "Home Loan Man Goes to Capital," ibid., July 13, 1933, p. 4. "Questions and Answers Explain How Home Loan Plan Operates," ibid., July 23, 1933, p. 3. "Home Loan Procedure Outlined Over Radio by State Manager," ibid., August 5, 1933, p. 5. "Home Loan Plan Operative Today," ibid., August 7, 1933, p. 3; "Rush of Applicants When Home Loan Relief Starts," ibid., August 8, 1933, p. 2; "Home Loan Agent to Be Selected in Near Future," ibid., August 9, 1933, p. 7; "Home Loan Office to Continue Here," ibid., August 27, 1933, p. 3.

8. "More Appraisers for Home Loans," Riverside *Daily Press,* January 1, 1934, p. 10; "Over 290 Federal Home Loans in Escrow Here; $580,000 Involved," ibid., February 9, 1934, p. 6; "County Home Loans Total $1,580,252," ibid., January 5, 1935, 1:3. "Uncle Sam in Role of Nation's No. 1 Realtor," ibid., August 13, 1938, p. 7.

9. "Some of the bright" quoted from "Real Estate Next on List to Move," editorial, *Riverside Enterprise,* July 13, 1933, p. 16. "Useless" quoted from "Nation-Wide Housing Program to Be Launched," Riverside *Daily Press,* March 23, 1934, p. 1. "Creation of Corporation Being Rushed," *Riverside Enterprise,* October 16, 1933, p. 2; "Home Loan Bill Given Approval," Riverside *Daily Press,* February 15, 1934, 1:4; "Federal Loans for New Houses," editorial, ibid., April 10, 1934, last section: 16. "Text of Roosevelt's Message," *Riverside Enterprise,* May 15, 1934, p. 1; "Roosevelt Plans New Home Finance," editorial, ibid., May 18, 1934, p. 18.

10. "We think" quoted from "Roosevelt Plans New Home Finance," editorial, *Riverside Enterprise,* May 18, 1934, p. 18. "With the injection" quoted from Robert Lynd and Helen Merrell Lynd, *Middletown in Transition: A Study in Cultural Conflicts* (New York: Harcourt, Brace, 1937), 125. On the role of savings and loans in control of local social order by the local property class, see ibid., pp. 477–479. For other classic descriptions of local property's maintenance of local social order through home ownership and housing allocation, see W. Lloyd Warner et al., *Democracy in Jonesville: A Study of Quality and Inequality* (New York: Harper & Brothers, 1949), 35–54; W. Lloyd Warner and Paul S. Lunt, *The Social Life of a Modern Community* (New Haven: Yale University Press, 1941), 108–109, 239–250; James West [Carl Withers], *Plainville, U.S.A.* (New York: Columbia University Press, 1945), 40–53, 117, 135. For a collective portrait of towns and small cities drawn from the classic stratification literature, see Richard Lingeman, *Small Town America: A Narrative History, 1620–The Present* (New York: G. P. Putnam's Sons,

1980), 392–440. For synopses and evaluation of the literature on social stratification from Middletown to the present, see Lawrence J. R. Henson and John M. Bolland, *The Urban Web: Politics, Policy, and Theory* (Chicago: Nelson-Hall, 1990), 181–212. Robert G. Barrows demonstrates a close association between the rate of home ownership in cities and "the percentage of families borrowing from local building and loan associations"; see Robert G. Barrows, "Beyond the Tenement: Patterns of American Urban Housing, 1870–1930," *Journal of Urban History* 9 (1983): 395–420. Richard Harris proved that this web included laboring classes, as well as middle classes; see Richard Harris, "Working Class Home Ownership in the American Metropolis," *Journal of Urban History* 17 (1990): table 5, p. 60. Doucet and Weaver provide the most extensive historical discussion of mortgage lending in their *Housing the North American City,* 243–304. Doucet and Weaver study Canada and note the New Deal only in passing. They observe that Canadian federal intervention in home financing after 1945 diminished the percentage of mortgages held by individuals (viz., individual lending for home owners) in place of institutional lending, but they decline to discuss at length the use of Canadian federal policies for social purposes; see ibid, pp. 283, 293, 298–304. Doucet and Weaver argue that local landlords exerted considerable social control over local renters. Since most households rented before 1950, local landlords were an important link in the chain binding local capital and the local social order. See ibid., p. 364 f.

11. "Rosy Reports Mark Meeting," *Riverside Enterprise,* September 2, 1933, p. 3; "Almost 5,000 Riversiders in N.R.A. Pledges," ibid., September 9, 1933, p. 3, "'Buy Now' Campaign Lauded as of Benefit to All Community," ibid., October 21, 1933, p. 5; "Are You Doing Your Share?" ad, ibid. October 25, 1933, p. 2. For a summary of scholarly literature on the NRA, see R. Biles, *A New Deal,* chap. 4, esp. pp. 83–84.

12. "We Deem It," ad, *Riverside Enterprise,* August 1, 1933, p. 5. "Supporting Our President," ad, ibid., August 4, 1933, p. 11. "Gen. Johnson Says," ad, ibid., September 10, 1933, p. 3.

13. "NRA to Start Great Effort for Business," ibid., October 9, 1933, p. 1.

14. "Adopted the NRA code" quoted from "Frigidaire Prices Are Still Down," ad, ibid., September 21, 1933, p. 7. "Leonard Electric Refrigerator," ad, ibid., October 26, 1933, p. 7; "The Latest Sensation in Electric Washers," ad, ibid., November 23, 1933, p. 4. "City Cooperates in Big Campaign," ibid., May 21, 1934, p. 5; "It's Great Fun to Cook with Electricity," ad for the cooking show, ibid., June 14, 1934, p. 6; "Plans Announced for Great All-Electric Riverside Cooking Institute," ibid. June 23, 1934, p. 5; "Riverside Women Throng," ibid., June 28, 1934, p. 15; "All Electric Cooking School," ad, ibid., October 21, 1934, p. 10; "Electrical Range Demonstration," ad, ibid., December 6, 1934, p. 14; "Riverside's Electrical Age Is Here," ad, ibid., June 8, 1937, p. 9. Curiously, Marchand's survey of national magazine advertising did not pick up magazine ads reflecting the New Deal effort to increase consumption; see Marchand, *Advertising the American Dream.*

15. "The time has come" quoted from "Spirit of NRA to Become Permanent," *Riverside Enterprise,* October 4, 1933, p. 16. "Important Part in NRA for Consumer," editorial, ibid., August 22, 1933, p. 16; "Household Workers Seek Place in NRA," ibid., September 2, 1933, p. 14; "Spirit of NRA to Become Permanent?" editorial, ibid., October 4, 1933, p. 16; "Consumers Hold Key to Recovery," ibid., October 21, 1933, p. 14.

16. "It is" quoted from "'Oh, Please don't sit on that Chair!'" editorial, ibid., October 29, 1933, p. 9. The Lynds observe the similar effect of the national government's campaign to spend and consume in *Middletown in Transition,* 479–482.

17. "Construction Activities Here Advance with Rapid Strides," *Riverside Enterprise,* January 29, 1922, p. 4. "Houses Built in City for 2,000 People," ibid., December 24, 1924, p. 7. "Riverside's Prosperity Is Proved in Building Total," ibid., January 1, 1927, p. 4. In 1928, 326 residential permits' estimated cost averaged $4,050, and in the first six months of 1929, when the building boom had collapsed, residential permits averaged $3,611. "Construction in Riverside for Last Twelve Months Is Reported Over Two Millions," ibid. January 1, 1929, p. 9; "Building Now Above Million," ibid., August 1, 1929, p. 3.

18. The source of the statistic was not mentioned; the tone of the article conveys the sense that a realtor judged 25 percent of housing needed painting on the basis of driving through neighborhoods. "25 Per Cent of Riverside's Homes Need Modernization," *Riverside Enterprise,* August 11, 1929, p. 6; "Modernize," ibid.; "Wake Up! Own Your Home!" ibid.; "Let Us Help You Modernize," ibid.

19. For modernization ads, see "Bring the Old Home up to Date," ad, ibid., June 29, 1930, p. 9; "Toward Prosperity," ibid., January 25, 1931, p. 4; "Don't Put Off Remodeling or Repair," ibid., April 5, 1931, p. 12. "Buy your building" quoted from "Give Employment to Home People," ibid., April 6, 1931, p. 5.

20. "Modern Home, Building Exhibit For Riverside, C. of C. Project," ibid., August 1, 1931, p. 13; "Booths All Reserved," ibid., September 30, 1931, p. 5; "Riverside Chamber of Commerce Invites You," ad for the show, ibid., October 4, 1931, p. 8. "Construction of Attractive Houses Urged," ibid., February 16, 1932, p. 4; "Riverside Small House Contest," announcement of contest, ibid., April 5, 1932, p. 3. "1933 Depends on Me," ad, ibid., March 5, 1933, p. 8–9.

21. Reports from Hoover's housing conference collected in John M. Gries and James Ford, eds., *Publications of the President's Conference on Home Building and Home Ownership,* 11 vols. (Washington, D.C.: President's Conference on Home Building and Home Ownership, 1932).

22. "Riverside Home Owners" quoted from "Recondition Unit in Los Angeles," Riverside *Daily Press,* September 10, 1934, p. 5. "Every effort" quoted from "Home Repairing Service Starts," ibid., September 12, 1934, p. 9. The HOLC had been criticized a year earlier for delays in processing mortgage refinancing. The agency stated that it took months to clear up the issues of title, since it was refinancing mortgages in default, and to appraise dwellings; see, "More Appraisers for Home Loans," ibid., January 1, 1934, p. 10, and "Complaint Probe Said Commenced," ibid., March 17, 1934, 1: 2.

23. "Moffett's job" quoted from "Federal Home Remodeling, Repairing Program Director Starts Job Today," *Riverside Enterprise,* July 9, 1934, p. 1; the story was by United Press. "Considerable promise" quoted from "Federal Housing Program Underway," editorial, ibid., August 17, 1934, p. 18; "Some hail" quoted from "Promising Plan of Ending Depression," ibid., September 9, 1934, p. 16.

24. On the FHA housing survey: "Better Housing Will Be Studied," *Riverside Enterprise,* July 4, 1934, p. 3; "Housing Census to be Parley Subject," ibid., July 24, 1934, p. 4; "Better Housing Drive Launched," p. ibid., September 19, 1934, p. 4; "Council Members Get Solidly Behind Better-Housing Campaign," ibid., p. 6; "Better Housing Campaign Started by C. of C. Building Trades Committee," ibid., October 6, 1934, p. 3; "Better Housing Group Will Meet," ibid., October 11, 1934, p. 5; "Housing Plan's Approval Asked," ibid., October 9, 1934, p. 5; "Better Housing Drive Launched." ibid., October 12, 1934, p. 4; "Housing Survey May Be Launched Soon," ibid., October 14, 1990, p. 5; "Housing Survey Planned in City," ibid., October 31, 1934, p. 9; "Riverside Needs

Homes Badly; Modernization Also Necessary," ibid., October 31, 1934, Chamber of Commerce Edition, p. 1; "Boom in Building of Homes Likely," ibid., November 6, 1934, p. 3; "Better Housing Program Scheduled to Be Launched on November 9," ibid., November 6, 1934, p. 9; "Better Homes Building Exhibit Will Open Here on Friday, November 16," ibid., November 11, 1934, p. 5; "Instruction Given Home Survey Crews," ibid., November 16, 1934, p. 15; "Riverside Better Housing Campaign Starts; Mayor Criddle Issues Official Proclamation," ibid., November 17, 1934, p. 5; "Proclamation," ibid., November 17, 1934, p. 5; "Community Challenge Voiced by Mayor," editorial, ibid., November 17, 1934, p. 14; "Reports on Federal Housing Plan Made," ibid., November 22, 1934, p. 3; "Better Housing Exhibit Viewed," ibid., November 22, 1934, p. 3; "Set-up of Housing Campaign Explained," ibid., November 22, 1934, p. 4; "Warning Issued by Better Housing Body," ibid., November 28, 1934, p. 4; "Housing Campaign Survey Progresses," ibid., November 26, 1934, p. 6; "Social, Economic Survey Finished," ibid., December 27, 1934, p. 9; "S.E.R.A. Survey of Riverside Soon Will Be Completed, Chairman States," Riverside *Daily Press,* January 3, 1935, 2:6. I could not locate the results of the survey in local, state, or national archives. I selected the following newspaper advertisements out of the deluge of such ads to illustrate the opening of the FHA modernization campaign: "Loans to Repair and Modernize Your Property," Bank of America ad, *Riverside Enterprise,* August 15, 1934, p. 5; "The United States Government . . . ," lumber and building supply stores ad with questions and answers on the Federal Housing Act, ibid., August 26, 1934, p. 10; "Free Information on the Federal Home Modernization Plan," ad announcing a special newspaper editor, the "Home Renovation Editor," ibid., September 2, 1934, p. 7; "You Can Get the Money," lumber and building supply store ad, ibid., September 2, 1934, p. 8; "Home Loan Special," lumber store ad, ibid., September 9, 1934, p. 4; "Home Owners!! The Money Is Ready for You," contractors ad, ibid., September 9, 1934, p. 5; "Loans up to $2,000," lumber and building supply store ad, ibid., September 9, 1934, p. 6; "Now You Can Borrow the Money," Sears, Roebuck and Co., ad, ibid., September 14, 1934, p. 5; "Loans for Repainting," paint store ad, ibid., September 15, 1934, p. 5; "Modernize Your Home Now," building suppliers ad, ibid., September 16, 1934, p. 5; "How's Your Bathroom?" plumbing dealer ad, ibid., September 16, 1934, p. 5; "The City Beautiful," building supplies ad, ibid., September 19, 1934, 2:6.

25. The theme persisted throughout the 1930s, well after the initial FHA campaign of 1934. For instance, see "Ten-Year-Old House Out-Moded Today," Riverside *Daily Press,* April 18, 1939, p. 3; "Modern Homes Have Many Improvements," ibid., June 10, 1939, p. 5, "Your Home," ad, ibid., August 4, 1936, p. 11. For a later similar discussion, see "How to Build a Home: Wiring the House," ibid., June 17, 1939, p. 5.

26. "First to meet" and "'Even'" quotations from "Faulty Electrical Wiring Exhibit at Utility Office Gets Attention," Riverside *Daily Press,* November 25, 1936, p. 7. "Defective Electrical Wiring in City Said Found in Survey," *Riverside Enterprise,* December 13, 1935, p. 3.

27. "How Both Renters and Home Owners Can Buy a General Electric Refrigerator," ad, Riverside *Daily Press,* July 16, 1935, p. 3; "New Financing Plan for Those Who Do Not Own Homes," ad, ibid., July 19, 1935, p. 5.

28. "1938 Big FHA Year in Riverside County," Riverside *Daily Press,* May 13, 1939, p. 4; "Few FHA Loans Made in Riverside," ibid., July 30, 1938, p. 5; "New Homes for Riverside," editorial, ibid., August 17, 1939, p. 14; "1941 One of City's Banner Home Years," ibid., January 3, 1942, p. 5; "FHA Home Financing Figures Announced," ibid.,

February 7, 1942, p. 5. The newspaper report on FHA loans in 1941 presented a confusing statistic on Riverside's participation in FHA programs. The February 7 article stated that the 246 FHA new dwellings constituted only 19.1% of permits, a regionally low statistic. However, the 19.1% figure is the percent of all permits—new dwellings and old—rather than just new dwellings. As a percentage of permits for all new dwellings, FHA-insured loans were 95%.

29. See Ronald C. Tobey and Charles Wetherell, "Labor in the Citrus Industry, 1887–1944," Report to the State of California, Department of Parks, Interpretive Division (Department of History, University of California, Riverside, 1993).

30. "Centralized," "These buildings," and "This seems" quotations from "Gigantic Housing Program Sought," *Riverside Enterprise,* October 17, 1934, p. 4; "Relief Bureau Housing Plan Is Given Blow," ibid., November 21, 1934, p. 2; "Home Funds Asked for Use in Valley," Riverside *Daily Press,* March 6, 1935, 1:4; "SERA Director Makes Report on Coachella Valley Housing," ibid., April 8, 1935, p. 6; "hovel" characterization by the newspaper, "Housing Project Brought Nearer," ibid., August 20, 1935, p. 3. "Work on Labor Camp Proceeds," ibid., October 1, 1937, p. 4.

31. "They had come" quoted from "Byproduct" (Editorial), Riverside *Daily Press,* May 7, 1940, p. 16. "140 Families at Migratory Camp," ibid., May 20, 1938, p. 4; "First Families Approved for Indio Housing Project," ibid., October 8, 1938, p. 5.

32. "100 Millions Added for Defense Housing," *Riverside Daily Press,* August 29, 1940, p. 1. "Cooperation of Citrus Belt in Army Housing Urged," ibid., November 2, 1940, p. 5. "Housing Shortage Foreseen by Air District Commander," ibid., December 9, 1940, p. 3; "Riverside Must House Army Depot Clerks," ibid., August 4, 1942, p. 1. The quartermaster depot was located to the northwest of the city, but the city had to meet its personnel housing needs. "Riverside Designated Defense Housing Area," ibid., January 30, 1942, p. 1. "Defense Housing Regulations in Southland Announced," ibid., April 11, 1942, p. 5.

33. "Increased interest" quoted from "Defense Housing to Receive FHA Aid," Riverside *Daily Press,* December 12, 1942, p. 5. "Each unit" quoted from "$160,000 Project Will Begin in Arlington," ibid., June 5, 1943, p. 3. "Defense Housing Regulations in Southland Announced," ibid., April 11, 1942, p. 5; "Riverside Must House Army Depot Clerks," ibid., August 4, 1942, p. 1; "800 More Rooms for Army Clerks Sought," ibid., August 26, 1942, p. 4. "125 War Units for City," ibid., February 4, 1943, p. 1. "Plans for Public Conversion Units in Riverside Discussed," ibid., February 6, 1943, p. 8. "Rezoning Approval Aids Housing Plan," ibid., April 27, 1943, p. 5.

34. "Crowding out" and "Race mixture" quotations from "Question of Race Survival," editorial, Riverside *Daily Press,* November 17, 1937, p. 16. "Without segregation" quoted from "Education as the Solution of the Negro Race Problem," editorial, ibid., June 3, 1944, p. 12. Henry Coil address reprinted in "City Planning Is Discussed at Public Affairs Dinner," *Riverside Enterprise,* March 27, 1930, p. 4.

35. R. B. Hampson (president, Riverside Chamber of Commerce), "Hampson Appeals for Help in Housing," Riverside *Daily Press,* January 1, 1946, p. 5; facts are rehearsed as background in the article, "Truman Cuts Major Housing Restrictions," ibid., December 16, 1946, p. 1; see also, "Creedon Junks Former Housing Priority System," ibid., December 24, 1946, p. 2. "Single Family House Shortage Shown after the United States Survey," ibid., July 19, 1937, p. 2; "3,000,000 New Homes Estimated Needed in Five-Year Period," ibid., July 27, 1937, p. 2. "Senate Gives Approval for Housing Bill," ibid., August 6, 1937, p. 1; "Slum Clearance Measure Signed," ibid., September 2, 1937,

p. 2. Editorial, "Housing Crisis Will Be Worse Before It Improves," ibid., February 21, 1946, p. 16; "Housing Shortage in State Remains Acute," ibid., April 11, 1947, p. 3; "State's Critical Need of Housing Shown to C of C," ibid., June 17, 1947, p. 7, which reported an estimate by the state legislature's housing committee of a need for 375,000 houses. Editorial, "End of National Housing Emergency Not Yet Foreseen," ibid., December 26, 1946, p. 20.

36. Housing figures of other nations were collected by the Riverside *Daily Press* from a variety of United Press wire stories. See "Lack of Postwar Housing Afflicting Entire World," Riverside *Daily Press,* December 28, 1946, p. 11. On U.S. statistics, see Series N156, "New Housing Units Started, by Ownership, Type of Structure, Location, and Construction Cost: 1889–1970," Census, *Historical Statistics of the United States* (1976), 2:639.

37. "City Beating Housing Problem," Riverside *Daily Press,* September 30, 1948, p. 4. See also, "Housing Shortage Seen Easing Up (in Minneapolis)," ibid., January 27, 1949, p. 6; "Housing Shortage in L.A. Claimed 'Thing of the Past,'" ibid., March 18, 1949, p. 2; "L.A. Realtor Says Housing Surplus Looms in City," ibid., October 4, 1950, p. 2. "Housing Normalcy Still Seen Distant as 1956," ibid., October 25, 1948, p. 18.

38. "OPA Freezes Rental Prices for Housing," Riverside *Daily Press,* April 29, 1942, p. 4. "Operation of Rent Control Explained," ibid., May 9, 1942, p. 3. "Roomers' Rents Now Under Control," ibid., July 11, 1942, p. 3. "Rent Control Office to Be Set Up Here," ibid., October 22, 1942, p. 9. "Control of Rents Extended," ibid., October 12, 1942, p. 2. "Rent Control Ended Here, Woods Says," ibid., November 16, 1949, p. 13. The organization of realtors and landlords against rent control should not be confused with tenants' movements to retain rent control or expand tenant rights. See Allan D. Heskin, *Tenants and the American Dream: Ideology and the Tenant Movement* (New York: Praeger, 1983), 3–37.

39. Miles Colean, technical director for the Federal Housing Administration, 1934–1937, and assistant administrator of the FHA, 1937–1940, confirmed the connection between top-down federal support of real estate capitalism and the potential for federal manipulation of monetary and credit policies for social purposes; see Miles L. Colean, *The Impact of Government on Real Estate Finance in the United States,* Financial Research Program, Studies in Urban Mortgage Financing (New York: National Bureau of Economic Research, 1950), 99–101. On Roosevelt's view of the need for national support of local real estate and home ownership, see Tobey, Wetherell, and Brigham, "Moving Out and Settling In," 1412–1420. Monkkonen's *America Becomes Urban* places my suggestion of a revolution in local property capitalism in the 1930s in the context of the history of the modern American city. Although historians see the New Deal as neglecting cities, as compared to agriculture, they do see it as having altered the growth game of local capitalism through intrusion of federal bureaucracy and regulations and through postwar sponsorship of suburbanization. See Monkkonen, *America Becomes Urban,* 5, 222–223; and Jackson, *Crabgrass Frontier,* 190–230.

40. The (now-classic) account of the corporate revolution in property that influenced the generation of New Deal economic thinking was provided by Adolf A. Berle and Gardiner C. Means, *The Modern Corporation and Private Property,* rev. ed. (New York: Harcourt, Brace & World, 1968).

41. "The multitude" quoted from Lynd and Lynd, *Middletown,* 22. "The mere fact" quoted from ibid., pp. 23–24.

42. "Those members" quoted from ibid., p. 489; "the thick blubber" quoted from ibid., p. 490.

Chapter 6. Political Paths to Electrical Modernization

1. The difference between average national use and Riverside's average use in the early 1920s is due to the difference in the average quality of electrified dwellings. A lower percentage of the nation's urban dwellings were electrified (38 percent in 1921) than Riverside's. Since higher-quality neighborhoods were electrified first, average national use would have been higher, because larger homes have more lights. With a higher percentage of electrified dwellings, Riverside's average would have been lower until the extent of urban electrification in the nation matched Riverside's later in the decade.

2. Riverside's and the nation's historical increase in electrical consumption are not statistically significantly different. Riverside's stepped growth best fits an exponential curve, as does the national consumption series. The differences between the national and the Riverside yearly monthly mean consumption for 1921 to 1950, using a one-way anova test, a Kolmogorov-Smirnow two-sample test, and a t-test for independent samples are not significantly different (probability = .24).

3. On the Riverside Sample Data, see chapter 3, note 7. Our basic sampling strategy in the utility billing records is technically termed a systematic random sample. For every year from 1921 to 1950, we looked at every fifth unit in randomly selected 80 percent of 512 meter-reader routes present in the city in 1950. We adjusted sampling for chronological bias (early years of the meter routes had fewer dwellings) and geographic dispersal. For further information, see Tobey, "Statistical Supplement."

4. We devised an analytical model of consumption to determine when Riverside households began using specific electric appliances. We distinguish between entry-level use and normal, modernized use of an appliance. To establish how much electricity an appliance or device, such as the radio, demands, we used published electrical industry tests from the 1920s and 1930s. The electrical utilities needed to determine future demand for electricity to plan generating capacity. Industry also conducted surveys of electrical consumption by devices in normal use by households. On the basis of these experiments, we established how much electricity a household would have to be using for us to be confident that it was using a particular appliance. To detect the presence of an appliance, we needed, not its average modernized use, but a minimal floor of use. Since households could build additional appliance consumption upon this floor, we considered it to be an "entry" floor establishing use. We employed the entry floor of use for the most popular appliances that surveys established as being in homes before 1950. These devices were lights, flatiron, radio, and refrigerator. Refrigerator use is less flexible than light, flatiron, and radio use. Rapid technological improvements in the 1930s reduced the amount of electricity demanded by refrigerator motors. We therefore adjusted the refrigerator demand year by year to reflect increased efficiency in the motors. We tested our model against four objective benchmarks of appliance ownership in Riverside. (1) The 1934 Real Property Inventory, conducted for the federal government's Department of Commerce, reported refrigerator ownership for Sacramento, to which we compared Riverside. (2) In 1940, the U.S. Census queried for possession of mechanical refrigerators and radios in dwellings. The census reported that 94.3 percent of Riverside homes owned radios. Our model predicts that 93.5 percent of Riverside homes used electric radios. (3) The 1940 Housing Census reports that 62.8 percent of Riverside dwellings had mechanical refrigeration. Our model predicts that 65.0 percent of Riverside's homes had electric refrigeration. (4) The 1950 Housing Census reported that 86.4 percent of River-

side homes had mechanical refrigeration; our model predicts 88.2 percent ownership. For a full description, see Tobey, "Statistical Supplement."

5. Cohen, *Making a New Deal.* The radio is not mentioned in Cowan, *More Work for Mother,* 172–191.

6. Studying only upper-income homes in Denver and Kansas in the 1920s, Mark Rose argues, on the basis of advertisements, that home owning and renting households shared electrical device ownership equally. In the 1930s, in the two cities, however, refrigerator ownership became differentiated between owners and renters as well as along the income scale. See Mark H. Rose, "Urban Environments and Technological Innovation: Energy Choices in Denver and Kansas City, 1900–1940," *Technology and Culture* 25 (July 1985): 503–539.

7. "State Benefits by FHA Loans," Riverside *Daily Press,* November 26, 1938, p. 5. In 1940, there were 11,073 dwelling units (houses, apartments, rental rooms) in the city of Riverside, of which 5,266 units were owner occupied; see Bureau of the Census, Sixteenth Census of the United States: 1940; *Housing, Vol. 2. General Characteristics,* California, Table 23, "Number of Rooms, Lighting Equipment, Size of Household, Etc., for Urban Places and Rural Areas, By Counties, 1940—con.," p. 279.

8. Political agitation for lower domestic electricity rates began in the 1920s, but was resisted by the city council, which did not want to lose its "profit" on electricity sales that could be transferred to the city's General Fund; see "Reduction of One Cent in Light Urged," *Riverside Enterprise,* November 8, 1927, p. 1, and "Council Declines to Act on Light Reduction Rates," ibid., November 9, 1927, p. 3. Reductions came during the depression, when Riverside followed the national trend. Political pressure on state regulatory boards, such as California's, pushed down the rates of private power utilities. In the nation as a whole, average residential electricity rates dropped from 7.04 cents for the first 25 kwh/mo. and 5.21 cents for the first 100 kwh/mo. in 1929 to 6.40 cents for the first 25 kwh/mo. and 4.67 cents for the first 100 kwh/mo. in 1935; see Series S 112–113, "Growth of Residential Service, and Average Prices for Electrical Energy: 1902 to 1970," in Bureau of the Census, *Historical Statistics of the United States* (1976), 1:827. Riverside followed the reductions provided to its privately supplied urban neighbors. See "Consumer Gets Break July 1," *Riverside Enterprise,* June 11, 1931, p. 5; "Reduction in Lighting Rate Now in Effect, Commercial Users Get Slash to Total of $17,000 Per Year Here," ibid., July 1, 1931, p. 13; "Slash in Power Charge Favored," Riverside *Daily Press,* March 15, 1935, p. 6; "Industrial Rate for Power Lower," ibid., May 17, 1935, p. 8. For heavy appliance sales figures, see "Electric Light Business Gains," ibid., July 12, 1935, p. 6; "Board of Utilities Authorizes Commercial Lighting Charge Cut," ibid., October 12, 1935, p. 10; "Board of Public Utilities Reduces Rates on Electricity for Domestic, Commercial Use Here," ibid., June 12, 1936, p. 10. California rates were compared in "Electricity Consumers in Riverside Pay Lower Rate than in Most Cities, Federal Study Shows," ibid., July 26, 1935, p. 11; "Electric Rates in City Among Lowest," ibid., December 28, 1938, p. 6; "City's Electric Rates Lowest in State for Small Consumer," ibid., June 20, 1939, p. 3. By the mid-1930s, Riverside tied its basic rate to the first 45 kwh/mo. of consumption, which corresponds to the consumption floor for an average house with lights, iron, radio, and refrigerator.

9. Fischer, *America Calling,* 110–121, 143–151.

10. On war rationing, see "OPM Orders Cut in Use of Electricity," Riverside *Daily Press,* October 30, 1941, p. 1; "Electricity for Homes May be Rationed, FPC Head Says," ibid., January 22, 1942, p. 1; "Electricity Curb Hits Riverside," ibid., January 29, 1945,

p. 1. Riverside lowered rates during the war in response to special interests; see "Commercial Lighting Rates to Be Lower," ibid., December 11, 1942, p. 4; "City Launches Move for Lower Power Rates," ibid., January 14, 1944, p. 3. On the rezoning, see "Hearing Looms on Extensive Apartment House Rezoning," ibid., December 2, 1939, p. 5; "Planning Body Approves New Apartment House Areas," ibid., December 8, 1939, p. 7; "Rezoning Notices Attain New High," ibid., December 18, 1939, p. 8; "Apartment House, Duplex Areas Approved for Rezoning," ibid., December 26, 1939, p. 4. On extending the apartment and duplex zone into the East Side, see "City Planning Commission Favors Rezoning Eighth," ibid., May 10, 1940, p. 6; "Council Overrules Planning Body on Duplex Rezoning," ibid., June 18, 1940, p. 4.

11. Baritz contends that World War II advanced the material prosperity of the civilian home front, on the grounds that half of the industrial productive output went to civilian consumption and that few Americans testified they had really sacrificed during the war; see Baritz, *The Good Life,* 178. See also, Sherna Berger Gluck, *Rosie the Riveter Revisited: Women, the War, and Social Change* (Boston: Twayne, 1987); George Lipsitz, *Rainbow at Midnight: Labor and Culture in the 1940s,* rev. (Urbana: University of Illinois Press, 1994), 19–44.

12. Tobey, Wetherell, and Brigham, "Moving Out and Settling In," 1395–1422.

13. In a multiple classification analysis of the tenure of households in months, the three factors accounted for only 19 percent of variation of length of residence (multiple R squared = .192). See Tobey, "Statistical Supplement."

14. For tables of residential tenure by tenure status, occupation, and neighborhood, see table 6.9 at the end of this chapter. See also Tobey, "Moving Out and Setting In," tables 2–5 and footnote 35 table. In this and the following paragraphs, we speak of owner and renter households, not about the dwellings.

15. For Los Angeles, see table 19, "Persons with Work Histories and Mean Number of Jobs Held, 1940–1949, by Occupation Group," p. 56, and table 26, "Mobility Measures for All Workers, 1940–1949, by Occupational Group, Six Cities Combined," p. 72, in Gladys L. Palmer, *Labor Mobility in Six Cities: A Report on the Survey of Patterns and Factors in Local Mobility, 1940–1950* (New York: Social Science Research Council, 1954).

16. Lynd and Lynd, *Middletown,* 60–62. Herbert S. Parnes, *Research on Labor Mobility: An Appraisal of Research Findings in the United States,* Social Science Research Council Bulletin 65 (New York: Social Science Research Council, 1954), 100–143; see especially pp. 107–109 on seniority. Migration research by social scientists in the 1940s and 1950s was primarily concerned with policy questions created by governmental social programs. In the 1960s, researchers shifted to investigate migration within the framework of theoretical (structural) social systems. For an introduction to this later literature see Martin Cadwallader, "Theoretical Frameworks," in Cadwallader, *Migration and Residential Mobility: Macro and Micro Approaches* (Madison: University of Wisconsin Press, 1992), 3–38.

17. Parnes, *Research on Labor Mobility,* 123–124, on home ownership.

18. Palmer, *Labor Mobility in Six Cities,* 125.

19. Mrs. Ralph Borsodi, "The Cost of Feeding a Family," *Electrical Merchandising* 53 (May 1935): 8. See also Cecile Tipton La Follette, *A Study of the Problems of 652 Gainfully Employed Married Women Homemakers,* Teachers College, Columbia University, Contributions to Education, no. 619 (New York: AMS, [1934] 1972), 83, 92, 174.

20. Cohen, *Making a New Deal,* passim.

Chapter 7. The Culmination of the New Deal
in Electrical Modernization, 1945–1960

1. On the African-American migration, see Nicholas Lemann, *The Promised Land: The Great Black Migration and How It Changed America,* reprint (New York: Vintage Books, 1991). Local wartime references to rising black consciousness included "Negro Legion Post to Be Formed Here," Riverside *Daily Press,* June 10, 1940, 2: 1; "Colored Soldiers Reception Guests," ibid., March 26, 1941, p. 10; "Veto Defeats Council's Move to Aid Settlement," ibid., August 19, 1941, p. 4; "Race Bans in Defense Denied," ibid., October 21, 1941, p. 2; "Riverside Men and Women on the Honor Roll of Air Raid Wardens in the Fourth Ward," ibid., May 18, 1942, p. 9; "Eighty Negro Soldiers Guests at Lincoln Park," ibid., January 14, 1943, p. 4; "Race Relations to Be Discussed by NAACP," ibid., July 19, 1943, p. 5; "Equal Opportunity for Whites and Negroes [editorial]," ibid., February 24, 1944, p. 16; "Race Problems Have Discussion," ibid., March 4, 1944, p. 8; "The Negro Vote as a Factor in the November Elections [editorial]," ibid., August 30, 1944, p. 14; "Negro Residents Active in Sales of War Bonds," ibid., June 24, 1944, p. 3.

2. John Hope Franklin, *From Slavery to Freedom: A History of Negro Americans,* 3d ed. (New York: Vintage Books, 1969), 572–607, and Richard Polenberg, *War and Society: The United States, 1941–1945* (Philadelphia: J. B. Lippincott, 1972), 99–130.

3. Robert C. Weaver, *The Negro Ghetto,* reprint with a new preface (New York: Russell & Russell, [1948] 1967), 77–98, 99–138. "The Negro lost" quoted from ibid., p. 104. Statistics on Detroit housing and population from ibid., p. 86; on Detroit's housing during wartime, see also ibid., pp. 114–116. For the statistics on African-American percentages of priority wartime housing, see ibid., pp. 144–145. See also Dominic J. Capeci, Jr., *Race Relations in Detroit: The Sojourner Truth Housing Controversy, 1937–1942* (Philadelphia: Temple University Press, 1984); Arnold R. Hirsch, *Making the Second Ghetto: Race and Housing in Chicago, 1940 to 1960* (Cambridge: Cambridge University Press, 1983); and Allan H. Spears, *Black Chicago: The Making of a Negro Ghetto, 1890–1920* (Chicago: University of Chicago Press, 1967).

4. Bredemeier, *The Federal Public Housing Movement;* Fish, *The Story of Housing;* Keith, *Politics and the Housing Crisis;* and May, *Homeward Bound,* 168–69. May locates the social forces that precipitated the federal policies favoring suburban family homes in the cold war, rather than in the depression of the 1930s; see ibid., pp. 169–172.

5. Findlay does not mention federal interference with local social control as a reason for the postwar panic of "cities out of control"; see John M. Findlay, *Magic Lands: Western Cityscapes and American Culture after 1940* (Berkeley, Los Angeles, and London: University of California Press, 1993), 33–51.

6. "If a neighborhood" quoted from Federal Housing Administration, *Underwriting Manual,* par. 937; see also, pars. 973, 1032. For racial covenant requirements, see par. 980.3.

7. Weaver, *The Negro Ghetto,* 166–170.

8. Ibid., pp. 148–154, 157–164; Eunice Grier and George Grier, *Privately Developed Interracial Housing: An Analysis of Experience,* Special Research Report to the Commission on Race and Housing (Berkeley: University of California Press, 1960), 143–155.

9. "One of the most" quoted from U.S. Committee on Civil Rights, Charles E. Wilson, Chairman, *To Secure These Rights* (New York: Simon and Schuster, 1946), 68; see also pp. 84–85, 89; "The right to housing" discussed, pp. 18–19, 40–47, 68, 83–87, 169. On

Truman's motivation, see William E. Leuchtenburg, "The Conversion of Harry Truman," pp. 274–288 in Leonard Dinnerstein and Kenneth T. Jackson, eds., *American Vistas, vol. 2: 1877 to the Present,* 7th ed. (New York: Oxford University Press, 1995); see also Kluger, *Simple Justice,* 249–253; Robert H. Ferrell, *Harry S. Truman and the Modern American Presidency* (Boston: Little, Brown, 1983), 96–99; Chafe, *Unfinished Journey,* 88–91; Hamby, *Liberalism and Its Challengers,* 66–69; William C. Berman, *The Politics of Civil Rights in the Truman Administration* (1970), as excerpted in Alonzo L. Hamby, ed., *Harry S. Truman and the Fair Deal* (Lexington, Mass.: D. C. Heath, 1974), 184–187; and David McCullough, *Truman* (New York: Simon and Schuster, 1992), 588–593.

10. Clement E. Vose, *Caucasians Only: The Supreme Court, the NAACP, and the Restrictive Covenant Cases* (Berkeley: University of California Press, 1959). Federal participation discussed, pp. 168–174. See also Kluger, *Simple Justice,* 250–255. "Both Presidents" quoted from the federal amicus brief, published as *Prejudice and Property: An Historic Brief Against Racial Covenants, Submitted to the Supreme Court By Tom C. Clark and Philip B. Perlman* (Washington, D.C.: Public Affairs Press, 1948), 70. "[Racially restrictive covenants] are responsible" quoted from ibid., p. 23. On the social disintegrative effects of covenants on African-Americans, see ibid., p. 14. On the role of covenants in barring minorities from modern postwar housing, see ibid., pp. 18–19.

11. Robert Weaver prepared the sociological data on the social and economic effects of racial covenants presented by NAACP lawyers to the Supreme Court. The sociological brief was drawn from materials published in 1948 as Robert C. Weaver, *The Negro Ghetto;* see Vose, *Caucasians Only,* 163–163.

12. Weaver, *The Negro Ghetto,* 66–138. See also Gunnar Myrdal, *An American Dilemma: The Negro Problem and Modern Democracy,* with the assistance of Richard Sterner and Arnold Rose (New York: Harper & Brothers, 1944), 618–627.

13. On the Court's decision, see Vose, *Caucasians Only,* 205–210. On the FHA's eligibility rule of 1950, see ibid., pp. 225–227.

14. See Jackson, *Crabgrass Frontier,* 224–228, for an overview of the history of public housing that focuses on the siting issue. See also Huthmacher, *Senator Robert Wagner and the Rise of Urban Liberalism,* 205–216, 299–302, 322–325, 335–336. Riverside's local press followed the national events. A few of the articles from the Riverside *Daily Press,* which establish continuity in local attention to the issue are D. Harold Oliver, "Slum Clearance Measure [the Wagner Act] Signed," September 2, 1937, p. 2; "Coalition Kills Housing Bill Too," August 3, 1939, p. 1; "Truman Housing Bill [Wagner-Ellender-Taft bill] Shelved by Congress," July 30, 1946, p. 2; "Low-Income Family Housing Problem Recognized in New Senate Bill [editorial]," March 21, 1947, p. 18; "Truman Outlines Vast Low-Rent Housing Plan," February 23, 1948, p. 1; "Failure of Housing Legislation Sure to Be Warm Campaign Issue [editorial]," June 28, 1948, p. 20; "Are Political Considerations, or Facts, to Govern the Housing Problem? [editorial]," July 20, 1948, p. 30; "Truman Signs Housing Bill," August 10, 1948, p. 1 [the bill referenced had been sponsored by Republican party opponents of publicly assisted low-rent housing and slum clearance and did not contain funding for these programs]; "Dewey Says New Deal Caused Housing Woes," October 8, 1948, p. 1; "Truman Awaits Recommendations on New Home, Foreign Policies," November 26, 1948, p. 1 [reviews legislation that would be part of Truman's Fair Deal]; "Housing Measure Goes to Senate Floor Tomorrow," February 24, 1949, p. 1 [unsuccessful effort of liberals to amend a housing bill to prohibit racial segregation in public housing projects]; "Truman Thinks Most of Program Will Pass; Pleas for Housing," March 21, 1949, p. 1; "Contractors Join

Demand to Kill Federal Housing," April 4, 1949, p. 20 [concerning support of Riverside chapter of Building Contractors' Association for efforts of congressional Republicans to defeat public housing bill]; "Housing Bill Passed by Senate," April 22, 1949, p. 1 [further efforts to amend bill to prohibit racial discrimination in public housing failed]; "Trumanites Exult as Housing Passes," June 30, 1949, p. 1; "Housing Bill Most Striking Action of This Session [editorial]," July 13, 1949, p. 24; "Slum Clearance Work May Start Here Soon," July 22, 1949, p. 9.

15. On the East Side housing survey of 1948 by the Riverside Council of Church Women, see "Forum to Feature Housing, Slum Clearance Films," Riverside *Daily Press,* October 19, 1948, p. 5. The report of results of the survey is in the Riverside Public Library Local History Collection. "Slum Clearance Work May Start Here Soon," ibid., July 22, 1949, p. 1; "Council Moves Toward Securing Housing Aid," ibid., August 16, 1949, p. 1.

16. "'The members walked'" quoted from "Colored People Ask for Private Plunge," *Riverside Enterprise,* May 24, 1922, p. 1. On the local hearings requirement of the 1937 and 1949 housing acts, see Jackson, *Crabgrass Frontier,* 224–225.

17. For the history of the Riverside County Housing Authority, see "County Housing Authority Urged," Riverside *Daily Press,* November 19, 1942, p. 1; "Housing Authority Organized for County," ibid., November 23, 1942, p. 8; "County Housing Authority Will Operate in City," ibid., April 27, 1943, p. 5. On privately constructed defense housing, see "Two City Projects Announced," ibid., September 23, 1942, p. 7. For the expectation that defense housing was temporary, see "Public, War Housing on Temporary Basis," ibid., April 24, 1943, p. 5. On local results in the 1948 California housing initiative, see "City Landlords Enter Public Housing Battle," ibid., December 3, 1949, p. 9. The story of Riverside's realty industry's effort to obtain a city housing authority can be followed in "Realtors Request Separate City Housing Authority," ibid., May 19, 1949, p. 1; "Realtors Urging Separate Local Housing Authority," ibid., August 25, 1949, p. 6; "City Landlords Enter Public Housing Battle," ibid., December 3, 1949, p. 9; "Landlords Prepare Attack on Public Housing Council," December 5, 1949, p. 13; "City Council Firm on Public Housing Plans," ibid., December 6, 1949, p. 13; "Housing Aid Foes Move to Kill Program Here," ibid., December 15, 1949, p. 6. On the estimate of federal funds that might come to the city, see "Housing Requests Go to Capital Soon," ibid., August 17, 1949, p. 9.

18. The Riverside *Daily Press* editorially summarized the opposition to public housing during the controversy over the November 1948 California public housing initiative, which would have authorized state loans to local housing authorities and was partly justified to provide housing for veterans; "No. 11 Promises Great Expense, But No Additional Housing," editorial, Riverside *Daily Press,* October 21, 1948, p. 32; see also "Are Political Considerations, or Facts, to Govern the Housing Problem," editorial, ibid., July 22, 1948, p. 30, which claimed that 75 percent of American families could afford housing in the private marketplace. The housing initiative is explained in "Initiative to Alleviate Housing Lack Explained," ibid., June 30, 1948, p. 5. Voters defeated the housing initiative—Proposition 11 on the California November 2 ballot—by better than 2 to 1; see table in "State Vote on Propositions," ibid., November 4, 1948, p. 4. On the continued contest over the New Deal, see "Is There Any Demurrer in the Resolution of the Election for the Nation's Press?" ibid., November 16, 1948, p. 24. The characterization of public housing as "socialistic" originated with its supporters, such as the city mayor, William C. Evans, but was soon repeated with acerbity by opponents; see the city council exchange between a Democratic councilman and Evans, "Council Votes to Seek Low-

Rent Housing Aid," ibid., November 29, 1949, p. 13, and "Tilden Says Beware of Housing Program Here," ibid., December 2, 1949, p. 9. For the eruption of anticommunism issues within the controversy over federal public housing in southern California, see Donald Craig Parson, "Urban Politics During the Cold War: Public Housing, Urban Renewal, and Suburbanization in Los Angeles" (Ph.D. dissertation, University of California, Los Angeles, 1985).

19. "Housing Bill Goes to Senate," Riverside *Daily Press,* August 25, 1949, p. 1. Public housing supporting coalition cited in "City Council Firm on Public Housing Plans," ibid., December 6, 1949, p. 13; "City's Ministers Okay Housing Plan," ibid., December 21, 1949, p. 13; "Labor Council of AFL Endorses Housing Program," ibid., January 11, 1950, p. 16. See also Patterson, *Colony for California,* 299–300.

20. Quotations from "Pro and Con on Housing Was Sharp," Riverside *Daily Press,* December 7, 1949, p. 13, and "Scott Defends Public Housing for Riverside," ibid., December 8, 1949, p. 5.

21. "Slum Clearance Work May Start Here Soon," Riverside *Daily Press,* July 22, 1949, p. 9. "Tilden Says Beware of Housing Program Here," ibid., December 2, 1949, p. 9; "Tilden Proposes Substitute for Federal Housing," ibid., December 15, 1949, p. 6; "Baltimore Plan Urged for Riverside's Slums," ibid., December 29, 1949, p. 9. "'You may have'" quoted from "Property Owner Group Blasts Housing Project," ibid., December 20, 1949, p. 18. "Public housing" quoted from "Proposition No. 10," ibid., October 30, 1950, p. 28. The editorial recommended a favorable vote on a November 1950 California statewide initiative to require approval of a majority of voters before a federal public housing project could be located in a community. Political alignments over slum clearance somewhat similar to Riverside were established in the 1930s in New York City; see Deborah S. Gardner, "Site Selection and the New York City Housing Authority, 1934–1939," *Journal of Urban History* 12 (1986): 334–352.

22. On receipt of grants by other cities, see "Beaumont Gets $4800 for Loan for Public Housing," Riverside *Daily Press,* August 24, 1950, p. 13, and "SB County Gets Big Housing Loan," ibid., October 30, 1950, p. 19. On statewide realty leadership, see "Contractors Ask Stop on U.S. Housing Plea," ibid., April 29, 1950, p. 7 (Marshal Tilden was president of the Building Contractors' Association); "Builders Hit Public Housing, Tighe Woods," ibid., November 18, 1950, p. 9. On the shift to defense housing, see "U.S. Housing Program Shifting Toward War," ibid., December 26, 1950, p. 6. See also Peter Kivisto, "A Historical Review of Changes in Public Housing and Their Impacts on Minorities," in Jamshid A. Momenti, ed., *Race, Ethnicity, and Minority Housing in the United States* (New York: Greenwood Press, 1986), 1–18.

23. "Home Building Boom Strong in Third Year," Riverside *Daily Press,* October 20, 1948, p. 7B; "Biggest Building Year in History," ibid., January 1, 1949, p. 3. "The area" and "should plan" quotations from "City Planners to Hear Multiple Dwelling Petition," ibid., April 6, 1949, p. 11; "Planners O.K. Housing Zone," ibid., April 8, 1949, p. 9; "Big Multiple Housing Area Created in City," ibid., April 20, 1949, p. 13, mentions that a new industrial zone had been created to the north of the rezoned area and workers in industries there would also probably rent in the newly rezoned area.

24. The minority enrollment statistics for Longfellow school were provided by the Eastside Settlement House to a newspaper reporter; see Beth Teters, "Fundamentals of Negro Life Probed in Series," Riverside *Daily Press,* February 15, 1950, p. 4. The publication of this series of articles on Riverside's African-American community in itself revealed the turmoil generated by local redistribution of minority population. The point

made about lack of wholesale white flight from North East Side is made only on the basis of racial identification. It does not address the question of shifting class composition of the area. Considering the long-term declining proportion of owner-resident, single-family houses, it is likely that the income level of Anglo residents declined. Huang brings forward evidence from the 1960 census—though block statistics are not available—that North East Side represented nearly the poorest census districts of the city, save only the poverty of the old East Side. See Hongwei Huang, "Historic Preservation at Eastside" (M.A. field report for the Program in Historic Resources Management, Department of History, University of California, Riverside, 1992). For a later assessment of subsequent progress in residential racial integration in Riverside, see "Integration in Riverside: What the Numbers Say," Riverside *Press-Enterprise,* August 27, 1989, B: 1. See also, Michael N. Danielson, *The Politics of Exclusion* (New York: Columbia University Press, 1976), 27–129.

25. William H. Chafe, *The Unfinished Journey: America since World War II,* 2d ed. (Oxford: Oxford University Press, 1991), 80; Kluger, *Simple Justice,* 253. "Consumer spending" quoted from Carolyn Shaw Bell, *Consumer Choice in the American Economy* (New York: Random House, 1967), 34. On President Truman's support for the Rooseveltian public power position, see John Richard Waltrip, *Public Power during the Truman Administration* (New York: Arno Press, 1979), 30–35, 79–81, 85–86. On Elaine May's thesis in *Homeward Bound,* see note 4, this chapter.

26. "It is especially" quoted from U.S. Housing and Home Finance Agency, *Housing of the Nonwhite Population, 1940–1950* (Washington, D.C.: Government Printing Office, 1951), 14; see also pp. 13–14. Owner occupancy rates from table 7, "Condition and Plumbing Facilities by Occupancy and Color of Occupants, for the United States, Urban and Rural: 1950," pp. 1–4, Bureau of the Census, *Census of Housing: 1950, Volume 1, General Characteristics, Part 1, United States Summary* (Washington, D.C., 1953); 1960 calculated from absolute data in table 9, "Tenure, Vacancy Status, and Condition and Plumbing Facilities for the United States, Inside and Outside SMSA's, Urban and Rural: 1960," p. 1–40, Bureau of the Census, *1960: Census of Housing, Volume 1, States and Small Areas, Part 1, United States Summary* (Washington, D.C., 1961). Home ownership rate of nonwhite households, 1940–1960, calculated from table 16, U.S. Housing and Home Finance Agency, *Housing of the Nonwhite Population,* p. 38; table 24, "Selected Population and Housing Characteristics By Color For The United States: 1950 and 1960," table 32, "Selected Characteristics of Urban Housing By Color of Occupants, United States: 1950 and 1960," table 33, "Selected Characteristics of Housing United By Color Of Occupants, For The United States, Urban and Rural: 1960," U.S. Housing and Home Finance Agency, *Our Nonwhite Population and Its Housing: The Changes Between 1950 and 1960* (Washington, D.C.: Government Printing Office, May 1963). Urban housing quality for nonwhite households, 1950 and 1960, from table 24, "Selected Population and Housing Characteristics By Color For The United States: 1950 and 1960," U.S. Housing and Home Finance Agency, *Our Nonwhite Population and Its Housing.*

27. FHA and VA housing starts, 1935–1960, from cols. 2, 3: Series N 180–185, "Private Owned Housing United in Major Federal Programs: 1935 to 1970," Bureau of the Census, *Historical Statistics of the United States* (1976), 2:641. Col. 4: Series N 157, "New Housing Units Started, by Ownership, Type of Structure, Location, and Construction Cost: 1889–1970," ibid., p. 639.

28. See table 1.1, chapter 1.

29. My inspiration for this view is Thomas S. Kuhn, "The Invisibility of Revolu-

tions," in Kuhn, *The Structure of Scientific Revolutions,* 2d ed. (Chicago: University of Chicago Press, 1970), 136–143.

30. Best and Cuttle quoted from "Riversiders Vitally Interested in Proposal to Enlarge Supreme Court," Riverside *Daily Press,* February 10, 1937, p. 1 f.; "Riverside Votes 20 to 1 Against," ibid., February 24, 1937, p. 9; "Vote Still Stands Two to One Against Roosevelt's Supreme Court Program," ibid., February 25, 1937, p. 2; "East Votes Heavily Against Roosevelt Court Change," ibid., February 26, 1937, p. 8; "Final Vote Shows 2 to 1 Opposed to Court Change," ibid., March 1, 1937, p. 8. The survey is not a scientific poll of Riverside's or the nation's electorate. The disaffection of Orange County, California, with Roosevelt similarly began with reaction against the court plan; see Robert L. Pritchard, "Orange County During the Depressed Thirties: A Study in Twentieth-Century California Local History," in Bernard Sternsher, ed., *Hitting Home: The Great Depression in Town and Country* (Chicago: Quadrangle Books, 1970), 261. Also see William E. Leuchtenburg, "Franklin D. Roosevelt's Supreme Court 'Packing' Plan," [1969 paper] reprinted in Dubofsky, *The New Deal,* 271–304, esp. pp. 280, 291–294. The court-packing controversy generated a large, partisan literature, but no titles I located examined local political opinion over the controversy. I found useful Edward S. Corwin, *Constitutional Revolution. Ltd.* (Claremont, Calif.: Pomona College, Scripps College, Claremont Colleges, 1941), esp. pp. 39–79, 80–177; and Robert H. Jackson [appointed to the U.S. Supreme Court by Roosevelt in 1941], *The Struggle for Judicial Supremacy: A Study of a Crisis in American Power Politics* (New York: Alfred A. Knopf, [1941] 1949). C. Herman Pritchett, *The Roosevelt Court: A Study in Judicial Politics and Values, 1937–1947* (New York: Macmillan, 1948), examines the Court after the court-packing controversy. For a historical reassessment of the "old Court," that sat before Roosevelt's Court appointments after 1937, defending the flexibility of the old Court on economic doctrine, see Arthur Shenfield, "The New Deal and the Supreme Court," in Eden, *The New Deal and Its Legacy,* 166–176. See Alan Brinkley, *The End of Reform: New Deal Liberalism in Recession and War* (New York: Alfred A. Knopf, 1995), on how the court-packing controversy and recession of 1937 changed the New Deal, esp. the overview, pp. 3–30.

31. On a related point, see Graham, *Toward a Planned Society,* 98–100.

32. For discussion of the collapse of labor-capital antagonism, see Steve Fraser, "The 'Labor Question,'" in Fraser and Gerstle, *Rise and Fall of the New Deal Order,* 55–84, and Nelson Lichtenstein, "From Corporatism to Collective Bargaining: Organized Labor and the Eclipse of Social Democracy in the Postwar Era," in ibid., pp. 122–152, both of which cite the relevant monographic literature. Cf. Gary Gerstle, *Working-Class Americanism: The Politics of Labor in a Textile City, 1914–1960* (Cambridge: Cambridge University Press, 1989), 263–264, 278–279, 310–330.

33. May, *Homeward Bound,* 162–182; Godfrey Hodgkin, *America in Our Time* (New York: Random House, 1978), 86–90; Lipsitz, *Rainbow at Midnight,* 252–278; Robert Eden, "Introduction: A Legacy of Questions," in Eden, *The New Deal Legacy,* 2–3; Charles R. Kesler, "The Public Philosophy of the New Freedom and the New Deal," in ibid., pp. 155–166; Morton J. Frisch, "An Appraisal of Roosevelt's Legacy: How the Moderate Welfare State Transcended the Tension Between Progressivism and Socialism," in ibid., pp. 190–198.

34. Brinkley, *The End of Reform,* 227–264, on the shift from state coordinated planning of investment and production of the 1930s for purpose of economic stabilization to state planning of national economic growth through regulating aggregate consumer demand in 1940s. See also Graham, *Toward a Planned Society,* 80–90.

35. Hodgkin, *America in Our Time,* 87. Hamby believes that since Roosevelt the institutional capability of the presidency for leadership has been tied to the broadcast media; see Alonzo L. Hamby, *Liberalism and Its Challengers: FDR to Reagan* (New York: Oxford University Press, 1992), vii. Elizabeth A. Foner-Wolf, *Selling Free Enterprise: The Business Assault on Labor and Liberalism, 1945–1960* (Urbana: University of Illinois Press, 1994).

36. Chafe, *The Unfinished Journey,* 112–113. Chafe does not make the point that home building represented a shift from a nation of renters to a nation of home owners as a policy goal of the New Deal and a Rooseveltian value. See also May, *Homeward Bound,* 167, 174–182. On the connection between automobiles, home ownership, and suburbia, see Jackson, *Crabgrass Frontier,* 246–271.

37. Fischer, *America Calling,* 175–192.

38. Cf. Albert Borgmann, *Technology and the Character of Contemporary Life: A Philosophical Inquiry* (Chicago: University of Chicago Press, [1984] 1987).

39. See Fischer's parallel, though not political, view; Fischer, *America Calling,* 265–268.

Selected Bibliography

Unpublished Materials

Birch, Eugenie Ladner. "Edith Elmer Wood and the Genesis of Liberal Housing Thought." Ph.D. dissertation, Columbia University, 1976.

Brigham, Jay Lawrence. "Public Power and Progressivism in the 1920s." Ph.D. dissertation, University of California, Riverside, 1992.

Cartland, Earl F. "A Study of the Negroes Living in Pasadena." M.A. thesis, Whittier College, 1948.

Duncan-Abrams, Marguerite. "The History of the Riverside Planning Commission, 1914–1928." M.A. field report [thesis], Department of History, University of California, Riverside, 1994.

Flint, Barbara J. "Zoning and Residential Segregation: A Social and Physical History, 1910–1940." Ph.D. dissertation, University of Chicago, 1977.

Hartmann, Heidi Irngard. "Capitalism and Women's Work in the Home, 1900–1930." Ph.D. dissertation, Yale University, 1974.

Kleinberg, Susan J. "Technology's Stepdaughters: The Impact of Industrialization upon Working-Class Women in Pittsburgh, 1870–1900." Ph.D. dissertation, University of Pittsburgh, 1973.

Myers, William Allan. "Electricity in Orange County, California, 1890–1914: A Case Study in the Socio-Economic Impact of Technology." M.A. thesis, California State University, Fullerton, 1991.

Parson, Donald Craig. "Urban Politics During the Cold War: Public Housing, Urban Renewal, and Suburbanization in Los Angeles." Ph.D. dissertation, University of California, Los Angeles, 1985.

Phelps, Robert. "Dangerous Class on the Plains of the Id: Ideology and Home Ownership in Southern California, 1880–1920." Ph.D. dissertation, University of California, Riverside, 1996.

Reccow, Louis. "The Orange County Citrus Strikes of 1935–1936: The 'Forgotten People.'" Ph.D. dissertation, Graduate School of the University of Southern California, 1972.

Riverside, City. Records of the City Attorney, Office of City Clerk, Light Department, Office of Mayor, Planning Department, and Police Department. Municipal Archives. Special Collections, Rivera Library, University of California, Riverside.

Sicilia, David B. "Selling Power: Marketing and Monopoly at Boston Edison, 1886–1929." Ph.D. dissertation, Brandeis University, 1991.

Tobey, Ronald C. "Statistical Supplement to *Technology as Freedom.*" 1995. 110 pp. Available from the author at the Department of History, University of California, Riverside 92521–0204.

Tobey, Ronald C., and Charles Wetherell. "Labor in the Citrus Industry, 1887–1944." Report to the State of California, Department of Parks, Interpretive Division. Department of History, University of California, Riverside, 1993.

Van Valen, N. S. "Power Politics: The Struggle for Municipal Ownership of Electric Utilities in Los Angeles, 1905–1937." Ph.D. dissertation, Claremont Graduate School, 1963.

Wheaton, William L. C. "The Evolution of Federal Housing Programs." Ph.D. dissertation, University of Chicago, 1953.

Woodyatt, Lyle J. "The Origins and Evolution of the New Deal Public Housing Program." Ph.D. dissertation, Washington University, St. Louis, 1968.

Government Documents

[California] Energy Resources Conservation and Development Commission. *An Assessment of Socioeconomic and Demographic Determinants of Electrical Energy and Gas Consumption in California.* 5 vols. Glastonbury, Conn.: Futures Group, 1976.

[California] Energy Resources Conservation and Development Commission. *California Plan for the Residential Conservation Service.* Sacramento: The Commission, 1980.

[California] Energy Resources Conservation and Development Commission. *Conservation as an Energy Resource: Policy Implications for California.* Sacramento: The Commission, 1978.

[California] Energy Resources Conservation and Development Commission. *Appliance Efficiency Program; Final Report.* Sacramento: The Commission, 1977.

[U.S.] Bureau of Labor Statistics. *Changes in Retail Prices of Electricity, 1923–1938.* Prepared by Retail Price Division, Stella Stewart, Chief, and Ruth J. Powers, Research Assistant. Bulletin no. 664. Washington, D.C.: GPO, 1939.

[U.S.] Bureau of the Census. *Historical Statistics of the United States, Colonial Times to 1970.* Bicentennial Edition. 2 vols. Washington, D.C.: GPO, 1976.

[U.S.] Bureau of the Census. *Biennial Census of Manufactures: 1921–1937.* 9 vols. in 8. Washington, D.C.: GPO, 1924–1939.

[U.S.] Bureau of the Census. *Census of Electrical Industries: 1902–1937.* U.S. Bureau of the Census. Washington, D.C.: GPO, 1905–1939.

[U.S.] Central Housing Committee. *Activities and Organization of Federal Agencies Concerned with Housing.* Washington, D.C.: GPO, 1936.

[U.S.] Federal Housing Administration. *The FHA Story in Summary, 1934–1959.* Washington, D.C.: Federal Housing Administration, 1959.

[U.S.] Federal Power Commission. *Statistics of Electric Utilities in the United States: 1937–1946.* Washington, D.C.: GPO, 1947.

[U.S.] Housing and Home Finance Agency. *Housing of the Nonwhite Population, 1940 to 1950.* Washington, D.C.: GPO, 1952.

[U.S.] Housing and Home Finance Agency. *Our Nonwhite Population and Its Housing: The Changes Between 1950 and 1960.* Washington, D.C.: GPO, [1962].

[U.S.] Housing and Home Finance Agency. *Housing of the Nonwhite Population, 1940–1950.* Washington, D.C.: GPO, 1951.

[U.S.] Housing and Home Finance Agency. *Our Nonwhite Population and Its Housing· The Changes Between 1950 and 1960.* Washington, D.C.: GPO, May 1963.

[U.S.] National Emergency Council. *Report on Economic Conditions of the South.* 1938. Reprint. New York: Da Capo Press, 1972.

Bibliographies

Beard, Belle Boone, and Other Members of the Seminary in Social and Industrial Research in the Carola Woerishoffer Graduate Department of Social Economy and Social Research, Bryn Mawr College. *Electricity in the Home: Being a List of Books and Articles with Brief Abstracts Prepared in Connection with a Survey of the Social and Economic Effects of the Wider Use of Electricity in the Home.* Foreword by Morris Llewellyn Cooke. New York: Workers Education Bureau Press, 1927.

Bedi, Joyce E., Ronald R. Kline, and Craig Semsel. *Sources in Electrical History: Archives and Manuscript Collections in U.S. Repositories.* New York: Center for the History of Electrical Engineering, 1989.

Beers, Henry Putney. *Bibliographies in American History, 1942–1978: Guide to Materials for Research.* Woodbridge, Conn.: Research Publications, 1982.

Boyce, Dr. Byrl N., and Dr. Sidney Turoff. *Minority Groups and Housing, A Bibliography, 1950–1970.* A d. h. mark publication of General Learning Press. [Center for Real Estate and Urban Economic Studies, University of Connecticut] [n.p.]: University of Connecticut, 1972.

Cutcliffe, Stephen H., Judith A. Mistichelli, and Christine M. Roysdon. *Technology and Values in American Civilization: A Guide to Information Sources.* Vol. 9 in the American Studies Information Guide Series. Detroit: Gale Research, 1980.

Ferguson, Eugene S. *Bibliography of the History of Technology.* Published jointly by the Society for the History of Technology and MIT Press. Cambridge: MIT Press, 1968.

Haber, Barbara. *Women in America: Guide to Books, 1963–1975, with Appendix on Books Published 1976–1979.* Urbana: University of Illinois Press, 1981.

Hay, Fred J. *African American Community Studies.* Garland Reference Library of Social Science, vol. 420. Applied Social Science Bibliographies, vol. 5. New York: Garland, 1991.

Kyvig, David E., and Mary-Ann Blasio, compilers. *New Day/New Deal: A Bibliography of the Great American Depression, 1929–1941.* Bibliographies and Indexes in American History, no. 9. New York: Greenwood Press, 1988.

Lovett, Robert W. *American Economic and Business History: A Guide to Information Sources.* Management Information Guide Series, no. 23. Detroit: Gale Research, 1971. [1980]: 95.

Lyford, Carrie Alberta. *Bibliography of Home Economics.* Bureau of Education. Bulletin no. 46. Washington, D.C.: GPO, 1919.

Mitcham, Carl, and Robert Mackey, eds. "Bibliography of the Philosophy of Technology." *Technology and Culture* 14 (April 1973): S1–S205.

Morrison, Denton E., et al. *Energy: A Bibliography of Social Science and Related Literature.* New York: Garland, 1975.

————. *Energy II: A Bibliography of 1975–76 Social Science and Related Literature.* New York: Garland, 1977.

Olson, David H. L., ed. *Inventory of Marriage and Family Literature, 1979.* [Beverly Hills]: Sage Publications, 1980.

Rogers, Everett M., Linda Williams, and Rhoda B. West. *Bibliography of the Diffusion of Innovations.* Monticello, Ill.: Council of Planning Librarians, 1977.

Shiers, George. *Bibliography of the History of Electronics.* Metuchen, N.J.: Scarecrow Press, 1972.

Shumsky, Neil L., and Timothy Crimmins, eds. *Urban America: A Historical Bibliography.* Santa Barbara, Calif.: ABC-Clio Information Services, 1983.

Articles

Allport, Floyd H., Lawrence K. Frank, Robert S. Lynd, Benjamin C. Gruenberg, and Sidonie Mastner, Chairman. "Housing and Family Life in Cities." In John M. Gries and James Ford, eds., 56–94. *Homemaking, Home Furnishing and Information Services.* Washington, D.C.: President's Conference on Home Building and Home Ownership, 1932.

American Home Economics Association. "Applications of Electricity to Domestic Use." *Journal of Home Economics* 22 (1930): 631–640.

Ando, Albert, and Franco Modigliani. "The 'Life Cycle' Hypothesis of Saving: Aggregate Implications and Tests." *American Economic Review* 53 (March 1963): 109–127.

Andrachek, Steven E. "Housing in the United States, 1890–1929." In Gertrude Sipperly Fish, ed., 123–176. *The Story of Housing.* New York: Macmillan, 1979.

Angus, Ian H. "Technology and Humanism: A Review-Essay on Edward G. Ballard's 'Man and Technology' (1978)." *Research in Philosophy and Technology* 6 (1983): 225–230.

Artle, Roland, and P. Varaiya. "Life Cycle Consumption and Homeownership." *Journal of Economic Theory* 18 (1978): 38–58.

Axelrod, Alan. "A Century of Light: The Development of Iowa's Electric Utilities." *Palimpsest* 60 (1979): 130–155.

Bailyn, Lotte, and Edgar Schein. "Life/Career Considerations as Indicators of Quality of Employment." In A. D. Biderman and T. F. Drury, eds., 151–168. *Measuring Work Quality for Social Reporting.* Beverly Hills, Calif.: Sage Publications, 1976.

Bandeen, Robert H. "Automobile Consumption, 1940–1950." *Econometrica* 25 (April 1957): 239–248.

Banner, Lois. "Women's History in the United States: Recent Theory and Practice." *Trends in History* 4 (Fall 1985): 93–123.

Barkan, Elliott, R. "Immigration Through the Port of Los Angeles." In M. Mark Stolarik, ed., 161–191. *Forgotten Doors: The Other Ports of Entry to the United States.* Philadelphia: Balch Institute Press, 1988.

Barmish, B. R. "A New Approach to the Incorporation of Attributes into Consumer Theory." *Journal of Economic Theory* 32 (1984): 93–110.

Barnes, R., et al. "Short-run Residential Demand for Electricity." *Review of Economics and Statistics* 63 (1981): 641–652.

Barrows, Robert G. "Beyond the Tenement: Patterns of American Urban Housing, 1870–1930." *Journal of Urban History* 9 (1983): 395–420.

Barten, A. P. "Systems of Consumer Demand Functions Approach: Review." *Econometrica* 45 (1977): 23–51.

Barton, S. G. "The Life Cycle and Buying Patterns." In L. H. Clark, ed., 53–57. *The Life Cycle and Consumer Behavior.* New York: New York University Press, 1955.

Basmann, R. L., et al."Budget Constraint Prices as Preference Changing Parameters Generalized Fechner-Thurstone Direct Utility Functions." *American Economic Review* 73 (1983): 411–413.

Bastian, Robert. "Urban House Types as a Research Focus in Historical Geography." *Environmental Review* 4 (1980): 27–34.

Beaune, Jean-Claude. "Philosophy of Technology in France in the Twentieth Century: Overview and Current Bibliography." *Research in Philosophy and Technology* 2 (1979): 273–292.

Bellante, Don, and Anne C. Foster. "Working Wives and Expenditures on Services." *Journal of Consumer Research* 11 (1984): 700–707.

Bengtson, Vern L. "Generations and Family Effects in Value Socialization." *American Sociological Review* 40 (1975): 358–371.

Bennett, Sheila Kishler, and Glen H. Elder, Jr. "Women's Work in the Family Economy: A Study of Depression Hardship in Women's Lives." *Journal of Family History* 4 (1979): 153–176.

Biola, Heather. "The Black Washer Women in Southern Tradition." *Tennessee Folklore Society Bulletin* 45 (1979): 17–27.

Birch, Eugenie Ladner. "Woman-made America: The Case of Early Public Housing Policy." *Journal of the American Institute of Planners* 44 (April 1978): 130–144.

Blitz, Rudolph C. "Women in the Professions, 1870–1970." *Monthly Labor Review* 97 (1974): 34–39.

Bloomenthal, Lawrence R. "Tax Exemptions; Part I—General Principles." *Taxation Magazine* 15 (May 1937): 269–274, 310.

———. "Tax Exemptions; Part II. Homestead Exemption." *Taxation Magazine* 15 (July 1937): 398–405, 440; (August 1937): 463–475.

Blundell, R., and I. Walker. "A Household Production Specification of Demographic Variables in Demand Analysis." *Economic Journal* 94 (Supplement 1984): 59–68.

Boocock, Sarane Spence. "Historical and Sociological Research on the Family and the Methodological Alternatives." In John Demos and Sarane Spence Boocock, eds., 366–394. *Turning Points: Historical and Sociological Essays on the Family. American Journal of Sociology,* Supplement 84 (1978). Chicago: University of Chicago Press, 1978.

Borgmann, Albert. "Orientation in Technology." *Philosophy Today* 16 (1972): 135–147.

Borsodi, Ralph. "What Should the Home Contribute?" *Journal of Home Economics* 28 (1936): 365–367.

Bose, C. E., Philip L. Bereano, and Mary Malloy. "Household Technology and the Social Construction of Housework." *Technology and Culture* 25 (1984): 53–82.

Boyer, M. "Rational Demand and Expenditure Patterns Under Habit Formation." *Journal of Economic Theory* 31 (1983): 27–53.

Bradford, Calvin. "Financing Home Ownership: The Federal Role in Neighborhood Decline." *Urban Affairs Quarterly* 14 (March 1979): 313–335.

Brady, Dorothy S. "Family Saving, 1888 to 1950." In Raymond S. Goldsmith, *A Study of Saving in the United States.* Vol. 3, pt. 2. Princeton: Princeton University Press, 1959.

Brems, Hans. "Long-run Automobile Demand." *Journal of Marketing* 20 (1956): 379–384.

Brown, D. Clayton. "Sam Rayburn and the Development of Public Power in the Southwest." *Southwestern Historical Quarterly* 78 (October 1974): 140–154.

Brownlee, W. Elliot, Jr. "Household Values, Women's Work, and Economic Growth, 1800–1930." *Journal of Economic History* 39 (1979): 199–209.

Bureau of the Census. "The Geographical Mobility of Americans: An International Comparison." *Current Population Reports: Special Studies,* no. 64.

Burk, M. C. "Survey of Interpretations of Consumer Behavior by Social Scientists in the Postwar Period." *Journal of Farm Economics* 49 (1967): 1–31.

Burstein, M. L. "The Demand for Household Refrigeration in the United States." In Arnold C. Harberger, ed., 99–145. *The Demand for Durable Goods.* Chicago: University of Chicago Press, 1960.

Burwell, Calvin C., and Blair G. Swezey. "The Home: Evolving Technologies for Satisfying Human Wants." In Sam H. Schurr, Calvin C. Burwell, Warren D. Devine, Jr., and Sidney Sonenblum, eds., 249–270. *Electricity in the American Economy: Agent of Technological Progress.* Contributions in Economics and Economic History, no. 117. Published under the auspices of the Electric Power Research Institute. Westport, Conn.: Greenwood Press, 1990.

Busch, Jane. "Cooking Competition: Technology on the Domestic Market in the 1930s." *Technology and Culture* 24 (April 1983): 222–245.

Button, K. J. "An Historical Survey of the Early Debate on Consumer's Surplus Theory." *Journal of Economic Studies* 6 (1979): 155–181.

Carey, James W., and John J. Quirk. "The Mythos of the Electronic Revolution." *American Scholar* 39 (Spring 1970): 219–241; (Summer 1970): 395–424.

Carpenter, Stanley R. "Review of Langdon Winner's Autonomous Technology." *Research in Philosophy and Technology* 3 (1980): 116–124.

Carse, Edith. "Relative Cost of Flamo and Electricity for Cooking." *Journal of Home Economics* 24 (1932): 537–538.

Chang, W. W., et al. "Dynamic Properties of a Simple Overlapping Generations Model." *Oxford Economic Papers* 35 (1983): 366–372.

Chapman, John M., and Associates. "Commercial Banks and Consumer Instalment Credit." *Studies in Consumer Instalment Financing,* no. 3. New York: National Bureau of Economic Research, 1940.

Charters, W. W. "The Traits of Homemakers." *Journal of Home Economics* 18 (1926): 673–685.

Chow, Gregory. "Statistical Demand Functions for Automobiles and Their Use for Forecasting." In Arnold C. Harberger, ed., 149–178. *The Demand for Durable Goods.* Chicago: University of Chicago Press, 1960.

Clark, Carroll D. "Evaluating Certain Equipment of the Modern Rural Home." *Journal of Home Economics* 22 (1930): 1005–1015.

Clower, Robert W. "Permanent Income and Transitory Balances," *Oxford Economic Papers* 15 (July 1963): 177–190.

Collier, B. J. "Sociological Foundations of Consumer Behavior: Their Implications for Economic Efficiency." *American Journal of Economics and Sociology* 37 (1978): 25–33.

Conkin, Paul K. "Intellectual and Political Roots [of TVA]." In Erwin C. Hargrove and Paul K. Conkin, eds., 3–34. *TVA: Fifty Years of Grass-Roots of Bureaucracy.* Urbana: University of Illinois Press, 1983.

Cook, S. W., and J. L. Berrenberg. "Approaches to Encouraging Conservation Behavior: A Review and Conceptual Framework." *Journal of Social Issues* 37 (1981): 71–107.

Coolidge, John. "The Modern House." *Atlantic Monthly* 159 (March 1937): 286 f.

Coppock, Joseph D. "Government as Enterpriser-Competitor: The Case of the Electric Home and Farm Authority." *Explorations in Entrepreneurial History,* 2d ser. (Winter 1964): 187–206.

Couto, Richard A. "New Seeds at the Grass Roots: The Politics of the TVA Power Program since World War II." In Erwin C. Hargrove and Paul Conkin, eds., 230–260. *TVA: Fifty Years of Grass-Roots Bureaucracy.* Urbana: University of Illinois Press, 1983.

Coverman, Shelley. "Gender, Domestic Labor Time and Working Women." *American Sociological Review* 48 (October 1983): 623–636.

Cowan, Ruth Schwartz. "The 'Industrial Revolution' in the Home: Household Technology and Social Change in the 20th Century." *Technology and Culture* 17 (1976): 1–23.

———. "Two Washes in the Morning and a Bridge Party at Night: The American Housewife Between the Wars." *Women's Studies* 3 (1976): 147–172.

Crockett, Jean, and Irwin Friend. "A Complete Set of Consumer Demand Relationships." In Irwin Friend and Robert Jones, eds., 1–92. *Proceedings of the Conference on Consumption and Savings.* Vol. 1. Philadelphia: University of Pennsylvania Press, 1960.

Cushman, Ella M. "A Study of Time Spent in Dishwashing." *Journal of Home Economics* 22 (1930): 295–297.

Davison, Eloise. "What the Homemaker Needs to Know about Electricity." *Journal of Home Economics* 22 (1930): 94–97.

Day, Tanis. "Capital-Labor Substitution in the Home." *Technology and Culture* 33 (April 1992): 302–327.

DeGraaf, Leonard. "Corporate Liberalism and Electric Power System Planning in the 1920s." *Business History Review* 64 (Spring 1990): 1–31.

De Graff, Lawrence B. "The City of Black Angeles: Emergence of the Los Angeles Ghetto, 1890–1930." *Pacific Historical Review* 39 (August 1970): 323–352.

Deutrich, Mabel, and Virginia C. Purdy. "Appendix: List of Numbered Bulletins of the Women's Bureau." In Mabel Deutrich and Virginia C. Purdy, eds., *Clio Was a Woman: Studies in the History of Women.* Washington, D.C.: Howard University Press, 1980.

DeWolff, P. "Demand for Motor Cars in the United States." *Econometrica* 6 (1938): 113–129.

Dilts, Madge E. "A Method for Determining Quantitatively the Comparative Ability of Electric Cleaners to Remove Dirt from Rugs and Carpets." *Journal of Home Economics* 26 (1934): 172–176.

Dorsey, Jean Muir. "Management of the Responsibilities of the Homemaker." In John M. Gries and James Ford, eds., 25–64. *Household Management and Kitchens.* Washington, D.C.: President's Conference on Home Building and Home Ownership, 1932.

Doucet, Michael J., and John C. Weaver. "Material Culture and the North American House: The Era of the Common Man, 1870–1920." *Journal of American History* 72 (1985): 560–587.

Douglas, Paul H. "Some Recent Social Changes and Their Effect upon Family Life." *Journal of Home Economics* 25 (1933): 361–370.

Dresslar, Martha E. "Relative Cost of Gas and Electricity." *Journal of Home Economics* 15 (February 1923): 71–80.

Droze, Wilmon H. "The TVA, 1945–80: The Power Company." In Erwin C. Hargrove and Paul K. Conkin, eds. 66–85. *TVA: Fifty Years of Grass-Roots Bureaucracy.* Urbana: University of Illinois Press, 1983.

DuBoff, Richard B. "The Introduction of Electric Power in American Manufacturing." *Economic History Review,* 2d ser. 20 (December 1967): 509–518.

Dudden, Faye E. "Experts and Servants: The National Council on Household Employment and the Decline of Domestic Service in the Twentieth Century." *Journal of Social History* 20 (1986): 269–289.

Durbin, Paul T. "Reviews of Bernard Gendron, Technology and the Human Condition, I." *Research in Philosophy and Technology* 3 (1980): 77–87.

Dyer, William G. "A Comparison of Families of High and Low Job Satisfaction." *Marriage and Family Living* 18 (1956): 58–60.

Edmonds, J. A. "Introduction to Behavioral Growth Models with Heterogeneous Consumer Goods." *Southern Economic Journal* 47 (1980): 444–462.

Edwards, Alba M. "A Social-Economic Grouping of the Gainful Workers of the United States." *Journal of the American Statistical Association* 28 (December 1933): 377–387.

Elder, Glen H., Jr. "Approaches to Social Change and the Family." In John Demos and Sarane Spence, eds., 1–38. *Turning Points: Historical and Sociological Essays on the Family. American Journal of Sociology,* Supplement 84 (1978). Chicago: University of Chicago Press, 1978.

Elder, Glen H., Jr., and Jeffrey K. Liker. "Hard Times in Women's Lives: Historical Influences Across Forty Years." *American Journal of Sociology* 88 (1982): 241–269.

Eliot, Thomas D. "Present-day Social Problems of the American Family." *Journal of Home Economics* 20 (1928): 229–237.

Federal Power Commission. "Best Scheme of Development of Colorado River Below Its Junction with the Green." By Chief Engineer of FPC, 177–200. *Second Annual Report of the Federal Power Commission,* Fiscal Year ended June 30, 1922. Washington, D.C.: GPO, 1922.

———. "Report to the Federal Power Commission in the Water Powers of California." By Frank E. Bonner, District Engineer, United States Forest Service. Washington, D.C.: GPO, 1928.

Ferber, Robert. "Family Decision Making and Economic Behavior: A Review." In Eleanor Bernert Sheldon, ed., 29–61. *Family Economic Behavior.* Philadelphia: J. B. Lippincott, 1973.

Ferguson, Eugene S. "Toward a Discipline of the History of Technology." *Technology and Culture* 15 (1974): 13–30.

Field, Gregory B. "'Electricity for All': The Electric Home and Farm Authority and the Politics of Mass Consumption, 1932–1935." *Business History Review* 64 (Spring 1990): 32–60.

Fish, Gertrude S. "Housing Policy During the Great Depression." In Gertrude Sipperly Fish, ed., 177–241. *The Story of Housing.* New York: Macmillan, 1979.

Fisher, Claude S., and Glenn R. Carroll. "Telephone and Automobile Diffusion in the United States, 1902–1937." *American Journal of Sociology* 93 (1988): 1153–1178.

Foner, Anne, and David Kertzer. "Transitions over the Life Course: Lessons from Age-Set Societies." *American Journal of Sociology* 83 (1978): 1081–1104.

Foner, Anne. "Age Stratification and Age Conflict in Political Life." *American Sociological Review* 39 (1974): 187–196.

———. "Age in Society: Structure and Change." *American Behavioral Scientist* 19 (1975): 144–166.

———. "Age Stratification and the Changing Family." In John Demos and Sarane Spence

Boocock, eds., 340–365. *Turning Points: Historical and Sociological Essays on the Family.* Chicago: University of Chicago Press, 1978.

Franks, Dean. "An Interpretation of Technology Through the Assertorical-Problematic Distinction." *Kinesis* 4 (1971): 22–30.

Freedman, Ronald, and Lolagene Coombs. "Childspacing and Family Economic Position." *American Sociological Review* 31 (1966): 631–648.

Furstenberg, Frank F. "Work Experience and Family Life." In J. O'Toole, ed., 341–360. *Work and the Quality of Life.* Cambridge: MIT Press, 1974.

Gendron, Bernard. "History, Dialectics, and the Prospects for Emancipation." Pp. 229–245 in *Technology and the Human Condition.* New York: St. Martin's Press, 1977.

———. "Reply: Growth, Power, and the Imperatives of Technology." *Research in Philosophy and Technology* 3 (1980): 102–116.

Gendron, Bernard, and Nancy Holmstrom. "Marx, Machinery, and Alienation. *Research in Philosophy and Technology* 2 (1979): 119–135.

Gilfillan, S. C. "Housekeeping in the Future." *Independent* 72 (1912): 1060–1062.

Glenn, E. N. "Occupational Ghettoization: Japanese American Women and Domestic Service, 1905–1970." *Ethnicity* 8 (1981): Bibliography, pp. 384–386.

Glick, Paul C., and Robert Parke, Jr. "New Approaches in Studying the Life Cycle of the Family." *Demography* 2 (1965): 187–202.

Goldin, Claudia. "Historians' Consensus on the Economic Role of Women in American History." *Historical Methods* 16 (1983): 74–81.

Goldschmidt-Clermont, L. "Does Housework Pay? A Product-related Microeconomic Approach." *Signs* 9 (1983): 108–119.

Gray, Greta. "The Nebraska Rural Kitchen." *Journal of Home Economics* 19 (1927): 504–512.

Gray, Greta, and Glasgow, Dorothy. "Conditions of Operation Affecting Current Consumption of Electric Refrigerators." *Journal of Home Economics* 25 (1933): 503–507.

Grether, D. M., and C. R. Plott. "Economic Theory of Choice and the Preference Reversal Phenomenon." *American Economic Review* 69 (1979): 623–638; discussion, 72 (1982): 569–584.

Grieves, R. "Demand for Consumer Goods." *Journal of Money, Credit and Banking* 15 (1983): 316–326.

Grossman, Allyson Sherman. "Women in Domestic Work: Yesterday and Today." *Monthly Labor Review* 103 (1980): 17–21.

Hader, Mathilde C. "The Effect of Electricity on the Life of Women in Norway." *Journal of Home Economics* 21 (1929): 248–253.

Hamermesh, D. S. "Consumption During Retirement: The Missing Link in the Life Cycle." *Review of Economics and Statistics* 66 (1984): 1–7.

Hancock, John. "The Apartment House in Urban America." In Anthony D. King, ed., 151–189. *Buildings and Society: Essays on the Development of the Built Environment.* London: Routledge & Kegan Paul, 1980.

Hanson, S. L., et. al. "Consequences of Involuntary Low Parity for Women's Perception of Homemaker and Work Roles: Findings from a 24-Year Longitudinal Study." *Sociology and Social Research* 68 (1984): 326–349.

Hareven, Tamara K. "The Family as Process: The Historical Study of the Family Cycle." *Journal of Social History* 7 (1974): 322–327.

———. "The Last Stage: Historical Adulthood and Old Age." *Daedalus* 105 (1976): 13–27.

———. "Cycles, Courses and Cohorts: Reflections on the Theoretical and Methodological Approaches to the Historical Study of Family Development." *Journal of Social History* 12 (1978): 97–109.

Harris, Richard. "Working-Class Home Ownership in the American Metropolis." *Journal of Urban History* 17 (1990): 46–70.

Hartman, R. S. "Note on the Use of Aggregate Data in Individual Choice Models: Discrete Consumer Choice Among Alternative Fuels for Residential Appliances." *Journal of Econometrics* 18 (1982): 313–335.

Haskel, Douglas. "Houses Like Fords." *Harper's* 168 (February 1934): 280.

Hattersley, J. F. "Rating Chart for Electric Cleaners." *Journal of Home Economics* 23 (1931): 642–645.

Havard, William C., Jr. "Images of TVA: The Clash over Values." In Erwin C. Hargrove and Paul K. Conkin, eds., 297–315. *TVA: Fifty Years of Grass-Roots Bureaucracy.* Urbana: University of Illinois Press, 1983.

Hawkins, Lucy B. "Wages for Household Tasks." *Journal of Home Economics* 15 (1923): 430–434.

Haynes, Elizabeth Ross. "Negroes in Domestic Servitude in the United States." *Journal of Negro History* 8 (1923): 384–442.

Heiner, Mary Koll, and N. Maude Vedder. "Studies in Dishwashing Methods: An Attempt to Apply Methods of Job Analysis to a Household Process." *Journal of Home Economics* 22 (1930): 393–407.

Hewes, Amy. "Electrical Appliances in the Home." *Social Forces* 2 (December 1930): 235–242.

Higgs, Robert. "Crisis, Bigger Government, and the Ideological Change: Two Hypotheses on the Ratchet Phenomenon." *Explorations in Economic History* 22 (1985): 1–28.

Hill, Reuben, and David M. Klein. "Understanding Family Consumption." In Eleanor Bernert Sheldon, ed., 3–22. *Family Economic Behavior.* Philadelphia: J. B. Lippincott, 1973.

Hill, Reuben, and Roy H. Rodgers. "The Developmental Approach." In Harold T. Christensen, ed., 171–211. *Handbook of Marriage and the Family.* Chicago: Rand McNally, 1964.

Holt, Charles. "Who Benefits from the Prosperity of the Twenties?" *Explorations in Economic History* 14 (July 1977): 277–289.

Hong, T. "Households and Markets: Theories and New Research on Consumption Activities." *Acta Sociologica* 23 (1980): 21–31.

Horowitz, Daniel. "Frugality or Comfort: Middle-Class Styles of Life in the Early Twentieth Century." *American Quarterly* 37 (1985): 239–259.

Horrigan, Brian. "The Home of Tomorrow, 1927–1945." In Joseph J. Corn, ed., 137–163. *Imagining Tomorrow.* Cambridge: MIT Press, 1986.

Hoselitz, Bert F. "Economic Growth: Noneconomic Aspects." *International Encyclopedia of the Social Sciences.* Vol 4: 422–429. New York: Macmillan Free Press, 1968.

Houthakker, H. S., and John Haldi. "Household Investment in Automobiles: An Intertemporal Cross-Section Analysis." In Irwin Friend and Robert Jones, eds., 175–224. *Proceedings of the Conference on Consumption and Saving,* vol. 1. Philadelphia: University of Pennsylvania Press, 1960.

Hughes, Thomas P. "The Industrial Revolution That Never Came." *American Heritage of Invention and Technology* (Winter 1988): 58–64.

Hypes, J. L. "The Physical Equipment of Homes in Relation to their Residential Holding Power." *Journal of Home Economics* 29 (1937): 397–404.

Ihde, Don. "The Historical-Ontological Priority of Technology over Science." In Paul
    T. Durbin and Friedrich Rapp, eds., 235–252. *Philosophy and Technology, Boston
    Studies in Philosophy of Science*. Vol. 80. Dordrecht: D. Reidel, 1983.

Inkeles, Alex. "Social Change and Social Character: The Role of Parental Mediation."
    Journal of Social Issues 11 (1955): 12–23.

———. "Industrial Man: The Relation of Status to Experience, Perception, and Value."
    American Journal of Sociology 66 (1960): 1–31.

Jensen, Joan M. "Cloth, Butter and Boarders: Women's Household Production for the
    Market." *Review of Radical Political Economics* 12 (1980): 14–24.

Johnson, Mary. "Women and Their Material Universe: A Bibliographic Essay." *Journal
    of American Culture* 6 (1983): 32–51.

Kahne, Hilda. "Economic Research on Women and Families." *Signs* 3 (1978): 652–665.

Kanter, Rosabeth Moss. "Families, Family Processes, and Economic Life: Toward Sys-
    tematic Analysis of Social Historical Research." In John Demos and Sarane Spence
    Boocock, eds., 316–339. *Turning Points: Historical and Sociological Essays on the
    Family*. Chicago: University of Chicago Press, 1978.

Katona, George, and Eva Mueller. "A Study of Purchase Decisions." In L. H. Clark, ed.,
    30–87. *Consumer Behavior: Research on Consumer Reactions*. New York: Arno
    Press, 1978.

Katz, Michael, and Ian F. Davey. "Youth and Early Industrialization in a Canadian City."
    American Journal of Sociology, Supplement 84 (1978): S81–S119.

Kearl, J. R., and C. L. Pope. "Life Cycle in Economic History." *Journal of Economic
    History* 43 (1983): 149–158.

Keller, R. R., et al. "Preference and Value Formation: A Convergence of Enlightened Or-
    thodox and Institutional Analyses." *Journal of Economic Issues* 16 (1982): 941–954.

Ketts, Joseph F. "Growing Up in Rural New England, 1800–1840." In Tamara K. Hareven,
    ed., 1–14. *Anonymous Americans: Explorations in Nineteenth-Century Social His-
    tory*. Englewood Cliffs, N.J.: Prentice-Hall, 1971.

King, M. A., and L. D. L. Dicks-Mireau. "Asset Holdings and the Life-Cycle." *Economic
    Journal* 92 (1982): 247–267.

Kivisto, Peter. "A Historical Review of Changes in Public Housing and Their Impacts
    on Minorities." In Jamshid A. Momeni, ed., 1–18. *Race, Ethnicity, and Minority Hous-
    ing in the United States*. New York: Greenwood Press, 1986.

Kneeland, Hildegarde. "Limitations of Scientific Management in Household Work."
    Journal of Home Economics 20 (1928): 311–314.

Koprowaki-Kraut, Gayle. "The Depression's Effects on a Milwaukee Family." *Milwau-
    kee History* 3 (1980): 84–92.

Lancaster, Kevin. "A New Approach to Consumer Theory." *Journal of Political Econ-
    omy* 74 (April 1966): 132–157.

Laslett, Barbara. "The Family as a Public and Private Institution: An Historical Per-
    spective." *Journal of Marriage and the Family* 35 (1973): 480–492.

Laurito, Pamela W. "The Message Was Electric." *IEEE Spectrum* 21 (September 1984):
    84–95.

Leach, William R. "Transformations in a Culture of Consumption: Women and Depart-
    ment Stores, 1890–1925." *Journal of American History* 71 (1984): 319–342.

Leuchtenburg, William E. "Franklin D. Roosevelt's Supreme Court 'Packing' Plan." In
    Melvyn Dubofsky, ed., 271–304. *The New Deal: Conflicting Interpretations and Shift-
    ing Perspectives*. New York: Garland, 1992.

————. "Roosevelt, Norris and the 'Seven Little TVAs.'" *Journal of Politics* 14 (August 1952): 418–441.

Lippitt, Vernon G. "Determinants of Consumer Demand for House Furnishing and Equipment." In Irwin Friend and Robert Jones, 225–246. *Proceedings of the Conference on Consumption and Savings.* Vol. 1. Philadelphia: University of Pennsylvania Press, 1960.

Lubell, Samuel. "That Generation Gap." *Public Interest* 13 (1968): 52–60.

Lubove, Roy. "Homes and a Few Well-Placed Fruit Trees: An Object Lesson in Federal Housing." *Social Research* 27 (Winter 1960): 469–486.

Lundgren, Nilo, ed. "Creating the Electrical Age." Special issue of *EPRI Journal* 4 (1979).

Luria, Daniel D. "Wealth Capital and Power: The Social Meaning of Home Ownership." *Journal of Intellectual History* 7 (1976): 261–282.

Lynd, Robert S., assisted by Alice C. Hanson. "The People as Consumers." In *Recent Social Trends in the United States; Report of the President's Committee on Social Trends,* 857–911. New York: McGraw-Hill, 1933.

Lynde, Carleton J. "The Dirt Lifting Efficiency and Wear Produced on Carpets by Different Types of Vacuum Sweepers." *Journal of Home Economics* 24 (1932): 257–261.

Macdonald, Elizabeth Stone. "Home Service Work in the Public Utilities." *Journal of Home Economics* 23 (1931): 719–723.

Mack, R. P., and T. J. Leigland. "Optimizing in Households, Toward a Behavioral Theory." *American Economic Review, Papers and Proceedings* 72 (1982): 103–108.

Mayer, T. "Consumption in the Great Depression." *Journal of Political Economy* 86 (1978): 139–145.

McClymer, John F. "The Federal Government and the Americanization Movement, 1915–1924." *Prologue: Journal of the National Archives* 10 (Spring 1978): 22–41.

McLaughlin, Virginia Yans. "Patterns of Work and Family Organization: Buffalo's Italians." *Journal of Interdisciplinary History* 2 (1971): 299–314.

Merz, J. "FELES: The Functionalized Extended Linear Expenditure System: Theory, Estimation Procedures and Application to the Individual Household Consumption Expenditures Involving Socioeconomic and Sociodemographic Characteristics." *European Economic Review* 23 (1983): 359–394.

Miller, Delbert C. "Theories of Social Change." In Francis R. Allen, Hornell Hart, Delbert C. Miller, William F. Ogburn, and Meyer F. Nimkoff, eds., 72–106. *Technology and Social Change.* New York: Appleton-Century-Crofts, 1957.

Miller, Roger. "Household Activity Patterns in Nineteenth-Century Suburbs: A Time-Geographic Exploration." *Annals of the Association of American Geographers* 72 (1982): 355–371.

Mishkin, F. S. "Household Balance Sheet and the Great Depression." *Journal of Economic History* 38 (1978): 918–937.

————. "Consumer Sentiment and Spending on Durable Goods." *Brookings Papers on Economic Activity,* no. 1 (1978): 217–232.

Modell, John, and Tamara K. Hareven. "Urbanization and the Malleable Household: An Examination of Boarding and Lodging in American Families." *Journal of Marriage and the Family* 35 (1973): 467–479.

Modell, John. "Suburbanization and Change in the American Family." *Journal of Interdisciplinary History* 9 (1979): 621–646.

Monroe, Day. "The Family in Chicago: A Study of Selected Census Data." *Journal of Home Economics* 19 (1927): 617–622.

———. "Levels of Living of the Nation's Families." *Journal of Home Economics* 29 (1937): 665–670.

Monroe, Day, Sarah J. MacLoed, Hildegarde Kneeland, Eloise Davison, and Helen W. Atwater. "Determination of Standards for the Establishment of Household Budgets, for the Expenditure of Money, Time, and Energy." *Journal of Home Economics* 25 (1933): 109–114.

Muth, Richard F. "The Demand for Non-Farm Housing." In Arnold C. Harberger, ed., 29–96. *The Demand for Durable Goods.* Chicago: University of Chicago Press, 1960.

Nerlove, M. "A Note on Long-run Automobile Demand." *Journal of Marketing* 22 (July 1957): 57–64.

Neufeld, John L. "Price Discrimination and the Adoption of the Electricity Demand Change." *Journal of Economic History* 47 (1987): 693–709.

Newman, J. W., and R. Staelin. "Multivariate Analysis of Differences in Buyer Decision Time." *Journal of Marketing Research* 8 (1971): 192–198.

Nielsen, Kai. "Technology as Ideology." *Research in Philosophy and Technology* 1 (1978): 131–147.

———. "Marx, the Primacy Thesis, and Technological Determinism." *Research in Philosophy and Technology* 5 (1982): 249–259.

Nimkoff, Meyer F. "Technology and the Family." In Francis R. Allen, Hornell Hart, Delbert C. Miller, William F. Ogburn, and Meyer F. Nimkoff, eds., 305–323. *Technology and Social Change.* New York: Appleton-Century-Crofts, 1957.

———. "Obstacles to Innovation." In Francis R. Allen, Hornell Hart, Delbert C. Miller, William F. Ogburn, and Meyer F. Nimkoff, eds., 56–71. *Technology and Social Change.* New York: Appleton-Century-Crofts, 1957.

Normile, J., and W. Adams. "Preview of Kitchens to Come." *Better Homes and Gardens* 21 (July 1943): 38.

Ogburn, W. F., assisted by S. C. Gilfillan. "The Influence of Invention and Discovery." In *Recent Social Trends in the United States: Report of the President's Research Committee on Social Trends.* Vol. 1: 122–166. New York: McGraw-Hill, 1933.

Ogburn, William Fielding. "Introductory Ideas on Inventions and the State." In William Fielding Ogburn, ed., 1–15. *Technology and International Relations.* Chicago: University of Chicago Press, 1949.

———. "How Technology Causes Social Change." In Francis R. Allen, Hornell Hart, Delbert C. Miller, William F. Ogburn, and Meyer F. Nimkoff, eds., 12–26. *Technology and Social Change.* New York: Appleton-Century-Crofts, 1957.

———. "The Meaning of Technology." In Francis R. Allen, Hornell Hart, Delbert C. Miller, William F. Ogburn, and Meyer F. Nimkoff, eds., 3–11. *Technology and Social Change.* New York: Appleton-Century-Crofts, 1957.

Olsen, Marvin E. "Consumer's Attitudes Towards Energy Conservation." *Journal of Social Issues* 37 (1981): 108–131.

Oppenheimer, Valerie Kincaide. "Structural Sources of Economic Pressure for Wives to Work: An Analytical Framework." *Journal of Family History* 4 (1979): 177–197.

Parsons, Talcott. "The Social Structure of the Family." In R. N. Anshen, ed., 13–201. *The Family: Its Function and Destiny.* New York: Harper & Brothers, 1949.

Patty, Ralph L. "Cost of Electricity for the Home Electric Refrigerator." South Dakota State College, Agricultural Engineering Experiment Station. *Bulletin,* no. 241.

Peterson, James L. "Work and Socioeconomic Life Cycles: An Agenda for Longitudinal Research." United States Labor Statistics Bureau. *Monthly Labor Review* 102 (1979): 2:23–27.

Peterson, R. D. "Problems in Estimating the Value of Household Services." *American Journal of Economics and Sociology* 37 (1978): 145–148.

Pommer, Richard. "The Architecture of Urban Housing in the United States during the Early 1930s." *Journal of the Society of Architectural Historians* 37 (1978): 235–264.

Potter, Ruth A., and Martha E. Dresslar. "Further Data on the Cost of Gas and Electricity for Cooking." *Journal of Home Economics* 23 (January 1931): 67–70.

Rainwater, Lee, and Gerald Handel. "Changing Family Roles in the Working Class." In A. Shostak and W. Gomberg, eds., 70–76. *Blue-Collar World: Studies of the American Worker.* Englewood Cliffs, N.J.: Prentice-Hall, 1964.

Raitt, Effie I. "Budgeting for Housing and Home Ownership." In John M. Gries and James Ford, eds., 100–143. *Household Management and Kitchens.* Washington, D.C.: President's Conference on Home Building and Home Ownership, 1932.

Ranis, Gustav. "Economic Growth: Theory." In *International Encyclopedia of the Social Sciences.* 4:408–417. New York: Macmillan/Free Press, 1968.

Ravetz, Alison. "Modern Technology and an Ancient Occupation: Housework in Present Day Society." *Technology and Culture* 6 (1965): 256–260.

Reid, Margaret. "Consumption, Savings, and Windfall Gains." *American Economic Review* 52 (September 1962): 728–737.

Reiff, Janice. "Documenting the American Family." *Midwestern Archivist* 3 (1978): 39–46.

Roberts, B. "Demand for Appliances: A Theoretical Structure." *Quarterly Review of Economics and Business* 18 (1978): 15–25.

Roos, C. F., and V. von Szeliski. "Factors Governing Changes in Domestic Automobile Demand." In *The Dynamics of Automobile Demand.* New York: General Motors Corporation, 1939.

Roosevelt, Franklin D. "The Real Meaning of the Power Problem." *Forum* 82 (December 1929): 327–332.

———. "How Will New York's Progressive Proposals Affect the Investor?" *Public Utilities Fortnightly* 7 (June 25, 1931): 810–812.

Rose, Mark H. "Urban Environments and Technological Innovation: Energy Choices in Denver and Kansas City, 1900–1940." *Technology and Culture* 25 (July 1985): 503–539.

Rose, Mark H., and John Clark. "Light, Heat, and Power: Energy Choices in Kansas City, Wichita, and Denver, 1900–1935." *Journal of Urban History* 5 (1979): 340–364.

Rosenberg, J. "American Family History." *Choice* 20 (1983): 674–684.

Rosenman, Samuel I. "Governor Roosevelt's Power Program." *Nation* 129 (September 18, 1929): 302–303.

———. "Governor's Theories About Power." *Review of Reviews* 88 (December 1931): 32.

Rossi, Alice S. "Transition to Parenthood." *Journal of Marriage and the Family* 30 (1968): 26–39.

Rotella, Elyce J. "The Transformation of the American Office: Changes in the Employment and Technology." *Journal of Economic History* 41 (1981): 51–57.

Rotenberg, Robert. "Community, Time, and the Technical Order." In Steven E. Goldberg and Charles R. Strain, eds., 133–144. *Technological Change and the Transformation of America.* Carbondale: Southern Illinois University, 1987.

Rurup, Reinhard. "Historians and Modern Technology: Reflections on the Development and Current Problems of the History of Technology." *Technology and Culture* 15 (1974): 161–193.

Ryan, A. H. "Fatigue Studies in Household Tasks." *Journal of Home Economics* 20 (1928): 637–644.

Sater, Lenore E. "The Cooking of Food with Heat Generated by the Resistance of the Food to the Passage of an Alternating Electric Current." *Journal of Home Economics* 23 (1931): 1050–1054.

Schott, Francis H. "Consumer Financial Management and Financial Institution Response—A Two-Decade Perspective." In Eleanor Bernert Sheldon, ed., 311–362. *Family Economic Behavior, Problems and Prospects.* Philadelphia: J. B. Lippincott, 1973.

Schroeder, Fred E. H. "More 'Small Things Forgotten': Domestic Electrical Plugs and Receptacles," *Technology and Culture* 27 (July 1989): 525–543.

Sheth, J. N. "A Review of Buyer Behavior." *Management Science* 13 (1967): B718–B757.

Skolnick, Arlene. "The Family and Its Discontents." *Society* 18 (1981): 42–47.

Smelser, Neil J., and Sydney Halpern. "The Historical Triangulation of Family, Economy, and Education." In John Demos and Sarane Spence Boocock, eds., 288–315. *Turning Points: Historical and Sociological Essays on the Family.* Chicago: University of Chicago Press, 1978.

Smith, Edgar C. "Some Pioneers of Refrigeration." *Transactions, Newcomen Society* 23 (1942–1943): 99–107.

Smith, James, and Stephen Franklin. "The Concentration of Personal Wealth, 1922–1969." *American Economic Review* 64 (May 1974): 162–167.

Soderstrom, L. "Life-Cycle Hypothesis and Aggregate Household Savings." *American Economic Review* 72 (1982): 590–596.

Soltow, Lee. "Evidence on Income Inequality in the United States, 1866–1965." *Journal of Economic History* 29 (June 1969): 279–286.

Spanier, Graham B., and Paul C. Glick. "The Life Cycle of American Families: An Expanded Analysis." *Journal of Family History* 5 (1980): 970–1012.

Sprenger, Elizabeth, and Pauline Webb. "Persuading the Housewife to Use Electricity? An Interpretation of Material in the Electricity Council Archives." *British Journal for the History of Science* 26 (March 1993): 63–64.

Stach, Patricia Burgess. "Deed Restrictions and Subdivision Development in Columbus, Ohio, 1900–1970." *Journal of Urban History* 15 (November 1988): 42–68.

Suits, B. "The Demand for New Automobiles in the United States, 1929–1956." *Review of Economics and Statistics* 40 (1958): 273–280.

Swartz, Verona. "Human Energy Cost of Operating a Vacuum Cleaner at Different Speeds." *Journal of Home Economics* 21 (1929): 439–447.

———. "Thermal Efficiency of Surface Units in Electric Ranges." *Journal of Home Economics* 23 (1931): 459–464.

Targa, Dena B. "Ideology and Utopia in Family Studies Since the Second War." *Women's Studies International Quarterly* 4 (1981): 191–200.

Thrall, C. A. "Who Does What: Role Stereotypy, Children's Work, and Continuity Between Generations in the Household Division of Labor." *Human Relations* 31 (1978): 249–265.

———. "The Conservative Use of Modern Household Technology." *Technology and Culture* 23 (1982): 175–194.

Tobey, Ronald, Charles Wetherell, and Jay Brigham. "Moving Out and Settling In: Resi-

dential Mobility, Home Owning, and the Public Enframing of Citizenship, 1921–1950."
    American Historical Review 95 (December 1990): 1395–1422.

Twombley, Robert C. "Saving the Family: Middle-Class Attraction to Wright's Prairie
    House, 1901–1909." *American Quarterly* 27 (1975): 57–72.

Udell, J. G. "Prepurchase Behavior of Buyers of Small Electrical Appliances." *Journal
    of Marketing* 30 (1962): 50–52.

Unger, Irwin. "The 'New Left' and American History: Some Recent Trends in United
    States Historiography." *American Historical Review* 72 (1967): 1237–1263.

Valadez, J. J., and R. Clignet. "Household Work as an Ordeal: Culture of Standards ver-
    sus Standardization of Culture." *American Journal of Sociology* 89 (1984): 812–835.

Van Rensselaer, Martha. "The Effect of Housing on Family Life." In John M. Gries and
    James Ford, eds., 1–55. *Homemaking, Home Furnishing and Information Services.*
    Washington, D.C.: President's Conference on Home Building and Home Ownership,
    1932.

Vanek, Joann. "Keeping Busy: Time Spent in Housework, United States, 1920–1970."
    Scientific American 231 (November 1974): 116–120.

———. "Household Technology and Social Status: Rising Living Standards and Status
    and Residence Differences in Housework." *Technology and Culture* 19 (1978):
    361–375.

Vickery, Clair. "Women's Economic Contribution to the Family." In Ralph E. Smith, ed.,
    159–200. *The Subtle Revolution: Women at Work.* Washington, D.C.: Urban Insti-
    tute, 1979.

Voeltz, Herman C. "Genesis and Development of a Regional Power Agency in the Pa-
    cific Northwest, 1933–1943." *Pacific Northwest Quarterly* 53 (April 1962): 65–76.

Waldman, Elizabeth, and Beverly J. McEaddy. "Where Women Work: An Analysis by
    Industry and Occupation." *Monthly Labor Review* 97 (1974): 3–13.

White, B. B. "Empirical Tests of the Life Cycle Hypothesis." *American Economic Re-
    view* 68 (1978): 547–560.

White, Eva Whiting, Chairman. "Housing and Citizenship, Recreation, and Education."
    Report of the Group on Housing and Citizenship, Prepared for the Committee on
    Housing and the Community. In John M. Gries and James Ford, eds., 86–104. *Hous-
    ing and the Community—Home Repair and Remodeling.* Washington, D.C.: Presi-
    dent's Conference on Home Building and Home Ownership, 1932.

Wiener, Jonathan M. "Radical Historians and the Crisis in American History, 1959–1980."
    Journal of American History 76 (1989): 399–434.

Wilk, R. R., and Rathje, W. L. "Household Archaeology." *American Behavioral Scien-
    tist* 25 (1982): 637–639.

Willey, Malcolm M., and Stuart A. Rice. "The Agencies of Communication." In *Recent
    Social Trends in the United States: Report of the President's Committee on Social
    Trends.* 2:167–172. New York: McGraw-Hill, 1933.

Wilson, Maud. "Laundry Time Costs." *Journal of Home Economics* 22 (1930): 735–740.

———. "Time Spent in Meal Preparation in Private Households." *Journal of Home Eco-
    nomics* 24 (1932): 10–16.

Woodhouse, Mrs. Chase Going. "The Field of Research on the Economic and Social
    Problems of the Home." *Journal of Home Economics* 20 (1928): 187–193, 272–280,
    355–360.

Books

Aaron, Henry J. *Shelter and Subsidies: Who Benefits from Federal Housing Policies.* Washington, D.C.: Brookings Institution, 1972.

―――. *Federal Housing Subsidies: History, Problems, and Alternatives.* Washington, D.C.: Brookings Institution, 1973.

Abel, Mary Hinman. *Successful Family Life on the Moderate Income: Its Foundation in a Fair Start.* 1921. 2d ed. Philadelphia: J. B. Lippincott, 1927.

Agan, Tessie. *The House: Its Plan and Use.* 1939. Philadelphia: J. B. Lippincott, 1948.

―――. *The House: Its Plan and Use.* 2d ed., rev. Philadelphia: J. B. Lippincott, 1948.

Aitken, Hugh. *Syntony and Spark: The Origins of Radio.* New York: Wiley, 1976.

―――. *The Continuous Wave: Technology and American Radio, 1900–1932.* Princeton: Princeton University Press, 1985.

Allen, Edith. *Mechanical Devices in the Home.* Peoria, Ill.: Manual Arts Press, 1922.

Anderson, Douglas D. *Regulatory Politics and Electric Utilities: A Case Study in Political Economy.* Boston: Auburn House, 1981.

Anderson, Oscar Edward, Jr. *Refrigeration in America: A History of a New Technology and Its Impact.* Princeton: Princeton University Press, 1953.

Andre, Rae. *Homemakers: The Forgotten Workers.* Chicago: University of Chicago Press, 1981.

Andrews, Benjamin R. *Economics of the Household; Its Administration and Finance.* 1923. Rev. 1935. Reprint. New York: Macmillan, 1938.

Angell, Robert C. *The Family Encounters the Depression.* New York: Charles Scribner's Sons, 1936.

Angly, Edward. *Fifty Billion Dollars: My Thirteen Years with the RFC.* New York: Macmillan, 1951.

Appadurai, Arjun, ed. *The Social Life of Things: Commodities in Cultural Perspective.* Cambridge: Cambridge University Press, 1986.

Appleyard, Rollo. *History of the Institution of Electrical Engineers, 1871–1931.* London: Institution of Electrical Engineers, 1939.

Arnold, Joseph L. *The New Deal in the Suburbs: A History of the Greenbelt Town Program, 1935–1954.* Columbus: Ohio University Press, 1971.

Aronovici, Carol. *Housing the Masses.* New York: J. Wiley, 1939.

Backman, Jules. *The Economics of the Electrical Machinery Industry.* New York: New York University Press, 1962.

Baker, Elizabeth Faulkner. *Technology and Women's Work.* New York: Columbia University Press, 1964.

Balderston, Lydia Ray. *Housewifery: A Manual and Text Book of Practical Housekeeping.* Philadelphia: J. B. Lippincott, 1921.

Ballard, Edward G. *Man and Technology: Toward the Measurement of a Culture.* Pittsburgh: Duquesne University Press, 1978.

Ballin, H. H. *The Organisation of Electricity Supply in Great Britain.* London: Electrical Press, 1946.

Banham, Reyner. *Theory and Design in the First Machine Age.* 2d ed. New York: Praeger, 1960.

Banner, Lois W. *Women in Modern America.* 1974. San Diego: Harcourt Brace Jovanovich, 1984.

Baritz, Loren. *The Good Life: The Meaning of Success for the American Middle Class.*
New York: Alfred A. Knopf, 1989.

Barnes, Joseph. *Willkie: The Events He Was Part Of, The Ideas He Fought For.* New York:
Simon & Schuster, 1952.

Barnouw, Erik. *A Tower in Babel: A History of Broadcasting in the United States.* Vol.
1.—To 1933. New York: Oxford University Press, 1966.

Barrett, William. *The Illusion of Technique: A Search for Meaning in a Technological
Civilization.* Garden City: Anchor Press, 1978.

Bartlett, Dana. *The Better City: The Sociological Analysis of a Modern City.* Los Angeles: Neuner Co. Press, 1907.

Bauer, Catherine. *Modern Housing.* 1934. Reprint. New York: Arno Press, 1974.

Bauer, John, and Nathaniel Gold. *The Electric Power Industry: Development, Organization, and Public Policies.* New York: Harper & Brothers, 1939.

Bauman, John T., and Thomas H. Coode. *In the Eye of the Great Depression: New Deal
Reports and the Agony of the American People.* DeKalb: Northern Illinois University Press, 1988.

Baxter, W. T. *Depreciation.* London: Sweet & Maxwell, 1971.

Beard, Charles A., and William Beard. *The American Leviathan: The Republic in the
Machine Age.* London: Cape, 1930.

Beard, Mary R. *Women as a Force in History: A Study in Tradition and Realities.* New
York: Macmillan, 1946.

———. *America Through Women's Eyes.* 1933. Reprint. New York: Greenwood Press,
1969.

Beecher, Catherine, and Harriet Beecher Stowe. *The American Woman's Home, Or, Principles of Domestic Science; being a Guide to the Formation and Maintenance of Economical, Healthful, Beautiful, and Christian Homes.* 1869. Reprint. New York: Arno
Press and New York Times, 1971.

Beito, David T. *Taxpayers in Revolt: Tax Resistance during the Great Depression.* Chapel
Hill: University of North Carolina Press, 1989.

Bell, Carolyn Shaw. *Consumer Choice in the American Economy.* New York: Random
House, 1967.

Bellamy, Edward. *Looking Backward.* 1888. Reprint. Foreword by Erich Fromm. New
York: New American Library, 1960.

Bellush, Bernard. *Franklin D. Roosevelt as Governor of New York.* New York: Columbia University Press, 1955.

Berg, Sanford V. *Innovative Electric Rates, Issues in Cost-Benefit Analysis.* Lexington:
Lexington Books, 1983.

Berk, Richard A., and Sarah Fenstermaker Berk. *Labor and Leisure at Home: Content
and Organization of the Household Day.* Beverly Hills: Sage Publications, 1979.

Berk, Sarah Fenstermaker, ed. *Women and Household Labor. Sage Yearbooks in Women's
Studies. Vol. 5.* [Beverly Hills]: Sage Publications, 1980.

Berkowitz, Edward, and Kim McQuaid, *Creating the Welfare State: The Political Economy of Twentieth-Century Reform.* 2d ed. New York: Praeger, 1988.

Berle, Adolf A., and Gardiner C. Means. *The Modern Corporation and Private Property.* 1932. Rev. ed. New York: Harcourt, Brace & World, 1968.

Bernstein, Barton J., ed. *Towards a New Past: Dissenting Essays in American History.*
New York: Pantheon Books, 1968.

Bernstein, Blanche. *The Pattern of Consumer Debt, 1935–36: A Statistical Analysis.* Studies in Consumer Instalment Financing, no. 6. New York: National Bureau of Economic Research, 1940.

Bernstein, Michael A. *The Great Depression: Delayed Recovery and Economic Change in America, 1929–1939.* Cambridge: Cambridge University Press, 1987.

Beyer, Glenn H. *Housing: A Factual Analysis.* New York: Macmillan, 1958.

———. *Housing and Society.* New York: Macmillan, 1965.

Bierstedt, Robert. *The Social Order.* New York: McGraw-Hill, 1963.

Bigelow, Howard French, and Benjamin Andrews, ed. *Family Finance: A Study in the Economics of Consumption.* Philadelphia: J. B. Lippincott, 1936.

Bijker, Wiebe E., Thomas P. Hughes, and Trevor J. Pinch, eds. *The Social Construction of Technological Systems: New Directions in the Sociology and History of Technology.* Cambridge: MIT Press, 1987.

Biles, Roger. *A New Deal for the American People.* DeKalb: Northern Illinois University Press, 1991.

Birch, Eugenie Ladner. *Edith Elmer Wood and the Genesis of Liberal Housing Thought.* New York: Division of Urban Planning, Columbia University, 1976.

Bird, Frederick L., and Frances M. Ryan. *Public Ownership on Trial: A Study of Municipal Light and Power in California.* New York: New Republic, 1930.

Birr, Kendall. *Pioneering in Industrial Research: The Story of the General Electric Research Laboratory.* Washington, D.C.: Public Affairs Press, 1957.

Blank, David M. *The Volume of Residential Construction, 1889–1950.* New York: National Bureau of Economic Research, n.d.

Bodnar, John. *Remaking America: Public Memory, Commemoration, and Patriotism in the Twentieth Century.* Princeton: Princeton University Press, 1992.

———. *The Transplanted: A History of Immigrants in Urban America.* Bloomington: Indiana University Press, 1987.

Bogardus, Emory S. *Essentials of Americanization.* Los Angeles: University of Southern California Press, 1919.

Bonbright, James C. *Public Utilities and the National Power Policies.* New York: Columbia University Press, 1940.

Bonbright, James C., and Gardiner C. Means. *The Holding Company: Its Public Significance and Its Regulation.* New York: McGraw-Hill, 1932.

Booth, William James. *Households: On the Moral Architecture of the Economy.* Ithaca: Cornell University Press, 1993.

Borgmann, Albert. *Technology and the Character of Contemporary Life: A Philosophical Inquiry.* Chicago: University of Chicago Press, 1987.

Bosanquet, Helen. *The Standard of Life, and Other Studies.* London, New York: Macmillan, 1898.

———. *The Family.* New York: Macmillan, 1923.

Bourdieu, Pierre. *Distinction: A Social Critique of the Judgment of Taste.* 1979. Cambridge: Harvard University Press, 1984.

Bowles, Samuel, and Herbert Gintis. *Democracy and Capitalism: Property, Community, and the Contradictions of Modern Social Thought.* New York: Basic Books, 1986.

Boydston, Jeanne. *Home and Work.* New York: Oxford University Press, 1990.

Braeman, John, Robert H. Bremmer, and David Brody, eds. *The New Deal.* Vol. 2. *The State and Local Levels.* Columbus: Ohio State University Press, 1975.

Bramson, Leon. *The Political Context of Sociology.* Princeton: Princeton University Press, 1961.

Brantlinger, Patrick. *Bread and Circuses: Theories of Mass Culture as Social Decay.* Ithaca: Cornell University Press, 1983.

Bredemeier, Harry C. *The Federal Public Housing Movement: A Case Study of Social Change.* New York: Arno Press, 1980.

Briggs, Asa. *Victorian Things.* 1988. Chicago: University of Chicago Press, 1989.

Bright, Arthur A., Jr. *The Electric-Lamp Industry: Technological Change and Economic Development from 1800 to 1947.* New York: Macmillan, 1949.

Brinkley, Alan. *The End of Reform: New Deal Liberalism in Recession and War.* New York: Alfred A. Knopf, 1995.

Brittain, James E., ed. *Turning Points in American Electrical History.* New York: IEEE Press, 1976.

Bronner, Simon J. *Grasping Things: Folk Material Culture and Mass Society in America.* Lexington: University Press of Kentucky, 1986.

————. *Consuming Visions: Accumulation and Display of Goods in America, 1880–1920.* New York: Winterthur/W. W. Norton, 1988.

Brown, D. Clayton. *Electricity for Rural America: The Fight for the REA.* Westport, Conn.: Greenwood, 1980.

Brown, Lawrence A. *Innovation Diffusion: A New Perspective.* New York: Methuen, 1981.

Bruce, Alfred, and Harold Sandbank. *A History of Prefabrication.* Original edition published under the title, *Housing Research.* Vol. 3. Reprint. New York: Arno Press, [1944] 1972.

Bruère, Martha Bensley, and Robert W. Bruère. *Increasing Home Efficiency.* 1911. New York: Macmillan, 1916.

Bryant, R. W. G. *Land: Private Property, Public Control.* Montreal: Harvest House, 1972.

Buder, Stanley. *Visionaries and Planners: The Garden City Movement and the Modern Community.* New York: Oxford University Press, 1990.

Burke, Robert E. *Olson's New Deal for California.* Berkeley: University of California Press, 1953.

Bureau of Internal Revenue. *Depreciation and Obsolescence. Bulletin F.* 1920. 3d ed. Washington, D.C.: GPO, 1942.

Burns, Arthur E., and Edward A. Williams. *Federal Work, Security, and Relief Programs.* Washington, D.C.: GPO, 1941.

Byatt, I. C. R. *The British Electrical Industry, 1875–1914.* Oxford: Clarendon Press, 1979.

Cadwallader, Martin. *Migration and Residential Mobility: Macro and Micro Approaches.* Madison: University of Wisconsin Press, 1992.

Cahn, Frances, and Valeska Bary. *Welfare Activities of Federal, State, and Local Governments in California, 1850–1934.* Berkeley: University of California Press, 1936.

California. Laws, Statutes, etc. *Public Utilities Act of California.* Compiled by Eugene R. Hallett [Managing Director, Louis Sloss & Co., Investment Securities]. San Francisco: Louis Sloss, 1912.

California Progressive Campaign Book for 1914: Three Years of Progressive Administration in California under Governor Hiram W. Johnson. San Francisco, 1914.

Callahan, North. *TVA: Bridge Over Troubled Waters.* South Brunswick: A. S. Barnes, 1980.

Campbell, Helen. *Household Economics: A Course of Lectures in the School of Economics of the University of Wisconsin.* Rev. New York: G. G. Putnam's Sons, 1896.

Campbell, Persia C. *Consumer Representation in the New Deal.* New York: Columbia University Press, 1940.

Canby, Edward Tatnall. *A History of Electricity.* New York: Hawthorn Books, 1963.

Capeci, Dominic J., Jr. *Race Relations in Detroit: The Sojourner Truth Housing Controversy, 1937–1942.* Philadelphia: Temple University Press, 1984.

Carlisle, Norman, and Frank B. Latham. *Miracles Ahead: Better Living in the Postwar World.* New York: Macmillan, 1944.

Cavan, Ruth Shonle. *The American Family.* 4th ed. New York: Crowell, 1969.

Cavan, Ruth Shonle, and Katherine Howland Ranck. *The Family and the Depression: A Study of One Hundred Chicago Families.* Chicago: University of Chicago Press, 1938.

Caywood, Russell E. *Electric Utility Rate Economics.* Sponsored and distributed by Electrical World. 1st ed., 1956. New York: McGraw-Hill, 1972.

Chafe, William H. *The American Woman, Her Changing Social, Economic, and Political Roles, 1920–1970.* New York: Oxford University Press, 1972.

Chandler, Alfred D., Jr. *The Visible Hand: The Managerial Revolution in American Business.* Cambridge: Belknap Press of Harvard University Press, 1977.

Child, Georgie Boynton. *The Efficient Kitchen: Definite Directions for the Planning, Arranging and Equipping of the Modern Labor-saving Kitchen—A Practical Book for the Home-Maker.* New York: McBride, Nast, 1914.

Childs, Marquis William. *The Farmer Takes a Hand: The Electric Power Revolution in Rural America.* Introduction by George G. Aiken. Reprint. New York: DaCapo Press, [1952] 1974.

Chow, Gregory. *Demand for Automobiles in the United States.* Amsterdam: North-Holland, 1957.

Clapp, Gordon R. *The TVA: An Approach to the Development of a Region.* Chicago: University of Chicago Press, 1955.

Clark, Clifford E., Jr. *The American Family Home, 1800–1960.* Chapel Hill: University of North Carolina Press, 1986.

Clark, John G. *Energy and the Federal Government: Fossil Fuel Policies, 1900–1946.* Urbana: University of Illinois Press, 1987.

Clark, Tom C., and Philip B. Perlman. *Prejudice and Property: An Historic Brief Against Racial Covenants.* Washington, D.C.: Public Affairs Press, 1948.

Clark, Victor Seldon. *History of Manufactures in the United States.* Contributions to the Economic History of the United States, Carnegie Institution of Washington. 3 vols. Rev. ed. New York: McGraw-Hill, 1929.

Cleveland Press. *Fourth Cleveland Kitchen Inventory.* Conducted by the Parent-Teacher Association. Cleveland: Cleveland Press, 1937.

Cobb, James C. *Industrialization and Southern Society, 1877–1984.* Lexington: University of Kentucky Press, 1984.

———. *The Selling of the South: The Southern Crusade for Industrial Development, 1936–1980.* Baton Rouge: Louisiana State University Press, 1982.

Cohen, Lizabeth. *Making a New Deal: Industrial Workers in Chicago, 1919–1939.* New York: Cambridge University Press, 1991.

Cohen, Wilbur, J., ed. *The Roosevelt New Deal: A Program Assessment Fifty Years After.* Lyndon B. Johnson School of Public Affairs, Lyndon Baines Johnson Library, Virginia Commonwealth University [Conference Sponsors]. Austin: University of Texas, 1986.

Cohn, Jan. *The Palace or the Poorhouse: The American House as a Cultural Symbol.* East Lansing: Michigan State University Press, 1979.

Colean, Miles Lanier. *Housing for Defense: A Review of the Role of Housing in Relation to America's Defense and a Program for Action; The Factual Findings*. Housing Committee [of] the Twentieth Century Fund. New York: Twentieth Century Fund, 1940.

———. *American Housing: Problems and Prospects*. New York: Twentieth Century Fund, 1944.

———. *Renewing our Cities*. New York: Twentieth Century Fund, 1953.

———. *Mortgage Companies: Their Place in the Financial Structure*. For the Mortgage Bankers Association of America. Monograph prepared for the Commission on Money and Credit. Englewood Cliffs, N.J.: Prentice Hall, 1962.

———. *A Backward Glance—An Oral History: The Growth of Government Housing Policy in the United States, 1934–1975*. Washington: The Fund, 1975.

Coleman, Charles M. *P. G. and E. of California: The Centennial Story of Pacific Gas and Electric Company, 1852–1952*. New York: McGraw-Hill, 1952.

Conkin, Paul K. *Tomorrow a New World: The New Deal Community Program*. Ithaca: Cornell University Press, 1959.

———. *FDR and the Origins of the Welfare State*. New York: Thomas Y. Crowell, 1967.

———. *TVA: Fifty Years of Grass-roots Bureaucracy*. Urbana: University of Illinois Press, 1983.

Consumer Purchases Study. U.S. Department of Agriculture, Bureau of Human Nutrition and Home Economics. Washington, D.C., 1939–1941.

Controllers Institute of America. *A Case Study of Management Planning and Control at General Electric Company*. Series II, Business Planning and Control, Report no. 3. New York: Controllership Foundation, 1955. "Based on Reports by Robert Paxton [et al.], of General Electric Company, Presented at the Annual National Conference, Controllers Institute, October 1954."

Coode, Thomas H., and John F. Bauman. *People, Poverty, and Politics: Pennsylvanians during the Great Depression*. Lewisburg: Bucknell University Press, 1981.

Cooke, Morris Llewellyn, ed. *Giant Power: Large-Scale Electrical Development as a Social Factor*. Annals of the American Academy of Political and Social Science, no. 118. Philadelphia: American Academy of Political and Social Science, 1925.

Cooley, Donald G., and editors of *Mechanix Illustrated*. *Your World Tomorrow*. [n.p.]: Essential Books, 1944. Distributed by Duell, Sloan and Pearce.

Coons, Alvin E., and Bert T. Glaze. *Housing Market Analysis and the Growth of Nonfarm Home Ownership*. Bureau of Business Research Monographs, no. 115. Columbus: Bureau of Business Research, College of Commerce and Administration, Ohio State University, 1963.

Coppock, Joseph D. *Government Agencies of Consumer Instalment Credit*. Studies in Consumer Instalment Financing, no. 5. New York: National Bureau of Economic Research, 1940.

Corn, Joseph J., ed. *Imagining Tomorrow: History, Technology, and the American Future*. Cambridge: MIT Press, 1986.

Corwin, Edward S. *Constitutional Revolution. Ltd*. Claremont, Calif.: Pomona College, Scripps College, Claremont Colleges, 1941.

Cowan, Ruth Schwartz. *More Work for Mother: The Ironies of Household Technology from the Open Hearth to the Microwave*. New York: Basic Books, 1983.

Cramer, J. S. *The Ownership of Major Consumer Durables: A Statistical Survey of Mo-*

torcars, Refrigerators, Washing Machines and Televisions Sets in the Oxford Savings Survey of 1953. Cambridge: Cambridge University Press, 1962.

Creese, Walter L. *TVA's Public Planning: The Vision, the Reality.* Knoxville: University of Tennessee Press, 1990.

Crocker, Ruth Hutchinson. *Social Work and Social Order: The Settlement Movement in Two Industrial Cities, 1889–1930.* Urbana: University of Illinois Press, 1992.

Croft, Terrell. *Wiring for Light and Power: A Detailed and Fully Illustrated Commentary on the National Electrical Code.* 4th ed. New York: McGraw-Hill, 1924.

Cross, William T., and Dorothy E. Cross. *Newcomers and Nomads in California.* Stanford: Stanford University Press, 1937.

Crouse, Joan M. *The Homeless Transient in the Great Depression: New York State, 1929–1941.* Albany: State University of New York Press, 1986.

Croxton, Frederick E. *A Study of Housewives Buying Habits in Columbus, Ohio, 1924.* Bureau of Business Research Monographs, no. 3. Columbus: Ohio State University, 1926.

Csikszentmihalyi, Mihaly, and Eugene Rochberg-Halton. *The Meaning of Things: Domestic Symbols and the Self.* Cambridge: Cambridge University Press, 1980.

Curl, James Stevens. *Victorian Architecture: Its Practical Aspects.* Newton Abbot: David & Charles, 1973.

Curtis, Isabel Gordon. *The Making of a Housewife.* New York: Frederick A. Stokes, 1906.

Daniel, Cletus E. *Bitter Harvest: A History of California Farmworkers, 1870–1941.* Berkeley: University of California Press, 1982.

Daniels, George H., and Mark H. Rose, eds. *Energy and Transportation: Historical Perspectives on Policy Issues.* Beverly Hills: Sage Publications, 1982.

Daniels, Roger. *The Politics of Prejudice: The Anti-Japanese Movement in California and the Struggle for Japanese Exclusion.* New York: Atheneum, [1967] 1970.

Danielson, Michael N. *The Politics of Exclusion.* New York: Columbia University Press, 1976.

Davidson, Donald. *The Tennessee.* 2 vols. New York: Rinehart, 1946–1948.

Davies, Pearl Janet. *Real Estate in American History.* Introduction by Miles L. Colean. Washington, D.C.: Public Affairs Press, 1958.

Davis, Allen F. *Spearheads for Reform: The Social Settlements and the Progressive Movement, 1890–1914.* New York: Oxford University Press, 1967.

Davis, J. Ronnie. *The New Economics and the Old Economists.* Ames: Iowa State University Press, 1971.

Davis, Kenneth S. *FDR: The New York Years, 1928–1933.* New York: Random House, 1985.

Davis, Mike. *City of Quartz: Excavating the Future in Los Angeles.* Reprint. New York: Vintage Books, [1990] 1992.

Davison, Jane. *Fall of a Doll's House: Three Generations of American Women and the Houses They Lived In.* New York: Holt, Rinehart, and Winston, 1980.

Dawley, Alan. *Struggles for Justice: Social Responsibility and the State.* Cambridge: Belknap Press of Harvard University Press, 1991.

De Bedts, Ralph F. *The New Deal's SEC: The Formative Years.* New York: Columbia University Press, 1964.

Dean, John P. *Home Ownership: Is It Sound?* New York: Harper & Row, 1945.

Deane, Albert Lytle. *The Deane Plan.* New York: Dependable Printing Company, 1933.

Deane, Albert Lytle, and Henry Kittredge Norton. *Investing in Wages; A Plan for Eliminating the Lean Years.* New York: Macmillan, 1932.

DeArmond, Fred. *The Laundry Industry.* New York: Harper & Brothers, 1950.

Deaton, Angus, ed. *Essays in the Theory and Measurement of Consumer Behavior, In Honor of Sir Richard Stone.* Cambridge: Cambridge University Press, 1981.

Demos, John. *Past, Present, and Personal: The Family and Life Course in American History.* New York: Oxford University Press, 1986.

Dewey, John, and James H. Tufts. *Ethics.* New York: Henry Holt, 1909.

Dollard, John. *Caste and Class in a Southern Town.* 1937. New York: Harper & Brothers, 1949.

Dorau, Herbert B., ed. *Materials for the Study of Public Utility Economics.* Social Science Texts. Edited by Richard T. Ely. New York: Macmillan, 1930.

Doucet, Michael, and John Weaver. *Housing the North American City.* Montreal: McGill-Queen's University Press, 1991.

Douglas, Ann. *The Feminization of American Culture.* New York: Avon Books, 1978.

Douglas, Harlan Paul. *The Suburban Trend.* Reprint. New York: Arno Press, [1925] 1970.

Douglas, Mary, and Baron Isherwood. *The World of Goods: Toward an Anthropology of Consumption.* New York: W. W. Norton, 1979.

Douglas, Susan J. *Inventing American Broadcasting, 1899–1922.* Baltimore: Johns Hopkins University Press, 1987.

Douglass, Harlan Paul. *The Suburban Trend.* New York: Century, 1925.

Dow, Joy Wheeler. *American Renaissance: A Review of Domestic Architecture.* New York: William T. Comstock, 1904.

DuBoff, Richard B. *Electric Power in American Manufacturing, 1889–1950.* Reprint. New York: Arno Press, [1964] 1979.

Dubofsky, Melvyn, ed. *The New Deal: Conflicting Interpretations and Shifting Perspectives.* New York: Garland, 1992.

Dudden, Faye E. *Serving Women: Household Service in the Nineteenth Century.* Middletown: Wesleyan University Press, 1983.

Duffus, Robert L. *The Valley and Its People: A Portrait of TVA.* New York: Knopf, 1944.

Dunsheath, Percy. *A History of Electrical Power Engineering.* Cambridge: MIT Press, 1962.

Durbin, Paul T., and Friedrich Rapp. *Philosophy and Technology.* Boston Studies in the Philosophy of Science. Edited by Robert S. Cohen and Marx W. Wartofsky. Vol. 80. Dordrecht: D. Reidel, 1983.

Dutton, Mark. *The Victorian Home.* London: Orbis, 1976.

Duvall, Evelyn. *Family Development.* 4th ed. Philadelphia: J. B. Lippincott, 1971.

Ebenstein, William. *The Law of Public Housing.* Madison: University of Wisconsin Press, 1940.

Eccles, Marriner S. *Beckoning Frontiers: Public and Personal Recollections.* Edited by Sidney Hyman. New York: Alfred A. Knopf, 1951.

———. *Economic Balance and a Balanced Budget: Public Papers of Marriner S. Eccles.* Edited by Rudolph L. Weissman. ca. 1940. New York: DaCapo Press, 1973.

Eden, Robert, ed. *The New Deal and Its Legacy: Critique and Reappraisal.* Contributions in American History, no. 132. New York: Greenwood Press, 1989.

Edison Electric Institute. *Historical Statistics of the Electric Utility Industry.* New York: Edison Electrical Institute, 1960.

Ehrenfeld, Louis. *The Story of Common Things.* New York: Minton, Balch, 1932.

Ehrenreich, Barbara, and Deirdre English. *For Her Own Good: 150 Years of the Experts' Advice to Women.* Garden City, N.Y.: Anchor Press, 1978.

Ehrenreich, John H. *The Altruistic Imagination: A History of Social Work and Social Policy in the United States.* Ithaca: Cornell University Press, 1985.

Elder, Glen, Jr. *Children of the Great Depression: Social Change in Life Experience.* Chicago: University of Chicago Press, 1974.

————. *Family Structure and Socialization.* New York: Arno Press, 1980.

Electric-Power Industry: Control of Power Companies. 69th Cong., 2d sess., 1927. S. Doc. 213.

Ellis, Clyde T. *A Giant Step.* New York: Random House, 1966.

Eltis, Walter. *The Classical Theory of Economic Growth.* New York: St. Martin's Press, 1984.

Ely, James W., Jr. *The Guardian of Every Other Right: A Constitutional History of Property Rights.* New York: Oxford University Press, 1992.

Evolution of Role of the Federal Government in Housing and Community Development: A Chronology of Legislative and Selected Executive Actions, 1892–1974. A Report for the Subcommittee on Banking, Currency and Housing, House of Representatives, 94th Cong., 1st sess., October 1975. Washington, D.C.: GPO, [1975].

Ewalt, Josephine Hedges. *A Business Reborn: The Savings and Loan Story, 1930–1960.* Chicago: American Savings and Loan Institute, 1962.

Federal Emergency Administration of Public Works. *Urban Housing: the Story of the PWA Housing Division, 1933–1936.* Federal Emergency Administration of Public Works Bulletin no. 2. Washington, D.C.: 1937.

Federal Housing Administration. *Underwriting Manual: Underwriting and Valuation Procedure under Title II of the National Housing Act.* Rev. ed. Washington, D.C.: Federal Housing Administration, February 1938.

Ferber, Robert. *Factors Influencing Durable Goods Purchases.* University of Illinois Bureau of Economic and Business Research. Urbana: University of Illinois, 1955.

Ferrell, Robert H. *Harry S. Truman and the Modern American Presidency.* Boston: Little, Brown, 1983.

Findlay, John M. *Magic Lands: Western Cityscapes and American Culture after 1940.* Berkeley, Los Angeles, and London: University of California Press, 1993.

Fish, Gertrude Sipperly, ed. *The Story of Housing.* New York: Macmillan, 1979.

Fischer, Claude S. *America Calling: A Social History of the Telephone to 1940.* Berkeley, Los Angeles, and Oxford: University of California Press, 1992.

Fisher, Ernest M. *Urban Real Estate Markets: Characteristics and Financing. Financial Research Program.* Studies in Urban Mortgage Financing. New York: National Bureau of Economic Research, 1951.

Fisher, Franklin M., and Carl Kaysen. *A Study in Econometrics: The Demand for Electricity in the United States.* Amsterdam: North-Holland, 1962.

Fisher, Jacob. *The Response of Social Work to the Depression.* Boston: G. K. Hall, 1980.

Fisher, Robert Moore. *Twenty Years of Public Housing.* New York: Harper & Brothers, 1959.

Fishman, Robert. *Bourgeois Utopias: The Rise and Fall of Suburbia.* New York: Basic Books, 1987.

Flagg, Ernest. *Small Houses: Their Economic Design and Construction; Essays on the Fundamental Principles of Design and Descriptive Articles on Construction.* New York: Charles Scribner's Sons, 1922.

Fogelson, Robert M. *The Fragmented Metropolis: Los Angeles, 1850–1930.* Cambridge: Harvard University Press, 1967.

Foner-Wolf, Elizabeth A. *Selling Free Enterprise: The Business Assault on Labor and Liberalism, 1945–1960.* Urbana: University of Illinois Press, 1994.

Foote, N. N., ed. *Household Decision-making.* New York: New York University Press, 1961.

Foster, Abram John. *The Coming of the Electrical Age to the United States.* New York: Arno Press, 1979.

Fox, Richard Wightman, and T. J. Jackson Lears. *The Culture of Consumption: Critical Essays in American History, 1880–1980.* New York: Pantheon, 1983.

Foy, Jessica H., and Thomas J. Schlereth, eds. *American Home Life, 1880–1930: A Social History of Spaces and Services.* Knoxville: University of Tennessee Press, 1992.

Franklin, John Hope. *From Slavery to Freedom: A History of Negro Americans.* 3d ed. New York: Vintage Books, 1969.

Fraser, Steve, and Gary Gerstle, eds. *The Rise and Fall of the New Deal Order, 1930–1980.* Princeton: Princeton University Press, 1989.

Frederick, Christine. *Household Engineering: Scientific Management in the Home. A Correspondence Course on the Application of the Principle of Efficiency Engineering and Scientific Management to the Every Day Tasks of Housekeeping.* Chicago: American School of Home Economics, 1919.

———. *Efficient Housekeeping or Household Engineering: Scientific Management in the Home. A Correspondence Course on the Application of the Principles of Efficiency Engineering and Scientific Management to the Every Day Tasks of Housekeeping.* Chicago: American School of Home Economics, 1925.

Freidel, Frank. *Franklin D. Roosevelt.* Vol. 4. *Launching the New Deal.* Boston: Little, Brown, 1973.

———. *Franklin D. Roosevelt: The Triumph.* Boston: Little, Brown, 1956.

Fried, Jacob, and Paul Molnar. *Technological and Social Change: A Transdisciplinary Model.* New York: PBI, a Petrocelli Book, 1978.

Friedman, Lawrence. *Government and Slum Housing: A Century of Frustration.* 1968. New York: Arno Press, 1978.

Friedman, Milton. *A Theory of the Consumption Function.* Princeton: Princeton University Press, 1957.

Friend, Irwin, and Robert Jones, eds. *Proceedings of the Conference on Consumption and Savings.* Vol. 1. *Study of Consumer Expenditures, Incomes and Savings.* Philadelphia: University of Pennsylvania Press, 1960.

Fuller, John Grant. *The Gentlemen Conspirators: The Story of the Price-fixers in the Electrical Industry.* New York: Grove Press, 1962.

Fuller, R. Buckminster. *Designing a New Industry: A Composite of a Series of Talks.* Wichita, Kan.: Fuller Research Institute, 1946.

Funigiello, Philip J. *Toward a National Power Policy: The New Deal and the Electric Power Industry, 1933–1941.* Pittsburgh: University of Pittsburgh Press, 1973.

Fusfield, Daniel G. *The Economic Thought of Franklin D. Roosevelt and the Origins of the New Deal.* New York: Columbia University Press, 1956.

Garland, J. V., and Theodore A. Brown. *The Crisis in the Electric Utilities.* Vol. 10. *The Reference Shelf.* New York: H. W. Wilson, 1936.

Garraty, John A. *The Great Depression: An Inquiry into the Causes, Course, and Consequences of the Worldwide Depression of the Nineteen Thirties as Seen by Contemporaries and in the Light of History.* San Diego: Harcourt Brace Jovanovich, 1986.

Gelfand, Mark I. *A Nation of Cities: The Federal Government and Urban America, 1933–1965.* New York: Oxford University Press, 1975.

Gendron, Bernard. *Technology and the Human Condition.* New York: St. Martin's Press, 1977.

General Motors Corporation. *The Dynamics of Automobile Demand.* New York: General Motors Corporation, 1939.

Gerstle, Gary. *Working-Class Americanism: The Politics of Labor in a Textile City, 1914–1960.* Cambridge: Cambridge University Press, 1989.

Getty, Cathleen, and Winnifred Humphreys, eds. *Understanding the Family: Stress and Change in American Family Life.* New York: Appleton-Century-Crofts, 1981.

Giedion, Sigfried. *Mechanization Takes Command.* New York: Oxford University Press, 1948.

Gilbreth, Lillian. *The Homemaker and Her Job.* 1927. New York: D. Appleton-Century, 1935.

Gilbreth, Lillian Evelyn, Orpha Mae Thomas, and Eleanor Clymer. *Management in the House: Happier Living Through Saving Time and Energy.* New York: Dodd, Mead, 1954.

Gilfillan, S. C. *The Sociology of Invention.* Chicago: Follett, 1935.

Gilman, Charlotte Perkins. *Woman and Economics: A Study of the Economic Relation Between Men and Women as a Factor in Social Evolution.* Reprint. New York: Harper Torchbooks, [1898] 1966.

———. *The Home, Its Work and Influence.* Reprint. New York: Source Book Press, [1903] 1970.

———. *The Man-made World; Or, Our Androcentric Culture.* London: T. Fisher Unwin, 1911.

Glaeser, Martin G. *Public Utilities in American Capitalism.* New York: Macmillan, 1957.

Glazer, Nathan, and Davis McEntire, eds. *Studies in Housing & Minority Groups.* Special Research Report to the Commission on Race and Housing. Berkeley: University of California Press, 1960.

Gloag, Joan. *A Social History of Furniture Design: From 1300 B.C. to A.D. 1960.* London: Cassell, 1966.

Gluck, Sherna Berger. *Rosie the Riveter Revisited: Women, the War, and Social Change.* Boston: Twayne, 1987.

Goldsmith, Raymond W. *A Study of Saving in the United States.* Princeton: Princeton University Press, 1956.

———. *Financial Intermediaries in the American Economy Since 1900.* A study published by the National Bureau of Economic Research, New York. National Bureau of Economic Research Studies in Capital Formation and Financing, no. 3. Princeton: Princeton University Press, 1958.

———. *The National Balance Sheet of the United States, 1953–1980.* A National Bureau of Economic Research Monograph. Chicago: University of Chicago Press, 1982.

Goode, Kenneth G. *California's Black Pioneers: A Brief Historical Survey.* Santa Barbara, Calif.: McNally & Loftin, 1974.

Gottlieb, Manuel. *Estimates of Residential Building, United States, 1840–1939.* National Bureau of Economic Research, Technical Paper 17. New York: National Bureau of Economic Research, 1964.

Gould, Jacob Martin. *Output and Productivity in the Electric and Gas Utilities, 1899–1942.* New York: National Bureau of Economic Research, 1946.

Gouldner, Alvin W. *The Dialectic of Ideology and Technology: The Origins, Grammar and Future of Ideology.* New York: Seabury, 1976.

Graham, Otis L., Jr. *Toward a Planned Society: From Roosevelt to Nixon.* New York: Oxford University Press, 1976.

Grant, Eugene L., and Paul T. Norton, Jr., *Depreciation.* Rev. New York: Ronald Press, 1955.

Grant, Nancy L. *TVA and Black Americans: Planning for the Status Quo.* Philadelphia: Temple University Press, 1990.

Gray, George Herbert. *Housing and Citizenship: A Study of Low-Cost Housing.* New York: Reinhold, 1946.

Gray, Greta. *House and Home.* Chicago: J. B. Lippincott, 1935.

Great Basin Foundation, ed. *Wong Ho Leun: An American Chinatown.* San Diego: The Foundation, 1987.

Grebler, Leo. *Mexican Immigration to the United States: The Record and Its Implications.* With contributions by Philip M. Newman and Ronald Wyse. Mexican-American Study Project, Division of Research, Graduate School of Business Administration, University of California, Los Angeles. Advance Report 2. January 1966. [Los Angeles]: Mexican-American Study Project, 1966.

Green, Constance McLaughlin. *The Secret City: A History of Race Relations in the Nation's Capital.* Princeton: Princeton University Press, 1967.

Green, Harvey. *The Light of Home: An Intimate View of the Lives of Women in Victorian America.* New York: Pantheon, 1983.

Greenwald, Maurine Weiner. *Women, War, and Work: The Impact of World War I on Women Workers in the United States.* Contributions in Women's Studies, no. 12. Westport, Conn.: Greenwood Press, 1980.

Grier, Eunice, and George Grier. *Privately Developed Interracial Housing: An Analysis of Experience.* Special Research Report to the Commission on Race and Housing. Berkeley: University of California Press, 1960.

Grier, Katherine C. *Culture and Comfort: People, Parlors, and Upholstery, 1850–1930.* Amherst: University of Massachusetts Press, 1988. Distributed for the Margaret Woodbury Strong Museum.

Gries, John M., and James Ford, eds. *The President's Conference on Home Building and Home Ownership.* 11 vols. Washington, D.C.: President's Conference on Home Building and Home Ownership, 1932.

Gruening, Ernest. *The Public Pays . . . And Still Pays: A Study of Power Propaganda.* New York: Vanguard Press, 1931.

Halbert, Blanche, ed. *Better Homes Manual.* Published in cooperation with Better Homes in America. Chicago: University of Chicago Press, 1931.

Halle, David. *Work, Home, and Politics among Blue-Collar Property Owners.* Chicago: University of Chicago Press, 1984.

Halttunen, Karen. *Confidence Men and Painted Women: A Study of Middle-Class Culture in America, 1830–1870.* New Haven: Yale University Press, 1982.

Halvorsen, Robert. *Econometric Models of U.S. Energy Demand.* Lexington: D.C. Heath Lexington Books, 1978.

Hamby, Alonzo L. *Beyond the New Deal: Harry S. Truman and American Liberalism.* New York: Columbia University Press, 1973.

———. *Liberalism and Its Challengers: FDR to Reagan.* New York: Oxford University Press, 1992.

Hamby, Alonzo L., ed. *Harry S. Truman and the Fair Deal.* Lexington, Mass.: D.C. Heath, 1974.

Hamilton, David. *The Consumer in Our Society.* Boston: Houghton Mifflin, 1962.

Hamish, W. *The Coming of the Mass Market, 1850–1914.* Hamden, Conn.: Archon Books, 1981.

Hammond, John Winthrop. *Men and Volts: The Story of General Electric.* Philadelphia: J. B. Lippincott, 1941.

Handlin, David P. *The American Home: Architecture and Society, 1815–1915.* Boston: Little, Brown, 1979.

Hannah, Leslie. *Electricity Before Nationalization: A Study of the Development of the Electricity Supply Industry in Britain 1948.* London: Macmillan Press, 1979.

———. *Engineers, Managers, and Politicians: The First Fifteen Years of Nationalised Electricity Supply in Britain.* Baltimore: Johns Hopkins University Press, 1982.

Harberger, Arnold C., ed. *The Demand for Durable Goods.* Chicago: University of Chicago Press, 1960.

Hareven, Tamara K. *Family Time and Industrial Time: The Relationship between the Family and Work in a New England Industrial Community.* Cambridge: Cambridge University Press, 1982.

Hargrove, Erwin C., and Paul K. Conkin, eds. *TVA: Fifty Years of Grass-Roots Bureaucracy.* Urbana: University of Illinois Press, 1983.

Harrison, D. Dex, J. M. Albery, and M. W. Whiting. *A Survey of Prefabrication.* London: Ministry of Works, 1945.

Harriss, C. Lowell. *History and Policies of the Home Owners' Loan Corporation.* New York: National Bureau of Economic Research, 1951.

Hartmann, Edward. *The Movement to Americanize the Immigrant.* New York: Columbia University Press, 1948.

Hartmann, Susan M. *The Home Front and Beyond: American Women in the 1940s.* Boston: Twayne, 1982.

Haskins, C. W. *How to Keep Household Accounts: A Manual of Family Finance.* New York: Harper & Brothers, 1903.

Havlik, Hubert Frank. *Service Charges in Gas and Electric Rates.* New York: Columbia University Press, 1938.

Hawley, Ellis W. *The New Deal and the Problem of Monopoly.* Princeton: Princeton University Press, 1966.

Hayden, Dolores. *The Grand Domestic Revolution: A History of Feminist Designs for American Homes, Neighborhoods, and Cities.* Cambridge: MIT Press, 1981.

Hecht, James L. *Because It Is Right: Integration in Housing.* Boston: Little, Brown, 1970.

Heinze, Andrew R. *Adapting to Abundance: Jewish Immigrants, Mass Consumption, and the Search for American Identity.* New York: Columbia University Press, 1990.

Hendricks, Gary, and Kenwood C. Youmans, with Janet Keller. *Consumer Durables and Installment Debt: A Study of American Households.* Survey Research Center, Institute for Social Research. Ann Arbor: University of Michigan, 1973.

Herbert, Gilbert. *Pioneers of Prefabrication: The British Contribution in the Nineteenth Century.* Baltimore: Johns Hopkins University Press, 1978.

Herling, John. *The Great Price Conspiracy: The Story of the Antitrust Violations in the Electrical Industry.* Washington, D.C.: R. B. Luce, 1962.

Heskin, Allan D. *Tenants and the American Dream: Ideology and the Tenant Movement.* New York: Praeger, 1983.

Higgs, Edward. *Domestic Servants and Households in Rochdale, 1851–1871.* New York: Garland, 1986.

Higham, John. *History: Professional Scholarship in America.* Updated paperback edition. Baltimore: Johns Hopkins University Press, 1989.

Hill, Reuben, and Associates. *Family Development in Three Generations: A Longitudinal Study of Changing Family Patterns of Planning and Achievement.* Cambridge: Schenkman, 1970.

Hirsch, Arnold R. *Making the Second Ghetto: Race and Housing in Chicago, 1940 to 1960.* Cambridge: Cambridge University Press, 1983.

Hirsh, Richard F. *Technology and Transformation in the American Electrical Utility.* Cambridge: Cambridge University Press, 1989.

Hobday, Victor C. *Sparks at the Grassroots: Municipal Distribution of TVA Electricity in Tennessee.* Knoxville: University of Tennessee Press, 1969.

Hodgins, Eric. *Mr. Blanding Builds His Dream House.* New York: Simon & Schuster, 1946.

Hodgkin, Godfrey. *America in Our Time.* New York: Random House, 1978.

Hofstader, Richard. *The Age of Reform, From Bryan to F. D. R.* Reprint. New York: Alfred A. Knopf/Vintage Books, 1955.

Holthausen, Duncan McC., Malcolm L. Merriam, and Rolf Nugent. *The Volume of Consumer Instalment Credit, 1929–38.* Studies in Consumer Instalment Financing, no. 7. New York: National Bureau of Economic Research, 1940.

Hoover, Frank G. *Fabulous Dustpan: The Story of the Hoover Company.* Cleveland: World, 1955.

Horowitz, Daniel. *The Morality of Spending: Attitudes toward the Consumer Society in America, 1875–1940.* Baltimore: Johns Hopkins University Press, 1985.

Hounshell, David. *From the American System to Mass Production, 1800–1932.* Baltimore: Johns Hopkins University Press, 1984.

Houthakker, H. S., and Lester D. Taylor. *Consumer Demand in the United States: Analyses and Projections.* Harvard Economic Studies. Vol. 74. 2d enlarged ed. Cambridge: Harvard University Press, 1970.

Howells, William Dean. *A Traveler from Alturia.* 1894. Reprint. Introduction by Howard Mumford Jones. New York: Hill and Wang, 1957.

Hubbard, Preston J. *Origins of the TVA: The Muscle Shoals Controversy, 1920–1932.* Nashville: Vanderbilt University Press, 1961.

Hughes, Charles Evans. *Addresses of Charles Evans Hughes.* With an Introduction by Jacob Gould Schurman, President of Cornell University. 1908. Rev. New York: G. P. Putnam's Sons, 1916.

———. *Public Papers of Charles E. Hughes, Governor.* 4 vols. State of New York [Publications]. Albany: J. B. Lyon Company, State Printers, 1908–1910.

———. *The Autobiographical Notes of Charles Evans Hughes.* Edited by David J. Danelski and Joseph S. Tulchin. Cambridge: Harvard University Press, 1973.

Hughes, James W., and George Sternlieb. *The Dynamics of America's Housing.* New Brunswick: Center for Urban Policy Research, Rutgers University, 1987.

Hughes, Thomas P. *Networks of Power: Electrification in Western Society, 1880–1930.* Baltimore: Johns Hopkins University Press, 1983.

———. *American Genesis: A Century of Invention and Technological Enthusiasm, 1870–1970.* Reprint. New York: Penguin Books, [1989] 1990.

Hundley, Norris, Jr. *Dividing the Waters: A Century of Controversy Between the United States and Mexico.* Berkeley, Los Angeles, and London: University of California Press, 1966.

―――. *Water and the West: The Colorado River Compact and the Politics of Water in the American West.* Berkeley, Los Angeles, and London: University of California Press, 1975.

―――. *The Great Thirst: Californians and Water, 1770s–1990s.* Berkeley, Los Angeles, and Oxford: University of California Press, 1992.

Hungerford, Edward. *The Story of the Public Utilities.* Reprint. New York: Arno Press, [1928] 1972.

Hunter, Burton L. *The Evolution of Municipal Organization and Administrative Practice in the City of Los Angeles.* Los Angeles: Parker, Stone & Baird, 1933.

Huthmacher, J. Joseph. *Senator Robert F. Wagner and the Rise of Urban Liberalism.* Reprint. New York: Atheneum, [1968] 1971.

Hyman, Sidney. *Marriner S. Eccles: Private Entrepreneur and Public Servant.* With a Foreword by G. L. Bach. Stanford: Graduate School of Business, Stanford University, 1976.

Ickes, Harold L. *The Autobiography of a Curmudgeon.* New York: Reynal & Hitchcock, 1943.

―――. *The Secret Diary of Harold L. Ickes: The First Thousand Days.* 3 vols. New York: Simon & Schuster, 1953–1954.

Ingels, Margaret. *Willis Haviland Carrier, Father of Air Conditioning.* Garden City, N.Y.: Country Life, 1952.

Jackson, Kenneth T. *Crabgrass Frontier: The Suburbanization of the United States.* New York: Oxford University Press, 1985.

Jackson, Robert H. *The Struggle for Judicial Supremacy: A Study of a Crisis in American Power Politics.* New York: Alfred A. Knopf, [1941] 1949.

Janowitz, Morris. *The Last Half-Century: Societal Change and Politics in America.* Chicago: University of Chicago Press, 1978.

Jay, Martin. *The Dialectical Imagination: A History of the Frankfurt School and the Institute of Social Research, 1923–1950.* Boston: Little, Brown, 1973.

Johnson, James M. *Handbook of Depreciation Methods, Formulas and Tables.* Englewood Cliffs, N.J.: Prentice Hall, 1981.

Jonas, Hans. *Philosophical Essays: From Ancient Creed to Technological Man.* Englewood Cliffs, N.J.: Prentice Hall, 1974.

Jones, Jesse H., with Edward Angly. *Fifty Billion Dollars: My Thirteen Years with the RFC.* New York: Macmillan, 1951.

Jones, Robert T. *Small Homes of Architectural Distinction: A Book of Suggested Plans Designed by the Architects' Small House Service Bureau, Inc.* New York: Harper & Brothers, 1929.

Josephson, Matthew, and Hannah Josephson. *Al Smith: Hero of the Cities: A Political Portrait Drawing on the Papers of Frances Perkins.* Boston: Houghton Mifflin, 1969.

Juster, F. Thomas. *Anticipations and Purchases: An Analysis of Consumer Behavior.* Study by the National Bureau of Economic Research. Princeton: Princeton University Press, 1964.

―――. *Household Capital Formation and Financing, 1897–1962.* National Bureau of Economic Research, General Series, no. 83, New York: Distributed by Columbia University Press, 1966.

Kaempffert, Waldemar. *Science Today and Tomorrow.* New York: Viking Press, 1939.

Kahn, Alfred E. *The Economics of Regulation: Principles and Institutions.* 2 vols. New York: John Wiley, 1971.

Kahn-Hut, Rachel, Arlene Kaplan Daniels, and Richard Colvard. *Women and Work: Problems and Perspectives*. New York: Oxford University Press, 1982.

Kahrl, William L. *Water and Power: The Conflict over Los Angeles' Water Supply in the Owens Valley*. Berkeley, Los Angeles, and London: University of California Press, 1982.

Kanter, Rosabeth Moss. *Commitment and Community*. Cambridge: Harvard University Press, 1972.

———. *Work and Family in the United States*. New York: Russell Sage Foundation, 1977.

Kantor, David, and William Lehr. *Inside the Family: Toward a Theory of Family Process*. San Francisco: Jossey-Bass, 1975.

Katz, Michael. *The People of Hamilton, Canada, West: Family and Class in a Mid-Nineteenth-Century City*. Cambridge: Harvard University Press, 1975.

———. *In the Shadow of the Poorhouse: A Social History of Welfare in America*. New York: Basic Books, 1986.

Keating, Paul W. *Lamps for a Brighter America: A History of the General Electric Lamp Business*. New York: McGraw-Hill, 1954.

Keezer, Dexter M., and Stacy May. *The Public Control of Business*. New York: Harper & Brothers, 1930.

Keith, Nathaniel S. *Politics and the Housing Crisis since 1930*. New York: Universe Books, 1973.

Keller, Morton. *Regulating a New Economy: Public Policy and Economic Change in America, 1900–1933*. Cambridge: Harvard University Press, 1990.

Kelly, Patrick, and Kranzberg, M., eds. *Technological Innovation: A Critical Review of Current Knowledge*. San Francisco: San Francisco Press, 1978.

Kerwin, Jerome G. *Federal Water Power Legislation*. 1926. New York: AMS Press, 1968.

Kessler-Harris, Alice. *Women Have Always Worked: A Historical Overview*. Old Westbury, N.Y.: Feminist Press, 1981.

Kessner, Thomas. *The Golden Door: Italian and Jewish Immigrant Mobility in New York City, 1880–1915*. New York: Oxford University Press, 1977.

King, H[enry] Churchill. *Rational Living: Some Practical Inferences from Modern Psychology*. New York: Macmillan, 1906.

Klein, Norman M., and Martin J. Schiesl, eds. *20th Century Los Angeles: Power, Promotion and Social Conflict*. Claremont, Calif.: Regina Books, 1990.

Kleinsorge, Paul Lincoln. *The Boulder Canyon Project, Historical and Economic Aspects*. Stanford: Stanford University Press, 1941.

Kline, Ronald R. *Steinmetz: Engineer and Socialist*. Baltimore: Johns Hopkins University Press, 1992.

Kloppenberg, James T. *Social Democracy and Progressivism in European and American Thought, 1870–1920*. New York: Oxford University Press, 1986.

Kluger, Richard. *Simple Justice: The History of Brown v. Board of Education and Black America's Struggle for Equality*. New York: Alfred A. Knopf, 1976.

Knapp, Joseph G. *The Advance of American Cooperative Enterprise: 1920–1945*. Danville, Ill.: Interstate Printers & Publishers, 1973.

Kolko, Gabriel. *The Triumph of Conservatism: A Reinterpretation of American History, 1900–1916*. 1963. Reprint. New York: Free Press, 1977.

Korman, Gerd. *Industrialization, Immigrants and Americanizers: The View from Milwaukee, 1866–1921*. Madison: State Historical Society of Wisconsin, 1967.

Kornhauser, William. *The Politics of Mass Society*. Glencoe: Free Press of Glencoe, 1959.

Kottke, Frank Joseph. *Electrical Technology and the Public Interest: A Study of Our Na-*

tional Policy Toward the Development and Application of Inventions. Washington, D.C.: American Council on Public Affairs, 1944.

Kyrk, Hazel. *Economic Problems of the Family.* New York: Harper & Brothers, 1930.

La Follette, Cecile Tipton. *A Study of the Problems of 652 Gainfully Employed Married Women Homemakers.* Teachers College, Columbia University, Contributions to Education, no. 619. Reprint. New York: AMS, [1934] 1972.

La Follette, Robert M. *La Follette's Autobiography: A Personal Narrative of Political Experience.* With a Foreword by Allan Nevins. Madison: University of Wisconsin Press, 1960.

Lancaster, Kevin. *Consumer Demand, A New Approach.* New York: Columbia University Press, 1971.

Langdon, William Chauncy. *Everyday Things in American Life, 1776–1876.* New York: Charles Scribner's Sons, 1941.

Lansing, John R. *New Homes and Poor People: A Study of Chains of Moves.* Ann Arbor: Institute for Social Research, University of Michigan, 1969.

Lapp, Rudolph M. *Afro-Americans in California.* 2d ed. San Francisco: Boyd & Fraser, 1987.

Laurenti, Luigi. *Property Values and Race: Studies in Seven Cities. Special Research Report to the Commission on Race and Housing.* Berkeley: University of California Press, 1960.

Layton, Edwin T., Jr. *Technology and Social Change in America.* Interpretations of American History Series. New York: Harper & Row, 1973.

Leavitt, Judith Walzer. *The Healthiest City: Milwaukee and the Politics of Health Reform.* Princeton: Princeton University Press, 1982.

———. *Brought to Bed: Childbearing in America, 1750–1950.* New York: Oxford University Press, 1986.

Lebergott, Stanley. *The American Economy.* Princeton: Princeton University Press, 1976.

Leff, Mark Hugh. *The Limits of Symbolic Reform: The New Deal and Taxation, 1933–1939.* Cambridge: Cambridge University Press, 1984.

Leiss, William. *The Limits to Satisfaction: An Essay on the Problem of Needs and Commodities.* Toronto: University of Toronto Press, 1976.

Lerner, Max. *America as a Civilization.* 2 vols. 1957. Reprint. New York: Simon & Schuster, 1961.

Levin, Jack. *Power Ethics: An Analysis of the Activities of the Public Utilities in the United States.* New York: Alfred A. Knopf, 1931.

Lifshey, Earl. *The Housewares Story: A History of the American Housewares Industry.* Chicago: National Housewares Manufacturers Association, 1973.

Lilienthal, David E. *TVA: Democracy on the March.* Rev. ed. New York: Harper & Brothers, 1953.

Lindquist, Ruth. *The Family in the Present Social Order: A Study of Needs of American Families.* Written and published with the cooperation of the American Home Economics Association. Chapel Hill: University of North Carolina Press, 1931.

Lingeman, Richard. *Small Town America: A Narrative History, 1620–The Present.* New York: G. P. Putnam's Sons, 1980.

Lipset, Seymour Martin, and Reinhard Bendix. *Social Mobility in Industrial Society.* Berkeley: University of California Press, 1959.

Lipsitz, George. *Rainbow at Midnight: Labor and Culture in the 1940s.* Rev. ed. Urbana: University of Illinois Press, 1994.

Long, Clarence D. *The Labor Force under Changing Income and Employment.* National Bureau of Economic Research, General Series, no. 65. Princeton: Princeton University Press, 1958.

Lord, Isabel Ely. *Getting Your Money's Worth: A Book on Expenditure.* New York: Harcourt, Brace, 1922.

Lotchin, Roger W. *Fortress California, 1910–1961.* New York: Oxford University Press, 1992.

Loth, David. *Swope of G.E.: The Story of Gerard Swope and General Electric in American Business.* New York: Simon & Schuster, 1958.

Low, A. M. *Science Looks Ahead.* New York: Oxford University Press, 1942.

Lowitt, Richard. *George W. Norris: The Making of a Progressive, 1861–1912.* Syracuse: Syracuse University Press, 1963.

———. *George W. Norris: The Persistence of a Progressive, 1913–1933.* Urbana: University of Illinois Press, 1971.

———. *George W. Norris: The Triumph of a Progressive, 1933–1944.* Urbana: University of Illinois Press, 1978.

Lowitt, Richard, and Maurine Beasley, eds. *One Third of a Nation: Lorena Hickok Reports on the Great Depression.* Urbana: University of Illinois Press, 1981.

Lubove, Roy. *Community Planning in the 1920s: The Contribution of the Regional Planning Association of America.* Pittsburgh: University of Pittsburgh Press, 1963.

———. *The Progressives and the Slums: Tenement House Reform in New York City, 1890–1917.* Pittsburgh: University of Pittsburgh Press, 1963.

Lukes Timothy J., and Gary Y. Okihiro. *Japanese Legacy: Farming and Community in California's Santa Clara Valley.* Local History Studies. Vol. 31. Cupertino: California History Center, 1985.

Lynd, Robert S., and Helen Merrell Lynd. *Middletown: A Study in American Culture.* Reprint. San Diego: Harcourt Brace Jovanovich, [1929] 1957.

———. *Middletown in Transition: A Study in Cultural Conflicts.* New York: Harcourt, Brace, 1937.

Lynes, Russell. *The Domesticated Americans.* New York: Harper & Row, 1963.

Maass, John. *The Victorian Home in America.* New York: Hawthorn Books, 1972.

MacFadden Publications, Inc. *86% of America: A Symposium on the Characteristics of the New American Prosperity as Related to the Wage Earning Masses.* New York: MacFadden Publications, Inc., 1927.

MacKenzie, Donald, and Judy Wajcman, eds. *The Social Shaping of Technology: How the Refrigerator Got Its Hum.* Stratford: Open University Press, 1985.

MacLaren, Malcolm. *The Rise of the Electrical Industry During the Nineteenth Century.* Princeton: Princeton University Press, 1943.

[MacLeish, Archibald]. *Housing America.* New York: Harcourt, Brace, 1932.

MacPherson, C. B. *The Political Theory of Possessive Individualism.* Oxford: Oxford University Press, 1965.

Mandelker, Daniel R., and Roger Montgomery. *Housing in America.* 1973. Indianapolis: Bobbs-Merrill, 1979.

Marchand, B. *The Emergence of Los Angeles: Population and Housing in the City of Dreams, 1940–1970.* London: Pion, 1986.

Marchand, Roland. *Advertising the American Dream: Making Way for Modernity, 1920–1940.* Berkeley, Los Angeles, and London: University of California Press, 1985.

Marshall, Alfred. *Principles of Economics.* 9th (Variorum) ed., with annotations by C. W. Guillebaud. 2 vols. 8th ed. 1920. London: Macmillan, 1961.

Martin, George Whitney. *Madam Secretary, Frances Perkins.* Boston: Houghton Mifflin, 1976.

Martin, Linda, and Kerry Segrave. *The Servant Problem: Domestic Workers in North America.* Jefferson, N.C.: McFarland, 1985.

Martin, Roscoe E., ed. *TVA: The First Twenty Years: A Staff Report.* University: University of Alabama Press, 1956. Copublished Knoxville: University of Tennessee Press, 1956.

Martinez, John. *Mexican Emigration to the U.S. 1910–1930.* San Francisco: R and E Research Associates, 1971.

Marvin, Carolyn. *When Old Technologies Were New: Thinking About Electric Communication in the Late Nineteenth Century.* New York: Oxford University Press, 1988.

Marx, Leo. *The Machine in the Garden: Technology and the Pastoral Ideal in America.* New York: Oxford University Press, 1964.

Matthaei, Julie A. *An Economic History of Women in America: Women's Work, the Sexual Division of Labor, and the Development of Capitalism.* New York: Schocken Books, 1982.

Matthews, Glenna. *'Just a Housewife': The Rise and Fall of Domesticity in America.* New York: Oxford University Press, 1987.

Maxwell, Robert S. *La Follette and the Rise of the Progressives in Wisconsin.* Madison: State Historical Society of Wisconsin, 1956.

May, Elaine Tyler. *Homeward Bound: American Families in the Cold War Era.* New York: Basic Books, 1988.

McBridge, Theresa. *The Domestic Revolution: The Modernisation of Household Service in England and France, 1820–1920.* London: Croom Helm, 1976.

McCracken, Grant. *Culture and Consumption: New Approaches to the Symbolic Character of Consumer Goods and Activities.* Bloomington: Indiana University Press, 1988.

McCraw, Thomas K. *Morgan vs. Lilienthal: The Feud within the TVA.* Chicago: Loyola University Press, 1970.

———. *TVA and the Power Fight, 1933–1939.* Philadelphia: J. B. Lippincott, 1971.

McCullough, David. *Truman.* New York: Simon & Schuster, 1992.

McDonald, Forrest. *Let There Be Light: The Electric Utility Industry in Wisconsin, 1881–1955.* Madison: American History Research Center, 1957.

———. *Insull.* Chicago: University of Chicago Press, 1962.

McDonnell, Timothy. *The Wagner Housing Act.* Chicago: Loyola University Press, 1957.

McEntire, Davis. *Residence and Race. Final and Comprehensive Report to the Commission on Race and Housing.* Berkeley: University of California Press, 1960.

McGuigan, Dorothy G., ed. *Women's Lives: New Theory, Research & Policy. Center for Continuing Education of Women.* [Ann Arbor]: University of Michigan, 1980.

McKinley, Donald Gilbert. *Social Class and Family Life.* New York: Free Press, 1964.

McMahon, Theresa S. *Social and Economic Standards of Living.* Boston: Heath, 1925.

McMurty, John. *The Structure of Marx's World-View.* Princeton: Princeton University Press, 1978.

McWilliams, Carey. *Southern California: An Island Upon the Land.* Reprint. Salt Lake City: Peregrine Smith Books, [1946] 1973.

———. *North from Mexico: The Spanish-speaking People of the United States.* New edition, updated by Matt S. Meier. New York: Praeger, [1948] 1990.

Meier, Richard L. *Science and Economic Development: New Patterns of Living.* 1956. Cambridge: MIT Press, 1966.

Melosi, Martin V. *Coping with Abundance: Energy and Environment in Industrial America.* Philadelphia: Temple University Press, 1985.

Mertz, Paul E. *New Deal Policy and Southern Rural Poverty.* Baton Rouge: Louisiana State University Press, 1978.

Mesthene, Emmanuel G. *Technological Change: Its Impact on Man and Society.* Cambridge: Harvard University Press, 1970.

Metcalf, Lee, and Vic Reinemer. *Overcharge.* New York: D. McKay, 1967.

Miller, Daniel. *Material Culture and Mass Consumption.* Oxford: Basil Blackwell, 1987.

Miller, John Thomas, Jr. *Foreign Trade in Gas and Electricity in North America: A Legal and Historical Study.* New York: Praeger, 1970.

Miller, Michael B. *The Bon Marche: Bourgeois Culture and the Department Store, 1869–1920.* Princeton: Princeton University Press, 1981.

Mitchell, Greg. *The Campaign of the Century: Upton Sinclair's Race for Governor of California and the Birth of Media Politics.* New York: Random House, 1992.

Mitchell, Sidney Alexander. *S. Z. Mitchell and the Electrical Industry.* New York: Farrar, Straus & Cuhady, 1960.

Mitchell, W. J. T. *Iconology: Image, Text, Ideology.* Chicago: University of Chicago Press, 1986.

Moeller, Beverley Brown. *Phil Swing and Boulder Dam.* Berkeley, Los Angeles, and London: University of California Press, 1971.

Moley, Raymond. *After Seven Years.* New York: Harper & Brothers, 1939.

Momenti, Jamshid A., ed. *Race, Ethnicity, and Minority Housing in the United States.* New York: Greenwood Press, 1986.

Monkkonen, Eric H. *America Becomes Urban: The Development of U.S. Cities and Towns, 1780–1980.* Berkeley: University of California Press, 1990.

Monkkonen, Eric H., ed. *Walking to Work: Tramps in America, 1790–1935.* Lincoln: University of Nebraska Press, 1984.

Monroe, Day. *Chicago Families: A Study of Unpublished Census Data.* Chicago: University of Chicago Press, 1932.

Montejano, David. *Anglos and Mexicans in the Making of Texas, 1836–1986.* Austin: University of Texas Press, 1987.

Moore, Joan W., and Frank G. Mittelbach. *Residential Segregation in the Urban Southwest.* With the Assistance of Ronald McDaniel. Mexican-American Study Project, Division of Research, Graduate School of Business Administration, University of California, Los Angeles. Advance Report 4. June 1966. [Los Angeles]: Mexican-American Study Project, 1966.

Moore, John R., ed. *The Economic Impact of TVA.* Knoxville: University of Tennessee Press, 1967.

Morgan, Arthur. *The Making of TVA.* Buffalo: Prometheus Books, 1974.

Morgan, Winona. *The Family Meets the Depression: A Study of a Group of Highly Selected Families.* 1939. Westport, Conn.: Greenwood Press, 1972.

Mosher, William E., and Finla G. Crawford. *The Electric Utilities: A Crisis in Public Control.* New York: Harper & Brothers, 1929.

———. *Public Utility Regulation.* New York: Harper & Brothers, 1933.

Motz, Marilyn Ferris, and Pat Browne, eds. *Making the American Home: Middle-Class*

Women and Domestic American Culture. Bowling Green, Ohio: Bowling Green University Popular Press, 1988.

Mowry, George E. *The California Progressives*. Berkeley: University of California Press, 1951.

Mukerji, Chandra. *From Graven Images: Patterns of Modern Materialism*. New York: Columbia University Press, 1983.

Muller, Herbert J. *The Children of Frankenstein: A Primer on Modern Technology and Human Values*. Bloomington: Indiana University Press, 1970.

Mumford, Lewis. *Technics and Civilization*. Reprint. New York: Harcourt, Brace & World, [1934] 1963.

————. *City Development: Studies in Renewal and Disintegration*. New York: Harcourt, Brace, 1945.

————. *The Myth of the Machine: The Pentagon of Power*. New York: Harcourt Brace Jovanovich, 1970.

Myers, William A. *Iron Men and Copper Wires: A Centennial History of the Southern California Edison Company*. Glendale, Calif.: Trans-Anglo Books, 1983.

Myerson, Abraham. *The Nervous Housewife*. 1920. Reprint. New York: Arno Press, 1972.

Myrdal, Gunnar. *An American Dilemma: The Negro Problem and Modern Democracy*. With the assistance of Richard Sterner and Arnold Rose. New York: Harper & Brothers, 1944.

National Consumer Finance Association. *The Consumer Finance Industry*. Monograph prepared for the Commission on Money and Credit. Englewood Cliffs, N.J.: Prentice Hall, 1962.

Nelson, George, and Henry Wright. *Tomorrow's House: How to Plan Your Post-War Home Now*. New York: Simon & Schuster, 1945.

Netting, Robert McG., Richard R. Wilk, and Eric J. Arnould, eds. *Households: Comparative and Historical Studies of the Domestic Group*. Berkeley, Los Angeles, and London: University of California Press, 1984.

New Deal Urban Housing: A Summary of Real Property Inventories Conducted as Work Projects, 1934–1936. Washington, D.C.: GPO, 1938.

Nixon, Richard. *Six Crises*. Reprint. New York: Simon & Schuster, [1962] 1990.

Noble, David F. *America By Design: Science, Technology, and the Rise of Corporate Capitalism*. New York: Knopf, 1977.

Norris, George W. *Fighting Liberal: The Autobiography of George W. Norris*. New York: Macmillan, 1945.

Nourse, Edwin G. *America's Capacity to Produce: Study of Consumption in the 1920s*. Institute of Economics of the Brookings Institution Publication no. 55. Washington, D.C.: Brookings Institution, 1934.

Novick, Peter. *That Noble Dream: The 'Objectivity Question' and the American Historical Profession*. Reprint. Cambridge: Cambridge University Press, 1988.

Nugent, Rolf. *Consumer Credit and Economic Stability*. New York: Russell Sage Foundation, 1939.

Nye, David E. *Electrifying America: Social Meanings of a New Technology, 1880–1940*. Cambridge: MIT Press, 1990.

Nye, F. Ivan, and Lois Wladis Hoffman, eds. *The Employed Mother in America*. Chicago: Rand McNally, 1963.

Nye, Russell B. *Midwestern Progressive Politics: A Historical Study of Its Origins and Development, 1870–1958*. East Lansing: Michigan State University Press, 1959.

Nystrom, Paul. *Economics of Consumption*. New York: Ronald Press, 1929.

O'Dea, William T. *A Social History of Lighting*. New York: Macmillan, 1959.

Oakley, Ann. *Woman's Work: The Housewife, Past and Present*. New York: Pantheon Books, 1975.

Ogburn, W. F. *Technological Trends and National Policy, including the Social Implications of New Inventions*. June 1937. Report of the Subcommittee on Technology to the National Resources Committee. Washington, D.C.: GPO, 1937.

Ogburn, William Fielding, ed. *Technology and International Relations*. Harris Foundation Lectures at the University of Chicago. Chicago: University of Chicago Press, 1949.

Ogburn, W. F., and M. F. Nimkoff. *Technology and the Changing Family*. Boston: Houghton Mifflin, 1955.

Ogden, Annegret S. *The Great American Housewife: From Helpmate to Wage Earner, 1776–1986*. Contribution to Women's Studies, no. 61. Westport, Conn.: Greenwood Press, 1986.

Olin, Spencer C., Jr. *California's Prodigal Sons: Hiram Johnson and the Progressives, 1911–1917*. Berkeley, Los Angeles, and London: University of California Press, 1968.

Ollman, Bertell. *Alienation: Marx's Concept of Man in Capitalist Society*. 1971. Cambridge: Cambridge University Press, 1976.

Olney, Martha L. *Buy Now, Pay Later: Advertising, Credit, and Consumer Durables in the 1920s*. Chapel Hill: University of North Carolina Press, 1991.

Olson, James S. *Historical Dictionary of the New Deal: From Inauguration to Preparation for War*. Westport, Conn.: Greenwood Press, 1985.

Oppenheimer, Valerie Kincade. *The Female Labor Force in the United States, Demographic and Economic Factors Governing Its Growth and Changing Composition*. Population Monograph Series 5. Berkeley: Institute of International Studies, 1970.

——. *Work and the Family: A Study in Social Demography*. New York: Academic Press, 1982.

Owen, Marguerite. *The Tennessee Valley Authority*. New York: Praeger, 1973.

Pachauri, R. K. *The Dynamics of Electrical Supply and Demand: An Economic Analysis*. New York: Praeger, 1975.

Palmer, Gladys L. *Labor Mobility in Six Cities: A Report on the Survey of Patterns and Factors in Labor Mobility, 1940–1950*. New York: Social Science Research Council, 1954.

Palmer, Phyllis. *Domesticity and Dirt: Housewives and Domestic Servants in the United States, 1920–1945*. Philadelphia: Temple University Press, 1989.

Parker, William Stanley, Chairman, Design Committee, Albert P. Greensfelder, Chairman, Construction Committee, and Collins P. Bliss, Fundamental Equipment Committee. *House Design Construction and Equipment*. Edited by John M. Gries and James Ford. Washington, D.C.: President's Conference on Home Building and Home Ownership, 1932.

Parnes, Herbert S. *Research on Labor Mobility: An Appraisal of Research Findings in the United States*. Social Science Research Council Bulletin 65. New York: Social Science Research Council, 1954.

Passer, Harold C. *The Electrical Manufacturers, 1875–1900: A Study in Competition, Entrepreneurship, Technical Changes, and Economic Growth*. Cambridge: Harvard University Press, 1953.

Patterson, James T. *America's Struggle Against Poverty, 1900–1980*. Rev. ed. Cambridge: Harvard University Press, 1986.

Patterson, Tom. *A Colony for California: Riverside's First Hundred Years*. Riverside: Press-Enterprise, 1971.

Pattison, Mary (Mrs. Frank A.), Colonia, New Jersey. *Principles of Domestic Engineering, Or The What, Why and How of a Home; An Attempt to Evolve a Solution to the Domestic 'Labor and Capital' Problem—To Standardize and Professionalize Housework—To Re-Organize the Home Upon 'Scientific Management' Principles—And To Point Out the Importance of the Public and Personal Element Therein, As Well As the Practical.* New York: [Women's Club of New Jersey], 1915.

Paul, Randolph. *Taxation in the United States.* Boston: Little, Brown, 1954.

Peel, C. S. *A Hundred Wonderful Years: Social and Domestic Life of a Century, 1820–1920.* London: Bodley Head, 1926.

———. *The Stream of Time: Social and Domestic Life in England, 1805–1861.* London: Bodley Head, 1931.

Peel, J. H. B. *An Englishman's Home.* 1972. Newton Abbot, Devon: David & Charles, 1978.

Peet, Louise J., and Lenore Sater Thye. *Household Equipment.* 4th ed. New York: John Wiley & Sons, 1955.

Peirce, Josephine. *Fire on the Hearth: The Evolution and Romance of the Heating Stove.* Springfield, Mass.: Pond-Ekberg, 1951.

Perin, Constance. *Everything in Its Place: Social Order and Land Use in America.* Princeton: Princeton University Press, 1977.

Perkins, Frances. *The Roosevelt I Knew.* New York: Viking Press, 1946.

Perry, Clarence. *Housing for the Machine Age.* New York: Russell Sage Foundation, 1937.

Pettitt, George Albert. *So Boulder Dam Was Built.* Berkeley, Calif.: Press of Lederer, Street & Zeus, 1935.

Pinchot, Gifford. *The Power Monopoly: Its Make-up and Its Menace.* Medford, Pa.: Privately printed, 1928.

Pink, Louis. *The New Day in Housing.* New York: John Day, 1928.

Pisani, Donald J. *From the Family Farm to Agribusiness: The Irrigation Crusade in California and the West, 1850–1931.* Berkeley, Los Angeles, and London: University of California Press, 1984.

Platt, Harold L. *City Building in the New South: The Growth of Public Services in Houston, Texas, 1830–1910.* Philadelphia: Temple University Press, 1983.

———. *The Electric City: Energy and the Growth of the Chicago Area, 1880–1930.* Chicago: University of Chicago Press, 1991.

Polenberg, Richard. *War and Society: The United States, 1941–1945.* Philadelphia: J. B. Lippincott, 1972.

Potter, David M. *People of Plenty: Economic Abundance and the American Character.* Chicago: University of Chicago Press, 1954.

Pritchett, C. H. *Tennessee Valley Authority: A Study in Public Administration.* Chapel Hill: University of North Carolina Press, 1943.

———. *The Roosevelt Court: A Study in Judicial Politics and Values, 1937–1947.* New York: Macmillan, 1948.

Putnam, Jack K. *Old-Age Politics in California, from Richardson to Reagan.* Stanford: Stanford University Press, 1970.

Raley, Dorothy, ed. *A Century of Progress in Homes and Furnishings.* Chicago: M. A. Ring, 1934.

Ramsay, M. L. *Pyramids of Power: The Story of Roosevelt, Insull and the Utility Wars.* New York: Bobbs-Merrill, 1937.

Ratcliffe, Richard A., Daniel B. Rathbun, and Junia H. Honnold. *Residential Finance.* New York: John Wiley & Sons, 1957.

Rauschenbush, H. S. *High Power Propaganda.* New York: New Republic, 1928.

————. *The Power Fight.* New York: New Republic, 1932.

Rauschenbush, H. S., and Harry W. Laidler. *Power Control.* New York: New Republic, 1928.

Rawitsch, Mark Howland. *No Other Place: Japanese American Pioneers in a Southern California Neighborhood.* Riverside: Department of History, University of California, Riverside, 1983.

Redinger, David H. *The Story of Big Creek.* Los Angeles: Angelus Press, 1949.

Reid, Margaret. *Economics of Household Production.* New York: John Wiley & Sons, 1934.

————. *Housing and Income.* New York: John Wiley & Sons, 1934.

Reinemeir, Vic, and Jack Doyle. *Lines Across the Land—Rural Electric Cooperatives: The Changing Politics of Energy in Rural America.* Washington, D.C.: Environmental Policy Institute, 1979.

Reiss, Ira F. *Family Systems in America.* 3d ed. New York: Holt, Rinehart and Winston, 1980.

Richards, Ellen H. *The Cost of Shelter.* New York: John Wiley & Sons, 1905.

Richards, Thomas. *The Commodity Culture of Victorian England: Advertising and Spectacle, 1851–1914.* Stanford: Stanford University Press, 1990.

Richardson, Bertha J. *The Woman Who Spends: A Study of Her Economic Function.* 1904. Rev. Boston: Whitcomb & Barrows, 1910.

Richmond, Mary E., and Fred S. Hall. *Marriage and the State.* New York: Russell Sage Foundation, 1929.

Roberts, Marc J., and Jeremy S. Bluhm. With the assistance of Margaret Gerteis. *The Choices of Power: Utilities Face the Environmental Challenge.* Cambridge: Harvard University Press, 1981.

Roberts, Peter. *The Problem of Americanization.* New York: Macmillan, 1920.

Robins, F. W. *The Story of the Lamp (and the Candle).* London: Oxford University Press, 1939.

Robinson, L. Eugene. *Domestic Architecture.* New York: Macmillan, 1917.

Rodgers, Daniel T. *The Work Ethic in Industrial America, 1850–1920.* Chicago: University of Chicago Press, 1978.

Rogers, Everett M. *The Diffusion of Inventions.* New York: Free Press of Glencoe, 1962.

————. *The Diffusion of Innovation.* 3d ed. New York: Free Press, 1983.

Rogers, Everett M., and F. Floyd Shoemaker. *Communication of Innovations: A Cross-Cultural Approach.* Second edition of *The Diffusion of Innovations.* New York: Free Press, 1971.

Roosevelt, Franklin D. *The Public Papers and Addresses of Franklin D. Roosevelt.* 13 vols. Compiled with Special Material and Explanatory Notes by Samuel I. Rosenman. New York: Random House, 1938–1950.

————. *F.D.R.: His Personal Letters, 1928–1945.* Vol. 1. Foreword by Eleanor Roosevelt. Edited by Elliott Roosevelt, assisted by Joseph P. Lash. New York: Duell, Sloan and Pearce, 1950.

Rose, Mark H. *Cities of Light and Heat: Domesticating Gas and Electricity in Urban America.* University Park: Pennsylvania State University Press, 1995.

Rosen, S. McKee, and Laura Rosen. *Technology and Society: The Influence of Machines in the United States.* New York: Macmillan, 1941.

Rosenberg, Nathan. *Perspectives on Technology.* New York: Cambridge University Press, 1976.

————. *Inside the Black Box: Technology and Economics*. New York: Cambridge University Press, 1982.

Rossi, Peter H. *Why Families Move*. 1955. Beverly Hills: Sage Publications, 1980.

————. *Why Families Move: A Study in the Social Psychology of Urban Residential Mobility*. Conducted under the joint sponsorship of the Bureau of Applied Social Research and the Institute for Urban Land Use and Housing Studies. Glencoe: Free Press, 1955.

Rotella, Elyce J. *From Home to Office: U.S. Women at Work, 1870–1930*. Ann Arbor: UMI Research Press, 1981.

Rudolph, Richard, and Scott Ridley. *Power Struggle: The Hundred-Year War over Electricity*. New York: Harper & Row, 1986.

Rybczynski, Witold. *Home: A Short History of an Idea*. New York: Penguin Books, 1987.

Sager, Daniel S., M.D. *The Art of Living in Good Health: A Practical Guide to Well-Being Through Proper Eating, Thinking, and Living in the Light of Modern Science*. New York: Frederick A. Stokes, 1907.

Salmon, Lucy H. *Progress in the Household*. Boston: Houghton Mifflin, 1906.

Schaefer, Herwin. *Nineteenth-Century Modern: The Functional Tradition in Victorian Design*. New York: Praeger, 1970.

Schaffer, Daniel. *Garden Cities for America: The Radburn Experience*. Philadelphia: Temple University Press, 1982.

Schaffer, Daniel, ed. *Two Centuries of American Planning*. Baltimore: Johns Hopkins University Press, 1988.

Schap, David. *Municipal Ownership in the Electric Utility Industry: A Centennial View*. Praeger Special Studies. Praeger Scientific, distributed by Greenwood Press, Westport, Conn. 1986.

Scharf, Lois. *To Work and To Wed: Female Unemployment, Feminism, and the Great Depression*. Contributions in Women's Studies, no. 15. Westport, Conn.: Greenwood Press, 1980.

Schivelbusch, Wolfgang. *Disenchanted Night: The Industrialization of Light in the Nineteenth Century*. Translated from the German by Angela Davies. Berkeley, Los Angeles, and London: University of California Press, 1988.

Schlesinger, Arthur M., Jr. *The Age of Roosevelt: The Crisis of the Old Order, 1919–1933*. Boston: Houghton Mifflin, 1957.

Schlesinger, Arthur Meyer. *The New Deal in Action, 1933–1938*. New York: Macmillan, 1939.

Schnedler, William A. *How to Get Ahead Financially*. New York: Harper & Brothers, 1926.

Schneider, David M. *American Kinship: A Cultural Account*. Englewood Cliffs, N.J.: Prentice Hall, 1968.

Scholten, Catherine M. *Childbearing in American Society, 1650–1850*. American Social Experience, no. 2. New York: New York University Press, 1985.

Schroyer, Trent. *The Critique of Domination: The Origins and Development of Critical Theory*. New York: Braziller, 1973.

Schulman, Bruce J. *From Cotton Belt to Sunbelt: Federal Policy, Economic Development, and the Transformation of the South, 1938–1980*. New York: Oxford University Press, 1991.

Schultz, Stanley K. *Constructing Urban Culture: American Cities and City Planning, 1800–1920*. Philadelphia: Temple University Press, 1989.

Schurr, Sam H., Calvin C. Burwell, Warren D. Devine, Jr., and Sidney Sonenblum. *Elec-

tricity in the American Economy: Agent of Technological Progress. Greenwood Press Contributions in Economics and Economic History, no. 117. Published under the auspices of the Electric Power Research Institute. Westport, Conn.: Greenwood Press, 1990.

Scott, William B. *In Pursuit of Happiness: American Conceptions of Property from the Seventeenth to the Twentieth Century*. Bloomington: Indiana University Press, 1977.

Seale, William. *The Tasteful Interlude: American Interiors Through the Camera's Eye, 1860–1917*. Nashville: American Association for State and Local History, 1982.

Segal, Howard P. *Technological Utopianism in American Culture*. Chicago: University of Chicago Press, 1985.

Selznick, Philip. *TVA and the Grass Roots: A Study in the Sociology of Formal Organization*. Reprint. New York: Harper & Row, [1949] 1966.

Sennett, Richard, and Jonathan Cobb. *The Hidden Injuries of Class*. New York: Knopf, 1972.

Severn, Bill. *Frances Perkins: A Member of the Cabinet*. New York: Hawthorn Books, 1976.

Shay, Robert Paul. *New-Automobile Financing Rates, 1924–62*. New York: National Bureau of Economic Research, 1963.

Sheldon, Eleanor Bernert, ed. *Family Economic Behavior, Problems and Prospects*. Philadelphia: J. B. Lippincott, 1973.

Shergold, Peter R. *Working-Class Life: The 'American Standard' in Comparative Perspective, 1899–1913*. Pittsburgh: University of Pittsburgh Press, 1982.

Sievers, Allen M. *Revolution, Evolution, and the Economic Order*. Reprint. Englewood Cliffs, N.J.: Prentice Hall, 1962.

Silver, Christopher. *Twentieth-Century Richmond: Planning, Politics, and Race*. Knoxville: University of Tennessee Press, 1984.

Simmons, Ralph B., comp. *Boulder Dam and the Great Southwest's Narrative History of the Boulder Canyon Project*. Los Angeles: Pacific Publishers, 1936.

Sinclair, Upton. *I, Governor of California, and How I Ended Poverty: A True Story of the Future*. Los Angeles: End Poverty League, 1933.

———. *The EPIC Plan for California*. New York: Farrar & Rinehart, 1934.

Sklar, Martin J. *The Corporate Reconstruction of American Capitalism, 1890–1916: The Market, the Law, and Politics*. New York: Cambridge University Press, 1989.

Skolnick, Arlene. *The Intimate Environment: Exploring Marriage and the Family*. Boston: Little, Brown, 1973.

Smith, Ron P. *Consumer Demand for Cars in the USA*. Cambridge: Cambridge University Press, 1975.

Smith, Wallace F. *Housing: The Social and Economic Elements*. Berkeley, Los Angeles, and London: University of California Press, 1971.

Sokoloff, Natalie J. *Between Money and Love: The Dialectics of Women's Home and Market Work*. New York: Holt, Rinehart and Winston, 1980.

Southern California Edison. *Southern California Edison, A History*. [Rosemead, Calif.: Privately printed by Southern California Edison] 1979.

Speare, Alden, Jr., Sidney Goldstein, and William H. Frey. *Residential Mobility, Migration and Metropolitan Change*. Cambridge: Ballinger, 1975.

Spears, Allan H. *Black Chicago: The Making of a Negro Ghetto, 1890–1920*. Chicago: University of Chicago Press, 1967.

Spiegel-Rosing, Ina, and Derek de Solla Price, eds. *Science, Technology and Society: A Cross-Disciplinary Perspective*. Beverly Hills: Sage Publications, 1977.

Stapp, Peyton. *Urban Housing: A Summary of Real Property Inventories Conducted as Work Projects, 1934–1936.* Division of Social Research, Works Progress Administration. Washington, D.C.: 1938.

Starr, Kevin. *Inventing the Dream: California Through the Progressive Era.* New York: Oxford University Press, 1986.

———. *Material Dreams: Southern California Through the 1920s.* New York: Oxford University Press, 1990.

Staudenmaier, John M. *Technology's Storytellers: Reweaving the Human Fabric.* Cambridge: MIT Press, 1985.

Sternsher, Bernard, ed. *Hitting Home: The Great Depression in Town and Country.* Chicago: Quadrangle Books, 1970.

Stevens, Joseph E. *Hoover Dam: An American Adventure.* Norman: University of Oklahoma Press, 1988.

Stevenson, Louis L. *The Victorian Homefront: American Thought and Culture, 1860–1880.* New York: Twayne, 1992.

Stigler, George. *Domestic Servants in the United States, 1900–1940.* Occasional Paper 24. New York: National Bureau of Economic Research, 1946.

Stock, Catherine McNicol. *Main Street in Crisis: The Great Depression and the Old Middle Class on the Northern Plains.* Chapel Hill: University of North Carolina Press, 1992.

Stokley, James. *Science Remakes Our World.* 1942. Rev. New York: Ives Washburn, 1946.

Stone, R. *The Measurement of Consumer's Expenditure and Behavior in the United Kingdom, 1920–1938.* Cambridge: Cambridge University Press, 1954.

Strasser, Susan. *Never Done: A History of American Housework.* New York: Pantheon Books, 1982.

———. *Satisfaction Guaranteed: The Making of the American Mass Market.* New York: Pantheon Books, 1989.

Straus, Nathan. *Two Thirds of a Nation: A Housing Program.* New York: Knopf, 1952.

Sultan, Ralph G. M. *Pricing in the Electrical Oligarchy.* Vol. 1. *Competition or Collusion.* Division of Research, Graduate School of Business Administration, Harvard University. Cambridge: Distributed by Harvard University Press, 1974.

Sussman, Herbert L. *Victorians and the Machine: The Literary Response to Technology.* Cambridge: Harvard University Press, 1968.

Sutherland, Daniel E. *Americans and Their Servants: Domestic Service in the United States from 1800 to 1920.* Baton Rouge: Louisiana State University Press, 1981.

Sypher, Wylie. *Literature and Technology: The Alien Vision.* New York: Random House, 1968.

Taber, C. W. *The Business of the Household.* 1918. 3d ed. Philadelphia: J. B. Lippincott, 1926.

Talbert, Roy, Jr. *FDR's Utopian: Arthur Morgan of TVA.* Jackson: University Press of Mississippi, 1987.

Talbot, Marion, and Sophonisba Preston Breckenridge. *The Modern Household.* Boston: Whitcomb & Barrows, 1912.

Tebbutt, Melanie. *Making Ends Meet: Pawnbroking and Working-Class Credit.* Leicester: Leicester University Press, 1983.

Tedlow, Richard S. *'New and Improved': The Story of Mass Marketing in America.* New York: Basic Books, 1990.

Temin, Peter. *Did Monetary Forces Cause the Great Depression?* New York: W. W. Norton, 1976.

Temple, Douglas M. *Real Estate Finance in California.* Santa Monica, Calif.: Goodyear, 1977.

Tentler, Leslie Woodcock. *Wage-earning Women: Industrial Work and Family Life in the United States, 1900–1930.* New York: Oxford University Press, 1979.

Thernstrom, Stephan. *The Other Bostonians: Poverty and Progress in the American Metropolis, 1880–1970.* Cambridge: Harvard University Press, 1973.

Thompson, Carl D. *Confessions of the Power Trust.* New York: E. P. Dutton, 1932.

Thorton, Jesse E. *Science and Social Change.* Washington: Brookings Institution, 1939.

Thrall, Charles A., and Jerold M. Starr, eds. *Technology, Power, and Social Change.* Lexington: D. C. Heath/Lexington Books, 1972.

Thring, M. W. *Man, Machines and Tomorrow.* London: Routledge & Kegan Paul, 1973.

Thwing, Leroy. *Flickering Flame: A History of Domestic Lighting Through the Ages.* Rutland, Vt.: Tuttle, 1958.

Time, Inc. *Markets by Incomes: A Study of the Relationships of Income to Retail Purchases in Appleton, Wisconsin.* New York: Time Incorporated, 1932.

Torbert, William R., with Malcolm P. Rogers. *Being for the Most Part Puppets: The Interaction of Men's Labor, Leisure, and Politics.* Cambridge: Schenkman, 1973.

Trachtenberg, Alan. *The Incorporation of America: Culture and Society in the Gilded Age.* New York: Hill & Wang, 1982.

Trattner, Walter. *From Poor Law to Welfare State: A History of Social Welfare in America.* New York: Free Press, 1974.

Trolander, Judith Ann. *Settlement Houses and the Great Depression.* Detroit: Wayne State University Press, 1975.

Trombley, Kenneth. *The Life and Times of a Happy Liberal, Morris Llewellyn Cooke.* New York: Harper & Brothers, 1954.

Tuan, Yi-Fu. *Space and Place: The Perspective of Experience.* Minneapolis: University of Minnesota, 1977.

Tucker, David M. *The Decline of Thrift in America: Our Cultural Shift from Saving to Spending.* New York: Praeger, 1991.

Tugwell, Rexford G. *The Diary of Rexford G. Tugwell: The New Deal, 1932–1935.* Edited by Michael Vincent Namorato. Westport, Conn.: Greenwood Publishing Group, 1992.

Twentieth Century Fund. *Electric Power and Government Policy: A Survey of the Relations Between the Government and the Electric Power Industry.* New York: Twentieth Century Fund, 1948.

[U.S.] President's Committee on Civil Rights. *To Secure These Rights: The Report of the President's Committee on Civil Rights.* Charles E. Wilson, Chairman. New York: Simon & Schuster, 1947.

University of California, Heller Commission. *Spending Ways of a Semi-Skilled Group.* Cost of Living Studies. Vol. 4. University of California Publications in Economics. Berkeley, 1931.

Uri, Noel D. *Towards an Efficient Allocation of Electrical Energy: An Essay in Applied Welfare Economics.* 1974. Lexington: Lexington Books, 1975.

Vance, Rupert B. *How the Other Half Is Housed: A Pictorial Record of Sub-minimum Farm Housing in the South.* Chapel Hill: University of North Carolina Press, 1936.

Vance, Rupert B., and Gordon W. Blackwell. *New Farm Homes for Old: A Study of Rural Public Housing in the South.* University: University of Alabama Press, 1946.

Vennard, Edwin. *Government in the Power Business.* New York: McGraw-Hill, 1968.

Vickery, Joyce Carter. *Defending Eden: New Mexican Pioneers in Southern California,*

1830–1890. Riverside: Department of History, University of California, Riverside, and the Riverside Museum Press, 1977.

Vietor, Richard H. K. *Energy Policy in America Since 1945: A Study of Business Government Relations.* New York: Cambridge University Press, 1984.

Vose, Clement E. *Caucasians Only: The Supreme Court, the NAACP, and the Restrictive Covenant Cases.* Berkeley: University of California Press, 1959.

Walker, Forrest A. *The Civil Works Administration: An Experiment in Federal Work Relief, 1933–1934.* New York: Garland, 1979.

Waltrip, John Richard. *Public Power during the Truman Administration.* New York: Arno Press, 1979.

Wandersee, Winifred D. *Women's Work and Family Values, 1920–1940.* Cambridge: Harvard University Press, 1981.

Ward, David. *Poverty, Ethnicity, and the American City, 1840–1925: Changing Conceptions of the Slum and the Ghetto.* Cambridge: Cambridge University Press, 1989.

Ware, Susan. *Holding Their Own: American Women in the 1930s.* Boston: Twayne, 1982.

Warner, George A. *Greenbelt: The Cooperative Community: An Experience in Democratic Living.* New York: Exposition Press, 1954.

Warner, Sam Bass, Jr. *The Way We Really Live: Social Change in Metropolitan Boston Since 1920.* Boston: Trustees of the Public Library of the City of Boston, 1977.

Warner, W. Lloyd, and Leo Srole. *The Social Systems of American Ethnic Groups.* New Haven: Yale University Press, 1945.

Warner, W. Lloyd, and Paul S. Lunt. *The Social Life of a Modern Community.* Yankee City Series. Vol. 1. New Haven: Yale University Press, 1941.

———. *The Status System of a Modern Community.* Yankee City Series. Vol. 2. New Haven: Yale University Press, 1942.

Warner, W. Lloyd, et al. *Democracy in Jonesville: A Study of Quality and Inequality.* New York: Harper & Brothers, 1949.

Waterman, Merwin H. *Financial Policies of Public Utility Holding Companies.* Ann Arbor: University of Michigan Press, 1936.

Watkins, G. P. *Electrical Rates.* New York: D. Van Nostrand, 1921.

Watson, Frank. *Been There and Back.* With Peggy Hoffman. Winston-Salem: J. F. Blair, 1976.

Watson, Frank. *Housing Problems and Possibilities in the United States.* New York: Harper & Brothers, 1935.

Weaver, Robert C. *The Negro Ghetto.* Reprint. New York: Russell & Russell, [1948] 1967.

Weiss, Marc A. *The Rise of the Community Builders: The American Real Estate Industry and Urban Land Planning.* New York: Columbia University Press, 1987.

Welfeld, Irving. *Where We Live: A Social History of American Housing.* New York: Simon & Schuster, 1988.

Wendt, Paul F. *Housing Policy—The Search for Solutions; A Comparison of the United Kingdom, Sweden, West Germany, and the United States since World War II.* Berkeley: University of California Press, 1962.

Wesser, Robert F. *Charles Evans Hughes: Politics and Reform in New York, 1905–1910.* Ithaca: Cornell University Press, 1967.

West, James [Carl Withers]. *Plainville, U.S.A.* New York: Columbia University Press, 1945.

West, Thomas Reed. *Flesh of Steel: Literature and the Machine in American Culture.* Nashville: Vanderbilt University Press, 1967.

Westin, Jeane Eddy. *Making Do: How Women Survived the '30s.* Chicago: Follett, 1976.

White, R. B. *Prefabrication: A History of Its Development in Great Britain.* London: Her Majesty's Stationery Office, 1965.

Whitten, Robert, and Thomas Adams. *Neighborhoods of Small Homes: Economic Density of Low-Cost Housing in America and England.* Cambridge: Harvard University Press, 1931.

Wiebe, Robert H. *Businessmen and Reform: A Study of the Progressive Movement.* Reprint. Chicago: Quadrangle Books, [1962] 1968.

Wik, Reynold M. *Henry Ford and Grass-Roots America.* Ann Arbor: University of Michigan Press, 1972.

Wilk, Richard R., ed. *The Household Economy: Reconsidering the Domestic Mode of Production.* Boulder: Westview Press, 1989.

Williams, Faith M., and Alice C. Hanson. *Money Disbursements of Wage Earners and Clerical Workers in Eight Cities in the East North-Central Region, 1934–1936.* United States Bureau of Labor Statistics Bulletin no. 636. Washington, D.C., 1940.

Williams, Faith M., and Carle C. Zimmerman. *Studies of Family Living in the United States and Other Countries.* U.S. Department of Agriculture. Miscellaneous Publication 223. Washington, D.C., 1935.

Williams, Rosalind H. *Dream Worlds: Mass Consumption in Late Nineteenth-Century France.* Berkeley, Los Angeles, and London: University of California Press, 1982.

Wilson, Margaret Gibbons. *American Woman in Transition: The Urban Influence, 1870–1920.* Contributions in Women's Studies, no. 6. Westport, Conn.: Greenwood Press, 1979.

Wilson, William H. *The City Beautiful Movement: Creating the American Landscape.* Baltimore: Johns Hopkins University Press, 1989.

Winner, Langdon. *Autonomous Technology: Technics-Out-of-Control as a Theme in Political Thought.* Cambridge: MIT Press, 1977.

Wise, George. *Willis R. Whitney, General Electric, and the Origins of U.S. Industrial Research.* New York: Columbia University Press, 1985.

Wood, Edith Elmer. *Recent Trends in American Housing.* New York: Macmillan, 1931.

Wood, Mildred Weigley, Ruth Lindquist, and Lucy A. Studley. *Managing the Home.* Boston: Houghton Mifflin, 1932.

Worster, Donald. *Rivers of Empire: Water, Aridity, and the Growth of the American West.* New York: Pantheon Books, 1985.

Wright, Gwendolyn. *Building the Dream: A Social History of Housing in America.* New York: Pantheon Books, 1981.

———. *Moralism and the Model Home: Domestic Architecture and Cultural Conflict in Chicago, 1873–1913.* Chicago: University of Chicago Press, 1981.

Wright, Lawrence. *Clean and Decent: The Fascinating History of the Bathrooms and the Water Closets, and of Sundry Habits, Fashions, and Accessories of the Toilet, Principally in Great Britain, France, & America.* New York: Viking Press, 1960.

———. *Home Fires Burning: The History of Domestic Heating and Cooking.* London: Routledge & Kegan Paul, 1964.

———. *Clean and Decent: The History of the Bath and the Loo.* London: Routledge & Kegan Paul, 1980.

Young, Louise B. *Power Over People.* New York: Oxford University Press, 1973.

Ziman, John M. *The Force of Knowledge: The Scientific Dimension of Society.* Cambridge: Cambridge University Press, 1976.

Zimmerman, Carle C. *Consumption and Standards of Living.* New York: D. Van Nostrand, 1936.

Index

Designer: U.C. Press Staff
Compositor: Integrated Composition Systems
Text: 10/12 Times Roman
Display: Helvetica
Printer & Binder: Thomson-Shore